DEMOCRACY AND CONSTITUTIONALISM
IN THE EUROPEAN UNION

Democracy and Constitutionalism in the European Union
Collected Essays

JUDGE G. F. MANCINI

Lately Judge of the European Court of Justice, Luxembourg

·HART·
PUBLISHING

OXFORD – PORTLAND OREGON
2000

Hart Publishing
Oxford and Portland, Oregon

Published in North America (US and Canada) by
Hart Publishing c/o
International Specialized Book Services
5804 NE Hassalo Street
Portland, Oregon
97213-3644
USA

Distributed in the Netherlands, Belgium and Luxembourg by
Intersentia, Churchillaan 108
B2900 Schoten
Antwerpen
Belgium

Hart Publishing Ltd is a specialist legal publisher based in Oxford, England.
To order further copies of this book or to request a list of other
publications please write to:

Hart Publishing Ltd, Salter's Boatyard,
Folly Bridge, Abingdon Road, Oxford OX1 4LB
Telephone: +44 (0)1865 245533 or Fax: +44 (0)1865 794882
e-mail: mail@hartpub.co.uk

British Library Cataloguing in Publication Data
Data Available
ISBN 1 84113–114–8 (cloth)

Typeset in Sabon 10pt
by Hope Services (Abingdon) Ltd.
Printed in Great Britain on acid-free paper
by Biddles Ltd, Guildford and King's Lynn

For Fulvia, of course

Contents

Preface

In the Spring of 1999, while working on this book, Professor Mancini left Luxembourg to return to Bologna where he was to undergo what he knew would be difficult medical treatment. He left with his characteristic good humour and strength of character intact and over the coming weeks we spoke regularly about draft judgments on which he was working, legal notes to be distributed and, of course, this book. He passed away not long afterwards, before the book was complete. It would have been his wish, and indeed it is the wish of his family, that this collection of essays see the light of day.

Having worked closely with Professor Mancini we know how dear this project was to him and how happy he was that the writings of the Court's most senior judge would be published by one of the law's youngest publishers. It has been with heavy hearts that we and his assistants in the Chambers—Angelica Lahure, Angela Parlanti and Simona Nobile—have put the finishing touches to the manuscript after his death. We know that the Introduction, the only unfinished part, does not shine as it would have had he completed it himself. We hope, however, that its shortcomings do not detract from the collection itself.

Professor Mancini was a person of extraordinary charisma and humanity. He will be dearly missed.

CARLO CURTI GIALDINO
VITTORIO DI BUCCI
SIOFRA O'LEARY
Luxembourg, December 1999

Acknowledgements

Chapter 1 is based on an address delivered at the Center for European Studies at Harvard University in November 1989. It was originally published under the same title in (1989) 26 *Common Market Law Review* 595–614 and then in R.O. Keohane and S. Hoffman (eds.), *The New European Community. Decisionmaking and Institutional Change* (Westview, Boulder Col.), pp. 177–194. Much gratitude is due to Professor David O'Keeffe who, then a *référendaire* at the Court of Justice, gave freely of his time and English prose.

Chapter 2, which originally appeared in (1991) 11 *Yearbook of European Law* 1–13 entitled "From *CILFIT* to *ERT*: the Constitutional Challenge Facing the European Court" was an expanded version of a speech delivered at the *Hojesteret* in Copenhagen on 30 April 1992. This article was one of two on which I collaborated with David Keeling, now a Member of the First Board of Appeal, Office of Harmonization in the Internal Market (Trademark and Designs), Alicante, then a *référendaire* at the Court of Justice.

An earlier version of Chapter 3 was originally delivered as the Shimizu Lecture at the London School of Economics in April 1993. It was then published as "Democracy and the European Court of Justice" in (1994) 57 *Modern Law Review* 175–190. It is also the product of my enjoyable and fruitful cooperation with David Keeling.

Chapter 4 was first presented on 1 November 1997 as an Inaugural Lecture at the University of New South Wales, Sydney, Australia and then published as "Europe: the Case for Statehood" in (1997) 4 *European Law Journal* 29–42. This article provoked an interesting debate with J.H.H. Weiler which in turn led to Chapter 5, "A Currency in Search of a State". The latter was originally presented as a Coudert Brother Lecture for the European Law Centre, University of New South Wales, on 2 November 1998 and was first published in G.C. Rodríguez Iglesias, O. Due, R. Schintgen and C. Elsen (eds.), *Mélanges en hommage à Fernand Schockweiler* (Nomos Verlagsgesellschaft, Baden-Baden, 1999), pp. 399–412. It was written in conjunction with one of my *référendaires*, Mr Vittorio Di Bucci, now a member of the European Commission's Legal Service. [Judge Mancini had intended that the arguments in this article be developed further but his untimely death meant that this was not possible.]

Chapter 6 is an early article on the protection of fundamental rights in the EC entitled "Safeguarding Human Rights: the Role of the Court of Justice of the European Communities" and to be found in F. Carpi and C. Giovannucci Orlandi (eds.), *Judicial Protection of Human Rights at the National and International Level* (Milan, 1991), pp. 497–517. It was written with the assistance of Professor Carlo Curti Gialdino who, for seventeen years, worked by my side in Luxembourg.

Chapter 7 is a revised version of my general report to the 13th FIDE Congress in Athens which was entitled "The Effect of Community Law on the Employment Law of the Member States: General Report" and was compiled with the assistance of Carlo Curti Gialdino. It was published in FIDE, *Reports of the 13th Congress* (Athens, 1988), Volume II, pp. 1–42.

Chapter 8 was written for the *Liber Amicorum* for my good friend and former colleague, T.F. O'Higgins, it was called "The Free Movement of Workers in the Case-law of the European Court of Justice" and was published in D. O'Keeffe and D. Curtin (eds.), *Constitutional Adjudication in European Community and National Law* (Butterworths, Dublin, 1992), pp. 68–77.

Chapter 9 is based on a speech delivered to the Australian Human Rights and Equal Opportunities Commission under the auspices of the European Law Centre of the University of New South Wales. It was written in conjunction with one of my last *référendaires*, Síofra O'Leary and was published as "The New Frontiers of EU Sex Equality Law" in (1999) 24 *European Law Review* 331–353.

Chapter 10 appeared as "The U.S. Supreme Court and the European Court of Justice" in K. Versluys (ed.), *The Insular Dream. Obsession and Resistance* (Amsterdam, 1995), pp. 113–124 and in D. O'Keeffe and N. Emiliou (eds.), *Legal Aspects of Integration in the European Union* (London–The Hague–Boston), pp. 3–17.

Chapter 11 was originally delivered as a lecture at the annual meeting of the American Law Schools Association in New Orleans on 6 January 1995. It was subsequently published as "Language, Culture and Politics in the Life of the European Court of Justice" in (1995) 1 *Columbia Journal of European Law* 397–413.

Chapter 12 was presented at the annual conference of the International Association of Procedural Law, held in Thessaloniki, Greece on 21–25 May 1997. It was entitled "A Case Study of the Court of Justice of the European Communities" and was reproduced in P. Yessiou-Faltsi (ed.), *The Role of the Supreme Courts at the National and International Level* (Thessaloniki, 1998), pp. 421–452. My thanks go to Síofra O'Leary who worked with me on the original version.

Chapter 13 was published as "Access to Justice: Individual Undertakings and EEC Antitrust Law—Problems and Pitfalls" (1989) 12 *Fordham International Law Journal* 189–203, and was written with the assistance of Ezio Perillo, then one of my *référendaires*, now a Director at the Secretariat General of the European Parliament.

Chapter 14 is another contribution to a collection of essays—this time in honour of my friend Bill Wedderburn—"The European Court of Justice and the External Competences of the Community" in *European Community Labour Law: Principles and Perspectives. Liber Amicorum Lord Wedderburn of Charlton* (Oxford, 1996), pp. 139–150. Once again, Vittorio Di Bucci gave willingly of his time to contribute to the article.

Chapter 15 is the slightly revised text of an article, written with the assistance of Carlo Curti Gialdino, entitled "The Incorporation of Community law into the Domestic Laws of the Member States of the European Communities" published in UNIDROIT, *International Uniform Law in Practice. Acts and Proceedings of the 3rd Congress on Private Law, Rome 7–10 September 1987* (Rome, 1988), pp. 13–27.

Introduction

The idea for this collection of essays came to me some years ago. My writings on European Community law had become increasingly focused on two or three areas—democracy, constitutionalism and the protection of individual rights—and I felt that, as my days at the European Court of Justice drew to a close, the time might have come to bring them together in one volume. An indulgent exercise for myself, perhaps, but an interesting one, I hope, for the reader. My intention was never to thoroughly update or alter the content of the essays and although some Treaty modifications and jurisprudential developments are indicated in the text, part of the aim of the collection is to emphasise how far Community law has progressed over the last fifteen years or so and where it might be heading.[1]

Having opted to study law at university rather than one of my other great passions, linguistics among them, I became increasingly interested, even at undergraduate level, in labour law and the dynamics of organized labour. Labour law was in fact to be my first chair and the subject of most of my early writings. Indeed this particular interest has survived to this day and many of the chapters in this book bear witness to my continued involvement with the subject during my time in Luxembourg.

When I finished my university studies, half a century ago, labour law was a veritable battlefield between those belonging to the *ancien regime*, innovators of all colours and hues, Communists, Christian Democrats, Social Democrats and Liberals. I was convinced at the time that the most pressing task was to get rid of our corporative heritage. The confrontation which marked that period was largely successful and opened the way for the developments of the 1960s and 1970s. This era is, of course, an easy one to recall to a European audience, some of whom probably still remember the passions of those times. With the exception of the authoritarian regimes still in power in Greece and the Iberian Peninsula, Western European countries shared largely similar experiences, marked by social reforms and the advancement of workers. I regret none of the enthusiasm which that period inspired in me and others, but I am perfectly aware that that ardour must now be reconsidered without too much indulgence in the light of the damage which it also produced in terms of public debt and rigidities in the labour market.

From the 1970s onwards, labour law began to "Europeanize" itself. The Council of Ministers adopted the first directives in the field, the Court of Justice

---

[1] Note also that the renumbering system introduced by Article 12 of the Amsterdam Treaty has not been applied in the various chapters. Reference should be made to the equivalence tables annexed to the Amsterdam Treaty.

began to elaborate on the scope and consequences of the status of migrant worker and the direct of effect of Community law ensured very concrete results for complainants. While modest progress resulted from the adoption of the Single European Act, the Maastricht Treaty reinforced the social dimension considerably with what was then a social agreement signed by eleven Member States, but which has since become the social chapter applicable to all following the Amsterdam Treaty. At the same time, the judgments of the Court on workplace equality between men and women, acquired rights, insolvency and collective redundancy created a *ius commune europeum* in social matters.

I am well aware that developments at European level do not exhaust the complex and composit reality of labour law which, already prior to the Maastricht Treaty, had discovered the principle of subsidiarity and begun to articulate itself with greater force. Nevertheless, the birth of collective bargaining at the Community level shows that the life forces of society feel the need for "more Europe". That is not all. Even when our countries take different paths on important questions—the long-running debate on the reduction of working time is but one case in point—they try to operate in concert and carry out parallel or common policies. This trend is likely to be strengthened by the guidelines to be adopted by the European Council pursuant to the new title on employment.

The globalization of the economy, the decline of heavy industry, the information revolution, the rapid expansion of distance work, the inexorable marginalization of the working classes and the dramatic persistence of structural unemployment, are all phenomena which oblige us to rethink entire sections of the social contract which has accompanied and rendered possible the social progress in our countries since the end of the Second World War. What will become of the European social model? What innovations and changes must be made to it and which of its elements remain viable? These are the most urgent questions facing today's young labour law scholars.

A number of the chapters in this volume discuss various of the social aspects of European Community law and the Court's jurisprudence. In line with the overall approach of this collection, they have not been updated and few changes have been made to their original content. With ten or more years gone by since the original publication of some of them and a host of decisions handed down by the Court since then, not to mention Treaty amendments and legislative enactments, it is for the reader to assess the progress made since they were written and whether or not the aspirations or predictions which they contain have materialized.

Having touched on my labour law origins I should perhaps move on to European Community law which, by the early 1980s, had become the path for my intellectual evolution as well as my professional future. Although I had always had a profound interest in different European cultures, in Europe's languages and its patrimony, it was not until 1982, with my appointment as Advocate General at the Court, that I dealt in my professional career with the political and legal construction of Europe.

For decades, European Community law had been regarded as a province of public international law. Many of my predecessors and those who were to be my colleagues at the Court, were and are renowned international lawyers. Looking back, I am convinced that becoming a member of the Court as a specialist in a subject other than international law can have its advantages. An international lawyer runs the risk of broaching the Community as a classic international organization, even a *sui generis* one, and, possibly, of not grasping as a result the essence of what has been developing over the years. A specialist in international law who is unprepared to reexamine in depth his or her patterns of thought risks lining up with the wrong side. The Union nowadays is a reality which must be studied first and foremost with the tools offered by the constitutional law of federal states.

In any case, since my arrival at the Court over seventeen years ago, I have had the privilege of experiencing at first hand the developments of the 1980s and 1990s—the adoption of the Single Act, the completion of the internal market, the great promises of Maastricht which, in 1999, led to the creation of a monetary union, and the changes introduced by the Amsterdam Treaty. Indeed, I am most grateful for this privilege to those who had not elected me as a Judge at the Italian Constitutional Court. Throughout my time at the Court of Justice my colleagues and I have had the chance to found our work on the fundamental principles which my far-sighted predecessors in Luxembourg had established in the 1960s and 1970s. In the 1990s, however, the disillusionment began. By this I do not refer to what I would call a "laicization" of the Court (in this respect someone has invoked the image of warrior monks who, in 1492, with the Moors evicted from Spain, threw off their tunics and laid down their arms only to adopt civilian garb). Of course, the blindness or excessive slyness which one finds in the occasional decision puts me in a bad mood. However, like Lord Devlin, I have never thought that enthusiasm is a judicial virtue and I am convinced that, at present, to limit ourselves to surveiling the borders which separate the competences of the Union from those of the Member States is perhaps a more sensible approach to adopt and, in any case, the only practicable one.

History alone can judge the stones which we contributed to the construction of the cathedral which our predecessors commenced. As with any construction, it is inevitable that, with time, original plans undergo alterations and are adapted to the tastes of the day—a gothic portal may come to enclose a Roman nave and a decision may even be made to demolish a pulpit which has become bothersome. What is important, nevertheless, is that the new architects and builders are conscious of the fact that they are simply adding their contribution to an edifice which surpasses them, which they have inherited from their ancestors and which they are bound to bequeath to future generations. It is in this context that the overall design must remain clear and intelligible so that a visitor to the cathedral and, equally, a reader of the Court's jurisprudence is able to grasp the grandeur and significance of the collective work. The architects, present and future, should thus take note of those voices of civil society which express concern if the jurisprudence acquires the speed and momentum of a pendulum.

The Judges of the Court of Justice have been described by some sources as unsung heroes of European integration and, by others, as "morbid megalomaniacs".[2] As one may well expect, the truth lies somewhere in between. Indeed, different perceptions of the truth depend both on the temporal context and the orientation of the beholding eye. At any given moment the opinion of the average citizen of the European Union may differ substantially from that of the European Commission, for example, or from that of a Member State government. Moreover, a national judge and a legal scholar are likely to focus on different aspects of the same judgment rendered by the Court. What follows in the coming pages is a historic overview of the varied reactions which the jurisprudence of the Court has elicited, on the one hand, from the general public and political actors (in both Member State governments and European Union institutions) and, on the other, from judicial actors, in particular, national judges and academics.

For a long time, the general public was virtually unaware of the very existence of the Court. This phenomenon was due in large part to the fact that the Court of Justice was originally established as the Court of the European Coal and Steel Community with a jurisdiction consequently limited to coal and steel undertakings. However, even after the establishment of the European Economic Community, which extended the Court's jurisdiction beyond that one specific sector, relatively few cases were brought before the Court and those judgments that were handed down did not attract the attention of the average citizen. Nonetheless, it is noteworthy that during this period the Court was busy establishing the basic principles of Community law, including the recognition of individuals as subjects of this new legal order which, according to the *Van Gend en Loos* ruling of 1963,[3] conferred upon them directly effective rights which became part of their legal heritage.[4] Thus, while the general public was not even fully aware of the Court, the Court assiduously kept the individual citizen in mind while laying the foundation of its jurisprudence.

Over time, individuals have grown to appreciate the practical effects of Community law in their daily lives: they cross borders between Member States more freely;[5] they may establish residence in another Member State and expect their professional qualifications to be fully recognized[6] and their pension duly

---

[2] See further Chapters 1 and 12.

[3] Case 26/62 *NV Algemene Transport- en expeditie Onderneming van Gend en Loos* v *Nederlandse Administratie der Belastingen* [1963] ECR 3.

[4] See, *inter alia*, Chapters 1, 2 and 8.

[5] See, for example, Case 118/75 *Lynne Watson and Alessandro Belmann* [1976] ECR 1185 and Case 265/88 *Lothar Messner* [1989] ECR 4209.

[6] See Case 222/86 *Union nationale des entraineurs et cadres techniques professionels du football (Unectef)* v *Georges Heylens and others* [1987] ECR 4097 or Case C-234/97 *Fernández de Bobadilla* v *Museo Nacional del Prado*, judgment of 8 July 1999.

rendered;[7] workers, as well as self-employed persons and members of their families can obtain the same level of medical care extended to residents when travelling in any Member State;[8] and if they fall victim to an assault on the Paris Métro, they are entitled to the same compensation from the French government as any French citizen.[9] The list goes on. Of course, legislative enactments and Treaty amendments have codified and extended the rights granted to individuals under Community law, but the Court, for its part, has often been the catalyst.

To a large extent, public reaction to the jurisprudence of the Court of Justice finds its source in the case law favourable to private individuals. Still, the quality of such reaction is to a large extent shaped by the media focusing on individual judgments. The press, of course, in its continual search for sensational news, is selective in its reporting and is obliged to give an immediate and superficial account of the Court's case law. The crowd of journalists which scampered through the courtroom when the ruling in the *Bosman*[10] case was handed down in December 1995 was more interested in the future composition of European football teams than in the development of the Community principle of the free movement of workers. The media's continued interest in that case is further evidence of the passion which sport can excite and of the powerful financial wheels which it can turn rather than an appreciation of the fundamental principles of free movement which a successful free market must respect. That said, the media is not the ideal forum for reasoned discussion of the Court's jurisprudence; not when the reporting is neutral but cursory, and certainly not when its avowed purpose is to suggest, as part of a larger anti-European campaign waged by the popular press, that the Court's wings should be clipped.

The politically charged nature of such journalistic reporting both mirrors and inspires criticism and reaction on the part of political actors. As I point out in the opening chapter, tucked away in the Grand Duchy of Luxembourg, the Court enjoyed, for at least twenty years, a period of benign neglect on the part of the media and national politicians. Only occasionally did the followers of General de Gaulle rise up against a particular judgment that they considered harmful to France's national interests. As time passed, national administrations and political groups began to realize the extent to which the evolution of European law was shifting the balance of powers in and between the European institutions and Member States. Moreover, it became increasingly apparent to

---

[7] Case C-443/93 *Ioannis Vougioukas* v *Idryma Koinonikon Asfalisseon (IKA)* [1995] ECR I-4033.

[8] See Case 75/63 *M.K.H. Unger, the wife of R. Hoecstra* v *Bestuur der Bedrijfsvereniging voor Detailhandel en Ambachten à Utrecht* [1964] ECR 347; Joined Cases 286/82 and 26/83 *Graziana Luisi and Giuseppe Carbone* v *Ministero del Tesoro* [1984] ECR 377; and, subsequently, Case C-158/96 *Raymond Kohll* v *Union des caisses de maladie* [1998] ECR I-1931 and Case C-120/95 *Nicolas Decker* v *Caisse de maladie des employés privés* [1998] ECR I-1831.

[9] Case 186/87 *Ian William Cowan* v *Trésor public* [1989] ECR 195.

[10] Case C-415/93 *Union royale belge des sociétés de football association ASBL and others* v *Jean-Marc Bosman* [1995] ECR I-4921.

them that their domestic legal systems were practically affected by Community law as interpreted in Luxembourg. Hence came allegations that the Court systematically favoured European integration over national sovereignty.[11] The Court was accused further of placing excessive financial burdens upon the Member States through its indiscriminate application of fundamental principles in matters of social and tax law.[12]

Discontent gradually grew into overt opposition. With the signature of the Maastricht Treaty in 1992, some Member States succeeded in persuading the Intergovernmental Conference to adopt three Protocols intended to force the hand of the Court and to prevent undesirable developments in its case law. First, while cases[13] were pending before the Court concerning the exact scope of a previous judgment on occupational pension schemes,[14] the Conference provided its binding interpretation of this issue,[15] thus presenting the Court with a *fait accompli*. Secondly, it was decided that Denmark could prohibit the acquisition of second homes by foreign nationals, although such a regime was contrary to Community case law.[16] Finally, Ireland could continue to ban distribution of information regarding abortion services in the United Kingdom,[17] notwithstanding the Treaty principle of free provision of services throughout the Community. Moreover, under the Maastricht Treaty the Court's jurisdictional reach was limited so as not to include the new areas governed by the European Union, namely, Common Foreign and Security Policy and Justice and Home Affairs. This last step was surely indicative of the mistrust that certain Member States felt for the Court of Justice.[18] The Court's powers could of course be said to have been strengthened in the Maastricht Treaty through the amendment of Article 171 of the EC Treaty, whereby the Court may impose upon Member States a lump sum or cumulative fine for non-compliance with one of its judgments. However, only the Commission may request such fines to be ordered,

---

[11] See further Chapters 1 and 3.

[12] See, for example, the political debate which followed the decisions in Case 41/84 *Pietro Pinna v Caisse d'allocations familiales de la Savoie* [1986] ECR 1; Case C-45/90 *Alberto Paletta and others v Brennet AG* [1992] ECR I-3423; and Case C-158/96 *Kohll* and Case C-120/95 *Decker*, *supra* n. 8.

[13] See, for example, Case C-109/91 *Gerardus Cornelius Ten Oever v Stichting Bedrijfspensioenfonds voor het Glazenwassers- en Schoonmaakbedrijf* [1993] ECR I-4879.

[14] Case C-262/88 *Douglas Harvey Barber v Guardian Royal Exchange Assurance Group* [1990] ECR I-1889.

[15] See Protocol (No 2) concerning Article 119 of the Treaty establishing the European Community.

[16] Protocol (No 1) on the acquisition of property in Denmark.

[17] Protocol (No 17) annexed to the Treaty on European Union and to the Treaties establishing the European Communities; although a subsequent Declaration of the High Contracting Parties of 1 May 1992 stipulated that it was not their intention that Protocol No 17 limit the freedom to travel between Member States.

[18] This limit on the jurisdiction of the Court did not succeed in totally excluding its competence. See the Court's decision in Case C-170/96 *Commission v Council* [1998] ECR I-2763, where the Court held that it would ensure that acts which, according to the Council, fall within the scope of the third pillar, do not encroach upon the powers conferred by the EC Treaty on the Community.

and it has rarely done so.[19] Thus, the new powers granted to the Court under Maastricht are subject to political control, and are not as dramatic as they appear to be at first glance. The most recent Intergovernmental Conference, which culminated in the signing of a Treaty in Amsterdam in 1997, has clearly enhanced the available judicial control mechanisms as regards the immigration and asylum provisions which now belong to the first pillar and the provisions on police and judicial cooperation in criminal matters which remain in the third pillar. However, it remains to be seen how the Court will handle the different degrees of jurisdiction which it has been admitted pursuant to the new Article 73p EC and the amended Article K.7 of the Treaty on European Union.

As for the European institutions, their relationship to the Court of Justice is perhaps best described by the title of Mendelssohn's overture, "Calm Sea and Prosperous Voyage". The Council, as a body representing national governments, may share their concern that national interests are not given the priority to which they are entitled, but it is unlikely to react strongly to any one judgment, even if a particular Member State finds it difficult to swallow. The European Parliament, for its part, saw its right to participate in legal proceedings recognized through the creative jurisprudence of the Court,[20] and more often than not, its substantive rights prevailed over the claims of the Member States or the Council. Finally, the Commission has long perceived the Court as an institutional ally *vis-à-vis* Member States and the Council. However, particularly after the establishment of the Court of First Instance, the internal practices and administrative decisions of the Commission have fallen victim to closer judicial scrutiny in cases brought by individuals or firms.[21]

As regards national courts, Joseph Weiler seems to have hit the nail on the head when he characterized their relationship with the Court of Justice as an "extended honeymoon, a mutually-empowering relationship". In large part, this success story flows from Article 177 of the EC Treaty, which enables any national judge—and obliges the judges in courts of last resort—to refer to the Court any question regarding the interpretation or validity of Community law. This reference procedure encourages dialogue, promotes cooperation, and avoids conflict between Member State judges and their European Union counterparts. The drafters of the Treaty preferred the Article 177 device to an appeals process, because the former would maintain the balance of powers in favour of the Member State courts by giving them the final word in any judicial procedure. Moreover, a reference proceeding permits national judges to seek

---

[19] At the time of writing only one case—Case C-387/97 *Commission* v *Greece* (compliance with Directives on toxic waste) has passed the oral stage of the procedure before the Court; see the Opinion of Advocate General Ruiz Jarabo of 28 September 1999. Cases C-197/97 *Commission* v *Greece* (compliance with the Directive on the mutual recognition of professional qualifications) and C-373/98 *Commission* v *France* (compliance with the Directive on the protection of wild birds) are also pending.

[20] Discussed in more detail in Chapters 2 and 3.

[21] See, for example, the annulment of the Commission's decision in Case C-137/92 P *Commission* v *BASF AG and others* [1994] ECR I-2555.

guidance from a specialized Court before making a definitive ruling—a ruling to which the parties are more likely to be receptive, since it is pronounced by a national, and not a European, judge.[22]

The goal of the national judge is to resolve the case pending before him, but the Court of Justice may see a reference proceeding as an opportunity to develop Community law incrementally.[23] The national judge can rely on the Luxembourg court to give him or her a sort of leverage through which to protect individual rights against national legislators or administrators. For example, the *Simmenthal* judgment of 1978 empowered *any* Italian judge to set aside a specific legislative provision deemed contrary to Community law,[24] even though the Italian Constitutional Court was the only body entitled to strike down national laws found contrary to its Constitution. Similarly, the *Factortame* ruling in 1990 allowed British judges to grant interim injunctions against the application of a statute to protect rights presumptively derived from Community law,[25] where such action would otherwise have been precluded by the unwritten British Constitution. Thus, the reference proceeding increases judicial protection of individual rights, empowers national judges within their respective jurisdictions, and assures the legitimacy and effectiveness of the Community legal order, thereby producing what economists might call a Pareto-optimal result for the judicial circuit.

Logical deduction predicts (and history has proven) that the judges sitting on lower national courts would be most receptive to the phenomenon of judicial empowerment just described. Article 177 provided lower court judges with a direct link to the judges in Luxembourg, which occasionally resulted in the setting aside of earlier case law created by superior national courts.[26]

This use by lower courts of a constitutional provision which enlarges their role in the judicial structure and the consequent straining of the relationship between lower courts and their superiors is not unprecedented and indeed is reminiscent of events in Italy in the 1950s and 1960s. In Italy, the 1948 Constitution entrusted judicial review of legislation to a special Constitutional Court of fifteen top-level judges, law professors and experienced lawyers. In 1959 the Higher Council on the Judiciary, also provided for in the Constitution, came into being with the task of making all decisions concerning judicial personnel in such areas as recruitment training, promotions, transfer from one office to another, discipline and so on. At the outset these bodies stirred heated controversies and were vehicles of conflict in the judiciary. The Constitutional Court acts by request of the courts below when, in adjudicating a case, the latter are called upon to enforce a statute of dubious validity. While the Court of

[22] See further Chapters 1 and 2.

[23] For a discussion of the public and private purposes of the Court's jurisprudence, particularly its Article 177 case law, see Chapter 12.

[24] Case 106/77 *Ammistrazione delle finanze dello stato v SA Simmenthal* [1978] ECR 629.

[25] Case C-213/89 *Regina v Secretary of State for Transport, ex parte Factortame* [1990] ECR I-2433.

[26] See, for example, Case 8/81 *Ursula Becker v Finanzamt Münster-Innenstadt* [1982] ECR 53.

Cassation, Italy's appeals court, did its best in those early years to keep the fifteen justices idle, the lower judges crowded their tables with hundreds of statutes or clauses, most of Fascist origin. The justices of the Constitutional Court responded favourably to this vicarious activism and even spurred it on by ruling out the doctrine which had virtually frozen the social provisions of the Constitution. The psychological foundations of the authority wielded by the senior courts were thus shaken.[27]

Understandably, in the EC as well, Member States' higher courts may have felt their own authority threatened by the reference procedure—or, more precisely, by its jurisprudential outcome, notably the principles of direct effect and supremacy. As a consequence, some of them initially refrained from referring questions to the Court of Justice under Article 177 or, in extreme cases, refused to comply with the Court's interpretation. In 1978, for example, in a politically-sensitive case dealing with the deportation order of Daniel Cohn-Bendit (the former leader of the 1968 student movement in Paris, currently the starring member of the Green Party in the European Parliament and the only MEP to have been elected in two different Member States) the French Conseil d'Etat staged an outright rebellion against Community jurisprudence by holding that Community directives cannot be relied upon by individuals in actions for annulment of individual administrative decisions.[28] Then, in its *Kloppenburg* decision in 1985, the German Bundesfinanzhof (Federal Supreme Fiscal Court) likewise denied that Community directives could have direct effect.[29] In France and Germany, as in Italy in the example given in the previous paragraph, national judicial defiance has since been brought to an end.[30]

Still today, a potential conflict exists between the Court of Justice, on the one hand, and the German and Italian Constitutional Courts and Danish Supreme Court on the other. While accepting the supremacy of EC law, the latter have repeatedly warned that they retain the authority to check the compliance of secondary European legislation with fundamental rights enshrined in their constitution,[31] thus posing an ominous threat to the Community-wide effectiveness of such legislation and usurping the role which is the exclusive domain of the European Court.

Legal scholars can be divided into two distinct groups: those specialized in Community law and those whose primary focus lies in another legal domain.

[27] See further G.F. Mancini, "Politics and Judges—The European Perspective" (1980) 43 *Modern Law Review* 1–17, at 6 and 7.

[28] Judgment of the Conseil d'Etat of 22 December 1978, *Rec. Lebon* 1978, p. 524.

[29] See the decision of the Bundesfinanzhof of 25 April 1985, VR 123/84.

[30] The Conseil d'Etat seemed to reconsider the *Cohn-Bendit* judgment in its judgment of 30 October 1996, *Cabinet Revert et Badelon*, *Rec. Lebon* 1996, p. 397 and in Germany the Bundesverfassungsgericht held that the position of the Bundesfinanzhof in *Kloppenburg* amounted to a violation of the German Basic Law—see Bundesgerichtshof, 28vR 687/85, judgment of 8 April 1987, in *BVerfGE*, 87, p. 223.

[31] See, for example, Bundesverfassungsgericht, judgment of 12 October 1993, in *BVerfGE*, 89, p. 155, the so-called Maastricht *Urteil*, or its judgment of 31 March 1998, in *BVerfGE*, 97, p. 350. For an English version of the Maastricht *Urteil* see [1994] *Common Market Law Reports* 57.

Generally speaking, the jurisprudence of the Court met with the approval and support of the experts, who were sympathetic to its goals and, therefore, welcomed its reasoning. Initially, few discordant voices were heard, and it is understandable that with anti-European sentiment growing in certain Member States such criticism has increased in reaction to the Court's coherent pursuit of "an ever closer union among the peoples of Europe" as prescribed in the Treaty preamble. But it is interesting to note that in spite of today's mixed political environment, most academics specialized in Community law continue to praise the Court's work; if they criticize anything, it is the fact that some judgments have not gone far enough.[32]

Non-specialists, it must be said, have been more critical. For the most part, their attitudes can be attributed to an inadequate understanding of the dynamics of European integration, and to an inability to conceptualize a legal system different from their own. Indeed, the European Union does not fit neatly into traditional political or legal moulds. Consequently, non-expert scholars, hindered by the notion that the Court of Justice is a judicial anomaly, are unable to see it for what specialists know it to be: an essential part of an unprecedented and unparalleled legal order which might become a model for other regions of the world.

Judicial confidentiality prevents Members of the Court from discussing how, if at all, these different reactions influence the Court's activities. The Court, however, does not function in a vacuum and it should come as no surprise that the Judges are aware of the political, legal and economic contexts surrounding the cases brought before the Court. It would be difficult to deny that the creative jurisprudence establishing the protection of fundamental rights within the Community was intended to prevent a clash with the constitutional courts in Italy and Germany, which, as a number of chapters discuss, could not accept that Community law overrides basic rights enshrined in their constitutions. In addition, it would be difficult to imagine that the Court did not have national judicial opposition to direct effect in mind (*Cohn-Bendit* and *Kloppenburg*) when it decided that directives can only be relied upon against states and not against private individuals.

The judicial perspective is, of course, far from providing an exhaustive overview of European integration. It can even induce excessive optimism, given the fact that the legal and jurisdictional system was the best-achieved element of the initial architecture of the Communities and that which the architects of the EC Treaty could define with most freedom, because it was farthest from the political power struggles which concerned most governments. Today we should pay tribute to the ingenuity of the negotiators of the Treaties, some of whom, like Riccardo Monaco and Pierre Pescatore, went on to serve as judges at the Court of Justice. While being compelled to stifle the federal ambitions inherent

---

[32] See, for example, the discussion in Chapter 9 of criticism of some of the Court's more recent decisions in the field of sex equality.

in the High Authority, they designed a strong Court capable of becoming a silent but effective motor of integration. The system which they created remains more or less intact. The addition of a Court of First Instance modernized the judicial system without upsetting its equilibrium and the Amsterdam Treaty, in providing for new competences, has enlarged the sphere of Community law and the protection of the rights of individuals. If the proof of the pudding is in the eating, the Community judicial system remains responsive to the demands of modern life, even if reforms appear to be necessary to enable the Court to respond to the quantity of demands for justice made to it.

Nowadays, what is perhaps most troublesome is the oft-criticized democratic deficit which, far from being resolved, looks in danger of being aggravated. It is the evil which has undermined the Community since its birth and whose origin lies precisely in the fact that the Community began life as an international organization. The Amsterdam Treaty does mark an important step for the European Parliament in the long march towards the status of co-legislator.[33] But the Council, the organ of the Member States, retains its pre-eminent position in numerous domains such as the second and third pillars, and in other areas, such as tax,[34] where it decides, in addition, by unanimity. These are legitimate choices which undoubtedly reflect the present stage of integration. But the Council reassembles a diplomatic round table more than a democratic assembly. Precisely because of this nature, it legislates behind closed doors and, in most cases, limits itself to rubberstamping texts prepared in the shadows by innumerable committees of experts.[35] The need to reach a consensus between fifteen different positions and the dilution of responsibility which results are bound to frustrate every inclination for control on the part of public opinion.

In 1999 a new Community body was added to the structure—the European Central Bank. The Bank, independent as it should be, will have enormous power; it will dictate European monetary policy and, as such, will condition the economic and social policies of the Member States. There is nothing wrong with this except that the only counterweight to such power will be the ECOFIN Council. The latter, based on Article 104c of the EC Treaty and the Stability Pact, can even sanction eventual deficits approved by national parliaments. Rest assured that the intention is not to sing the praises of high-spending politics. But that said, was the control of its own budget not the very first of the demands which the mother of all parliaments, the House of Common, addressed to the Stuarts at the beginning of the seventeenth century. Since the European Parliament will have no voice in this respect, how is one not to fear the drying up of the river of democracy in Europe. Has the moment not come to cry loud

---

[33] See the streamlined co-decision procedure in Article 189b EC and its extension to many new areas.
[34] See, for example, Article 93 EC on the adoption of harmonizing legislation in the field of indirect taxation.
[35] See further Chapter 4.

and clear that the neo-functionalist approach, for all its previous successes, risks becoming an exercise of apprentice sorcerers?[36]

I have made few attempts in my writings to hide the fact that my hopes and dreams for European integration are of a federalist nature. I have no doubt that one source of these aspirations dates back to my experiences in Italy during the Second World War and thereafter. But that is not all. Italians, unlike most other Europeans, do not seem to fear losing their identity in a more closely-knit and more powerful Union. The attraction that a European Union destined to remain multicultural even if it evolved into a state is bound to exert on a country which has been a state for 140 years, but whose cultural identity is still in the making should not be lightly dismissed. Defined by Prince Metternich, with both accuracy and a whiff of disparagement, as no more than "a geographical expression", Italy was slowly transformed into a nation by the state which a diminutive intellectual elite had succeeded in establishing on her soil. It was a fragile nation, evincing at every major crisis that it had become one not of its own free will, but by virtue of a will settled upon it under extra-ordinary circumstances and deaf to the kicking and screaming that its commands aroused.

Many have questioned whether there could actually be a European identity and, if there could, what atrocious kind of homogenization it would involve. Out multiple "selves", our diversity, which even state borders define inadequately, together with our long past and ingrained sense of tragedy are the factors that make Europe European, and I suspect that they constitute the best tools we possess to tackle the future. What advantages would we draw from becoming a nation that could make up for the loss of our present, sometimes uneasy, but so very fruitful rubbing of shoulders with one another knowing that our roots, cultures and primeval loyalties are different? Perhaps interesting or useful pointers for such a discussion can be found in some of the chapters within.

In the *Festschrift* dedicated to me by colleagues—old and new—friends and pupils—young and not so young—on the occasion of my 70th birthday, Pieter VerLoren Van Themaat described the paradigm of federalism with his usual clarity as the simultaneous perception of the need for unity, for coherent action and for the respect of the prerogatives of the constituent elements *dans ce qu'elles ont de primaire et d'originaire*.[37] I share his ideas when I dream of a European political entity organized along the lines of a state—a state, of course, without a nation—respectful of the identity of the peoples of which it is composed but provided with its two chambers, its executive branch and its guaranteeing organs. It may of course be the case that the European Union becomes a democratic entity without taking the form of a federal state and, in that case,

[36] See further Chapter 5.

[37] See P. VerLoren Van Themaat, "The Institutional System of the European Union: Between Some Lessons from the Past and Challenges of the Future" in *Scritti in onore di Giuseppe Federico Mancini* (Giuffrè Editore, 1998), pp. 1003–1031.

believe me, I will be delighted. The objective is democracy; states are but the means and the history of this century has shown to what point they can turn out to be catastrophic when they become an end in themselves.

G.F. MANCINI
Bologna 1999

1

The Making of a Constitution
for Europe

I. INTRODUCTION

FOR EDUCATED OBSERVERS of European affairs, whether friends or foes of a strong Community, the magnitude of the contribution made by the Court of Justice to the integration of Europe has almost become a byword. It is unnecessary to quote the friends, which in any event, since they tend to be enthusiastic, would be somewhat embarrassing for a member of the Court. Far more interesting are the enemies or the less than lukewarm supporters of a united Europe. In England politicians who openly criticize judges are frowned upon; Mrs Thatcher, a barrister, is aware of this rule and cannot therefore be quoted, though her private reactions to judgments encroaching on British sovereign rights and interests are easy to visualize. But that old, unredeemed Gaullist, the former Prime Minister Michel Debré, is eminently quotable: "J'accuse la Cour de Justice", he said as late as 1979, "de mégalomanie maladive", by which, of course, he meant insufficient deference to the sovereign rights and interests of France.

If one were asked to synthetize the direction in which the case law produced in Luxembourg has moved since 1957, one would have to say that it coincides with the making of a constitution for Europe. Unlike the USA, the EC was born as a peculiar form of international organization. Its peculiarity resided in the unique institutional structure and the unprecedented law-making and judicial powers it was given. But these features—admittedly reminiscent of a federal State—should not overshadow two essential facts. First: while the American Declaration of Independence spoke of "*one people*" dissolving the bonds which connected them with "*another people*", the preamble of the EC Treaty recites that the contracting parties are "determined to lay the foundations of an ever closer union among the *peoples* of Europe".[1] Secondly and more important: the instrument giving rise to the Community was a traditional multilateral *treaty*.

Treaties are basically different from constitutions. In many countries (and "many" includes even some of the founding States of the EC) they do not enjoy the status of higher law. The interpretation of treaties is subject to canons unlike

---

[1] See F. Jacobs and K. Karst, "The 'Federal' Legal Order: The U.S.A. and Europe Compared: Juridical Perspective" in M. Cappelletti, M. Seccombe and J.H.H. Weiler (eds.), *Integration through Law*, Volume I, Book 1 (de Gruyter, Berlin-New York, 1986), p. 169 at p. 171.

all others (such as, for example, the principle according to which limitations of states' sovereignty shall not be presumed and shall be construed restrictively, the presumption that states do not lose their sovereignty). As a rule, treaties devise systems of checks and balances whose main function is to keep under control the powers of the organization which they set up. In the case of the EC Treaty these differences are emphasized by two highly significant characteristics. The Treaty does not safeguard the human rights of the individuals affected by its application, nor does it recognize, even in an embryonic form, a constitutional right to European citizenship. Europe cannot confer citizenship; this remains the prerogative of the Member States. By the same token, individual citizens of a Member State are entitled to move from their State to another Member State exclusively by virtue of their being workers, self-employed persons or providers of services, that is *qua* units of a production factor.

The main endeavour of the Court of Justice has precisely been to remove or reduce the differences just mentioned. In other words, the Court has sought to "constitutionalize" the Treaty, that is to fashion a constitutional framework for a federal-type structure in Europe. Whether this effort was always inspired by a clear and consistent philosophy is arguable, but that is not really important. What really matters are its achievements—and they are patent to all.

To be sure, the Court has been helped by favourable circumstances. The combination of being, as it were, out of sight and out of mind by virtue of its location in the fairy-tale Grand Duchy of Luxembourg and the benign neglect of the media has certainly contributed to its ability to create a sense of belonging on the part of its independent-minded members and, where necessary, to convert them into confirmed Europeans.[2] Furthermore, the Judges and Advocates General have usually been middle-aged and at least half of them have been academics. As a group, therefore, they have never met the three conditions of Lord Diplock's famous verdict: "by training, temperament and age judges are too averse to change to be entrusted with the development of rules of conduct for a brave new world".[3]

Nevertheless, these circumstances do not explain the whole story. The Court would have been far less successful had it not been assisted by two mighty allies: the national courts and the Commission. The institutional position of the former will be clarified below. It is sufficient to mention here that by referring to Luxembourg sensitive questions of interpretation of Community law they have been indirectly responsible for the boldest judgments the Court has made. Moreover, by adhering to these judgments in deciding the cases before them, and therefore by lending them the credibility which national judges usually enjoy in their own countries, they have rendered the case law of the Court both effective and respected throughout the Community.

---

[2] See E. Stein, "Lawyers, Judges and the Making of a Transnational Constitution" (1981) *American Journal of International Law* 1.

[3] Diplock, "The Courts as Legislators" in B.W. Harvey (ed.), *The Lawyer and Justice* (1978), p. 263 at p. 280.

As to the Commission, the founding fathers and especially Jean Monnet conceived it as a sort of "Platonic embodiment of Communitarian spirit, with Gallic élan, self-confidence and expertise".[4] As the executive-political branch of the Community, the Commission may not have always lived up to those expectations, but as "watchdog of the Treaty", that is both as the prosecutor of Member State infractions and as an *amicus curiae* in cases referred by the national courts, it has undoubtedly played a most positive role. In other words, the Commission has led the Court—particularly by assuaging the concern some of the Judges may have felt regarding the acceptability of their rulings[5]—on the path toward further integration and increased Community power.

On the other hand, the Parliament and the Council are not natural allies of the Court. The Parliament evinced great sympathy for the Court in the 1960s and the 1970s, but then its function was simply that of a debating forum. More recently, however, the Parliament has been involved in a permanent trial of strength with the Council: the stake is a new allocation of power in the budgetary and legislative areas. The Court is a victim of this (in itself entirely legitimate) turbulence. The reason is obvious. Luxembourg is more and more encumbered by increasingly political and emotion-loaded intra-Community controversies: hence a visibility and an exposure to scrutiny by the media that are in sharp contrast with the conditions under which progress was made in the past.

The Council, the Community legislative body, is bound not to be an ally of the Court. Although formally an institution with supranational characteristics like the others, it was drawn by its very composition—a gathering of national Ministers—into resembling an intergovernmental round table often characterized by all the warmth of a love match in a snake-pit. In other words, its members regularly speak, and no doubt think, in terms of negotiating with their partners much as they would do in any other international context.[6] The observation that "decisionally, the Community is closer to the United Nations than it is to the United States" is therefore particularly telling.[7]

This situation is heightened by the weight acquired in the area of law-making by COREPER (the Committee of Permanent Representatives of the Member States) and its many subcommittees. The permanent representatives are ambassadors and the subcommittees are composed of national officials. While a minister may occasionally be expected to deal with a given problem in a supranational spirit, it would be naïve to expect an ambassador or a national bureaucrat, whatever his leanings, to assist wilfully in the process of the wasting away of Member State power, thereby blighting his own career.

---

[4] S. Krislov, C.-D. Ehlermann and J.H.H. Weiler, "The Political Organs and the Decision-Making Process in the United States and the European Communities" in Cappelletti *et al., supra* n. 1, Volume I, Book 2, p. 3 at p. 18.

[5] See Stein, *supra* n. 2.   [6] See Jacobs and Karst, *supra* n. 1, at p. 186.

[7] Cappelletti, Seccombe and Weiler, "A General Introduction", *supra* n. 1, p. 3 at p. 29.

2. JUDICIAL CONSTITUTIONALIZATION

(a) Supremacy

It was noted above that, unlike federal constitutions, treaties creating inter-national organizations do not usually enjoy higher-law status with regard to the laws of the contracting powers. Article VI of the American Constitution reads: "the laws of the United States . . . shall be the supreme law of the land; and the Judges in every State shall be bound thereby; any thing in the constitution or laws of any State to the contrary notwithstanding". In the same vein section 109 of the Australian Constitution provides that "When a law of a State is inconsistent with a law of the Commonwealth the latter shall prevail and the former shall be . . . invalid", and the German Fundamental Law stipulates just as clearly that *Bundesrecht bricht Landesrecht.* On the contrary, the EC Treaty, while including some hortatory provisions to the same effect (Article 5), fails to state squarely whether Community law is pre-eminent *vis-à-vis* prior and subsequent Member State law.

The now undisputed existence of a supremacy clause in the Community framework is therefore a product of judicial creativeness. In *Costa* v *ENEL*,[8] a case which arose in the early 1960s before a *giudice conciliatore* (local magistrate) in Milan, a shareholder of a nationalized power company challenged as being contrary to the EC Treaty the Italian law nationalizing the electric industry. The Italian Government claimed before the Court of Justice that the Court had no business to deal with the matter: the magistrate, it said, should apply the nationalization law as the most current indication of parliamentary intention and could not avail of the reference procedure provided for by the Treaty. But the Court ruled that "by creating a Community of unlimited duration, having its own institutions, its own personality . . . and, more particularly, real powers stemming from a limitation of sovereignty or a transfer of powers from the States to the Community, the Member States have limited their sovereign rights . . . and have thus created a body of law which binds both their nationals and themselves".[9]

Is this line of reasoning entirely cogent? Some legal writers doubt it and a few have regarded *Costa* v *ENEL* as an example of judicial activism "running wild".[10] Yet, the Court's supremacy doctrine was accepted by the judiciaries and the administrations of both the original and the new Member States, with the exception of some grumblings by the French Conseil d'Etat, the Italian Corte costituzionale and a couple of English Law Lords. Lord Denning, a majestic but irritable elderly gentleman, was caught intimating that "once a bill is passed by

---

[8] Case 6/64 [1964] ECR 585.

[9] *Ibid.*, at 593.

[10] H. Rasmussen, *On Law and Policy in the European Court of Justice: A Comparative Study in Judicial Policymaking* (Martinus Nijhoff, Dordrecht-Boston-Lancaster, 1986).

Parliament, that will dispose of all this discussion about the Treaty".[11] A few years later, however, Lord Diplock admitted that even subsequent acts of Parliament must be interpreted in line with Community law, no matter how far-fetched the interpretation.[12] Lord Diplock, and many other national judges before him, obviously realized that the alternative to the supremacy clause would have been a rapid erosion of the Community; and this was a possibility that nobody really envisaged, not even the most intransigent custodians of national sovereignty. Actually, the "or else" argument, though not fully spelled out, was used by the Court, and it was this argument, much more than the one just quoted, that led to a ready reception of the doctrine in *Costa* v *ENEL*.

But the recognition of Community pre-eminence was not only an indispensable development, it was also a logical development. It is self-evident that in a federal or quasi-federal context the issue of supremacy will arise only if federal norms are to apply directly, that is to bear upon the federation's citizens without any need of intervention by the Member States.[13] Article 189 of the EC Treaty identifies a category of Community norms that do not require national implementing measures but are binding on the States and their citizens as soon as they enter into force: the founding fathers called them "regulations" and provided them principally for those areas where the Treaty itself merely defines the thrust of Community policy and leaves its elaboration to later decisions of the European Parliament, the Council and the Commission. One year before *Costa* v *ENEL*, however, the Court had enormously extended the Community power to deal directly with the public by ruling in *Van Gend en Loos*[14] that even Treaty provisions may be relied upon by private individuals if they expressly grant them rights and impose on the Member States an obligation so precise and unconditional that it can be fulfilled without the necessity of further measures.

(b) Direct Effect

Costa v *ENEL* may be regarded therefore as a sequel of *Van Gend en Loos*. It is not the only sequel, however. Eleven years after *Van Gend en Loos*, in *Yvonne Van Duyn* v *Home Office*[15] the Court took a further step forward by attributing direct effect to provisions of directives not transposed into the laws of the Member States within the prescribed time limit, so long as they met the conditions laid down in *Van Gend en Loos*. In order to appreciate fully the scope of this development it should be borne in mind that while the principal subjects

[11] *Felixstowe Dock and Ry Co.* v *British Transport Docks Board* [1976] 2 *Common Market Law Reports* 655.

[12] *Garland* v *British Rail Engineering* [1982] 2 All ER 402.

[13] D.J. Elazar and I. Greilsammer, "Federal Democracy: the USA and Europe Compared—A Political Science Perspective" in Cappelletti *et al.*, *supra* n. 1, Volume I, Book 1, p. 71 at p. 103.

[14] Case 26/62 *NV Algemene Transport- en Expeditie Onderneming van Gend en Loos* v *Nederlandse Administratie der Belastingen* [1963] ECR 3.

[15] Case 41/74 [1974] ECR 1337.

governed by regulations are agriculture, transport, customs and the social security of migrant workers, Community authorities resort to directives when they intend to harmonize national laws on such matters as taxes, banking, equality of the sexes, protection of the environment, employment contracts and organization of companies. Plain cooking and haute cuisine, in other words. The hope of seeing Europe grow institutionally, in matters of social relationships and in terms of quality of life rests to a large extent on the adoption and the implementation of directives.[16]

Making directives immediately applicable poses, however, a formidable problem. Unlike regulations and the Treaty provisions dealt with by *Van Gend en Loos*, directives resemble international treaties, in so far as they are binding *only* on the States and *only* as to the result to be achieved. It is understandable therefore that, whereas the *Van Gend en Loos* doctrine established itself within a relatively short time, its extension to directives met with bitter opposition in many quarters. For example, the French Conseil d'Etat and the German Bundesfinanzhof bluntly refused to abide by it and Rasmussen, in a most un-Danish fit of temper, went so far as to condemn it as a case of "revolting judicial behaviour".[17]

Understandable criticism is not necessarily justifiable. It is mistaken to believe that in attributing direct effect to directives not yet complied with by the Member States, the Court was only guided by political considerations, such as the intention of by-passing the States in a strategic area of law-making.[18] Non-compliance with directives is the most typical and most frequent form of Member State infraction; moreover, the Community authorities often turn a blind eye to it and, even when the Commission institutes proceedings against the defaulting State under Article 169 of the EC Treaty, the Court cannot impose any penalty on that State.[19] This gives the directives a dangerously elastic quality: Italy, Greece or Belgium may agree to accept the enactment of a directive with which it is uncomfortable knowing that the price to pay for possible failure to transpose it is non-existent or minimal.

Given these circumstances, it is sometimes submitted that the *Van Duyn* doctrine was essentially concerned with assuring respect for the rule of law. The Court's main purpose, in other words, was "to ensure that neither level of government can rely upon its malfeasance—the Member State's failure to comply, the Community's failure or even inability to enforce compliance", with a view to frustrating the legitimate expectation of the Community citizens on whom

---

[16] For a further elaboration of this idea see my article "The Incorporation of Community Law into the Domestic Laws of the Member States of the European Communities" in Unidroit (ed.), *International Uniform Law in Practice* (Unidroit and Oceana, Rome-New York, 1988), p. 13 at p. 23, reproduced as Chapter 15.

[17] Rasmussen, *supra* n. 10, at p. 12.

[18] This and the following remarks are drawn from Cappelletti *et al.*, *supra* n. 1, at p. 38 ff.

[19] The Maastricht Treaty added two paragraphs to Article 171 empowering the Court to impose financial penalties on a Member State which fails to comply with an earlier judgment of the Court declaring that the Member State is in breach of the EC Treaty.

the directive confers rights. Indeed, "if a Court is forced to condone wholesale violation of a norm, that norm can no longer be termed law"; nobody will deny that "directives are intended to have the force of law under the Treaty".[20]

Doubtless, in arriving at its judgment in *Van Duyn*, the Court may also have considered that by reducing the advantages Member States derived from non-compliance, its judgment would have strengthened the "federal" reach of the Community power to legislate and it may even have welcomed such a consequence. But does that warrant the revolt staged by the Conseil d'Etat or the Bundesfinanzhof? The present author doubts it; and so did the German Constitutional Court, which sharply scolded the Bundesfinanzhof for its rejection of the *Van Duyn* doctrine.[21] This went a long way towards restoring whatever legitimacy the Court of Justice had lost in the eyes of some observers following *Van Duyn*. The wound, one might say, is healed and the scars it has left are scarcely visible.

(c) Pre-emption

Supremacy and direct effect are usually regarded as two of the three principal doctrines encapsulating the judicial constitutionalization of the EC Treaty. The third notion is pre-emption, which may be dealt with very briefly. A familiar notion to American lawyers, pre-emption plays a decisive role in the allocation of power and it is an essential complement of the supremacy doctrine since it determines "whether a whole policy area has been actually or potentially occupied by the central authority so as to influence the intervention of the States in that area".[22] The Court of Justice discovered this problem at a rather early stage and has tended to solve it in an increasingly trenchant way.

It may be useful to give two illustrations which are indicative of this attitude. Under the common agricultural policy the Community has adopted for most products a Community-wide marketing system; the Court has taken the view that the very existence of such a system precludes Member States from legislating within the field covered by it.[23] Even more telling are the British fishery cases involving conservation measures in the North Sea. After lengthy consideration of the way in which powers to adopt these rules had been transferred to the Community, the Court held that Member States were no longer at liberty to enact conservation laws even though no Community measures had been taken.[24]

---

[20] Cappelletti *et al.*, *supra* n. 1 at p. 39.
[21] Bundesverfassungsgericht, judgment of 8 April 1987, in *BVerfGE*, 75, p. 223, reproduced in [1988] 3 *Common Market Law Reports* 1.
[22] Cappelletti *et al.*, *supra* n. 1, at p. 32.
[23] Jacobs and Karst, *supra* n. 1, at p. 238.
[24] Case 804/79 *Commission* v *United Kingdom* [1981] ECR 1045. See T. Koopmans, "Federalism, the European Community and the Case Law of the Court of Justice", text of a speech delivered on 27 March 1987 at the University of Leuven.

3. JUDICIAL REVIEW OF COMMUNITY LEGISLATION

Let us now turn to a different, but no less important achievement of the Court's case law. An essential feature of all federal systems is the judicial review of legislation. Striving as it did to endow the Community with a constitutional framework for a federal-type structure, the Court was bound to come to grips with this "conundrum to democracies", as Cappelletti has aptly called it.[25] Under Article 173 of the EC Treaty, the Court has the power to review the legality of acts of the European Parliament, the Council and the Commission in actions brought by those institutions, by the Member States and even, albeit within certain limited circumstances, by "natural and legal persons". But this is tantamount to solving only a part—indeed the smaller part—of the problem. As Oliver Wendell Holmes said: "I do not think the United States would come to an end if the Supreme Court lost its power to declare an Act of Congress void, but the Union would be imperilled if the courts could not make that declaration as to the laws of the several States".[26]

The EC Treaty does not empower the Court to review Member State laws. It provides, however, for a machinery which, although overtly conceived for a different function (securing the uniform application of Community law throughout the Member States), has been utilized by the Court in such a way as to enable it to monitor national laws for incompatibility with the Treaty and with secondary legislation. Under Article 177 of the EC Treaty, the Court of Justice is given jurisdiction to rule, on a reference from courts and tribunals of the Member States, on any question of interpretation and validity of Community law raised before them; while lower courts *may* request the Court of Justice to give a preliminary ruling, courts of last resort *must* send the matter to Luxembourg.

How effective is the preliminary rulings procedure? In comparing it with a fully-fledged dual system of federal courts as can be found in the USA, some learned writers have described it as legally frailer, but politically more faithful to the federal ethos.[27] While the latter opinion is disputable, the former is no doubt correct since the Community system of review requires, much more than the American one, the cooperation and goodwill of the State courts. The reason is twofold: under Article 177, litigants do not have *locus standi* to appeal national judicial decisions to the Court of Justice and the Court lacks coercive powers to enforce its judgments.[28]

The Court's first preoccupation was therefore to win that cooperation and that goodwill. The early results were frustrating. It took almost four years

[25] See M. Cappelletti, *The Judicial Process in Comparative Perspective* (Clarendon Press, Oxford, 1989), p. 149.

[26] O.W. Holmes, Jr., "Law and the Court", *Collected Legal Papers* (Peter Smith, New York, 1952), p. 291, at pp. 295–296.

[27] Cappelletti *et al.*, *supra* n. 1, at p. 23.

[28] Cappelletti, *et al.*, *supra* n. 1, at p. 367.

before the first reference made by a national judicial body—the Gerechtshof in The Hague—was received at the Court and legend has it that on that day there was abundant popping of champagne corks in the deliberation room. As time went by, however, requests for a preliminary ruling began to arrive in increasing numbers and by the end of the 1980s they amounted to 150 a year on average. More importantly, most national courts—about 95 per cent according to a survey carried out at that time—accepted the rulings they sought and some went so far as to accept even rulings requested by other courts when they had to decide a similar case. In short, the interpretations given at Luxembourg have acquired a binding authority and, at least to some extent, they have been attributed precedential value.

Why did this happen? The only reason I can see, much as expounding it may sound awkward, is the cleverness of my predecessors. If what makes a judge "good" is his awareness of the constraints on judicial decision-making and the knowledge that rulings must be convincing in order to evoke obedience, the Luxembourg Judges of the 1960s and the 1970s were obviously *very* good. In other words, knowing that the Court had almost no powers that were not traceable to its institutional standing and the persuasiveness of its judgments, they made the most of these assets.[29] Thus, they developed a style that may be drab and repetitive, but explains as well as declares the law and they showed unlimited patience *vis-à-vis* the national judges, reformulating questions couched in imprecise terms or extracting from the documents concerning the main proceedings the elements of Community law which needed to be interpreted with regard to the subject matter of the dispute.

It was by following this courteously didactic method that the Luxembourg Judges won the confidence of their colleagues from Palermo to Edinburgh and from Bordeaux to Berlin; and it was by winning their confidence that they were able to transform the procedure of Article 177 into a tool whereby private individuals may challenge their national legislation for incompatibility with Community law. It bears repeating that under Article 177 national judges can *only* request the Court of Justice to interpret a Community measure. The Court never told them they were entitled to overstep that bound; in fact, whenever they did so—for example, whenever they asked if national rule A is in violation of Community Regulation B or Directive C—the Court answered that its only power is to explain what B or C actually mean. But, having paid this lip service to the language of the Treaty and having clarified the meaning of the relevant Community measure, the Court usually went on to indicate to what extent a *certain type* of national legislation can be regarded as compatible with that measure.[30] The national judge is thus led hand in hand as far as the door; crossing the threshold is his job, but now a job no harder than child's play.

---

[29] See Cappelletti, *et al.*, *supra* n. 1, at p. 371.
[30] See Koopmans, *supra* n. 24. See further Chapter 2.

[handwritten marginalia: Constitution requires a citizenship, so strengthen? go through here?]

4. COMMUNITY CITIZENSHIP

Let us now return to the issues of Community citizenship and the human rights of Community citizens. As pointed out at the beginning, the EC Treaty guarantees labour mobility and the right of the migrant worker and his family to share, on a par with national workers, the social benefits of the host country, including housing, medical care, education and social security rights. But this system, although a remarkable advance by comparison with the time when the migration of workers was handled by the authorities of the host State, does not entail any recognition of a common citizenship status. Individuals may be said to derive their transnational rights from their constitutional position of being nationals of a Member State and from their functional status of being workers.[31]

In recent times, however, an evolution has been clearly detectable. Since 1979 the European Parliament is elected by popular vote, on the cover of passports issued by the Member States the words "European Community" are printed above the name of the issuing country and college students are granted scholarships enabling them to get credit in any other EC country. Even more significantly, the Commission has proposed directives under which the right to stay or settle in another Member State and enjoy the same privileges as its nationals (including the right to vote in local elections) would be conferred on *all* Europeans, whether workers or not.[32] The Court has of course been aware that certain progressive forces are trying to give rise to a form, albeit still imperfect, of European citizenship and seizing the opportunity offered, it legitimized their efforts with one of its shrewdest judgments.[33]

In June 1982, Mr Ian William Cowan, a United Kingdom national, was paying a visit to his son in Paris. At the exit of a metro station he was thrashed by a gang of rowdies and the assault caused him severe physical damage for which he asked compensation under article 706/15 of the French Code of Criminal Procedure. As far as foreigners are concerned, however, this provision requires the victim of an assault to hold a residence permit or to be the national of a country which has entered into a reciprocal agreement with France. As he met neither condition, Mr Cowan was not indemnified. He therefore brought the case before the Commission d'indemnisation des victimes d'infractions [Compensation

---

[31] Cappelletti *et al.*, *supra* n. 1, at p. 48. See also M. Garth, "Migrant Workers and Rights of Mobility in the European Community and the United States: a Study of Law, Community and Citizenship in the Welfare State" in Cappelletti *et al.*, *supra* n. 1, Volume I, Book 3, p. 85, at p. 103 *et seq.*

[32] See the proposal for a Council Directive on voting rights for Community nationals in local elections in their Member States of residence, OJ 1988 C 246, p. 4; Proposal for a Council Directive on the right of residence for students, OJ 1989 C 191, p. 2; Proposal for a Council Directive on the right of residence for employees and self-employed persons who have ceased their occupational activity, OJ 1989 C 191, p. 3; Proposal for a Council Directive on the right of residence, OJ 1989 C 191, p. 5.

[33] Case 186/87 *Ian William Cowan* v *Trésor public* [1989] ECR 195.

Board for Victims of Crime), a body attached to the Paris Tribunal de Grande Instance. The Commission stayed the proceedings and asked the Court to rule on the interpretation of the principle of non-discrimination as set out in what was then Article 7 of the EEC Treaty in order that it could assess whether the French measure was compatible with Community law.

The Court stressed that the prohibition of discrimination on grounds of nationality applies not only to goods and workers moving throughout the common market, but also to the movement of services and noted that the latter includes both the freedom to provide and the freedom to receive a service anywhere in the Community. A corollary of this finding is that a person who goes to another country in order to receive such a service must be guaranteed protection on the same basis as the nationals of that country and the aliens residing there. A tourist is by definition a recipient of services; hence, when a State grants protection against the risk of assault and, if the risk materializes, financial compensation, the tourist is obviously entitled to both. Mr Cowan was probably a tourist and this is why the Court insisted on that notion. However, since leaving one's country without resorting to services provided in the host country (means of transportation, hotels, restaurants etc.), is impossible, it is safe to conclude that the *Cowan* judgment does not fall much behind the words of Justice Jacksons's concurring opinion in *Edwards* v *California*: "it is a privilege of citizenship of the United States, protected from state abridgment, to enter any state of the Union, either for temporary sojourn or for the establishment of permament residence therein".[34]

5. THE PROTECTION OF HUMAN RIGHTS

Human rights is the next area for consideration. In the same way as they ignored the issue of citizenship, the framers of the EC Treaty did not envisage the need to protect human rights) Presumably they knew that bills of rights are in the long run a powerful vehicle of integration and in 1957, when the European climate was already tinged with scepticism and in any event was no longer virginal, they were not eager to see the integration process speeded up by a central authority empowered to safeguard the civil liberties of the Community citizens first in Brussels and later, perhaps, in the six countries concerned.[35] But there is a further possibility: the founding fathers may have thought that the scope of Community law was essentially limited to economic issues and, as such, did not

---

[34] 314 U.S. (1941) 160 at 183. For the developments in the Court's case law since the establishment of Union citizenship in Article 8 of the EC Treaty see Case C-85/96 *María Martínez Sala* v *Freistaat Bayern* [1998] ECR I-2691 and Case C-274/96 *Criminal proceedings against Horst Otto Bickel and Ulrich Franz* [1998] ECR I-7637.

[35] This theme has been developed at some length in "Safeguarding Human Rights: the Role of the Court of Justice of the European Communities" in F. Carpi and C. Giovannucci Orlandi (eds.), *Judicial Protection of Human Rights at the National and International Level* (Milan, 1991), pp. 497–517; reproduced as Chapter 6.

involve human rights problems. If this is the reason why they omitted to guarantee those rights, no American observer should be shocked by their attitude as he only has to recall that, in arguing for the ratification of the constitution despite the absence of a bill of rights, Hamilton and Madison took the view that the limited powers of the federal government made such a bill unnecessary.[36] Indeed, it is well known that the American Supreme Court did not issue any important opinion in the area of free speech until well into this century.

Europe, however, experienced a quicker development. As Community law came to govern diverse and sometimes unforeseen facets of human activity, it encroached upon a whole gamut of old and new rights with both an economic and a strictly "civil" content. Thus, a problem which in 1957 might have appeared to be of practical insignificance turned ten years later into one of the most controversial questions of Community law; so much so that it ended by taking on the character of a major judicial conflict. On 18 October 1967 the Constitutional Court of the Federal Republic of Germany decided that the Community order, lacking any protection for human rights, had no lawful democratic basis. The transfer of powers from Germany to the Community could therefore not deprive German citizens of the protection accorded to them by their Constitution; it followed that Community law had to be examined at national level to ensure that it was compatible with internal constitutional provisions.[37]

It was a brutal blow, a blow jeopardizing not only the supremacy but the very independence of Community law. Something had to be done and the Court did it, both for fear that its hard-won conquests might vanish and because of its own growing awareness that a "democratic deficit" had become apparent in the management of the Community. Thus, initially in *dicta* and finally in the *Nold* judgment of 1974, the Luxembourg Judges declared that "fundamental rights form an integral part of the general principles of law, the observance of which it ensures". But what book would they have to consult for the identification and the protection of such rights? *Nold* answered this question too: "The Court is bound to draw inspiration from constitutional traditions common to the Member States . . . International treaties for the protection of human rights on which the Member States have collaborated . . . can supply guidelines which should be followed within the framework of Community law".[38]

There were to be two sources in other words: common constitutional values and human rights conventions. In the fifteen years following *Nold* the Court extracted from both of them, but increasingly from the second one whatever elements could contribute to the preservation of minimum human-rights standards in the legislative output and the administrative practice of Brussels. More specif-

---

[36] Cappelletti, *supra* n. 1, at p. 171.

[37] Bundesverfassungsgericht, judgment of 18 October 1967, in *BVerfGE*, 22, p. 293, reproduced in [1968] *CMLRev* 483.

[38] Case 4/73 *J. Nold, Kohlen- und Baustoffgrosshandlung* v *Commission* [1974] ECR 491 at para. 13.

ically, and disregarding rights of a purely economic nature, the Court concerned itself with procedural and substantive due process,[39] respect for private life,[40] lawyers' business secrecy,[41] the fact that criminal law provisions cannot be made retroactive,[42] the principle of review by courts,[43] the inviolability of domicile and the right not to incriminate oneself. These last two, it should be noted, were dealt with in cases brought by multinationals complaining about some antitrust searches and inquiries made by Commission officials under Article 85 of the EC Treaty.[44]

How should one assess this case law? According to Cappelletti, watching "those thirteen little men unknown to most of the 320 million Community citizens, devoid of political power, charisma and popular legitimation" who claim "for themselves the . . . capacity to do what the framers did not even think of doing, and what the political branches of the Community do not even try to undertake", is a fascinating spectacle.[45] Though perhaps guilty of artistic licence, Cappelletti may not be mistaken. Reading an unwritten bill of rights into Community law is indeed the most striking contribution the Court has made to the development of a constitution for Europe. This statement, however, should be qualified in two respects. First, as said above, that contribution was forced on the Court from outside, by the German and, later, the Italian Constitutional Courts.[46] Secondly, the Court's effort to safeguard the fundamental rights of the Community citizens stopped at the threshold of national legislations.

So far, in other words, Europe has not experienced anything resembling *Gitlow* v *New York*, the judgment in which the American Supreme Court held that the limitations laid down in the United States Bill of Rights are not only applicable to the federal government but extend to the laws and administrative practices of the individual states.[47] In *Cinéthèque* v *Fédération nationale des cinémas français*, the Court of Justice made it clear that "it has no power to examine the compatibility" with its human rights catalogue of laws concerning

---

[39] Case 98/79 *Josette Pecastaing* v *Belgium* [1980] ECR 691; Case 209/78 *Heintz van Landewyck Sàrl and others* v *Commission* [1980] ECR 3125; Joined Cases 100–103/80 *SA Musique Diffusion française and others* v *Commission* [1985] ECR 1825.

[40] Case 136/79 *National Panasonic UK Limited* v *Commission* [1980] ECR 2033; Case 145/83 *Stanley George Adams* v *Commission* [1985] ECR 3539.

[41] Case 155/79 *AM & S Europe Limited* v *Commission* [1982] ECR 1575.

[42] Case 63/83 *Regina* v *Kent Kirk* [1984] ECR 2689.

[43] Case 141/84 *Henri de Compte* v *European Parliament* [1985] ECR 1951; Case 222/84 *Marguerite Johnston* v *Chief Constable of the Royal Ulster Constabulary* [1986] ECR 1651; Case 222/86 *Union nationale des entraîneurs et cadres techniques professionnels du football (Unectef)* v *Georges Heylens and others* [1987] ECR 4097.

[44] Joined Cases 46/87 and 227/88 *Hoechst AG* v *Commission* [1989] ECR 2859; Joined Cases 97, 98 and 99/87 *Dow Chemical Iberica, SA and others* v *Commission* [1989] ECR 3165; Case 85/87 *Dow Benelux N.V.* v *Commission* [1989] ECR 3137; Case 27/88 *Solvay & Cie* v *Commission* [1989] ECR 3355; Case 374/87 *Orkem* v *Commission* [1989] ECR 3283.

[45] Cappelletti *et al.*, *supra* n. 1, at p. 174.

[46] *Corte costituzionale*, judgment of 27 December 1973, No 183, *Frontini*, in *Giurisprudenza costituzionale*, 1973, 2401, reproduced in [1974] 2 *Common Market Law Reports* 381.

[47] 268 U.S. (1925), 652.

areas which fall "within the jurisdiction of the national legislator".[48] For a self-inflicted restriction, this is rather severe. It is however compensated by the fact that, in terms of respect for human rights, no Member State is comparable with Noriega's Panama or, for that matter, Huey Long's Louisiana. Moreover, one can safely assume that since Community law penetrates directly the legal systems of the Member States national courts interpreting the laws of their own State in the light of a fundamental freedom are unlikely to remain below the standards set at Luxembourg.[49]

6. CONCLUSION

The foregoing survey—which is incomplete since it has not dealt with the case law of the Court in such crucial matters as the movement of goods and the international posture of the Community—should leave no doubt as to the degree of activism the Court displayed in fostering the integration of Europe and forging a European identity. Judicial activism, however, is not necessarily a good thing. Judges are usually incompetent as law-makers and their inventiveness is incompatible with the values of certainty and predictability; it is indeed unfair, since the findings of inventive courts catch the litigants by surprise.[50] Worse still, as a former Judge at the Court, Thijmen Koopmans, has put it, courts "are not designed to be a reflex of a democratic society".[51] If this is true, adventurous enterprises of the kind described above are only acceptable under very particular conditions. Listing such conditions would serve no purpose, but those prevailing in Europe during the Gaullist revolt and the dark age of stagnation that followed it should certainly be counted amongst them: above all, there were the inexistence of a body both representative and genuinely legislative, and the obdurate reluctance of the Member States to fully implement the EC Treaty which they themselves had framed.

In these circumstances, does it have any meaning to raise the problem of the Court's activism? The fact is that things have changed: the Parliament is now able to exert a considerable influence on the law-making process, the Commission was headed in the 1980s and 1990s by a dedicated European who also happened to be a consummate politician, hundreds of directives have been enacted and, last but not least, we have witnessed a heated debate on whether

---

[48] Joined Cases 60 and 61/84 [1985] ECR 2605 at para. 26. This judgment has been criticized by J.H.H. Weiler in "The European Court at a Crossroads: Community Human Rights and Member State Action" in F. Capotorti *et al.*, *Du droit international au droit de l'intégration* (Nomos, Baden-Baden, 1987), p. 821 *et seq*. See, however, *infra* n. 52.

[49] J.A. Frowein, "Fundamental Human Rights as a Vehicle of Legal Integration in Europe", in Cappelletti *et al.*, *supra* n. 1, Volume I, Book 3, p. 300 at p. 302.

[50] See generally Cappelletti, *supra* n. 1, at p. 35 *et seq*.

[51] T. Koopmans, "The Roots of Judicial Activism" in *Protecting Human Rights: the European Dimension, Studies in Honour of Gérard J. Wiarda* (Carl Heymans, Köln-Berlin-Bonn-München, 1988), p. 317 at p. 321.

an integrated Europe should be a giant consumers' union with goods, services and capital flowing unhindered or a political entity directing economic change into socially beneficial channels.

Some observers argued in the light of these changes that the time had come for the Court to reconsider its philosophy. When democracy advances and politics asserts its claims, judges are bound to take a pace back. The reason for their being in the van has waned, and if they insist on remaining there, they risk to become so embroiled in the passions of the day as to imperil their most precious resource, their independence.

These remarks contain more than a kernel of truth and the Court itself seems to have grasped this. *Cinéthèque* might indeed have signalled the opening of a new trend in its jurisprudence, and a similar attitude was detectable in *Comitology*, a judgment which refused to equalize the jurisdictional status of Parliament to that of the Commission and the Council by giving it standing to bring an action under Article 173 of the EC Treaty.[52] Accepting a measure of self-restraint, however, does not mean embarking on a course of strict constructionism. The Court is likely to extend the area of problems which it feels should be solved by the political institutions, but in other areas it will undoubtedly go on feeling that it can, or rather must, exercise guidance.

There are essentially two such areas. The first includes a number of issues which the Council is obliged or empowered to regulate under the EC Treaty, but did not regulate on purpose, so as to avoid for as long as possible their adjustment to Community criteria. State aids to industry are a case in point. Deciding whether they are compatible with the common market falls to the Commission, but the surveillance power of its officials is seriously impaired by the lack of rules imposing on the States a timely and accurate notification of the subsidies they grant.[53] Sooner or later, therefore, such rules will have to be written by the Court.

The second area is a result of the Single European Act. The words of Article 7a ("The internal market shall comprise an area without internal frontiers in which the free movement of goods, persons, services and capital is ensured") have by now rung all over the world. Only specialists, however, know that they are accompanied by manifold derogations, sometimes in the form of joint declarations appended to the Act, which deprive them of much of their scope and effectiveness. The binding force and the meaning of such declarations are often uncertain. What should one make, for example, of the most incisive one which stipulates that "setting the date of 31 December 1992 does not create an

---

[52] Case 302/87 *European Parliament v Council* (*"Comitology"*)[1988] ECR 5615. Although, with hindsight, the Court's reluctance on the one hand to review Member States' compliance with fundamental rights standards and, on the other, to extend standing to the European Parliament to bring an action under Article 173 was shortlived: see respectively, Case 260/89 *Elliniki Radiophonia Tiléorassi and others v Dimotiki Etairia Pliroforissis and others* (*"ERT"*) [1991] ECR I-2925; and Case C-70/88 *European Parliament v Council* (*"Chernobyl"*) [1991] ECR I-4529.

[53] See generally J. Pelkmans, "The Institutional Economics of European Integration" in Cappelletti *et al.*, *supra* n. 1, Volume I, Book 1, p. 318 at p. 373 *et seq.*

automatic legal effect"? Is this a formal rule governing the decisions of a court of law? And if it is, does it mean that Article 7a is incapable of instituting legal obligations or can it be read in a less disruptive way?[54]

The Court still has ample room to mould the destiny of the Community both by writing new rules and by cutting a number of Gordian knots. The most difficult challenge will be to reconcile this prospect with the necessity of a retreat from the daring of old—or, one might say, with the need for a little rest, all the more pleasant for being so richly deserved. But, of course, one always expects judges to know how to conceal a contradiction.

---

[54] See A.S. Toth, "The Legal Status of the Declarations annexed to the Single European Act" (1986) 23 *CMLRev* 803 *et seq.*

2

The Constitutional Challenges Facing the European Court of Justice

1. THE INHERENT WEAKNESS OF ARTICLE 177

T HE OUTSTANDING FEATURE of the procedure established by Article 177 of the EC Treaty is that it is entirely dependent on the goodwill of national courts. It is true that the third paragraph of Article 177 *obliges* national courts, against whose decisions there is no judicial remedy under domestic law, to seek a preliminary ruling from the Court of Justice whenever a question concerning the interpretation or validity of Community law is raised before them. That paragraph, however, lays down an obligation of a special kind; the litigant who seeks to invoke Community law, but whose plea for a "compulsory" reference falls on deaf ears in the national court of last instance, has no direct access to the Court of Justice in Luxembourg and finds himself in the unfortunate position of possessing a right without a remedy. The consequences of this can be truly dramatic, perhaps even shocking for those of us who have been nurtured on the comforting notion that Western society is founded upon the rule of law. A dealer may be sued on a contract that is null and void under Article 85 of the EC Treaty because it restrains trade. An importer of magazines may be prosecuted under an obscenity law that is caught by Article 30 and not saved by Article 36 of the Treaty because it amounts to arbitrary discrimination. The former may be compelled to perform the contract or pay damages; the latter may be fined or sent to prison. In both cases the individual's rights under Community law will be violated and he will have no redress. If he is British, he will probably write to his Members of Parliament, both national and European. If he is French, he will be likelier to complain to the Commission. If he is Italian, learned professors in ancient universities will write scholarly articles suggesting that the failure to refer the case to Luxembourg was a breach of the citizen's right to his "legal judge" under Article 25 of the Constitution. Only in Germany, it seems, would he have a better chance of success, since the Bundesverfassungsgericht has held that the corresponding provision of the *Grundgesetz* (Article 101) is infringed by a wrongful failure to refer.[1]

Even if the recalcitrant national court is persuaded to make a grudging reference and the Court of Justice solemnly pronounces a ruling that establishes the

---

[1] Bundesverfassungsgericht, judgment of 8 April 1987 (*Kloppenburg*), in *BVerfGE*, 75, p. 223, reproduced in [1988] 3 *Common Market Law Reports* 1.

litigant's rights under Community law, there is no way of ensuring that the ruling will be applied by the national court. The latter may not be familiar with, or may not accept,[2] the Court of Justice's established case law on the binding nature of preliminary rulings; or it may simply misconstrue the ruling and apply it incorrectly. Once again there is little that the litigant can do, other than console himself with the knowledge that his experiences may have served to enrich surveys on the implementation of preliminary rulings conducted in various European universities.

This fundamental weakness in the system of judicial protection established by Article 177 is all the more striking inasmuch as the reference procedure plays a crucial role in ensuring the uniform interpretation and application of Community law. And no one should be mistaken about the need for such uniformity. It is not just a question of achieving an aesthetic symmetry that is pleasing to the eye; uniformity of interpretation and application is vital for the continued existence of the European Community. Suppose, for example, that Article 177 did not exist and that the German courts held that Article 119 of the EC Treaty, laying down the principle of equal pay for men and women workers, had direct effect, but that the courts in the other Member States came to the opposite conclusion; the result would be a crippling, competitive disadvantage for German manufacturers. Or suppose that in relation to the free movement of goods the French and Italian courts held that restrictive measures applicable without distinction to domestic and imported goods were caught by Article 30 of the EC Treaty, but that the British and German courts took the view that only discriminatory measures were prohibited; the resulting distortions in competition would shake the very foundations of the Community.

The vital role of Article 177 was recognized by the Court in the *Van Gend en Loos* judgment,[3] where it held that one of the reasons for upholding the direct effect of certain provisions of Community law was the existence of the reference procedure. With devastatingly simple logic the Court observed that there would be little point in allowing national courts to seek rulings on the interpretation of provisions of Community law if those provisions could not be invoked before them. If the doctrines of direct effect and supremacy are, as two distinguished authors have said, the "twin pillars of the Community's legal system",[4] the reference procedure laid down in Article 177 must surely be the keystone in the edifice; without it the roof would collapse and the two pillars would be left as a

---

[2] Not, however, in Italy; by Order of 23 April 1985, No 113, *BECA SpA*, in *Giurisprudenza Costituzionale*, 1985, I, 694, reproduced in [1990] *CMLRev* 83, the Constitutional Court placed interpretative rulings of the Court of Justice on a par with Community regulations, which the Italian courts are obliged to apply. In the United Kingdom a similar result should be achieved by s. 3(1) of the European Communities Act 1972. But such provisions cannot prevent the national court from misconstruing a preliminary ruling.

[3] Case 26/62 *NV Algemene Transport- en Expeditie Onderneming van Gend en Loos* v *Nederlandse Administratie der Belastingen* [1963] ECR 3.

[4] D. Wyatt and A. Dashwood, *The Substantive Law of the EEC*, 2nd edn. (Sweet and Maxwell, London, 1987), p. 28.

desolate ruin, evocative of the temple at Cape Sounion—beautiful but not of much practical utility.

Those two essential points—namely, the vital importance of Article 177 and the ultimate unenforceability of the obligations imposed by it on national courts, must always be borne in mind when reading the two judgments, *Da Costa*[5] and *CIFLIT*,[6] in which the Court interpreted the third paragraph of Article 177. The two judgments are not entirely homogeneous: *Da Costa* admits of a single exception to the obligation to refer (the fact that the Court has already ruled on a question that is "materially identical"), while *CILFIT* is more permissive (the national court may refrain from referring, albeit in narrowly defined circumstances, even in the absence of a previous ruling), and learned writers have expatiated about this difference. In fact, it is easily explained. The two judgments differ because they were given in different circumstances. In *Da Costa* the Court was asked to rule on a question that was in substance identical to the one answered by it in *Van Gend en Loos* a month earlier. The Commission urged the Court to dismiss the case as lacking substance. The Court rejected that argument, observing that a national court of last instance was dispensed from its obligation to refer in such circumstances but that it retained the power to refer if it so wished.[7]

In *CILFIT*, on the other hand, the Italian Court of Cassation—a court normally subject to the obligation imposed by the third paragraph of Article 177— asked the Court of Justice whether it was obliged to refer a question of interpretation when the meaning of the relevant provision was clearly, in its view, beyond doubt. The Court replied that the obligation to refer may be waived if the correct application of Community law is so obvious as to leave no scope for any reasonable doubt as to the manner in which the question raised is to be resolved. But the Court then defined the condition of obviousness so narrowly that it would rarely, if ever, be satisfied. After all, could any national court reasonably be expected to compare the nine language versions of a Community provision and satisfy itself that the matter would be equally obvious to the courts of the other Member States and to the Court of Justice, having regard to the characteristic features of Community law, to the context of the provision in

---

[5] Joined Cases 28–30/62 *Da Costa en Schaake NV, Jacob Meijer NV, Hoechst Holland NV v Nederlandse Belastingadministratie* [1963] ECR 31.

[6] Case 283/81 *Srl CILFIT and Lanificio di Gavardo SpA v Ministry of Health* [1982] ECR 3415.

[7] The Court could hardly have ruled otherwise, given that it does not apply a rigid doctrine of *stare decisis*. Notable examples of the Court's willingness to reconsider earlier rulings include Case C-10/89 *SA CNL-SUCAL NV v HAG GF AG ("HAG II")* [1990] ECR I-3711 and Case C-269/90 *Technische Universität München v Hauptzollamt München-Mitte* [1991] ECR I-5469. In the latter case the German Bundesfinanzhof expressly invited the Court to reconsider a number of earlier rulings.

the light of Community law as a whole and the objectives of Community law and its state of evolution at the time in question? One is reminded of Oliver Wendell Holmes' paradox: "We need education in the obvious more than investigation of the obscure."[8]

CILFIT has many detractors. They accuse the Court of having capitulated in the face of the resistance that its role under Article 177 encountered in the late 1960s and early 1970s on the part of some of Europe's great courts.[9] Like Shakespeare's shrew, Katherine, the Court surrendered, at the end of a long and painful taming process, having verified its evident inability to "seek for rule, supremacy and sway".[10]

Such criticism is misconceived. It fails to appreciate the subtlety displayed by the Court in *CILFIT*, together with an acute understanding of judicial psychology. It is true that at least three supreme courts—the French Conseil d'Etat, the equivalent Greek organ, and the German Bundesfinanzhof—blatantly defied the authority of the Court of Justice. It is equally certain that, without reaching that extremity, the supreme courts of all the other Member States simply ignored the obligation imposed by Article 177 on at least one or two occasions.[11] But the Court of Justice was not "tamed" by such conduct, nor can it be said to have rendered more than lip service to the argument—the so-called doctrine of *acte clair*—with which the national courts sought to justify their attitude. For proof of that one need only look at the most notorious instance of a breach of the third paragraph of Article 177: namely, the French Conseil d'Etat's refusal to make a reference in the *Cohn-Bendit* case.[12] Such a refusal would clearly not have been justified under the *CILFIT* guidelines, no matter how liberally they are construed.

The correct analysis of *CILFIT* was given by Rasmussen, who maintains that the judgment was based on an astute strategy of "give and take". The Court, recognizing that it could not in any case coerce the national courts into accepting its jurisdiction, concedes something—a great deal in fact, nothing less than the right not to refer if the Community measure is clear—to the professional or national pride of the municipal judge, but then, as we have just seen, restricts the circumstances in which the clarity of the provision may legitimately be sustained

---

[8]   O.W. Holmes, *Collected Legal Papers* (New York, 1952), pp. 292–296.

[9]   See in particular G. Bebr, "The Rambling Ghost of 'Cohn-Bendit': *Acte Clair* and the Court of Justice" (1983) 20 *CMLRev* 439 *et seq.*; A.M. Arnull, "Article 177 and the Retreat from *Van Duyn*" (1983) 10 *ELRev* 365; but see also A. Saggio "Aspetti problematici della competenza pregiudiziale della Corte di giustizia delle Comunità europee messi in luce dalla giurisprudenza" (1987) *Rivista di diritto europeo* 179–189.

[10]   W. Shakespeare, *The Taming of the Shrew*, Act 5, scene 2, line 163.

[11]   See the Sixth Annual Report to the European Parliament on Commission Monitoring of the Application of Community Law (1988), Appendix, "The Attitude of National Supreme Courts to Community Law", OJ 1989 C 330, p. 146.

[12]   Judgment of 22 December 1978, *Rec. Lebon* 1978, p. 524, reproduced in [1980] 1 *Common Market Law Reports* 562. On the attitude of the French Conseil d'Etat before that ruling, see M.F. Conniff, "The French Conseil d'Etat and Article 177 of the Treaty of Rome: A Case Analysis" (1972) *Virginia Journal of International Law* 377 *et seq.*

to cases so rare that the nucleus of its own authority is preserved intact (or rather consolidated because it voluntarily divested itself of a part of its exclusive jurisdiction). The objective of the Court is plain: by granting supreme courts the power to do lawfully that which they could in any case do unlawfully, but by subjecting that power to stringent conditions, the Court hoped to induce the supreme courts to use willingly the "mechanism for judicial cooperation" provided by the EC Treaty. The result is to eliminate sterile and damaging conflicts and to reduce the risk that Community law might be the subject of divergent interpretations.[13]

That there can be no talk of a surrender was to be proved, moreover, a few years later by *Foto-Frost*,[14] in which the Court held that even the lower courts are under a duty to refer if they are of the view that the provision in question must be declared invalid. The thread that links the *ratio* of that judgment (namely, to ensure that the same provision is not applied in one Member State and disapplied in another) to the *ratio* of *CILFIT* (ensuring, as we have pointed out, the uniform application of Community law) is evident. And it is in any event obvious that the Court could not have forced the letter of the second paragraph, according to which the national court *"may . . . request the Court of Justice to give a ruling,"* if it had been conscious of having greatly diluted the expression *"shall bring the matter before the Court of Justice"* in the third paragraph, rather than simply accepting that the obligation indicated by those words must be performed with open eyes and thus within reasonable limits.

3. CONSOLIDATING THE COURT OF JUSTICE'S ROLE AS HELMSMAN

Having thus established the philosophy underlying *CILFIT*, it would seem that the line followed by the Court in *Da Costa*, *CILFIT*, and *Foto-Frost* was the only course open to it. The Court could not have ruled otherwise without calling in question the juridical nature of rules of Community law—that is to say, the ability of such norms to be termed law. It is not necessary to be a legal realist in the image of Jerome Frank or Alf Ross in order to recognize that a rule can only be considered valid if it is possible to predict that it will, for a reasonable period of time, be interpreted and applied in much the same way by the majority of judges in a particular geographical space. It is clear that such a prediction will have a greater probability of being well founded if the area in question is small, if the judges to be reckoned with are few in number and if they subscribe to the same judicial ideology.[15] Such conditions doubtless exist in relatively

---

[13] See H. Rasmussen, "The European Court's Acte Clair Strategy in *CILFIT* (Or: Acte Clair, of course! But what does it mean?)" (1984) 10 *ELRev* 342 *et seq*.

[14] Case 314/85 *Foto-Frost v Hauptzollamt Lübeck-Ost* [1987] ECR 4199.

[15] See A. Ross, *On Law and Justice* (London, 1974), chs 2, 3 and 4; but see also H. Rasmussen, "The Court of Justice of the European Communities and the Process of Integration" in E. Orban (ed.), *Fédéralisme et Cours Suprêmes* (Brussels-Montreal, 1991), p. 217 *et seq*.

small, homogeneous countries; but in the Community as a whole they cannot be said to exist.

The area of the Community is enormous, the judges number tens of thousands and their ideological cohesion is zero. This last characteristic which is decisive—is brought about by a number of factors, which are too well-known to require detailed examination; it suffices here to mention the fundamental dichotomy between common law countries and civil law countries (with Denmark somewhere in between), the different systems of recruiting judges in the Member States, and the development of the phenomenon of politicization which in some of those countries (in particular, France, Italy and, to a lesser degree, Spain) has led to the division of the judiciary into organized groups engaged in constant struggle one against the other, even as regards the development of case law.[16]

If all that is true, it seems indisputable that the only way of preventing Community law from disintegrating as a result of divergent interpretations— and thus losing its validity or rather its nature as law—was to safeguard as much as possible the role of helmsman conferred upon the Court by Article 177, especially in relation to the national supreme courts which, for their part, have the institutional task of steering the administration of justice and, in particular, monitoring the development of case law in the Member States. The accuracy of that observation will become more apparent if it is borne in mind that Community law has peculiar characteristics and that those characteristics accentuate the need for a central steering.

Community law is in fact still in its adolescence, more or less as American constitutional law was in the age of Marshall and, like American constitutional law, it is suffering all the pangs of nation-building. Moreover, the last decade had seen a continuous broadening and deepening of the Community's competences, including at times the discovery and activation of competences established by the EC Treaty but insufficiently explored or utilized until recently, such as for example the transnational provision of services. That process generates amongst individuals, Member States, and even the organs of the Community, new expectations and new interests with respect to which the primary and secondary rules of law turn out to be outdated, incomplete, or in need of reinterpretation, sometimes in fields of great economic, social, and political importance.

To mention but a few examples, the founding fathers could never have imagined that the Court of Justice would be asked to legalize in Ireland the dissemination of information about British clinics in which abortions are carried out,[17] to prohibit non-discriminatory restrictions on cross-border television pro-

---

[16] See G.F. Mancini, "Politics and the Judges: The European Perspective" (1980) 43 *Modern Law Review* 1 *et seq.*

[17] Case C-159/90 *The Society for the Protection of Unborn Children Ireland Ltd* v *Stephen Grogan* [1991] ECR I-4685.

grammes,[18] to order the compensation of citizens who suffer damage as a result of the failure to implement a directive,[19] and, on a different level, to recognize the *locus standi* of the European Parliament when it is in dispute with the other institutions.[20] Of course one is aware that in 1957 the United Kingdom and Ireland had no intention of joining the Community, that abortion was in any event not legal in Britain and that not even a latter day Jules Verne could have foreseen the development of satellite and cable television; but these facts, far from disproving the point, corroborate it because they clearly show that the interpretation of the EC Treaty must necessarily be dynamic, lest its provisions be overtaken by social and technological change.

4. THE EVOLUTION OF THE COURT OF JUSTICE INTO A CONSTITUTIONAL COURT

Thus, by means of *CILFIT*, that is to say by consolidating the rules that govern cooperation between the national supreme courts and the Court of Justice, the latter provided itself with a sort of safety net in order to be able to face, without fear of further traumatic clashes with national supreme courts, the challenges posed by the development of Community law. Can the operation be described as a success? All things considered, the reply must be affirmative. There have been no outright clashes since *CILFIT* and the resistance that some supreme courts continue to show towards the reference procedure[21] has not prevented the Court from reacting to such challenges ever more vigorously. Those reactions have allowed the continuation of a process initiated before *CILFIT* whereby the Court has little by little transformed itself into a genuine constitutional court with at least some of the basic attributes that such bodies possess when they operate in a federal system.

One should of course be clear what is meant by such terms. A power to review legislation was certainly conferred upon the Court by the EC Treaty, namely by Articles 173, 175, and 177, in so far as the latter empowers or obliges national courts to refer to the Court of Justice questions concerning the validity of provisions, at issue in a case pending before them. But the subject matter of the

---

[18] Case C-288/89 *Stichting Collectieve Antennevoorziening Gouda and others* v *Commissariaat voor de Media* [1991] ECR I-4007.

[19] Joined Cases C-6/90 and C-9/90 *Andrea Francovich and Danila Bonifaci and others* v *Italy* [1991] ECR I-5357.

[20] Case 294/83 *Parti écologiste "Les Verts"* v *European Parliament* [1986] ECR 1339; Case 302/87 *European Parliament* v *Council* ("*Comitology*") [1988] ECR 5615; Case C-70/88 *European Parliament* v *Council* ("*Chernobyl*") [1990] ECR I-2041.

[21] Typical of this ambivalent attitude, which none the less represents progress in comparison with the past, is the stance of the French Conseil d'Etat. That court has in fact modified the more objectionable aspects of its earlier case law (see the *Nicolo* judgment of 20 October 1989, *Rec. Lebon*, 1989, p. 190, reproduced in [1990] 1 *Common Market Law Reports* 101), but continues to look upon Community law as a branch of international law: see H. Calvet, "Le Conseil d'Etat et l'article 55 de la Constitution: une solitude révolue" in *La Semaine Juridique* of 7 February 1990, and more recently L. Cohen-Tanugi, *L'Europe en Danger* (Paris, 1992), p. 90 et *seq*.

power of review thus possessed by the Court is exclusively the law produced in Brussels by the Council, Commission and, more recently, the European Parliament. On the other hand, no provision of the Treaty grants the Court express power to test the legality, in the eyes of Community law, of national laws, apart that is from Articles 169 to 171 which, however, in an approach still largely coloured by international law, make the effectiveness of the review dependent on the acquiescence of the Member States. (The modal "shall" in Article 171 has the same hortatory value as in the third paragraph of Article 177).

One should not underrate the importance of the first type of review: it suffices to mention the role played by some direct actions brought by the European Parliament under Articles 173 and 175 in prompting the Court to update the institutional balance of the Community (in particular, the *Chernobyl* case and the cases on the legal basis of certain directives[22]) or to rouse the Community legislature from its lethargy in the realm of transport.[23] Yet, it cannot be doubted that this type of review is strategically less significant—or, in plainer words, less essential for the survival of the Community—than the other one. Once again Justice Holmes may be quoted: "I do not think" he wrote, "the United States would come to an end if the Supreme Court lost its power to declare an Act of Congress void, but the Union would be imperilled if the Court could not make that declaration as to the laws of the several Member States".[24]

It thus becomes clear what is meant when we say that the Court of Justice has gradually evolved into a fully-fledged constitutional court. That evolution, which was motivated at least in part by the need to eliminate or reduce the danger alluded to by Holmes, has taken place essentially through:

(a)   the transformation of the procedure established by Article 177 into an instrument which makes it possible for the Court to rule *de facto* on the compatibility of domestic law with Community law; and

(b)   the use of that same procedure in such a way as to reinforce *indirectly* the procedure established by Article 169.

In addition, the Court has used Article 177—following an example set by the Supreme Court of the United States in the best moments of its history—to reduce the democratic deficit which has blighted the Community since its inception and to enhance the democratic content of a number of national measures in a variety of fields. These aspects of the Court's work will be examined one by one.

---

[22] Case C-70/88, *supra* n. 20. For cases on the legal basis of legislation, see the thorough review conducted by G.M. Roberti, "La giurisprudenza della Corte di giustizia sulla 'base giuridica' degli atti comunitari" in (1991) *Foro Italiano* IV col. 99 *et seq.*

[23] Case 13/83 *European Parliament* v *Council* [1985] ECR 1513.

[24] Holmes, "Law and the Court" in *Collected Legal Papers, supra* n. 8, p. 291, at p. 295 *et seq.*

5. REVIEWING THE COMPATIBILITY OF NATIONAL LAW WITH COMMUNITY LAW

The first aspect is perhaps the most significant and many members or former members of the Court have highlighted it. The division of labour on which Article 177 is based (the European Court's role being to interpret Community law, leaving to the national court the task of applying the interpretation obtained to the facts of the case) is rather sophisticated and may cause difficulty not only for judges who operate in a system to which the reference procedure is unknown (e.g. the United Kingdom and Denmark) but also for judges in countries in which reference procedures exist but are organized in simpler and more direct fashion (e.g. Germany, Italy, Spain, and Portugal). Thus it happens that national courts, called upon to apply a national law whose compatibility with Community law seems doubtful to them, ask the Court whether their doubts are well-founded or, in other words, whether there exists a conflict between the national law and some provision of Community law.

Naturally the Court has never accepted this form of raising a preliminary question, which is, however, extremely frequent; whenever the issue is put to it in that form its reaction has been to reformulate the question. Yet, aware of the difficulties faced by the national judge, the Court does not confine itself to interpreting the Community rule; instead it enters into the heart of the conflict submitted to its attention, but it takes the precaution of rendering it abstract, that is to say it presents it as a conflict between Community law and a hypothetical national provision having the nature of the provision in issue before the national court. The technique thus described, which is formally impeccable and of great use to the national court, results in the Court of Justice acquiring a power of review which is analogous to—though of course narrower than—that routinely exercised by the Supreme Court of the United States and the constitutional courts of some Member States.[25]

6. THE REINFORCEMENT OF ARTICLES 169 TO 171 OF THE EC TREATY

The second achievement—namely, the reinforcement of the mechanism provided by Article 169 EC—was not, in contradistinction to the first, the chemical precipitate, as it were, of countless judgments, but the consequence of a number of specific rulings. The first such ruling was *Defrenne II*.[26] In the eighteen years that preceded that decision the Commission had made use of Article 169 in thirty-two cases only, well aware that the Member States, under whose suspicious guardianship it was operating at the time, might regard infringement

---

[25] For a fuller treatment of the argument, see G.F. Mancini, "The Making of a Constitution for Europe" (1989) 26 *CMLRev* 604 *et. seq.* and Chapter 1.

[26] Case 43/75 *Gabrielle Defrenne* v *Société anonyme belge de navigation aérienne Sabena* (*"Defrenne II"*) [1976] ECR 455.

proceedings as an offence to their dignity. In *Defrenne II* the Court observed that the principle of equal pay for men and women laid down by Article 119 of the EC Treaty was being flagrantly breached in many Member States and, in an unusually outspoken mood, it placed the blame on the laxness of the Commission. The Member States—declared the Court—had been led to form an erroneous opinion about the binding effect of Article 119 as a result of a lack of vigilance on the part of the Community's executive. If the Commission had done its job properly, female workers in the Community would not have suffered such serious and widespread discrimination.[27]

The Court's criticisms hit the mark. After 1976, under the leadership of Roy Jenkins, the Commission set to work and actions based on Article 169 multiplied on such a scale as to become matters of routine, attaining by the mid-1980s the dimensions of an avalanche that now accounts for approximately one-fifth of the actions pending before the Court. The multiplication of such actions has not, however, done anything to make the procedure more effective. On the contrary, the frequent use of Article 169, and the consequent trivialization of the procedure, have had a perverse effect: the greater the number of actions, the less probable it is that the Member States will succeed in executing the resulting judgments; the more cases of non-compliance, the less credible becomes the organ whose decisions are thus disregarded; the weaker those decisions become, the greater is the temptation not to implement them.

Action was therefore required in order to break that vicious circle; and the Court took the necessary step in 1991 in response to a preliminary question referred to it by two Italian courts which asked it whether a worker could claim compensation from his Member State for damage suffered as a result of its failure to implement the Directive on the insolvency of employers.[28] Italy's failure to implement the Directive had already been established by a judgment of the Court under Article 169 of the EC Treaty[29] and there was no doubt that the worker had been prevented by that failure from exercising his rights under the Directive. The Court of Justice ruled in *Francovich*[30] that such a person was entitled to claim compensation from the Member State. To many commentators the judgment appeared revolutionary. That assessment is not accurate because the principle that the individual may claim compensation for damage sustained as a result of a Member State's breach of Community law was recognized in *Russo v AIMA*,[31] which dates back to January 1976; it is true, however, that *Francovich* gave to Article 169, and thus to the power of review over national

---

[27] Case 43/75 *Gabrielle Defrenne v Société anonyme belge de navigation aérienne Sabena* ("*Defrenne II*") [1976] ECR 455 at para. 73.

[28] Council Directive 80/987/EEC of 20 October 1980 on the approximation of the laws of the Member States relating to the protection of employees in the event of the insolvency of their employer, OJ 1980 L 283, p. 23.

[29] Case 22/87 *Commission v Italy* [1989] ECR 143

[30] Joined Cases C-6/90 and C-9/90 *supra* n. 19.

[31] Cf. Case 60/75 *Carmine Antonio Russo v Azienda di Stato per gli interventi sul mercato agricolo AIMA* [1976] ECR 45 at para. 9.

legislation, claws and teeth that are far sharper and more incisive than those concocted by the authors of the Maastricht Treaty.

7. THE PROTECTION OF FUNDAMENTAL RIGHTS

The aspects of the EC Treaty that have led so many politicians and academic commentators to regard the democratic deficit as the one true original sin of the Community are many in number. But none is as serious as the failure to recognize the fundamental rights of the citizens to whom the legislative provisions and administrative measures emanating from Brussels are addressed; or rather, none appeared so obvious after *Van Gend en Loos*,[32] in so far as that judgment marks the definitive rupture between Community law, which directly involves the citizens of the Member States in its application, and international law, under which the provisions of treaties may be invoked only by, or against, the contracting States.[33] It would be superfluous to analyse the reasons for this lacuna or to describe the process whereby the Court has sought to remedy it, because a year seldom goes by without at least ten authors having aired this theme.[34] It need merely be observed that the Court's case law in this field—case law which has played a crucial part in the developments that have seen the Court transform itself into a supreme court of a federal nature—was provoked by the national courts.

In particular, the German and Italian constitutional courts goaded the Court of Justice into confronting the problem squarely by threatening to carry out their own review of the compatibility of Community provisions with the bills of rights enshrined in their respective Constitutions; in addition, there were various lower or intermediate courts that offered the Court of Justice the opportunity to recognize that fundamental rights form part of the general principles of law, the observance of which it ensures,[35] and to establish, step by step, the criteria that serve to identify those rights and their scope. Nowadays the main source of enrichment for the Community bill of rights is probably provided by direct actions brought by companies complaining about antitrust searches and inquiries made by Commission officials under Articles 85 and 86 of the EC Treaty; but it should not be forgotten that, if the ground on which those companies litigate had not been ploughed and fertilized by the inter-judicial cooperation provided for in Article 177, the actions of the Commission in the delicate sector of competition law would in large measure escape the constraints of the rule of law.

[32] Case 26/62, *supra* n. 3.
[33] See Cohen-Tanugi, *supra* n. 21, at p. 93.
[34] See G.F. Mancini and V. Di Bucci, "Le développement des droits fondamentaux en tant que partie du droit communautaire" in Academy of European Law (ed.), *Collected Courses of the Academy of European Law*, Volume I, Book 1 (Deventer, Kluwer 1991), p. 27. See also Chapters 1 and 6.
[35] See Article 164 of the EC Treaty.

Even more significant, however, is the role played by the dialogue between the national courts and the Community court with regard to the testing of national laws against the Community charter of fundamental rights. That remark may seem absurd to anyone who considers that the question was definitively disposed of by *Cinéthèque*, the judgment in which the Court ruled that "it had no power to examine the compatibility" with the European Human Rights Convention of laws concerning areas which fall "within the jurisdiction of the national legislator".[36] But the fact is that since *Cinéthèque* the case law has progressed enormously, though in judgments less conspicuous than that ruling. The Court began by deciding, on a reference from a German court, that it lacks the aforesaid power only if the national law "lies outside the scope of Community law".[37] Another court from the same country then led it to declare that a national measure implementing a Community provision must not disregard fundamental rights protected in Community law.[38] Finally, in response to a preliminary question from Greece, the Court went so far as to affirm, in the *ERT* case, that, among the conditions that a Member State must satisfy in order to be able to invoke the derogations provided for in Articles 36 and 56 of the EC Treaty from the free movement of goods and services, there must be included compliance with fundamental rights.[39] Anyone who reflects for a moment about how intimately some of those derogations (public policy, security, morality, etc.) are bound up with fundamental notions governing the relationship between Member States and their citizens cannot fail to appreciate the potential impact of that judgment on national sovereignty.

8. CONCLUSION

It will be clear from the preceding pages that the Court of Justice does not yet exercise a fully federal review of the constitutionality of national legislation or of compliance with human rights on the part of national parliaments and administrative authorities; and yet the powers that it has acquired, with the active collaboration of thousands of judges scattered in every corner of the Community, have already enabled it to make large strides in that direction. Hence it is true, as was written by Buxbaum,[40] as early as 1969 and from the

---

[36] Joined Cases 60 and 61/84 *Cinéthèque SA and others v Fédération nationale des cinémas français* [1985] ECR 2605 at para. 26. The mention of the Human Rights Convention both in the national court's order for reference and in the judgment of the Court of Justice is justified by the use which the Court makes of that instrument as a source of guidelines in the realm of fundamental rights.

[37] Case 12/86 *Meryem Demirel v Stadt Schwäbisch Gmünd* [1987] ECR 3747 at para. 28.

[38] Case 5/88 *Hubert Wachauf v Bundesamt für Ernährung und Forstwirtschaft* [1989] ECR 2609 at para. 19.

[39] Case 260/89 *Elliniki Radiophonia Tiléorassi AE v. Dimotiki Etairia Pliroforissis and others* (*"ERT"*) [1991] ECR I-2925 at paras. 42 and 43.

[40] See R.M. Buxbaum, "Article 177 of the Rome Treaty as a Federalizing Device" (1969) *Stanford Law Review* 104 *et seq.*

other side of the Atlantic, that Article 177, notwithstanding its inherent weakness, is a federalizing device. But that device is not yet achieving its full potential. It will only do so if the supreme courts of the Member States employ it in accordance with the spirit of *CILFIT*, with the confidence and goodwill displayed over so many years by their junior colleagues. No one is asking them to become enthustiasts: "Enthusiasm" observed Lord Devlin, "is not and cannot be a judicial virtue."[41] All that is asked is that they should show still greater generosity in contributing their prestige and their wisdom to the institutional progress of the Community.

[41] "Judges and Lawmakers" (1976) 39 *Modern Law Review* 5.

3

Democracy and the European Court of Justice

T HE DEBATE ABOUT the democratic deficit in the European Community which for some time now, and especially since the referenda of 1992 and 1993, has engaged the attention of politicians and scholars in the twelve Member States, seems to ignore one fundamental fact: shocking though it may seem the Community was never intended to be a democratic organization. That is proved above all by the preamble and the first part of the EC Treaty in which the word "democracy" is not used at all and "liberty" is spoken of, like "peace", as a value to be defended; so those terms are used not with reference to the form of government of the new international organization but in the light of the challenges and threats to which the founding States and the entire Western world were subject in the 1950s. What is perhaps even more surprising is that the founders of the Community did not feel it necessary expressly to reserve membership of the Community to the democratic States. The old Article 237 of the EC Treaty envisaged the accession of "Any European State", which seems that it would have been technically possible for even Franco's Spain and Salazar's Portugal to apply for membership.[1] Decisive proof that the Community was not made in the democratic image of its creators is to be found in the guiding principles of its original constitution.

The Assembly, composed of members chosen by the national Parliaments, was involved in the exercise of legislative power solely as the addressee of information and as a consultative organ. The power to legislate, though admittedly only on the basis of proposals submitted by the Commission, belongs to the Council of Ministers, an institution composed paradoxically of the leading members of the national executives.[2] As for the executive power at Community

---

[1] See, however, Article O of the Treaty on European Union, as amended in Amsterdam, which specifies that "Any European State which respects the principles set out in Article F(1) [liberty, democracy, respect for human rights and fundamental freedoms, and the rule of law] may apply to become a Member of the Union".

[2] J.H.H. Weiler, "Problems of Legitimacy in Post-1992 Europe" (1991) 46 *Aussenwirtschaft* 180. R. Bieber, "Democratization of the European Community through the European Parliament", *ibid.*, 164, observes, however, that the members of the Council "usually have been elected to their national Parliaments or derive their mandate therefrom. Hence they possess a proper legitimacy". See also P. Pescatore, "L'Exécutif communautaire: justification du quadripartisme institué par les traités

level, that was (and still is) discharged principally by the Commission, whose members are appointed by the Parliament of the Member States. The Commission is of course accountable to the Assembly; however, the accountability is enforceable through a sanction (collective dismissal upon a motion of censure) which is so drastic that, like the hydrogen bomb, it is of little practical use.[3] Less unorthodox, at least in appearance, is the judicial branch of government: but here too the legitimacy of the organ which embodies judicial power, the Court of Justice, could hardly be weaker. The Judges and Advocates General, like the Commissioners, are appointed by common accord of the governments of the Member States. They hold office for six years and may be reappointed (or, of course, not reappointed). Few supreme courts in the Western world are so lacking in links, direct or indirect, with the symbols of democratic government[4] and in few countries is the judiciary so bereft of formal guarantees of its independence.

Thus—at least under the original Treaties—power is firmly concentrated at all levels in the hands of the governments of the Member States. They possess a virtual monopoly on legislative power, through the Council of Ministers, and hold in addition the exclusive, uncontrolled power to appoint and reappoint the members of the Community's executive and judiciary. If the history of democracy can be seen as a process whereby parliaments wrested power from monarchs, autocrats and executives, the signing of the EC Treaty must to some extent be regarded as a backward step. The willingness of the national parliaments to ratify the Treaty shows how strong the urge for European integration must have been in the 1950s.

2. THE REASONS FOR THE LACK OF DEMOCRACY

Before proceeding to examine the progress made since 1957 in terms of democratizing the Community, one should briefly consider why its founders did not make it more democratic from the outset. At least four reasons can be identified. First, the Community began life as an international organization founded on a treaty between sovereign states. Such organizations do not normally provide for much direct democracy in their decision-making apparatus; whatever democ-

de Paris et de Rome" (1978) *Cahiers de droit européen* 391–393. On the Commission's exclusive power to initiate legislation, see K. Lenaerts, "Some Reflections on the Separation of Powers in the European Community" (1991) 28 *CMLRev* 21.

[3] Although events from Brussels in January to March 1999 and the resignation of the Commission due, in part, to intense parliamentary pressure, indicate that the European Parliament is becoming increasingly willing and able to use its powers under the EC Treaty.

[4] See Gibson and Caldeira, "Legitimacy, Judicial Power and the Emergence of Transnational Legal Institutions", Report presented at the Conference of the Research Committee on Comparative Judicial Studies of the International Political Science Association, held at Forlì from 14 to 17 June 1992, under the aegis of the University of Bologna, at 10. See also A. Bzdera, "L'Enjeu politique de la réforme institutionelle de la Cour de justice de la Communauté européenne" (1992) *Revue du marché commun et de l'Union européenne* 240.

racy there is will normally be indirect in the sense that the governments of the states concerned are accountable to their national parliaments for their conduct whithin the international organization.

Secondly, although from the beginning the Community contained supranational elements and provided for some pooling of sovereignty, the Member States were anxious to circumscribe the surrender of national sovereignty within clearly defined limits. It would have been much more difficult to control the transfer of sovereignty if a Community parliament had been endowed with important legislative powers. By keeping legislative power within the Council of Ministers and by requiring unanimity in areas that might have a substantial impact on national level (e.g. Articles 99 and 100 of the EC Treaty, which deal with the harmonization of laws), the governments of the Member States were able to ensure that sovereignty could be transferred in small, controllable doses.

Thirdly, the European model of parliamentary democracy is generally based on an executive composed of members of the party or parties that have a majority in parliament; hence European governments are traditionally able, within limits, to impose their will on the national parliament and are removed from office if they lose the confidence of parliament. The American model of the democracy based on a strong version of the separation of powers, under which the head of the executive does battle with an independent-minded legislature and both are equally legitimized by direct popular election, has never flourished in Europe. Since it would be impossible to recreate the European model of parliamentary democracy at Community level (unless we had a Community executive drawn from the ranks of the European Parliament), the only realistic alternative was the one chosen by the Community's founding fathers: namely, a parliamentary assembly with a consultative role.

Fourthly, because of the fear of an uncontrollable loss of sovereignty, the only type of legislative power that might have been granted to the Community Parliament in 1957 was a purely negative power of review; that is to say, the power to reject regulations or directives but not the power to initiate or amend legislation. The objection to that is that it might have paralysed the development of the Community. It would have been very debilitating for the Community, especially in the early days, if a hard-won consensus arrived at within the Council of Ministers could not be translated into legislation because of opposition from the Community's parliament.

3. THE GRADUAL DEMOCRATIZATION OF THE COMMUNITY SINCE 1957

Between 1957 and the present day the situation has changed considerably. The Community is no longer an organism that pursues economic and social objectives with institutional mechanisms that are indifferent to the requirements of democracy; instead it has at last been infected with the democratic traditions of the Member States. In fact the differences between it and the great Western federations is gradually diminishing, and as they do so, the more the Community provokes passionate debates not only in the refined milieux of the experts but also in the pubs, bistros and pavement cafés of the entire continent, inflaming political parties and mobilizing electorates. Although the democratic deficit still exists, and continued to do so even after the entry into force of the Maastricht and Amsterdam Treaties, there is no doubt that it has been reduced considerably since the foundation of the Community. The purpose of this chapter is to examine the surpisingly important contribution of the Court of Justice to the process by which the Community has evolved into a more democratic structure than its founders apparently envisaged.

4. CONSOLIDATING THE ROLE OF THE EUROPEAN PARLIAMENT

A good starting point is the relations between the Assembly, Council and Commission. The first authoritative call for a thorough revision of the institutional balance established by the EC Treaty was made by the Heads of State and government at the Paris summit of 1974,[5] when the Belgian Prime Minister (Leo Tindemans) was invited to prepare a report on the institutional problems facing the Community.[6] The Gaullist revolt of the 1960s had withered away, the power of veto that the Member States claimed in 1966 (for which there is no foundation whatsoever in the Treaty)[7] had not achieved its full potential for paralysing the Community and the Community had acquired new fields of action thanks to an incisive use of Article 235 of the EC Treaty, which allows the Council to take action in pursuit of the aims of the Treaty even where the necessary powers have not been conferred on the Community expressly. Clearly such an extension of the Community's powers had to be given some form of political legitimacy. The areas removed from the sovereignty of the national Parliaments without their express consent could not be placed under the exclusive decision-making power of a technocratic élite such as the Commission and an intergovernmental conference such as the Council of Ministers: hence the imperative need for reforms granting the Assembly a more active role in the Community's legislative process and providing for its direct election by universal suffrage in order to endow it with democratic legitimacy.

The second of these reforms was approved in 1976; the first had to wait until the signing of the Single European Act in 1986 and took the form of a "cooperation procedure" involving the European Parliament (as the Assembly was at last officially renamed) in ten of the areas in which the EC Treaty had previously

---

[5] See B. Olivi, *L'Europa difficile* (Il Mulino, Bologna, 1993), p. 168.

[6] The Tindemans Report is published in *Bulletin of the EEC*, Suppl. 1/1976.

[7] The veto, which could be invoked whenever a Member State's vital interests were in issue, was part of the so-called "Luxembourg Compromise", the text of which is published in the *Bulletin of the EEC*, March 1966, 8–10.

allowed it to do no more than issue opinions.[8] That was undoubtedly an important advance; but, as Altiero Spinelli once said, in European affairs each step forward is generally followed by a "long and persistent deterioration".[9] The conquests first recommended by the Tindemans Report might have suffered the same fate; by defending them and overcoming the danger that they would be tacitly reversed, the Court made a crucial contribution to the democratic development of the Community.

The issue that first brought the Court of Justice into play—several years before the signing of the Single European Act—was the Parliament's right to be consulted before legislation is adopted under certain provisions of the EC Treaty. One such provision is Article 43, under which the legislation establishing and amending the common agricultural policy is enacted. In 1979 the Council passed a Regulation fixing production quotas for isoglucose. Roquette Frères, a French company which manufactures isoglucose, was dissatisfied with its quota and challenged the Regulation before the Court of Justice. One of its arguments was that the Council had failed to obtain the opinion of the Parliament before legislating. The Council had in fact asked the Parliament for its opinion. It did so in a letter dated 19 March 1979 in which it stressed the urgency of the matter and politely suggested that the Parliament might like to consider the matter at its April session. The Parliament was unable to do so and the Council adopted the contested Regulation on 25 June.

In annulling the Regulation the Court employed language of unaccustomed solemnity:

> "The consultation provided for in the . . . Treaty is the means which allows the Parliament to play a . . . part in the legislative process of the Community. Such power represents an essential factor in the institutional balance intended by the Treaty. Although limited, it reflects at Community level the fundamental democratic principle that the peoples should take part in the exercise of power through the intermediary of a representative assembly. Due consultation of the Parliament therefore constitutes an essential [procedural requirement] disregard of which means that the measure concerned is void".[10]

An interesting feature of the case is that the Court did not base its judgment solely on the need to maintain the institutional balance established by the EC Treaty. It chose also to invoke the "fundamental democratic principle" of popular participation in the exercise of legislative power—a principle for which there is scant support in the text of the Treaty. What, then, is the authority for

---

[8] See J.C. Gautron, "Le Parlement européen ou la lente émergence d'un pouvoir normatif" in *Etudes Offertes à Jean-Marie Auby* (Paris, Dalloz, 1992), p. 528, in particular at p. 539. It should also be remembered that the Parliament had in the meantime acquired greater powers in relation to the budget (by Treaties of 22 April 1970 and 22 July 1975) and that it had used those powers aggressively. On this subject, which is of great importance in the process of democratization of the Community, see the Opinion of Advocate General Mancini in Case 34/86 *Council v European Parliament* [1986] ECR 2155.

[9] A. Spinelli, *Diario europeo 1976/1986* (Il Mulino, Bologna, 1992), p. 320.

[10] Case 138/79 *SA Roquette Frères v Council* [1980] ECR 3333 at para. 33.

that principle? The answer must be that, like respect for human rights; the "fundamental democratic principle" forms an inherent part of the Community legal order which finds its roots in the constitutional traditions of the Member States, in natural law and in the common legal heritage of Western civilisation. There are of course limits on how far the Court may go with such an approach. It could hardly have invented a European Parliament if none was provided for in the Treaty. But since there was no provision in the Treaty—however limited—for a representative assembly to participate in the legislative process, the Court was able to stress the importance of the democratic element, and elevate it to the status of a fundamental principle to strike down legislation not sanctified with even a whiff of democratic legitimacy.

Roquette Frères v *Council* was only a foretaste of what was to come. The Court's conviction that the EC Treaty had established a system of checks and balances based on democratic principles did not emerge fully until some years later. The introduction of the cooperation procedure by the Single European Act in 1986 was a significant conquest in the Parliament's struggle to gain a legislative role commensurate with its status, after 1979, as a democratic organ directly elected by universal suffrage. But the value of that conquest was immediately called into question by the self-same Single European Act, whose authors, resisting pressure from many quarters, refused to amend the first paragraph of Article 173 of the EC Treaty[11] so as to allow the Parliament to challenge the acts of the other institutions before the Court of Justice.

Of course, so long as the Parliament was a purely consultative body, the failure to give it title to sue could be justified. But, once it had conquered a bridgehead in the legislative process, leaving it out in the procedural cold made no sense. The Council might be tempted to undermine that bridge-head by choosing as the legal basis[12] of its acts a provision of the Treaty under which the cooperation procedure does not apply. How, then, could the Parliament hope to prevent the subversion of its position if it was unable to challenge unlawfully adopted measures before the Court of Justice?

In 1987, convinced that that was exactly what the Council had attempted to do, the Parliament sought the protection of the Court in what came to be known as the *Comitology* case.[13] Necessary though it was, it was acutely difficult to

---

[11] Article 173 EC allows certain institutions, the Member States and natural and legal persons (provided the latter can establish a sufficient interest) to bring proceedings in the Court of Justice for annulment of acts adopted by the Community institutions. The first paragraph of Article 173 provides: "The Court of Justice shall review the legality of acts of the Council and the Commission other than recommendations or opinions. It shall for this purpose have jurisdiction in actions brought by a Member State, the Council or the Commission on grounds of lack of competence, infringement of an essential procedural requirement, infringement of this Treaty or of any rule of law relating to its application, or misure of powers".

[12] On the subject of legal basis in general, see G.M. Roberti, "La giurisprudenza della Corte di giustizia sulla 'base giuridica' degli atti comunitari" (1991) *Foro Italiano*, IV col. 99–119; and G.C. Rodríguez Iglesias, "La Constitución de la Comunidad Europea" (1993) *IX Noticias CEE* No 100, 93–99.

[13] Case 302/87 *European Parliament* v *Council* ("*Comitology*") [1988] ECR 5615.

give the Parliament *locus standi* in actions for annulment since it entailed the performance of a surgical operation on the body of a perfectly clear Treaty rule: the first paragraph of Article 173 allowed the Commission, the Council and the Member State to sue for annulment, but made no mention of the European Parliament. Admittedly, the Court had already appeared to rewrite—or rather—"creatively reinterpret"—Article 173 in 1986 when it had allowed an action for annulment to be brought *against* the Parliament by the French Green Party.[14] But the "creative reinterpretation" now called for would have been far more daring: it is one thing to say that the Parliament's own acts must be subject to judicial review whenever they affect the rights of others; it is quite another to say that the Parliament must itself be entitled to challenge acts adopted by the other institutions. Moreover, there was an obvious justification for allowing the Parliament to be sued, notwithstanding the wording of Article 173. Under the 1957 version of the Treaty, the Parliament lacked the power to adopt binding legal acts, so there was no reason to provide an annulment action against it; when the Treaty was amended so as to empower the Parliament to adopt binding acts, the failure to make a concomitant amendment allowing those acts to be challenged in court could be regarded as an oversight.[15] Such an argument could not, of course, justify giving the Parliament title to sue. A decision to do so was likely to cause an interinstitutional earthquake. It was perhaps not surprising then, that in the *Comitology* case, decided in 1988, the Court declared the Parliament's action inadmissible. With remarkable determination the Parliament tried again two years later and this time, in the *Chernobyl* case,[16] the Court held that, in order to maintain the institutional equilibrium created by the EC Treaty as amended by the Single European Act, the Parliament should be able to safeguard its newly won prerogatives and therefore have standing to commence proceedings against acts of the Council and Commission.

Technically, the Court managed by means of an ingenious—though perhaps unconvincing—sleight of hand, to avoid expressly overruling the *Comitology* judgment, delivered only 20 months earlier. Instead of holding that the Parliament may initiate proceedings under the first paragraph of Article 173, the Court stated that the Parliament must be allowed, in order to safeguard its prerogatives, to bring an action for annulment governed by procedural rules identical to those laid down in the first paragraph of Article 173. The Court did, however, expressly recognize that it had been wrong to hold in the *Comitology* case that the task of safeguarding the Parliament's privileges before the Court could be entrusted to the Commission: the *Chernobyl* case showed that such a guarantee was illusory because the Commission shared the Council's position as to the validity of the contested Regulation and could hardly be expected to defend the Parliament's prerogatives by challenging a measure that it agreed with.

---

[14] Case 294/83 *Parti écologiste "Les Verts"* v *European Parliament* [1986] ECR 1339.
[15] See para. 24 of the judgment in *Les Verts*.
[16] Case C-70/88 *European Parliament* v *Council* (*"Chernobyl"*) [1990] ECR I-2041.

By any standards, the *Chernobyl* ruling constituted a momentous *volte-face*, which doubtless explains why it was so fiercely criticized in some quarters ("one of the most blatantly policy-based judgments ever", wrote a member of the Bruges group).[17] But, more importantly, *Chernobyl* also represented a step towards endowing the Community with a less incongruous system of checks and balances, and, hence, strengthening its democratic legitimacy. It is signifi-cant that even the indirect victims of *Chernobyl*, the Member States, saw the advantages of this development. Thus, while a legion of academic writers were still busy predicting a growing problem of compliance with the decisions of a Court so unbridled and aggressive, the authors of the Maastricht Treaty incor-porated almost *verbatim* the operative part of the judgment into the new version of Article 173.

Of course, constitutional lawyers immersed in the familiar paradigms of their national systems must find it strange that the Community's Parliament should seek to assert its rights in court proceedings. After all, the national legislatures do not often descend into the judicial arena and none can have been such an habitual litigant as the European Parliament. But the comparison is misleading and merely serves to underline the unique, *sui generis* nature of the Community's constitution. The peculiar features of the Community legal order are, first, that legislative power is formally shared out between the representa-tive, parliamentary body and two unelected organs (the Council and Commission), according to elaborate formulae enshrined in the EC Treaty; and, secondly, that the scope of the Parliament's powers varies enormously—from a right of consultation to a power of co-decision after Maastricht—depending on the subject-matter of the proposed legislation. To speak of checks and balances in such a context is an understatement. The entire system is founded on that concept and on a principle of limited powers expressly laid down in Article 4 of the EC Treaty. The task of ensuring that each institution acts within the con-fines of its powers and does not trespass on the prerogatives of the other insti-tutions could only be performed by the Court of Justice. If the Court had continued to deny the Parliament the right to challenge such trespasses, it would have been abdicating its duty, under Article 164 of the EC Treaty, to ensure that the law is observed.

5. THE OTHER ASPECT OF DEMOCRACY: SAFEGUARDING THE RIGHTS OF THE INDIVIDUAL

By vigilantly protecting the rights of the European Parliament in the complex institutional scheme established by the EC Treaty, the Court of Justice has undoubtedly made a significant contribution to bolstering democracy in the

---

[17] G. Smith, *The European Court of Justice: Judges or Policy Makers?* (The Bruges Group, London, 1990).

Community. But in a constitutional system founded on checks and balances and on the principle of limited government under the rule of law, democracy is not just a matter of ensuring that the people's elected representatives play a full role in the process of law-making; democracy is also about protecting the rights of the individual. No society can be considered truly democratic if its citizens are denied the possibility of vindicating their legal rights in judicial proceedings, whether against the oppressive acts of a powerful legislature—even a democratically elected one—or against the unlawful practices of an overweening administration.

And let there be no mistaking the impact of Community law on the citizens of Europe. Natural and legal persons are intimately involved in the application of the EC Treaty by the Community institutions and the Member States. They are the ones who profit directly by an unhindered flow of goods, services and capital thoroughout the common market; they are the beneficiaries of the rules on labour mobility and of the right to share, on a par with local workers, the social advantages available in the country to which they move. By the same token, their jobs and their investments may be wiped out by the abolition of a state aid found incompatible with the Treaty; the protection of their health, working conditions and environment may be impaired by a harmonizing directive if it imposes a lower standard than national law; and even their fundamental rights may be encroached upon by a Community normative or administrative measure.

Those are salient and mundane interests. Yet the EC Treaty does not seem to take them seriously as their weight requires—not, at any rate, in terms of remedies for their non-observance. The most notorious lacuna, of course, is the lack of a catalogue of fundamental rights. But that is not the only weakness of the Treaty. The second paragraph of Article 173 empowers natural and legal persons to impugn before the Court *only* such Community acts as are specifically addressed to them or apt to affect them directly and individually. And even weaker, at least on paper, is the protection which the Treaty affords against national legislation infringing Community rights. Under Articles 169 and 170 of the EC Treaty, only the Commission or another Member State may institute proceedings for a declaration that by maintaining the legislation in force the Member State in question has infringed the Treaty. There are no circumstances in which an individual may sue a Member State directly in the Court of Justice. All the individual can do is to invoke the rights conferred on him by Community law before a national court. This court, in turn, may—or, if its judgment is not subject to appeal, must—refer the matter to the European Court under Article 177 of the EC Treaty, requesting it to give a preliminary ruling on the interpretation of the relevant Community provision.

How, then, has the Court set about the task of ensuring an adequate level of judicial protection for the individual in spite of the sometimes deficient terms of the Treaty? In some areas it has shown courage, foresight and imagination, for example, by endowing the Community with a highly flexible catalogue of fundamental rights borrowed from the national constitutions and from the European Human Rights Convention. But perhaps the Court's outstanding achievement has been in relation to the reference procedure established by Article 177, which on the face of things is flawed and fragile because it does not grant litigants direct access to the Court of Justice and because its effectiveness is entirely dependent on the good will of the national courts.[18] In spite of the inherent—one might say "built-in"—weakness of the procedure, the Court of Justice has made it spectacularly successful, amplifying its incisiveness through the doctrine of direct effect and transforming it into a quasi-federal instrument for reviewing the compatibility of national legislation with Community law.

6. THE DOCTRINE OF DIRECT EFFECT

The Court's achievements in relation to direct effect need a few words of explanation. Invoking a Community right before a national court obviously postulates that the measure conferring that right is directly applicable in the national legal order. Under the EC Treaty (Article 189) only regulations are expressly endowed with such a quality; the Treaty itself, whose rules are mostly addressed to Member States, does not appear to possess it, nor do directives, which are apparently enforceable only if and when the national authorities implement them. But in two famous cases decided in 1963[19] and 1974,[20] the Court revolutionized this situation by holding that Treaty rules and provisions of directives not implemented on time may be relied upon by private individuals if they grant them rights and impose on the State an obligation so clear-cut that it can be fulfilled without the necessity of further measures.

The epithet "landmark" is sometimes bestowed too frivolously on judicial decisions that do not deserve it. But surely no-one would contest the claim of the *Van Gend en Loos* judgment to be described thus. It is rare that judges are given a chance to change the course of history. But if the European Community still exists 50 or 100 years from now, historians will look back on *Van Gend en Loos* as the unique judicial contribution to the making of Europe. If the Court had held in 1963 that the Treaty provision prohibiting increases in customs duties could not be relied on by an importer who challenged a customs assestment in the national courts, the subsequent development of the Community would have been very different. Doubtless the common market, then in the transitional stage, would still have been completed in the technical sense. But would it have been enforced? Would it have withstood the protectionist tendencies that are

---

[18] For further discussion of this subject, see G.F. Mancini and D. Keeling, "From *CILFIT* to *ERT*: The Constitutional Challenge Facing the European Court" (1991) 11 *Yearbook of European Law* 1 and Chapter 2.

[19] Case 26/62 NV *Algemene Transport- en Expeditie Onderneming Van Gend en Loos* v *Nederlandse Administratie der Belastingen* [1963] ECR 3.

[20] Case 41/74 *Yvonne Van Duyn* v *Home Office* [1974] ECR 1337.

always ready to resurface, manifesting themselves in the form of non-tariff barriers and disguised restrictions on trade, especially during an economic recession? And the same is true of other fundamental freedoms provided for in the EC Treaty—the freedom for individuals to take up employment or pursue a trade or profession in another Member State or to provide cross-frontier services—and of great principles such as the right for men and women to receive equal pay for equal work.

Without the doctrine of direct effect the enforceability of the basic rights created by the Treaty would have been dependent on the willingness of the Council of Ministers to adopt the necessary implementing regulations or on the readiness of the Commission to pursue Member States under Article 169 of the EC Treaty (which was of course a toothless remedy in the pre-Maastricht version of the Treaty).[21] Without direct effect, we would have a very different Community today, a more obscure, more remote Community barely distinguishable from so many other international organizations whose existence passes unnoticed by ordinary citizens. As a result of *Van Gend en Loos*, the unique feature of Community law is its ability to impinge directly on the lives of individuals, who are declared to be the "subjects" of the new legal order, entitled as such to invoke rights "which become part of their legal heritage".[22] The effect of *Van Gend en Loos* was to take Community law out of the hands of politicians and bureacrats and to give it to the people. Of all the Court's democratizing achievements none can rank so highly in practical terms. Moreover, the Court recognized in *Van Gend en Loos* that the two aspects of democratic legitimacy, namely, the right of the people to participate in the law-making function through representative bodies and the ability of individuals to vindicate their rights in judicial proceedings, are intimately linked: one of the reasons given for upholding direct effect was that "the nationals of the States brought together in the Community are called upon to cooperate in the functioning of this Community through the intermediary of the European Parliament and the Economic and Social Committee".[23]

This is not the place for a thorough analysis of the doctrine of direct effect or for an appraisal of its fidelity to the EC Treaty and to the original intention of the people who drafted its terms. It is sufficient to observe that, as regards directives, the Court might be—and indeed has been—accused of gross infidelity by those who look only at the letter of Article 189; but fidelity in a nobler sense of the term there certainly was, if it is borne in mind that the Member States could easily have compromised the binding nature of directives, by implementing them late or not at all, which would clearly be contrary to the express intent of

---

[21] The Maastricht Treaty added two paragraphs to Article 171 empowering the Court to impose financial penalties on a Member State which fails to comply with an earlier judgment of the Court declaring that the Member State is in breach of the EC Treaty.

[22] Case 26/62, *supra* n. 19, at 12.

[23] *Ibid.*

Article 189.[24] As for the provisions of the EC Treaty (and indeed other provisions of Community law), the Court demonstrated in *Van Gend en Loos* that they are in the final analysis intended to confer rights on individuals by means of an argument that is simple but unanswerable: it would be pointless for Article 177 to empower or require national courts to seek rulings on the interpretation of provisions of Community law if those provisions could not be invoked in national proceedings. It may be added that the idea of direct effect had already been developed by the Permanent International Court in The Hague in an advisory opinion in 1928:[25] thus, although *Van Gend en Loos* is rightly regarded as having established the original character of Community law, it none the less has a sound pedigree in international law.

7. THE SURPRISING SUCCESS OF ARTICLE 177

The involvement of Europe's citizens in the enforcement of Community law, as a result of the doctrine of direct effect, is, as we have said, a dramatically important democratizing factor; but it could not have borne full fruit if the reference procedure under Article 177 had not been transformed in the course of the years into the quasi-federal instrument for reviewing the compatibility of national laws with Community law. The reasons for this phenomenon are easy to understand.

The division of labour on which Article 177 is based (the European Court's role being to interpret Community law, leaving to the national court the task of applying the interpretation to the facts of the case) is rather sophisticated and may cause difficulty not only for judges who operate in a system to which the reference procedure is unknown, but also for judges in countries in which reference procedures exist but are organized in simpler and more direct fashion. Thus it happens that national courts, called upon to apply a national law whose compatibility with Community law seems doubtful to them, ask the Court whether there exists a conflict between the national law and some provision of Community law.

Naturally the Court has never accepted this form of raising a preliminary question, which is however extremely frequent; whenever the issue is put to it in that form, its reaction has been to reformulate the question. Yet, aware of the difficulties faced by the national judge, the Court does not confine itself to interpreting the Community rule; instead it enters into the heart of the conflict submitted to its attention, but it takes the precaution of rendering it abstract, that is to say it presents it as a conflict between Community law and a hypothetical national provision having the nature of the provision in issue before the national

---

[24] See G.F. Mancini, "The Making of a Constitution for Europe" (1989) 26 *CMLRev* 602 and Chapter 1.

[25] Advisory Opinion No 15 of 3 March 1928, Publications of the Permanent Court of International Justice, Series B, Collection of Advisory Opinions.

court.[26] The technique thus described, which is formally impeccable and of great use to the national court, results in the Court of Justice acquiring a power of review which is analogous to—though of course narrower than—that routinely exercised by the Supreme Court of the United States and the constitutional courts of some Member States.

The consequence is a virtuous circle. More and more Europeans are aware that a law higher than the statutes enacted by their Parliaments bestows upon them rights which are, in the last analysis, protected by the body interpreting that law. This growing awareness increases the visibility of the Court (according to a Community-wide survey of 1988, the latter was perceived as a very important policy-making institution by 18 per cent of respondents).[27] Visibility, in turn, is the first precondition of legitimacy, at least for judicial organs;[28] and the legitimacy thus acquired by the Court reverberates on the law which the Court administers and enlarges the expectations which ordinary people found on its provisions. Whether these expectations coincide with a sense of common citizenship is doubtful; but they are certainly a prelude to it and, as is evidenced by the constant growth in the number of references, they come ever closer to the real thing.

8. THE DANGER FACING THE EUROPEAN COURT

The Court emerged unscathed from the *Chernobyl* case; the political earthquake which that and subsequent judgments on the choice of legal basis[29] failed to provoke may yet be brought about by the routine dialogue between the Court of Justice and national judges via the route opened up by *Van Gend en Loos* and *Van Duyn*. The steady flow of judgments from Luxembourg establishing that some provision of national legislation is incompatible with the rules of the EC Treaty, in response to questions raised by industrial tribunals, pretori, tribunaux de grande instance and Landgerichte, has provoked first displeasure and later open disapproval in certain Member States. The Court has often been the object of ferocious attacks articulated on the front pages of newspapers and echoed, especially in Germany, in the speeches of politicians, even at the most

---

[26] See Mancini, "The Making of a Constitution for Europe", *supra* n. 24, at 605.

[27] The results of the survey are published by Gibson and Caldeira, *supra* n. 4, p. 10. The three countries in which the Court was most "visible" were Ireland (32.2 per cent), Great Britain (29.5 per cent) and Luxembourg (25.3 per cent); it was least "visible" in Greece (12.9 per cent), Portugal (9.7 per cent) and Spain (9.2 per cent).

[28] See Murphy and Tanenhaus, "Public Opinion and the United States Supreme Court: A Preliminary Mapping of Some Prerequisites for Court Legitimation of Regime Changes" (1968) 2 *Law and Society Review* 357–382.

[29] In particular, the judgment in Case C-300/89 *Commission v Council* (*"Titanium Dioxide"*) [1991] ECR I-2867. That judgment annulled a Council Directive based on Article 130S of the EC Treaty, which merely required consultation of the Parliament, rather than Article 100A, which prescribed the cooperation procedure. The formula used in para. 20 of the judgment corresponds word-for-word with that used in *Roquette Frères*.

senior level.[30] A favourite target has been a number of judgments benefiting Italian and non-Community migrant workers. Moreover, the critics soon began to lament the erosion of national sovereignty which the Court's judgments inevitably produce. The process has culminated in an outright threat: if—it is implied—the Court is not able to resist the pressure exerted on it by lower-ranking national judges who are politically motivated or in search of publicity, there will be nothing for it but to deprive those judges of the power to refer questions to the Court of Justice. In 1996 and 1997 an Intergovernmental Conference took place at which key points in the European constitutional system were to be re-examined. Some regarded it as an excellent occasion for the deletion of the second paragraph of Article 177[31] although such reforms did not in the end materialize.

There is, however, a grave danger facing the Court—and, more importantly, there is a grave danger facing the relationship between the European Court and the national courts, a relationship which is rich in democratic promise. To counter that danger the Court will need much wisdom, which in this context means first of all a willingness to practice self-criticism. The irritation of the German authorities' cannot be ascribed entirely to protectionist nostalgia, to the desire to soothe the ethnic resentment of a section of the population or to the understandable fear of surrendering sovereignty in more and more areas without the consent of the national Parliament. Their irritation is fuelled by an additional element: namely, the impression that the Court is one-sided; that, faced with a choice between the interests of the Member States and the interest of the Community, the Court systematically favours the latter. "Im Zweifel für Europa" ("When in doubt, opt for Europe") was the title of an article in the *Frankfurter Rundschau*. That slogan encapsulates the anxiety with which the political class in Germany and in other Member States contemplates the philosophy which seems to guide the Court whenever it is called upon to resolve the most classical of conflicts inherent in federal and confederal organizations.

That is not to suggest that the Court must necessarily bow to such anxieties. The preference for Europe is determined by the genetic code transmitted to the Court by the founding fathers, who entrusted to it the task of ensuring that the law is observed in the application of a Treaty whose primary objective is an "ever closer union among the peoples of Europe".[32] But it is suggested that the Court might seek to placate its critics by demonstrating that the rights of

---

[30] In addition to the article published in the *Frankfurter Rundschau* of 7 December 1992, see "Die Europa-Richter stellen das deutsche Betriebsverfassungsgesetz auf den Kopf", *Handelsblatt*, 13 October 1992; "Die Leise Übermacht", *Der Spiegel*, 30 November 1992 (signed by the Minister for Social Affairs, Norbert Blüm); and "Dem EuGH auf die Finger Geschaut", *E G Magazin*, No 5, 1993 (signed by P. Clever). Threatening allusions to the Court were also uttered by Chancellor Kohl in his speech to the Bundestag of 4 December 1992 (Bulletin No 130/s, 1193).

[31] The suggestion that only courts against whose decision there is no appeal should be allowed to seek a preliminary ruling has been advanced by a senior German civil servant; see P. Clever, "Grundsätzliche Bemerkungen zur Rechtsprechung des EuGH" *Die Angestelltenversicherung*, 2/93.

[32] Article 164 of the EC Treaty and the preamble.

European citizens are equally close to its heart not only when they are breached by the Member States but also when they are encroached upon by legislation emanating from Brussels.[33] So far the jurisprudence of the Court contains few signs of equal solicitude in the two situations.

9. THE CREATION OF A CATALOGUE OF FUNDAMENTAL RIGHTS

The outstanding exception to the phenomenon described above is undoubtedly the definition of a catalogue of fundamental rights by reference to which the Court reviews the legality of the Community's legislative and administrative acts. That achievement, which was initiated in 1969 and 1970 with the judgments in *Stauder*[34] and *Internationale Handelsgesellschaft*[35] and has continued step by step to the present day, is one of the greatest contributions that the Court has made to democratic legitimacy in the Community. The enormous attention devoted to the subject by students of the judicial process is fully justified. There is, however, one fact that should not be forgotten. The Court's discovery that European citizens have fundamental rights was provoked by a well-founded fear that in Germany and Italy the constitutional courts would assume power to test Community laws for compliance with the fundamental rights enshrined in their own constitutions. In fact, before the judges in Karlsruhe and Rome let it be known that they were willing to act in that way, the Court had held that it had no powers in the field of human rights.[36]

It would be an exaggeration to say that the European Court was bulldozed into protecting fundamental rights by rebellious national courts. It is, however, clear that the Court did not embark upon that course in a spontaneous binge of judicial activism. The fact that the Court was forced to recognize fundamental rights in order to prevent the Community's laws from being tested for compatibilty with national constitutions should suffice to exonerate the Court from a charge of wilfully exceeding its powers by rewriting the EC Treaty. It also demonstrates what an impeccable pedigree the Community's catalogue of fundamental rights has. The Court's case law on fundamental rights is founded on the constitutional traditions of the Member States, natural law and the common legal heritage of western civilization. The justification for interpreting the EC Treaty as protecting fundamental rights in spite of the silence of its terms is strong. It is inconceivable that the national Parliaments would have ratified a

---

[33] A.M. Burley, "Democracy and Judicial Review in the European Community" (1992) *University of Chicago Legal Forum* 81.

[34] Case 29/69 *Erich Stauder* v *Stadt Ulm* [1969] ECR 419.

[35] Case 11/70 *Internationale Handelsgesellschaft mbH* v *Einfuhr- und Vorratsstelle für Getreide und Futtermittel* [1970] ECR 1125.

[36] For summary of this fascinating chapter of legal history, see G.F. Mancini and V. Di Bucci, "Le développement des droits fondamentaux en tant que partie du droit communautaire" in Academy of European Law (ed.) *Collected Courses of the Academy of European Law*, Volume I, Book 1 (Kluwer, Deventer, 1991), p. 27.

treaty which was capable of violating the fundamental tenets of their own constitutions. Logically, a law ratifying such a treaty might itself have been unconstitutional, which would remove the entire legal basis for the foundation of the Community.

Moreover, the Court's approach to the question of fundamental rights has been approved consistently by the other institutions and by the Member States. In a Joint Declaration on Fundamental Rights,[37] adopted on 5 April 1977, the European Parliament, the Council and the Commission cited the Court's case law and stressed "the prime importance they attach to the protection of fundamental rights, as derived in particular from the constitutions of the Member States and the European Convention for the Protection of Human Rights and Fundamental Freedoms". In the preamble to the Single European Act the Member States expressed their determination to work together to promote democracy on the basis of fundamental rights. Finally, Article F(2) of the Maastricht Treaty commits the European Union to respecting fundamental rights, as guaranteed by the European Human Rights Convention and the constitutional traditions common to the Member States.[38] What is striking about all these documents is that—as occurred after the *Chernobyl* judgment—the rulings of the Court have been more than an inspiration; they have been taken over *verbatim*.

10. TWO AREAS IN WHICH THE COURT OF JUSTICE HAS LET THE INDIVIDUAL DOWN

Although the Court of Justice has been bold in relation to fundamental rights and has subjected the Community's legislative and administrative organs to a high standard, there are other areas in which the Court has been surprisingly cautious and has shown excessive indulgence towards the Council and Commission. What is even more puzzling is that the high level of judicial protection established by the Court on the basis of the complex, inherently defective reference procedure provided for in Article 177 has not always been equalled in areas where the Court's jurisdiction is direct, in the sense that actions are commenced in Luxembourg without passing through the intermediary of a national court.

Two examples of that disparity may be offered. The first concerns the *locus standi* of natural and legal persons under the second paragraph of Article 173 of

---

[37] OJ 1977 C 103, p. 1. All the documents cited in this passage, together with numerous declarations issued by the Member States and the Council and a catalogue of fundamental rights promulgated in a declaration of the European Parliament, are available in a booklet published by the Commission (C. Duparc, *The European Community and Human Rights*, October 1992).

[38] A commitment which was subsequently rendered justiciable by the modification of Article L in the Amsterdam Treaty.

the EC Treaty.[39] Such persons may only challenge a regulation if it is of direct and individual concern to them. A generous and not unreasonable reading of that provision would allow Joe Smith, the turnip-grower, to challenge a regulation that was particularly detrimental to the interests of turnip-growers. But the Court has opted for a parsimonious construction: in order to have *locus standi* Joe Smith, the turnip-grower, must show that the regulation singles him out and affects him more severely than it affects turnip-growers as a category.[40] It is obvious that in most cases Joe Smith's action will founder on the reef of inadmissibility.

The results of this narrow construction of what is in any event a restrictive provision may be bizarre and paradoxical, if not downright perverse. A regulation may, as a matter of substance, be patently and outrageously unlawful; it may breach the principles of non-discrimination and proportionality, violate fundamental rights and inflict huge financial loss on large numbers of persons; but unless one of those persons can show that he is somehow singled out by the regulation and injured more severely than the category to which he belongs, he will be unable to challenge it directly before the European Court. All that he can do is to defy the regulation and wait till an attempt is made to enforce it against him in the national courts, where he may of course contest the validity of the regulation and succeed in having the issue referred to the European Court under Article 177.

So at the end of the day justice will be done and the regulation will be struck down. But does it make sense to force the individual in such a scenario to suffer years of uncertainty as to his legal rights, to explore the highways and byways of national procedural law and to adopt an essentially defensive line of conduct when logic and justice command that he should be allowed to launch a full-frontal assault on an act so detrimental to his interests? One can of course understand the familiar arguments about opening the floodgates and admitting a deluge of actions by disgruntled individuals who are adversely affected by

---

[39] The paragraph is worded as follows: "Any natural or legal person may, under the same conditions [i.e. on grounds of lack of competence, infringement of an essential procedural requirement, infringement of the Treaty or of any rule of law relating to its application, or misuse of powers], institute proceedings against a decision addressed to that person or against a decision which, although in the form of a regulation or a decision addressed to that person or against a decision which, although in the form of a regulation or a decision to another person, is of direct and individual concern to the former".

[40] See, for example, Case 26/86 *Deutz and Geldermann, Sektkellerei Breisach (Baden) GmbH* v *Council* [1987] ECR 941, which is a typical example of a restrictive approach dating back to Case 25/62 *Plaumann & Co.* v *Commission* [1963] ECR 95. For criticism of the Court's approach, see A. Barav, "Direct and Individual Concern: An Almost Insurmountable Barrier to the Admissibility of Individual Appeal to the EEC Court" (1974) 11 *CMLRev* 191; E. Stein and J.G. Vining, "Citizen Access to Judicial Review of Administrative Action in a Transnational and Federal Context" (1976) 70 *American Journal of International Law* 219; and H. Rasmussen, "Why is Article 173 Interpreted Against Private Plaintiffs?" (1980) 5 *ELRev* 112. On the same subject, see also C. Harding, "The Private Interest in Challenging Community Action" (1980) 5 *ELRev* 354 and R. Greaves, "*Locus Standi* under Article 173 EEC when Seeking Annulment of a Regulation" (1986) 11 *ELRev* 119.

Community legislation;[41] but surely it would not have been beyond the ingenuity of the Court to devise a test that would bar frivolous or tenuous claims while allowing direct actions by those who can demonstrate with a sufficient degree of plausibility that they are likely to suffer serious loss as a result of a normative act of the Community.

The second example of the Court's excessive caution and indulgence towards Community institutions concerns the action for damages for non-contractual liability. It occasionally happens, especially in the agricultural sector, that individuals suffer economic loss as a result of an unlawful regulation. In principle, Article 215 of the EC Treaty requires the Community to compensate persons who suffer damage as a result of the unlawful acts of its institutions. However, the Court will only award compensation for damage caused by normative acts if the victim of the illegality can prove that the institutions have committed a sufficiently serious breach of a "superior rule of law" for the protection of the individual. It is not enough for their conduct to be knowingly unlawful, although that would doubtless suffice in the laws of most of the Member States, laws to which Article 215 refers specifically: instead, the conduct must verge on the arbitrary or the capricious.[42] It is hardly surprising, then, that only a handful of actions for damages have succeeded and that the test applied by the Court has been widely criticized.[43] The criticism is particularly understandable since the recent *Francovich* judgment. In that case, the Court held that Member States which have failed to implement a directive in good time must compensate individuals who suffer damage as a result, provided that the directive was intended to create rights for the individual, even though it does not have direct effect; as regards the conditions governing liability the Court referred to the laws of the Member States, which, as emerged above, are much less demanding than the case law of the Court.[44]

11. CONCLUSION

To sum up, there are many points in the case law of the Court that are in need of further refinement and there are many gaps waiting to be filled; the more so

[41] The "floodgates" argument, which was never wholly convincing, looks weaker still since the establishment of the Court of First Instance and the extension of its jurisdiction by Council Decision 93/350 of 8 June 1993 (OJ 1993 L 144, p. 21). It is not inconceivable that the Court of First Instance, whose specific task is to hear and determine actions brought by natural and legal persons, will be able to develop more flexible criteria regarding the *locus standi* of individuals.

[42] See, in particular, Joined Cases 116 and 124/77 *G.R. Amylum NV and Tunnel Refineries Limited* v *Council and Commission* [1979] ECR 3497 at para. 19.

[43] See, for example, Fuss, "La responsabilité des Communautés européennes pour le comportement illégal de leurs organes" (1981) 1 *Revue trimestrelle de droit européen* 31; J. Rideau and J.L. Charrier, *Code de procédures européennes* (Paris, Litec, 1990), p. 189; and F. Fines, *Etudes de la responsabilité extracontractuelle de la Communauté économique européenne* (Paris, L.G.D.J, 1990), p. 338 *et seq.*

[44] Joined Cases C-6/90 and C-9/90 *Andrea Francovich and Danila Bonifaci and others* v *Italy* [1991] ECR I-5357.

because circumstances have changed vastly since the years when the Court delivered its first judgments on the *locus standi* of individuals and on the liability of the Community institutions in damages. In those days, when it was a question of imposing scanty and sporadic items of legislation on a hostile, reluctant world, a degree of indulgence could be tolerated; in fact, it performed a useful balancing function. Nowadays that function is no longer required. In 1991, according to a study by the French Conseil d'Etat, 1,564 legal measures originated in Brussels, against 1,417 which emanated from Paris.[45]

Little, however, has changed in the decision-making procedures of the Community. The main innovation, before Maastricht, was the enhanced role granted to the European Parliament under the cooperation procedure: the importance of that should not be underestimated, though it has yielded results that are meagre and disproportionate to the energy and time consumed. It remains to be seen whether the power of co-decision granted to the Parliament under the Maastricht Treaty and extended under the Amsterdam Treaty will bring about a significant shift in the balance of power. For the present, real power is still in the hands of the Council, which legislates behind closed doors on the basis of drafts prepared by an ambassadorial college (COREPER)[46] and, at a lower level, by numerous committees of national experts, who are faceless and unaccountable. Even the Commission has sins to atone for. Jean Monnet once said: *d'abord on décide, puis on explique.* Most past and present Commissioners and the élite group of senior officials seem to have taken this dubious dictum all too seriously. As a journalist wrote in *Le Monde*, mapping out measures and blueprints in the bosom of a coterie which pursues lofty aims with rites, codes and a language of its own is intoxicating,[47] but it is hardly consistent with the rules of democracy, even in the eyes of those who understand that in the formation of legislative proposals there is limited scope for transparency.

That is all very well, some will say, but there are too many risks; that greater democracy and more power for Brussels are objectives that can only be reconciled in the Elysian fields of rhetoric; that in the real world, the pursuit of one will make the other more difficult to attain. Worse still: in the Community edifice breaches will open up which, rather than benefiting the citizens of Europe, will appeal only to those elements in the Member States whose deepest aspiration is to substitute, wherever possible, the intergovernmental for the supranational. In stimulating those tendencies the Court, it could be argued, will have safeguarded its competences but at the price of abdicating from the task

---

[45] Conseil d'Etat, *Rapport public* 1992, Etudes et documents, No 44.

[46] See, however, Article 151 of the EC Treaty which was introduced by the Amsterdam Treaty, which requires the Council to establish in its Rules of Procedure the conditions under which the public shall have access to Council documents and Article 191a EC on the right of Union citizens to have access to European Parliament, Council and Commission documents generally subject, of course, to conditions.

[47] Servent, "Déboires et Espoirs de la Construction Européenne", *Le Monde*, 5 December 1992.

entrusted to it by the founding fathers. What can one say in response to such an objection? Perhaps only this: the risks are there but they must be faced. If Europe is not to grow as a democratic organism, that which will be left for us to organize will no longer be Europe.

4

Europe: The Case for Statehood

"IN PRINCIPLE", WRITES Jürgen Habermas, "the rule of law can exist without the concomitant existence of democracy", that is to say without political rights empowering the citizen to bring influence to bear on changes of his own status.[1] The model of less than democratic governance which the German philosopher has in mind is probably the British Raj or something akin to it: a "paternalistic authority", as he puts it. Yet Habermas' remark seems to apply no less accurately to a polity which, both in its conception and operation, has little that is paternal about it: the one brought into being in 1957 by the EC Treaty.

Treaties, as happened in the case of the German Empire at the end of 1870, may give rise to federal states, but what they usually produce are alliances, leagues, confederations and, when the goals pursued are confined to a specific area, international organizations.[2] The European Community differed from the latter in many respects, by far the most significant of which was the fact that the relationships established between its institutions and its Member States, including their citizens, were subjected to the rule of law. Nevertheless, there were weightier reasons which led both politicians and scholars to deny that the Community possessed a federal character and therefore to number it with the other and looser entities: namely, the chiefly economic nature of the competences transferred to it and, even more telling, its substantially undemocratic structure. Indeed, the correlation between federalism and democracy (or, at the least, constitutionalism) is generally deemed to be so necessary[3] that most authorities agreed to designate the Soviet Union and certain Latin American

---

[1] J. Habermas, "Citizenship and National Identity: Some Reflections on the Future of Europe" (1992) 12 *Praxis International* 1, at 10. In a not dissimilar context see I. Berlin, *Four Essays on Liberty* (1969), p. 129 *et seq.*

[2] See C. Leben, "A propos de la nature juridique des Communautés européennes" (1991) 14 *Droits* 61, at 63. According to some writers, by contrast, confederations have, in principle, political and defensive objectives. A.D. Pliakos, "La nature juridique de l'Union européenne" (1993) 29 *Revue trimestrielle de droit européen* 187, at 209 *et seq.* writes that, while an international organization implies a pooling of sovereignty by its Member States, their sovereignty remains intact in a confederation.

[3] The necessary "coincidence" between federalism and democracy has been convincingly demonstrated by O. Kimminich, "Der Bundesstaat" in *Handbuch des Staatsrechts der Bundesrepublik Deutschland*, I (C.F. Muller, 1987), p. 1128; but see also the eloquent remarks of H. Kelsen, *General Theory of Law and State* (Harvard University Press, 1949), p. 310 *et seq.* On the relation between federalism and constitutionalism see C.J. Friedrich, *Limited Government. A Comparison* (Prentice Hall, 1974), p. 54 *et seq.*

states in some phases of their history as sham federations.[4] International organizations, by contrast, are supposedly non-democratic, since they reserve central normative power to the body representing the contracting states which, as a rule, exercises it unanimously.[5] "Diplomacy not democracy" governs their decision-making mechanisms.[6]

The EC Treaty is technically still in force; but the case law of the Court of Justice and a series of constitutional reforms begun in 1976 have deeply affected the scheme established by its authors. As a consequence of the jurisprudence of the European Court, especially those judgments which read into the Treaty an open-ended charter of fundamental rights, the area covered by the rule of law in the operation of the Community is now so spacious and well-guarded as to pillory for its gratuitous arrogance a sentence uttered in 1974 by Raymond Aron: "genuine civil rights do not reach beyond national boundaries".[7] As for the reforms to which reference has already been made—the election of the European Parliament by universal suffrage and its modest but increasing involvement in the Community's law-making machinery—they were clearly prompted by the awareness that the growing range of the Community's powers had significantly detracted from the sovereignty of national parliaments, removing ever wider matters from their purview in an incremental process to which national parliamentarians had not consented and over which they had no control.[8] The legislative monopoly accorded to the body representing the states had therefore to be diluted at the Community level in ways reminiscent, even if only faintly, of the federal model under which the power to make laws is shared by the states' council and a house representing the people.[9]

These developments, together with other institutional steps taken in order to ensure the efficiency of the Community (for example, a considerable increase in majority voting within the Council of Ministers) as well as the forthcoming

---

[4] On the Soviet Union see Z. Gitelman, "Federalism and Multiculturalism in Socialist Systems" in D.J. Elazar (ed.), *Federalism and Political Integration* (Turtledove, 1974), p. 157 *et seq.* On Argentina, Brazil, Mexico and Venezuela, see J. Carpizo, *Federalismo en Latinoamérica* (UNAM, 1973), p. 76 *et seq.* For a general survey of the cases of "sham" federalism see also G. de Vergottini, "Stato federale" in *Enciclopedia del Diritto*, XLIII, 1990, p. 831 *et seq.*

[5] Leben, *supra* n. 2, at 65; G.F. Mancini and D.T. Keeling, "Democracy and the European Court of Justice" (1994) 57 *Modern Law Review* 175 *et seq.* and Chapter 3; A. La Pergola, "L'Unione europea tra il mercato comune e un moderno tipo di confederazione. Osservazioni di un costituzionalista" (1993) *Rivista trimestrale di diritto e procedura civile* 1, at 3.

[6] D.M. Curtin, "Postnational Democracy. The European Union in Search of a Political Philosophy", Inaugural Lecture, University of Utrecht, at p. 9.

[7] R. Aron, "Is Multinational Citizenship Possible?" (1974) 4 *Social Research* 638.

[8] Mancini and Keeling, *supra* n. 5, at 177 *et seq.* A further argument that helped to strengthen the case for direct elections was the Parliament's acquisition of budgetary powers in 1970 and 1975: see J. Pinder, *European Community. The Building of a Union* (Oxford University Press, 1991), at p. 35.

[9] Leben, *supra* n. 2; La Pergola, *supra* n. 5, at 7. For a comprehensive survey of the evolution of the European Parliament up to the Maastricht Treaty, which in the last analysis conferred on it a negative right to block a legislative proposal in ten policy areas (the so-called "co-decision procedure"), see M. Newman, *Democracy, Sovereignty and the European Union* (Hurst, 1996), at p. 174 *et seq.*

acquisition of monetary sovereignty[10] and, under the frailer label of the European Union, a growing European capacity to assume "almost all the core functions of the nation state"[11] have undoubtedly modified the primitive nature of the polity born in 1957. Today, insisting on defining it as an international organization and describing all that does not fit well with this definition as "frills and rhetorics"[12] is much like trying to push the toothpaste back into the tube.[13] Those who indulge in such an exercise are either die-hard acolytes of the neo-realist school in political science, eager to prove that any further progress on the part of the Union will falter in the face of unsurmountable barriers,[14] or professors of international law anxious to maintain their hold on a luscious province increasingly coveted by constitutional lawyers.[15] However, if this point is indisputable, there is much doubt as to whether constitutional lawyers might, without further ado, annex and lord over the province which they so covet. I personally believe that their time has yet to come. While the Maastricht Treaty has conquered a large and important territory, it has nevertheless not led the Union across the threshold wherein lies the federal state. I shall say more: it seems to me that the closer the Union moves towards statehood, the greater the resistance to the attainment of this goal becomes.

Two recent examples will support this suggestion. Any upholder of the functionalist philosophy which profoundly informed one of the Community's founding fathers, Jean Monnet, as well as any subscriber to the Madisonian dictum "federalise their wallets and their hearts and minds will follow",[16] is given to think that the implementation of monetary union will inevitably so unbalance the system as to require a counterpoise in terms of a genuine and democratically accountable economic government. Yet the Amsterdam Treaty fell

---

[10] Which, as Baroness Thatcher once remarked, is "the core of the core of national sovereignty": see W. Wallace, "Rescue of Retreat? The Nation State in Western Europe, 1945–1993" (1994) XLII *Political Studies* 52, at 67. According to P.C. Schmitter, "Imagining the Future of the Euro-Polity with the Help of New Concepts" in G. Marks *et al.* (eds.), *Governance in the European Union* (Sage, 1996), at p. 122 *et seq.*, if monetary union is successful, "Member States will have 'pooled' [the right] to pursue any macro-economic policy independent of the other participating Member States".

[11] Wallace, *supra* n. 10, at 65. See also Schmitter, *supra* n. 10, at p. 124: "There is no issue area that was the exclusive domain of national policy in 1950 and that has not somehow and in some degree been incorporated within the authoritative purview of the EC/EU".

[12] See Pinder, *supra* n. 8, at p. 4.

[13] J.H.H. Weiler, and U.R. Haltern, "The Autonomy of the Community Legal Order—Through the Looking Glass" (1996) 37 *Harvard International Law Journal* 411, at 423.

[14] On the neo-realist school and its belief in the immutable role of the nation state and the unreality of proposals for the transfer of sovereignty to common institutions see Pinder, *supra* n. 9, at p. 203 *et seq.* and Newman, *supra* n. 9, at p. 17 *et seq.* See also H.H. Koh, "Why Do Nations Obey International Law?" (1997) 106 *Yale Law Journal* 2599, at 2615, who devotes a highly sophisticated analysis to the origins, the development and the present decline of this group of scholars.

[15] For a perfect example of this attitude see A. Pellet, "Les fondements juridiques internationaux du droit communautaire" in Academy of European Law (ed.), *Collected Courses of the Academy of European Law*, Volume I, Book 1 (Deventer, Kluwer, 1997), p. 193 *et seq.*. A similar, albeit less loaded, approach is adopted by T. Schilling, "The Autonomy of the Community Legal Order: An Analysis of Possible Foundations" (1996) 37 *Harvard International Law Journal* 389.

[16] Oxford University, Final Honour School of Jurisprudence, European Community Law Paper, 1980.

demonstrably short of this expectation. Its authors decided that the college of the fifteen Finance Ministers (including representatives from countries which might not necessarily join the single currency) will be a sufficient match for the power of a future Central Bank and that the extent of such power does not itself settle the case in favour of granting the European Parliament a greater role. Equally indicative of this hard-nosed attitude, however, was their curt opposition to any enrichment of the stingy catalogue of rights—no more than "mirrors and beads" for the natives[17]—which Articles 8 to 8e of the Treaty on European Union attached to Union citizenship. Obviously, an expansion of this status, not unlike an enlargement of the Parliament's prerogatives, would strengthen European democracy or, more accurately, would contribute to its transformation from "liturgy" to "substance".[18] By the same token, however, it would enfeeble *national* identities;[19] this, or a residual clinging to the concept of nationhood, seems to be precisely the reason why the negotiators of the Amsterdam Treaty not only shied away from it, but even emphasized that Union citizenship may complement but in no way replaces Member State nationality.

2. STATES AND NATIONS

In spite of appearances, which suggest that the main issue at stake is the safe-guarding of national sovereignty, the reasons accounting for the hostility of the powers that be to European statehood are in essence more down-to-earth than ideological.[20] Old hands identify them in the self-preserving interests of the political and bureaucratic élites in the fifteen Member States and, in a worthier vein, the awareness of the latter that in the eyes of their constituencies the national community remains the broadest focus for political life and group identity.[21] In recent times, however, the same élites have found an unexpected (and

---

[17] H.U.J. D'Oliveira, "Union Citizenship: Pie in the Sky?" in A. Rosas and E. Antola (eds.), *A Citizens' Europe in Search of a New Legal Order* (Sage, 1995), p. 58, at p. 64. For an even harsher judgment see J.H.H. Weiler *et al.*, *Certain Rectangular Problems of European Integration*, Volume I, Political Series, Working Paper W-24, at 20: "the Citizenship clause in the TEU is little more than a cynical exercise in public relations". On the weaknesses and limitations of Articles 8—8e see generally, S. O'Leary, *The Evolving Concept of Community Citizenship* (Kluwer, 1996).

[18] La Pergola, *supra* n. 5, at 7.

[19] For a clear-sighted analysis of this contradiction see G. de Búrca, "The Quest for Legitimacy in the European Union" (1996) 16 *Oxford Journal of Legal Studies* 349, at 359. According to K. Lenaerts and E. De Smijter, "The Question of Democratic Representation" in J.A. Winter, D.M. Curtin, A. Kellermann and B. De Witte (eds), *Reforming the Treaty on European Union: the Legal Debate* (Kluwer, 1996), p. 173 at p. 177, the fear that, in the long run, Union citizenship could lead to a shift of social loyalty from the national to the supranational level was the immediate incentive for the Edinburgh Decision of December 1992.

[20] See the eloquent examples which Newman, *supra* n. 9, at p. 2 *et seq.* draws from the attitudes of the opponents of Norway's accession to the EU and of the Eurosceptics in the House of Commons' debate on Britain's contribution to the EU budget. In both cases, both of which took place in 1994, the slogans and the political priorities involved were quite different.

[21] Wallace, *supra* n. 10, at 55 *et seq.*

in this case unequivocally ideological) ally in those academic and judicial circles which only a few years ago drummed and fifed for the speedy political integration of Europe. Having been myself a member of both circles I am particularly interested in exactly what motivates these views and will seek to identify their underlying causes.

To this end, a premise is indispensable. The new mood which pervades many of the courthouses and the law faculties of Europe (but also some of their off-shoots in America) is far from homogeneous. These are intellectual worlds and accordingly the discursive scenery is host to a myriad of details and nuances. With a touch of simplification, however, two streams of thought may be discerned which are not only unlike one another, but also at odds with each other on most qualifying points. The first has thus concluded that "the safest . . . option is simply to retreat to what we are familiar with, the nation state" and that any notion of democracy beyond this horizon is "at best sheer Utopianism, at worst downright dangerous".[22] The second, in the words of its most prestigious spokesman, Professor Joseph Weiler, is opposed to a "statal Europe albeit of a federal kind"[23] because such a polity would assemble and perpetuate all that is "excluding"—namely hindering outsiders from entrance and refusing them participation—in both the history and the practice of the European nation states, and would thus betray the promises implicit in the vision of a merely supranational, rather than statal, Europe. In this respect, the Maastricht Treaty, "having appropriated the deepest symbols of statehood (citizenship, foreign policy, defence) was a deception".[24]

On a first reading, it would seem readily apparent that these views are nothing if not highly contradictory. However, I intend in the next two paragraphs to delve deeper and argue that, differences apart, both these stem from a common root: the inability to conceive of statehood in any terms other than *nation* statehood, or, in a nutshell, to divorce the state from the nation.

3. THE HIDDEN ETHNOS?

(a) Homogeneity and Political Communication

Let me begin with the school of thought according to which any attempt to strengthen the democratic dimension of the European Union is either illusory or likely to jeopardize the roots of democracy where they are at their deepest and firmest—the nation state. Although traces of this opinion can be detected within

---

[22] Curtin, *supra* n. 6, at p. 13.

[23] J.H.H. Weiler, "Europe After Maastricht—Do the New Clothes Have an Emperor?" Harvard Jean Monnet Working Paper 12/95, at p. 13.

[24] *Ibid.*, at p. 20; Curtin, *supra* n. 6, at p. 16, referring succinctly to Europe as the first "post-modern" that is fragmentary and fluid, polity, seems to share, given the positive connotation usually attached to "post-modern", at least some aspects of Weiler's position.

various legal and political cultures,[25] Germany is its native land and the decision delivered by the German Constitutional Court on the compatibility of the Maastricht Treaty with German Basic Law[26] is its best-known, if not subtlest, expression. The section of this judgment relevant for our discussion can be easily summarized: the principle of democracy, as enshrined in Article 20 of the Basic Law, requires that each and every execution of sovereign rights derives directly from the "people of the State" (*Staatsvolk*), the framing of whose political will postulates the existence of a form of public opinion which can only be created through the free exchange of ideas and an ongoing process of interaction between social forces and interests. Today, such conditions exist only within the nation state where the people may express and have an influence on what concerns them "on a relatively homogeneous basis, spiritually, socially and politically".

In Europe—here I shall draw less upon the Judgment and more upon the many comments, some by Justices of the German Court, which it has stimulated—the "thickening economic and social intercourse"[27] brought about by forty years of integration has certainly yielded a limited harvest in terms of social cohesion; but the discrepancy between this intercourse and the degree of communication which is required for an authentic democratic discourse is still large. As Justice Grimm points out, neither a European public nor a European political debate are detectable;[28] and the biggest obstacle to their development, the factor which dooms to failure any attempt to Europeanize the social substructure on which the functioning of a political system and the performance of a parliament are contingent, is the absence of a common language. Certainly, multilingual states—Belgium, Switzerland, Finland—do exist; but they have five to ten million inhabitants and two or three languages, while the figures in the European Union are 370 million and eleven, respectively. Europe's democratic deficit—as we somewhat piously call the inability of the Union to ferry itself beyond the rites and the catchwords of democracy—is therefore *inborn* and cannot realistically be removed within a time-frame which is other than geological or, at the very least, epochal.[29]

Reforms aiming to stop the "formidable gaps" which still exist in the legislative powers of the Parliament[30] or seeking to require its assent to EC Treaty

---

[25] See, in Italy, G.E. Rusconi, "La cittadinanza europea non crea il 'popolo europeo'" *Il Mulino* 5/96, at p. 831 *et seq.*

[26] Bundesverfassungsgericht, judgment of 12 October 1993, *BVerfGE*, 89, p. 155, the so-called Maastricht *Urteil*, reproduced in [1994] *Common Market Law Reports 57.*

[27] J.H.H. Weiler, "Does Europe Need a Constitution? Demos, Telos and the German Maastricht Decision" (1995) 1 *European Law Journal* 219, at 229.

[28] D. Grimm, "Does Europe Need a Constitution?" (1995) 1 *European Law Journal* 282, at 295.

[29] These adjectives have been used, ironically but quite correctly in my opinion, by Weiler, "Does Europe Need a Constitution? . . . " *supra* n. 27, at 227. More warily, Justice Grimm uses expressions such as "as yet", "for the time being" etc.

[30] See Weiler *et al.*, "Certain Rectangular Problems of European Integration", *supra* n. 17, at p. 6. As Corbett has pointed out, "Representing the People" in A. Duff, *et al.* (eds.), *Maastricht and Beyond. Building the European Union* (Routledge, 1995), p. 207, at p. 223, even in the areas of

amendments, would therefore have little impact on the democracy deficit. In fact, as is often the way with institutional shortcuts, they might even be fraught with risks. Since there is now—and this is the gist of the argument—no European people, the assembly in Strasbourg is by definition not a popular representative body. Accordingly, promoting it to a fully-fledged legislature would not be an adequate balance for the loosening of the ties between the citizens of the fifteen Member States and their parliaments which such an enterprise would necessarily entail.[31] The upshot of these remarks is plain and Justice Grimm states it with remarkable candour: democracy in its plenitude can only be achieved within a national framework and, if this be the case, "converting the European Union into a federal state is not a desirable goal".[32]

The authors of the Maastricht judgment and their fellow-travellers in German constitutional law certainly do not lack sagacity. They are aware that the *Staatsvolk*, which they regard as the only basis for democratic authority and legitimate law-making, might be understood in the light of the elements used to define the notion of *Volk* by the Romantic movement dominant at the beginning of the last century (a "natural whole" having an origin and a destiny of its own) and they consequently spare no efforts in trying to avoid this risk. The emphasis which they place on the indispensable nature of a political discourse and the conditions that make it possible—that is to say a widespread and elaborate communications system or the existence of "mediatory" agencies (political parties, institutes of learning, interest groups of all sorts)[33]—clearly reflects their intention to strip the *Staatsvolk* of any organic connotation and present it as a *demos*, a mundane community of political animals endowed with interests as often divergent as convergent.

Yet, as a host of scholars with Weiler in the vanguard[34] have seen, this endeavour fails. The most eloquent evidence of such failure is provided by the academic works of the selfsame jurist who wrote the German constitutional decision, Justice Kirchhof.[35] It is not necessary, however, to scrutinize these

Community law-making where the co-decision procedure applies, the onus in adopting a measure will normally be in obtaining a qualified majority (and sometimes unanimity) in Council rather than a simple majority in Parliament.

[31] See Grimm, *supra* n. 28, at 296.

[32] *Ibid.*, at 297.

[33] See, primarily, Grimm, *supra* n. 28, at 294 *et seq.*, and the authors he quotes in notes 33 and 39.

[34] See B.O. Bryde, "Die bundesrepublikanische Volksdemokratie als Irrweg der Demokratietheorie" (1994) 5 *Staatswissenschaften und Staatspraxis* 305, at 309; C. Joerges, "Taking the Law Seriously: On Political Science and the Role of Law in the Process of European Integration" (1996) 2 *European Law Journal* 105, at 115 *et seq.*; M. Zuleeg, "The European Constitution under Constitutional Constraints: the German Scenario" (1997) 22 *ELRev* 19, at 28 *et seq.* Most of the criticisms made by these and other commentators are taken up by a Resolution adopted in plenary session by the European Parliament with an overwhelming majority on 2 October 1997. The Resolution incorporates a report drafted by Deputy Siegbert Alber, (who thereafter became an Advocate General at the European Court of Justice), on the relationships between international law, Community law and the constitutional law of the Member States.

[35] See, in particular, his *Handbuch des Staatsrechts der Bundesrepublik Deutschland*, *supra* n. 3, VII, para. VII. Weiler quotes abundantly from this and other writings of Justice Kirchof.

works in detail. A crucial passage of the decision itself—the "spiritual, social and political homogeneity" which must characterize the people of the state—and the inordinate importance which a scholar as accomplished and level-headed as Justice Grimm attaches to the necessity of a common language (wasn't language the "primeval social link" according to the greatest German Romanticist, Johann Gottfried von Herder?) prove that hiding behind the *demos* lies, irreducibly, the metaphysical *Volk* enjoying an "eternal existence" that Savigny theorized in 1840, Gierke revamped at the end of the century and Carl Schmitt rendered sinister in 1927.[36] Democracy is possible in the Member States because an organic, ethnically homogeneous construction renders them socially coherent; it is not possible in Europe, with the consequence of making its conversion into a state inadvisable, because Europe lacks ethnic uniformity and is therefore denied cohesion. When dealing with some of the premises of German public law, one is at times reminded of the Cheshire cat: the body, beginning with the end of the tail, has vanished, but the grin remains.

(b) Democracy and Multicultural Societies

Disproving these propositions or, one might say, exorcizing the grin, is not a daunting task; provided, of course, that one resists the temptation to appeal to half-truths such as the existence of a common European culture dating back to the Middle Ages and recently given new life by the Erasmus student exchange programme and the postgraduate institutes in Florence and Bruges. True enough, "large numbers of young people across Europe treat their Continent, rather than their country, as the space within which they expect to move" (and, why not, to find a partner); no less true, "a certain diffusion of loyalties, a certain expansion of horizons from the national to the European . . . are evident both among élites and, more faintly, among mass publics".[37] However, to draw from these developments the conclusion that Europe has already acquired "a sense of shared identity and collective self" is an exercise in self-deception.[38] On this score Kirchhof and Grimm are right. They are wrong, however, in not seeing that a European State composed of a plurality of nations and yet founded on a *demos*, deriving its legitimacy from consent rather than descent and its chances of survival from civic rather than primordial loyalties is indeed con-

[36] See M.D. Dubber, "The German Jury and the Metaphysical *Volk*: From Romantic Idealism to Nazi Ideology" (1995) 43 *American Journal of Comparative Law* 227, at 248, 259. The author notes that this concept retains, sometimes with overtones reminiscent of its Nazi version, a considerable pull in several areas of contemporary German law and jurisprudence, at 267–271.

[37] Wallace, *supra* n. 10, at 55 and 59.

[38] Weiler, "Does Europe Need a Constitution? . . ." *supra* n. 27, at 239. See also Newman, *supra* n. 9, at 151: "It seems probable that the majority of the population in the majority of Member States retain a far stronger sense of common citizenship within the 'nation-state' than with the EU as a whole. If this is so, it is hardly surprising since states have far greater power over people's lives than the EU".

ceivable. They are wrong in rejecting such a prospect for a simple, empirical reason: the existence and survival of several polities corresponding to the model which I have outlined. I would like to add that ignoring this fundamental objection or cursorily ridding itself of it is, for German scholarship, an alarming signal of parochialism.

Let us pass over the USA and Australia whose multiethnic characters are (as yet) not reflected at the level of language and are anyhow strongly tempered by the cultural hegemony of one group, the descendants of the first colonists. Let us dwell instead on Belgium and Canada. As a consequence of the ethnic revival which torments our age and has grating overtones in their case, both federations are wobbly, though not necessarily doomed to dismemberment. In any event, both are democracies as impeccable as can be in this imperfect world. Their communications systems, however, are no longer common and their "mediatory" agencies—parties, trade unions, universities—have split, fully in Belgium, partly in Canada, along language lines. Indeed, it might be argued that the linguistic provisions applying to large areas of either country have one basic object: precluding the ethnic group for the benefit of whom they have been enacted from using or even learning the language of the other. Thus the Charter of the French language in Québec and various decrees of the Flemish Community impose deterring penalties, the former on the employers who fire, downgrade and transfer their employees for speaking only French, the latter on those who do not confine themselves to Dutch when offering jobs.[39]

The history of my own country provides us with a more positive example, although from a different angle. The unification of Italy between 1859 and 1861 was the result of the work of thin political and intellectual elites aided and abetted by two powerful nation states, France and Britain. The claim, sometimes to be found in our primary-school textbooks, that the *Risorgimento* sprang from popular demand and involved popular participation is a pious untruth. In any case, at a time when tens if not hundreds of mutually unintelligible vernaculars peppered the Italian countryside, it was not possible to speak of a collective "Italian self". Indeed, so distinct were the dialects used in the peninsula that when, on what would today be regarded as a fact-finding mission, two eminent Milanese intellectuals, Emilio and Giovanni Visconti Venosta, visited the *Mezzogiorno* on horseback, they were thought by passing peasants to be Englishmen on their grand tour simply because the language tripping from their tongues was the cultivated Italian which the ruling classes learnt in their homes and exclusive schools.[40] Nonetheless, while it never acquired a more than wavering national identity, Italy consolidated and has lived on as a state for over

[39] S. Mancini, *Minoranze autoctone e stato tra composizione dei conflitti e secessione* (Giuffrè, Milan, 1996), pp. 97 and 135.
[40] See T. De Mauro, *Storia linguistica dell'Italia unita*, 3rd edn. (Laterza, 1995), p. 43. In the years following the unification of Italy, outside of Tuscany and Rome where Italian was spoken, as it were, by definition, only 160,000 in over 20 million individuals could be defined as Italophones. For further information see ch. 2 of De Mauro's remarkable book, p. 15 *et seq.*

one hundred and thirty years, the last fifty of which were under a fully democratic form of government.

But the most spectacular among the cases which might have prompted German constitutional lawyers to engage in some hard thinking if they had been less inward-looking are undoubtedly those of South Africa since 1994 and India since 1947. The South African population is composed of eight black ethnic groups, a large number of "coloureds", two Asian communities and two white "tribes", as they are sometimes called, while the official languages of the Republic are eleven. In India, which has 2.5 times more inhabitants than the European Union, the ethnic groups are countless, the religions with more than three million followers are six, the regional languages are fifteen, while the official language of the State, Hindi, is spoken by 38 per cent of the population and only four persons out of one hundred can read English, the language of the influential newspapers.

Given such circumstances—and indeed a number of other divisive or debilitating factors might be added to them (the memories of apartheid, the still vital caste system, the sharp antagonism between Zulus and Xhosas or Hindus, Sikhs and Muslims, illiteracy rates ranging from 39 to 49 per cent)—how do Kirchhof and Grimm explain the form of political governance adopted and kept alive—in India for as long as the *Bundesrepublik*—by the two countries? Where is the spiritual and social homogeneity which should make it possible? Where are the preconditions of a rich exchange of ideas supposedly vital for the birth and prospering of full-blown public opinion? Yet, however huge the obstacles put in their way may be and however weak are the values and the understanding of rights and duties shared by the citizens, the democracies of South Africa and India have survived all manner of challenges and seem ready to enter the coming millennium with a not unreasonable degree of self-assurance.[41]

4. THE EXCLUSIONARY DEMOS?

Let us then revert to Europe. Why couldn't a European State, which would of course be based upon material and social conditions incomparably more favourable than those present within South Africa and India, attain a level of democracy higher and denser than the latter? Stripped of its comparative dimension, this question should also be addressed to Weiler who is similarly convinced—although, as we have seen, for very different reasons—that a statal Europe is not a desirable goal. "It would be more than ironic" he says in the key passage of one of his recent essays, "if a polity set up as a means to counter the excesses of statism ended up by coming round full circle and transforming itself into a (super)state. It would be equally ironic if the ethos which rejected the

---

[41] On the tremendous economic and social progress made by India in the last few years (India is now the sixth largest world economy) see the dossier "L'Inde aussi s'est éveillée", *Le Monde-Economie*, 17 June 1997.

boundary abuse of the nation state gave birth to a polity with the same potential for abuse".[42]

The first of these hypotheses strikes me as unrealistic. There is in Weiler a deeply-rooted and, as far as I am concerned, entirely justified conviction that our political world is still dominated by the ethics of sovereignty and might;[43] but I do not believe that it reaches so far as to lead him to include in the notion of "excesses of statism" the accepted monopoly of violence within the boundaries and the willingness to use violence against outsiders attacking those boundaries, which are the irreducible minimum of the concept of state.[44] I think rather that what worries Weiler is the possible recourse by the authorities of a statal Europe to more or less coercive pressures aimed at imposing a single or hegemonic culture, such as a tendentious teaching of history in the schools, the brazen fostering of a specific language etc., or, in other words, a replica of the policies which a number of those unitary (but also federal) nation states which are bedevilled by one or more untamed ethnic minorities have adopted and continue to adopt with a view to creating an overarching and all-encompassing identity, a *homo americanus, gallicus, hispanicus* and so forth.[45]

As for myself, my unassuming guess is that such policies, originating as they do from the assertiveness or the anxieties of an ethnic majority (the Wasps, the speakers of the *langue d'oïl*, the Castilians), would be simply unthinkable in a European Union endowed with statehood. At most, its authorities might, following in the footsteps of the present-day European Commission, launch campaigns designed to instil and fortify what Professor Habermas calls the citizens' "constitutional patriotism", that is the only feeling of belonging which an identity as loose and frigid as the European one can be expected to engender. Any brasher step than this in the direction of integration or assimilation, if it were really to be attempted, would be repelled by those antibodies which history has rendered all too effective.[46]

But Weiler is not only short on realism. If my interpretation of his formula is correct, he is also strangely unable, much like his German antagonists, to conceive of a state not rooted in, and coinciding with, a nation. And even more revealing of this inability is his assumption that a statal Europe would have the same potential for boundary abuse as the nation states of old. Why on earth the

---

[42] Weiler, "Does Europe Need a Constitution? . . ." *supra* n. 27, at 248. Newman, *supra* n. 9, at p. 210 seems to go even further when he writes that: "it is not clear that regional supranational entities would necessarily be any less expansionist than the nation-states that they replaced."

[43] On this attitude see Newman, *supra* n. 9, at p. 10 *et seq.*

[44] Wallace, *supra* n. 10, at 62.

[45] S. Mancini, *supra* n. 39, at p. 26 *et seq.*

[46] See K. Reif, "Cultural Convergence and Cultural Diversity as Factors in European Identity", quoted by Newman, *supra* n. 9, at p. 207: "Any conceivable 'European Political Union' would be . . . a multinational and multilingual political system . . .; it would not be transformed into a one-nation-state aimed at homogenizing societies and cultures". These sensible remarks should dispel C. Gamberale's fear that "the abstract construction of fortress Europe . . . [could be transformed] into a concrete new ethnic Europe": see "National Identities and Citizenship in the European Union" (1995) 1 *European Public Law* 633, at 659.

same potential if the *only possible* basis for a statal Europe would be a *demos* relying merely on the bond of civic loyalty? José Ortega y Gasset wrote that Isabel of Castilia and Fernando of Aragon joined body, soul and forces in order "to flood the planet with the energies" of the new Spanish nation.[47] Flood the planet Spain actually did as soon as the *Reconquista* was completed, as did England and France after the accession of Elizabeth and Napoleon, or Germany after the proclamation of Empire. But how could Europe do so, considering that its energies would not draw their sap from any emotional form of nationhood and would coalesce not as a result of a stirring event, but in the course of a slow, laborious and desperately matter-of-fact process of convergence on the part of its Member States?

A state, of course, but also the merely supranational entity which Weiler seems to prefer, has boundaries—and boundaries include and exclude, that is to say they divide if not always friends from foes, as Carl Schmitt claimed, then certainly "us" from "them". At this point, however, I will make one more unassuming guess. In the case of a European State, the "us-them" dichotomy would primarily take shape in the areas of free trade and movement of persons—and not necessarily in forms more rigid or "excluding" than at present.[48] In particular, as far as immigration is concerned, a central authority empowered to distribute refugees and asylum-seekers over the whole territory of the Union would probably be in a position to host more rather than fewer of them and, at the same time, to intervene to mitigate those conflicts which are currently flaring up in all the Member States. As for a single foreign policy and its obvious bedfellow, a united defence apparatus, I, though no expert, would welcome them as a blessing. One need not recall how much the conflicting interests and historical memories of the Member States contributed to the mismanagement of the crisis which led to the dissolution of Yugoslavia and to the civil war that ravaged Bosnia. It suffices, in a more recent context, to imagine how many horrors Rwanda, Burundi and the Congo might have been spared if the Union, and not one or other of its states with post-imperial interests in mind, had had the power to promote effective humanitarian action under the aegis of the United Nations.

5. A FEDERAL EUROPE

A European federal state capable of steering clear of the excesses and the abuses which have marked the history of its constituent units is in short conceivable. If—and this is a big if—the force of circumstances were to kindle the necessary

---

[47] J. Ortega y Gasset, *España invertebrada. Bosquejo de Algunos Pensamientos Historicos*, Revista de Occidente en Alianza Editorial, 7th edn. (Alianza Editorial, 1996), at p. 41.

[48] For the "bleak record" of the Community institutions in dealing with would-be migrants and refugees even after the establishment of the "Third Pillar" in the Maastricht Treaty, see Newman, *supra* n. 9, at p. 163 *et seq.*

political will, it could even be feasible.[49] But how desirable is it? So far I have not faced this question squarely. I shall do so now: if, as promised by the Treaties of Rome, Maastricht and now Amsterdam, the march towards an ever closer union between the peoples of Europe is to continue and if, in the course of this march, the peoples of Europe are to preserve the constellation of values informing their ways of life, then Europe needs those well-tested institutions and procedures which only statehood can provide.

The federalists of the 1930s and 1940s—the Marquis of Lothian, Lionel Robbins, Altiero Spinelli, François Bondy—raised a number of arguments in favour of this proposition, many of which are still topical. Of course, they could not predict the most topical issue, namely the threat which a denationalization of the economy, especially of the financial markets and of industrial production itself, would pose at the end of the century to Europe's employment policies and social security schemes.[50] It has become almost a commonplace to state that, under the thrust of international competition, our countries are faced with a dramatic choice: either to retain the generous entitlements resulting from the welfare state and thus to accept a permanently high level of unemployment, or to speed up deregulation and "corporate rightsizing",[51] leaving profit as the sole arbiter of virtue and so marginalizing the least skilled and least educated or the most vulnerable of our citizens.

These remarks should not be taken as a reflection of a hostile attitude on my part towards globalization. I am aware of its benefits and I find it extraordinary that within the European left even respected scholars such as Hobsbawm voice regret that we no longer have recourse to protectionism as a means to counter its social effects.[52] Those effects cannot be denied, however, nor is it possible to ignore the fact that they do tend to undermine the loyalty of large segments of the population. How else, indeed, might one explain such highly visible developments as the revival of extreme right-wing populism, the rampant egotism of most interest groups and the burgeoning of identity politics and xenophobia (Le Pen, Haider, Bossi, Kjærsgård, Hagen), disquieting movements built upon the ruins of the old ideologies?[53] Forced with their backs to the wall by a world economy which they cannot control, some of our nation states are at a loss to manage the aftermaths of the upheaval which globalization has brought about without resorting to coercion. A European State, by contrast, were it only

---

[49] Schmitter, *supra* n. 10, suspects instead that an integrated Europe will move increasingly in the direction of a multi-layered government, without clear lines of demarcated jurisdiction and identity, for which he coins the term "*condominio*".

[50] J. Habermas, "Remarks on Dieter Grimm's 'Does Europe Need a Constitution?'" (1995) 1 *European Law Journal* 303, at 304.

[51] See R. Hughes, *Culture of Complaint. The Fraying of America* (Oxford University Press, 1993), p. 27.

[52] E. Hobsbawm, *Age of Extremes. The Short Twentieth Century 1914—1991* (1995), at pp. 572–574.

[53] Régis Debray has brilliantly telescoped the relation between globalization and the upsurge of identity politics with the phrase: "les objets se mondialisent, les sujets se tribalisent"; see S. Mancini, *supra* n. 39, at p. 4.

because of the broader vision and the single-mindedness which it could bring to the exercise of Europe's vast economic power, would probably be able to influence the global market. Our social contract would still have to be restyled, but its core values might thus be salvaged with the possible result of toning down the loyalty crises which seem to have arisen by virtue of their impairment.[54]

Forceful as this argument is, however, it is not the most cogent one which can be advanced in support of statehood for Europe. It is in fact based on the social rights of the European citizens, while something even more precious is at stake: their political rights or, in one word, democracy. Some data will cast light on the magnitude of this problem both in quantitative and qualitative terms. The prediction usually attributed to Jacques Delors that, by the year 2000, 80 per cent of the economic and social regulation applicable in the Member States will originate in Brussels is probably spurious[55] and surely exaggerated. Nevertheless, according to a study by the Conseil d'Etat, of the 2981 legal measures which came into force in France in 1991, 1,564, that is almost 53 per cent, emanated from the Community's capital,[56] while a more recent statistic shows that 30 per cent of the legislation produced in the Netherlands is composed of provisions implementing Community directives.[57] On the other hand, it is true that the members of the body (the Council of Ministers) which enacts those directives and the more important regulations possess a proper legitimacy, having been elected to their national parliaments or deriving their mandate from them; but, as everyone knows, they often confine themselves to rubber-stamping, in most cases behind closed doors, drafts prepared by an ambassadorial college (COREPER) and, at a lower level, by numberless,[58] faceless and unaccountable committees of senior national experts.[59]

---

[54] See also O'Leary, *supra* n. 17, at p. 314, who suggests that to proceed, even at this stage of integration, without deepening the social legitimacy of the Community would be a grave error.

[55] J.H.H. Weiler, "The European Union Belongs to its Citizens" (1997) 22 *ELRev* 150.

[56] Conseil d'État, *Rapport Public* 1992, Etudes et documents, No 44.

[57] For an interesting comparison of the legislative output of the Council of Ministers and the German Bundestag and Bundesrat between 1958 and 1993 see D. Rometsch, and W. Wessels, "The Commission and the Council of Ministers" in G. Edwards and D. Spence (eds.), *The European Commission* (Carter Mill, 1994), at p. 212.

[58] According to F. Hayes-Renshaw, and H. Wallace, *The Council of Ministers* (MacMillan, 1997), p. 97: "The exact dimensions of the base of the Council hierarchy is one of the EU's great unsolved mysteries. Hardly anyone knows how many working groups exist at any one time".

[59] Mancini and Keeling, *supra* n. 5, at 190. According to W. Wessels, "The EC Council: the Community's Decisionmaking Center" in R.O. Keohane, and S. Hoffmann, (eds.), *The New European Community. Decisionmaking and Institutional Change* (Westview, 1991), p. 133, at p. 140: "[i]n a rough estimation, 80% of the Council's acts are decided on a professional bureaucratic basis. Some documents . . . can even pass the Council without a political debate". Hayes-Renshaw and Wallace estimate that "in practice [the] committees are the last actual arbiters in Council negotiations of roughly 70% of the legislative output", *supra* n. 58, p. 15. It is interesting to note that, although obviously aware of this state of affairs, national governments have done little if anything to improve it. According to J. Lodge, "Transparency and Legitimacy" (1994) 32 *Journal of Common Market Studies* 343, some of them prefer to lay the blame on the Commission, depicting it as an autocratic and distant Eurocracy which dictates policy to the Member States and ignores the public's desire for openness.

6. CONCLUSION

So, that is the situation. Today's European Union *presupposes democracy* as a heritage of values and institutions shared by its Member States in all of which the representatives of the people control the action of the executive branch;[60] *but it is not itself democratic.* Indeed, the Union is doomed never to be truly democratic as long as not only its foreign and security policies, which are openly carried out on an intergovernmental basis, but the very management of its supranational core, the single market, are entrusted, with or without a circumscribed control by the European Parliament, to diplomatic round tables. In other words, democracy will elude Europe as long as its form of government includes rules and legitimizes practices moulded on those of the international community.

All this looks sombre enough; but a further consideration makes it appear even gloomier. As evidenced by the figures which I have just quoted, the application of such rules and practices also threatens to reinforce the governments' predominance over domestic parliaments and therefore to infect the constitutions of the Member States, that is the very democracy *presupposed* by the Union.[61] This very serious danger is even regarded with growing anxiety by the many who wish the Union to remain what it is. The remedies which they offer, however, are either ineffectual or disruptive. Thus, a tighter control exercised by the national parliaments on the legislative process in Brussels by means of rigid guidelines imposed on the respective governments would restrict the bargaining power of the latter, consigning them, whenever decisions are taken by a majority vote, to a splendid but sterile isolation.[62] As for nation-wide referenda, the Danish experience in 1992–1993 has shown that, if their outcome is negative, they may have such ruinous consequences as to force the Union and the Member State concerned to sidestep the popular will by working out some fudged compromise. Finally, the testing by Member State courts of Community provisions against the values enshrined in their constitutions runs the risk of undermining the major advances made during the integration process: namely, supremacy of European law and its corollaries, undistorted competition and equal treatment for all Union citizens.[63]

The truth is therefore that the problem of democracy cannot be tackled at national level. It must be confronted where it was engendered, in the very fabric

[60] La Pergola, *supra* n. 5, at 19.

[61] A particular aspect of this infection is revealed by the fact that Member State governments use the Union as a scapegoat. To borrow from Schmitter, *supra* n. 10, at p. 150: "[s]ending intractable issues abroad to Brussels and blaming it for the need to implement unpopular policies at home has become a standard feature of European politics".

[62] For a perceptive discussion of this state of affairs see Newman, *supra* n. 9, at p. 191 *et seq.*

[63] On this danger, which has been smouldering throughout the whole history of Community law and which became red-hot in 1993, see the remarkable article by S. Boom, "The European Union after the Maastricht Decision: Will Germany be the 'Virginia of Europe'?" (1995) 43 *American Journal of Comparative Law* 177.

of the Union, and it may only be solved by ridding the Union of the last—but still how powerful!—vestige of its original constitution: the essentially international nature grafted onto its policy-making machinery. In 1941 Clement Attlee uttered five words of glorious political folly which were soon forgotten and were destined never to be repeated in England or elsewhere: "Europe" he said, "must federate or perish". The following decades proved him patently wrong. Europe opted for a set-up verging on the confederal and this choice did not prevent it from making the idea of war unthinkable within its boundaries and from becoming economically prosperous. Unless I am entirely mistaken, however, Attlee's folly sounds much like wisdom today. While yielding its crop, the confederal set-up has given rise to contradictions which grow in direct proportion to the growth of the Union's powers and which only a leap towards federalism can hope to overcome. The alternative, I am afraid, is a withering of the worthiest reasons which justify Europe's role as a protagonist in world affairs— its democratic integrity and hence its right to preach democracy to those who do not practise it.

Of course, as Karl Marx put it, no tailor can hope to try his breeches on history. Hard as it may be to visualize, the Union might after all evolve into a democratic entity without becoming a federal state, even as minimal and open a state as it could possibly be in a world order which is light-years distant from Kant's vision. If this were to happen, I would certainly not be vexed; in fact, I would rejoice. Democracy is the end, states, as we have known them, are but means. Achieving a stateless democracy has been one of mankind's most recurrent and noblest dreams. How could the miracle of its coming true be felt as a discomfiture?

5

The Euro: A Currency in Search of a State

"The transfer of functions to a monetary union involves the corresponding decline of the powers of the States who become its constituent members. It does not matter whether the union is equiparated to a federal State or whether the members continue to be called States or are described as *Laender*, cantons or provinces. What matters is that numerous functions traditionally vested in the nation State are transferred to the union and that such transfer has far-reaching direct and indirect financial, economic, budgetary, and fiscal consequences for the member States . . . There cannot . . . be any doubt that a monetary union presupposes a constitutional organisation which is or approximates that of a single (federal) State".

F.A. Mann, *The Legal Aspect of Money*, 5th edition (Oxford, 1992).

I. INTRODUCTION

THE DECISION TO enter the third stage of European Monetary Union (EMU) and the ensuing establishment of the European Central Bank in June 1998 have opened a new and exciting phase in the long-running debate on democracy and political unity in Europe. That the Economic Community of old suffered and today's European Union still suffers from a serious democratic deficit has been a commonplace in academic writing, the media and, increasingly, the political élites of some Member States for at least two decades. As everyone knows, its most disturbing aspects are usually identified in the fact that the Council of Ministers, Europe's dominant institution, lies beyond the reach of the citizens voting in European elections, in the still limited powers of the European Parliament as a legislative body, in the utter opaqueness of the decision-making machinery and in the overwhelming role which technocrats, both unaccountable and devoid of popular legitimation, play in the operation of that machinery.

In Chapter 4, it is argued (a) that these aspects stem from the original nature of the European Union as a *sui generis* international organization, namely as a polity where governance is by definition based not on democracy, but on diplomacy, (b) that they have undergone a certain attenuation—especially in terms of an improvement of the Parliament's status—which signals a progressive absorption by the Union of doses of federalism and statehood and (c) that they will further dilute and perhaps waste away only if and when the evolution of the

Union into a fully-fledged federation ejects the traces of international law and practice which still linger in its fabric. Resorting to a formula instigated by the former President of the European Commission, Jacques Delors, to which I entirely subscribe, I might add that such a federation is conceivable only as a unit assembling *nation states* and, therefore, not *itself* as a nation.[1] In the European polity, statehood and nationhood are destined not to be concomitant. What O.W. Holmes wrote about the "begetters" of the American Constitution, namely that "it was enough for them to realise or to hope that they had created an organism", is all that can be envisaged for our continent; the words which follow—"it has taken a century and has cost their successors much sweat and blood to prove that they had created a nation"[2]—have no reasonable chance of being reiterated on our side of the Atlantic. Regardless of how its powers and cohesion increase, the EU is in all likelihood bound to remain an "organism".

These views have been criticized for a variety of reasons, the most pertinent of which coincide in essence with the arguments of those political scientists who tend to belittle the weightiness and the anomalous nature of the democratic deficit in the EU.[3] In their words, the latter is but an instance of post-parliamentary governance epitomizing or, at most, emphasizing trends which are clearly detectable in the evolution of all advanced Western societies. Such societies have become too complex and differentiated for policy-making, with its monitoring and deliberative processes, to take place in the single setting or forum which a parliament is by definition. The monitoring and deliberative settings are now as numerous as the various policy areas, each of which engages multiple, self-representative interest groups and requires specialized technical expertise. Parliamentary democracy tends, as a consequence, to be superseded by a *de facto* democracy of organized interests and parliamentary sovereignty makes way for expert sovereignty. Policies and the rules embodying them are not only shaped, but "legitimised . . . by expert knowledge, as opposed to (the) popular, common-sensical, everyday knowledge"[4] which is as much as traditional parliaments are able to muster.

Taking issue with these remarks would be pointless. Once stripped of the sometimes irksome complacency of their authors, they reflect an undeniable reality, just as the unflattering comparison drawn by Weiler between the "netherworld" inhabited by the European experts and the elitism of the higher

---

[1] G.F. Mancini, "Europe: the Case for Statehood" (1998) 4 *European Law Journal* 29–42, reproduced as Chapter 4.

[2] *Missouri v Holland*, 252 U.S. (1920) 416, 433. For a more specific use of this quotation see D.A.O. Edward, *Europe and America: A European Lawyer's View* (1979) 65 *A.B.A. Journal* 913 (June).

[3] J.H.H. Weiler, "Europe: the Case against the Case for Statehood" (1998) 4 *European Law Journal* 43–62.

[4] S.S. Andersen and T.R. Burns, "The European Union and the Erosion of Parliamentary Democracy: A Study of Post-parliamentary Governance" in S.S. Andersen and K.A. Eliassen (eds.), *The European Union: How Democratic is It?* (Sage, London, 1996), pp. 227–253, especially p. 229 *et seq.* See also R. Ladrech, "Parliamentary Democracy and Political Discourse in EC Institutional Change" (1993) XVII *Revue d'Intégration européenne—Journal of European Integration* 53, at 56.

French civil servants, the entrenched secrecy of their British brethren and the rigidity of the German *Beamten* wittily hits the nail on the head. It is even possible, as Weiler suggests, that the transnational character of that netherworld makes its discourses and negotiations more democratic than those of its national counterparts;[5] although I suspect that by "democratic" he means "dialectical", which is not necessarily the same thing.

2. EXPERT SOVEREIGNTY AND INTEREST REPRESENTATION

This, however, is only part of the picture. The other part, which the believers in the primacy of executive bureaucracies minimize or do not see, is the fact that experts in the national contexts are accountable to the ministers they serve who, in turn, account for the actions of the former to the national parliamentary majority from which they derive their mandate. In Europe, by contrast, the technocrats debating and preparing the Union's legislative acts are much freer from the ministers' control, were it only for the reason that ministers flit in and out of Brussels becoming, in the process, highly dependent on the advice they receive. The experts are, therefore, the real co-legislators which, given their greater competence, blunts the effectiveness of the European Parliament's contribution to the law-making process. But the situation is even worse when it comes to the implementation of those same acts. In contrast to what happens at least in some Member States, the Parliament is entirely estranged from this all important task which is carried out exclusively by the experts, whether appointed by the Member States or belonging to the European civil service. In both cases they are democratically accountable to no one.

If these observations are correct, expert sovereignty in the EU is clearly more absolute than in its Member States. As for the other major feature of post-parliamentary democracy—the representation of organized interests—there seems to be no doubt that its European version[6] is far less balanced than the forms it takes in the national contexts. When one thinks of the role that trade unions play, even formally, in the "organic" economic governance of many a European country (Italy, since 1993, being perhaps the most conspicuous example in this respect), Schattschneider's metaphor according to which in all national liberal democracies the "interest group chorus" sings in an upper class accent[7] appears, to say the least, exaggerated. But even if its pessimism were justified, one would have to agree with other commentators when they argue that the EU is a rather extreme case of weakness in the self-organization of large scale and/or more diffuse interests such as wage-earners, women, consumers, patients, pensioners, the unemployed and the environmentally aware.[8] It is a well-known fact that of

---

[5] See Weiler, *supra* n. 3, at 55.

[6] For a comprehensive analysis of which see Andersen and Eliassen, *supra* n. 4, at p. 41 *et seq.*

[7] E.E. Schattschneider, *The Semi-Sovereign People* (Dryden Press, Hinsdale, Ill., 1975).

[8] W. Streeck and P.C. Schmitter, "From National Corporatism to Transnational Pluralism: Organised Interests in the Single European Market" (1991) 10 *Politics & Society* 133–164.

the myriad Euro-lobbies which have flooded Brussels since the Single European Act, individual companies and accountancy and law firms have the easiest access to the *sancta sanctorum* of the COREPER, the Commission and even the Parliament. All available evidence, as Schmitter points out, suggests a mobilization of bias on the part of the powers that be in favour of business and business-related interests.

A very recent example of this mobilization, all the more telling as it concerns a particularly passionate issue and is embodied in a formal administrative measure, was provided by a Commission decision of 24 February 1997 on the setting-up of a consultative forum on the environment and sustainable development.[9] Of the twelve to twenty-two seats allotted to social movements, seven to twelve are assigned to business figures, four to seven to representatives from environmental protection and consumer organizations and one to three to trade union representatives. Even supposing that the latter will as a rule side with the delegates of the groupings representing diffuse interests, which is far from a foregone conclusion, sheer numbers would relegate such a red-green coalition to a role of inane sermonizing. Business interests are bound to prevail and therefore to be the real interlocutors of the Commission whenever it asks the forum for an opinion.

3. DEMOCRACY AND THE INSTITUTIONAL FRAMEWORK OF EMU

Of course, further arguments and instances could be found to demonstrate the structural deficiencies affecting popular sovereignty in the EU. What has been said so far, however, seems to me sufficient to prove that the solace which one may draw from analyzing the EU as just another case of post-parliamentary governance is short-lived and in any event scant. The democratic deficit of the Union is to the democratic "imperfections, contradictions and dilemmas"[10] of most advanced Western societies what the beam is to the mote.

Or, rather, it was. The accomplishment of Monetary Union and the Stability Pact which was added to it in 1996 oblige the observer to look for analogies even more powerful than those of Matthew's Gospel. For reasons which I shall not review but which I assume to be entirely justified, the primary function of the European Central Bank (ECB) has been conceived by the authors of the Maastricht Treaty as providing an uncompromising guarantee of price stability and therefore requiring a watertight insulation of the new body from the pressures of politics and partisanship.[11] Such insulation and the ensuing depoliticization of monetary union could of course be achieved only by granting the ECB a status of independence. But while this choice was of itself orthodox, central

[9] See OJ 1997 L 58, p. 48.

[10] See Andersen and Eliassen, *supra* n. 4, Preface.

[11] See H.-P. Frohlich, "European Economic and Monetary Union Without Political Union" (1993) V *De Pecunia* 207, at 219.

bank autonomy having evolved into an accepted feature of modern constitutionalism as an expansion of the doctrine of separation of powers,[12] the degree of independence conferred on the ECB is, both in terms of its scope and depth, unprecedented and unparalleled. A simple comparison between the ECB statute and the provisions governing the German *Bundesbank*, which admittedly served as its model and are rightly regarded as the world's most rigorous and effective in shielding a central bank from political influences, will easily prove this point.[13]

There is no need to insist on the terms of office of the Members of the respective executive boards—which are in both cases eight years, but in Germany shorter and in the EU longer than those of constitutional judges, namely the members of the other great counter-majoritarian institution operating in the two polities; nor on the no less significant divergences which the German and the European regimes evince as regards the monitoring of the two Banks' decision-making process by representatives of the legislative and/or executive branches. It will suffice to point to the fact that the protocol setting out the statute of the ECB has constitutional dignity—an unheard-of occurrence in the realm of law—and to the rules concerning the overriding of the Bank's policy. Thus, while the German government has a temporary veto (two weeks) on the taking of decisions by the *Bundesbank*[14] and the German Parliament can at any time change the mandate of the latter if it deems that the Bank has failed to comply with its duties, the mandate of the ECB can only be altered by amending the EC Treaty, which implies a unanimous vote of the Member States and a cumbersome ratification procedure in their national Parliaments. In addition, since Article 88 of the German Basic Law was amended in 1992 with a view to entrenching the independence and the anti-inflationary function of the ECB, any fundamental alteration of the latter's status and objectives at the European level would in turn require an amendment of the Basic Law.

A system so conceived consciously sacrifices the idea of reconciling, as many observers had hoped it would,[15] the independence and the democratic accountability of the ECB, despite the Member States' clear awareness of the preponderant role which that body is bound to play in the government of the EU. Nor is it imaginable that such accountability could at least be partly retrieved by informally persuading the Bank's leadership to share responsibility with a political authority[16] or to submit of its own free will to a hail of hearings, reports,

---

[12] See P. Brentford, "Constitutional Aspects of the Independence of the European Central Bank" (1998) 47 *International and Comparative Law Quarterly* 75, at 77 and 88.

[13] For a more comprehensive comparison, covering the Nederlandsche Bank and the Reserve Bank of New Zealand, see L. Gormley and J. de Haan, "The Democratic Deficit of the European Central Bank" (1996) 21 *ELRev.* 95 *et seq.*

[14] As Gormley and de Haan point out, however, *supra* n. 13, at 98, this right has so far never been exercised.

[15] See, for example, R.M. Lastra, "European Monetary Union and Central Bank Independence" in M. Andenas, L. Gormley, C. Hadjiemmanuil, I. Harden (eds.), *European Economic and Monetary Union: the Institutional Framework* (Kluwer, 1997), p. 291, at p. 323 *et seq.*

[16] See F. Riccardi, (*EU*) *A Look Behind the News*, Agence Europe of 10 June 1998.

inquiries and obligations such as publishing the minutes of its meetings or disclosing how its members voted.[17] I would go further: in addition to being examples of wishful thinking (and in one case—the disclosure of the Directors' votes—smacking more of voyeurism than of a keenness on transparency and legitimacy), those mitigations of the Bank's autonomy are not desirable. Whether one shares the philosophy of the framers or one just regards the product of their efforts as final and unchangeable, the only reasonable option is to let the Bank act as they wished: namely, as a body totally devoted to safeguarding the value of the common currency and willing to carry out this task with all the stubbornness, stiffness or even surliness which that might entail.[18] It is for European politicians to take up the challenge posed by such an organ and do their job—ensuring that the might of monetary federalism be balanced by an equally powerful political federalism.

4. MONETARY UNION WITHOUT POLITICAL UNION

I am of course aware that a number of European politicians are reluctant to embark on this enterprise. As will be specified at a later stage, the governments of at least two of the eleven Member States which form Euroland rejected the prospect of a democratic counterpoise to the ECB and tended to belittle the scope and the powers of its possible embryo, the semiformal club of Euroland's Finance Ministers (Euro-11). Even more eloquent is the recent statement of the President of the Commission, Jacques Santer, to the effect that Europe must prove that a federal Bank may function in the absence of a federal government.[19] These views are not without a respectable cultural hinterland. Several economists have indeed maintained that, as evidenced by the success story of the gold standard, the world-wide supranational currency system in force until 1914, the parallel development of a monetary and a political union is not indispensable for the effective implementation of the former and, in the specific case of EMU, may actually jeopardize its basic premise, namely the immunity of the ECB from the pressures of political actors. In one word, the perfect guarantee for the primacy of monetary policy over the other areas of economic policy, which still are and will continue to be the domain of partisan politics, is "a currency without a State".[20]

The intellectual respectability of this argument, however, does not conceal its intrinsic weakness. History, of course, demonstrates that whereas no monetary union unsupplemented by a political union has survived a major crisis among its

---

[17] Some of these requests were indeed made by the European Parliament in the Resolution of 2 April 1998, based on a report by the German MEP Christa Randzio-Plath (OJ 1998 C 138, p. 177).

[18] See G. Ruffolo, *Una Maastricht per l'ambiente*, in *La Repubblica* of 17 June 1998.

[19] See B. De Peretti, *Duisenberg plaide pour une BCE responsable et citoyenne*, in *La Tribune* of 1 July 1998. It has been surmised in various quarters that Santer's true motive in making this statement was to accredit the Commission as the sole political interlocutor of the ECB.

[20] See Frohlich, *supra* n. 11, 208–221.

participants (the outbreak of the First World War in 1914 is a telling example), all monetary unions concomitant with a political union have proven irreversible:[21] but, in the words of Aldous Huxley, "that men do not learn very much from the lessons of history is the most important of all the lessons that history has to teach". Economic logic and constitutional reasons will therefore be more relevant for our purposes.

In this context, it should be pointed out first that, even if a stateless environment were shown to provide the best background for a stable currency, the latter would only be one among the many economic aims of the EU as a whole. The Maastricht Treaty puts price stability on a par with sustainable growth which respects the environment, the raising of the standard of living and quality of life, economic and social cohesion including solidarity among Member States and—most crucial in a continent plagued by jobless masses—a high level of employment and social protection.[22] Does this list warrant the conclusion that the institutional framework of EMU is inherently lame if not downright contradictory?

I believe it does. Indeed, on the one hand, monetary policy has been entirely pooled at the Union level and entrusted to a powerful Central Bank, which is uniquely committed to price stability, with the result that all the other EC Treaty objectives become subordinate to it[23] in so far as any use of monetary instruments to pursue them at the risk of unleashing inflation is effectively ruled out. Moreover, an independent and counter-majoritarian Central Bank might be tempted to neglect its secondary duty to support the general economic policies of the Community and refrain from any measure that might even remotely affect price stability. Indeed, it is often submitted that the ECB will adopt a particulary tough stance during the initial years of its existence, in order to establish its reputation on the financial markets and strengthen the perception of the Euro as a strong currency.

On the other hand, the Maastricht Treaty provides that economic policy—the only tool still at hand to boost economic growth and promote employment—remains within the province of national governments and is merely coordinated at the European level, that is subject to an extremely fragile constraint as the soft wording of Article 103 (which speaks of "common concern", "broad guidelines") patently proves. The consequence of this state of affairs is evident. Since the size of the Community budget (roughly 1.2 per cent of the Union's GDP) is insufficient to achieve significant macroeconomic results and Member States are loath to see an increased share of taxpayers' money going to the European Union, the "policy mix" in the latter will result from a combination of centralized monetary policy and varying national fiscal policies: a combination all the more peculiar and risky as the institutions in Brussels, unlike the

---

[21] Frohlich, *supra* n. 11, 222.
[22] See Article 2 of the EC Treaty.
[23] See Article 105(1) of the EC Treaty.

American federal authorities (who may have resort to financial inducements),[24] have virtually no power to influence spending choices by individual Member States. This impotence has been forcefully stressed by Cameron: the authors of the Maastricht Treaty provisions on EMU, he wrote "ignored a simple and obvious fact of political life—that no central bank, independent or otherwise, has ever operated, or could ever operate, without a political counterpart that is responsible for shaping the overall contours of economic policy".[25]

The above considerations are worrisome enough; but the picture becomes positively frightening if one reflects that the third stage of EMU will marry a single monetary target for Euroland with large cross-country differences in economic conditions, enhanced by structural disharmony between national business cycles, and thereby provides a sure recipe for region-specific—or, as economists say, asymmetric—shocks. To give you an example, a restrictive monetary stance adopted by the ECB, say, to counteract inflationary trends in some over-heated Euroland economies, may trigger recession and reduce employment in an already stagnating Italian context. Even worse, socio-cultural conditions prevailing in continental Europe—insufficient labour and capital mobility, relatively rigid labour legislation—may prevent the market from reacting promptly and efficiently to such regional imbalances. In the past, all these factors led a host of economic writers to argue that the EU was far from being an optimal currency area. The authors of the Maastricht Treaty were obviously aware of this warning, but did nothing to endow the monetary union which they created with the institutional instruments required to achieve homogeneity in the pursuit of economic policies. I therefore tend to share the conclusion put forward by one of the leading economists in this field: "if . . . we have cause for concern about the life expectancy of . . . monetary union, it is not because [of] the objectives or governance of the ECB, but because individual countries may have too much trouble adjusting to its monetary policy".[26]

This remark seems to carry even more truth since, in the area of economic policy, the Maastricht Treaty only shows teeth when prohibiting excessive deficits of individual Member States. The relevant provisions, strengthened by the aforementioned Stability Pact, empower the Council of Ministers to impose heavy sanctions—fines of up to 0.5 per cent of the annual GDP—on those countries which run deficits in excess of 3 per cent of their GDP: an extraordinary prerogative, if it is true, as claimed by Jean-Claude Trichet, the Governor of the Banque de France, that it exceeds by far the power of the US federal adminis-

---

[24] G.A. Bermann, "Regulatory Federalism: European Union and United States" in *Collected Courses of the Hague Academy of International Law* (1997), pp. 9–148, at p. 106.

[25] See D.R. Cameron, "EMU after 1999: the Implications and Dilemmas of the Third Stage" (1998) 4 *Columbia Journal of European Law* 425, at 441.

[26] See Cameron, *ibid.*, at 441.

[27] See P.-A. Delhommais and E. Leser, "Selon M. Trichet, la France a une économie efficace mais souffre de son 'mental' ", in *Le Monde* of 18 February 1998.

tration to ensure that Texas or California run balanced budgets.[27] However—and this is a big however—what may well be a necessary precaution against profligate national policies really amounts to imposing an unelected watchdog on budgets voted by democratically elected Parliaments. Those who recall that the House of Commons first laid the foundations of modern constitutionalism by obtaining as early as the fourteenth century the right to authorise taxation and control public expenditure may have some cause for concern.

Nor is that all. The situation described above warrants even more fundamental concerns about the impact of EMU on democracy in the context of the European Union. As we have seen, the broad guidelines for economic policy adopted by the Council will be of limited help in shaping a homogenous economic background and avoiding asymmetrical shocks. At the same time, the ECB may only use those monetary tools which are consistent with price stability and, since it is bound to implement a single policy for the Union as a whole, it cannot tailor its interventions to suit the specific needs of individual countries. Finally, because of the limits imposed on deficit spending, an individual Member State may prove unable to pursue an expansive fiscal policy in order to counteract a serious recession.

Are these factors not bound to remove such basic issues as the general state of the economy or unemployment from the responsibility of political actors and hence from the electoral arena? In the event of an economic slump national politicians will no doubt try to get out of such a scrape by blaming the central bankers for pursuing a policy unsuited to their own country and question the wisdom of joining EMU in the first place; they will, however, miss the point, the cause of their woes being not the independence of the Bank and its duty to defend price stability across the Union, but the absence of a European economic policy to match a European monetary policy. It is because of this absence that no political body will be able to influence the economy by its choices, public debates at the national level will become little more than a shadow of democracy, as futile as television talk shows, and voters unhappy with the employment situation, their income taxes or mortgages, will be deprived of their time-honoured right to throw out the "scoundrels" who have provoked or accentuated these ills.

5. THE QUEST FOR INSTITUTIONAL REFORM

The need for an effective political counterweight to the ECB was widely felt and prompted proposals, particularly from the French government, of a Euro Council empowered to pursue an effective European economic policy. Unfortunately, the French bid was perceived as a disguised assault on the independence of the ECB, stirring up fierce opposition from the German and Dutch sides. The inevitable compromise gave birth to a half-baked creature, the aforementioned Euro-11, intended as a forum for the Finance Ministers of participating Member States to discuss issues relating to the single currency while excluding the four countries composing the more or less sceptic "Eurofringe" which do not take part in monetary union.[28]

Such a forum may well be an appropriate response to the bizarre demands of Prime Minister Blair and the other Eurofringe leaders to, as it were, put their mouth where they failed to put their money; nor can one exclude, especially after Schröder's victory in Germany, that Euro-11 acquires more power in the future. At this stage, however, it falls far short of providing Euroland with a genuine economic government. And yet, calls for a counterweight to the ECB do not only come from academics and congenitally statist French officials. The need not to leave the new bank in a political vacuum has also been stressed by such a respected central banker as Tommaso Padoa-Schioppa, currently a Member of the ECB Executive Board. Purporting to express the views of his colleagues, he argued with even greater verve than Cameron that "The ECB's birth evokes, postulates and makes it indispensable to create rapidly a European political counterpart. We want it; we need it as much as the air we breathe. The Bank's independence presupposes a political power to establish a constant relationship of information and exchange of views. Failing that, there would be no independence, but just navel-gazing and solitude".[29] Furthermore, Padoa-Schioppa aptly observed that while the EU, under the excessive deficit procedure, can prevent participating Member States from doing evil, it is itself prevented from doing good by developing a fiscal policy of its own.[30]

Once again, the incremental or "spill-over" logic which has so far ensured the institutional progress of Europe obliges further steps to be taken on the path towards integration. If national governments are no longer individually in control of their economies, then the necessary powers must be conferred upon a central political organ. This is not to imply that large portions of tax-raising and public spending ought to be transferred from the Member States to Europe. What I do mean is that the fundamental economic options for Euroland must be taken at the European level; and any notion of democracy, parliamentary or for that matter post-parliamentary, would then require that the body empowered to take such options must be accountable to public opinion. In this respect, even the French proposals for a stronger Euro Council were inherently defective. Had they been accepted, the technocracy of the central bankers would have been adequately balanced; but the balancing force, the technocracy of the national Finance Ministries, would itself have eluded any serious form of democratic control.

To sum up, Europe's democratic deficit as exacerbated by the design of EMU cannot be remedied by subjecting the ECB to disclosure and reporting require-

[28] See European Council, Luxembourg, 12–13 December 1997, Presidency conclusions, point 44, and Annex 1, point 6, in *EU Bulletin* 12/1997, pp. 13 and 19.

[29] See his interview with E. Scalfari, "L'Europa ha bisogno di politica", in *La Repubblica* of 23 May 1998 (author's own translation).

[30] T. Padoa-Schioppa, "Il passo più lungo", in *Il Corriere della Sera* of 5 May 1998.

ments. For both economic and constitutional reasons, Monetary Union calls for bold steps towards the creation of robust European economic governance. The political debate in economic affairs will have to move significantly from the national to the European level and issues of democracy must be addressed in that context. Furthermore, these conclusions are confirmed by a brief overview of the external aspects of European integration.

6. DEMOCRACY AND THE EXTERNAL ACTION OF THE EUROPEAN UNION

Only in one case does the Maastricht Treaty provide a political organ with sufficient powers to govern the economy. Ironically, that happens in the very area which may cause a serious disturbance to the activities of the ECB in the pursuit of its institutional tasks, namely external monetary affairs. One of the most arcane EMU provisions empowers the Council of Ministers, by a qualified majority of participating Member States, to map out general orientations for exchange-rate policy in relation to foreign currencies and, arguably, to conclude such informal arrangements as the Plaza or Louvre Accords of the Eighties.[31] But, whatever the exact balance of powers between the ECB and the Council may be in this area, one thing is evident, namely that the European Parliament remains shut out. Of course, by their very nature, monetary arrangements are discussed and concluded behind closed doors and no popular representative body is called to ratify them. Yet, what makes the case of the EU unparalleled is that whoever, in the future, strikes those arrangements in its name will not be accountable before its own representative body—and ultimately before the Union's electorate—for their impact on domestic economies.

This situation is by no means unique: consider the external projection of the Community in the realm of commerce. The Amsterdam Treaty reinforced the role of the European Parliament in decision-making; it made, however, some important exceptions, the common trade policy being the most important. Yet, in a globalized market, trade policies are often decisive for the long-term prosperity of undertakings and of the economy in general, so that one can hardly contend that they are best left to the netherworld of experts and should escape any form of democratic supervision.

The Parliament's position is equally marginal in the so-called second pillar of the Amsterdam Treaty, the common foreign and security policy (CFSP). Based on the recognition that individual European states have become unable to play a significant role on the international stage, the CFSP presently amounts to

[31] See Article 109(2) and (3) of the EC Treaty. Admittedly, the general orientations to be adopted by the Council "shall be without prejudice to the primary objective of the ECB to maintain price stability"; however, the Council will have the last word. It is interesting to note that the European Council has decided that the power to formulate general orientations shall only be used under exceptional circumstances: see European Council, Luxembourg, 12–13 December 1997, Presidency conclusions, point 45, and Annex 1, point 8, in *EU Bulletin* 12/1997, pp. 13 and 20.

little more than coordination between national diplomacies in the discrete venue of the Council's meeting rooms. Admittedly, unlike the establishment of a European economic government, the reinforcement of CFSP and the transfer to a supranational authority of a number of powers in this context bear no direct link with the creation of the ECB. It has been authoritatively argued, however, that EMU may bring conflict or, in extreme circumstances, even war between the USA and the EU.[32] Although such fears are clearly implausible, they show that a single currency will have, to say the least, some bearing on European foreign and security policy. It is therefore highly regrettable that, here too, the authors of the Amsterdam Treaty have done no more than provide for a mere consultation of the European Parliament on the main aspects and the basic choices of that policy. Indeed, if a common foreign policy is needed for Europe to be heard in the international arena, it cannot be designed and decided by national officials out of the public eye, subject to a parliamentary debate, or rather a parody thereof, which could in no way affect their determinations.

In all of the areas mentioned, the European Union shows a blatant inconsistency between the extent of competence in international affairs already transferred to Brussels, or soon to be pooled together, and the shortcomings of its democratic structures. It follows from what was said at the outset that this inconsistency is a product of the peculiar nature of the Union, which makes it both so intriguing and prey to the sophisticated mindgames of academics on either side of the Atlantic. But that peculiar nature is also at the root of another and no less momentous shortcoming, namely the Union's built-in weakness in the international sphere.

In any international organization or in any major negotiation, those speaking on behalf of the EU must invariably solve preliminary questions concerning the forms of the Union's representation and participation. As we all know, in spite of its growing flexibility, present-day international law bears more than a glaring reminder of the era when sovereign states were its only legal subjects; it is not surprising, therefore, that it should not really welcome an odd figure such as the European Union, which variously appears as one, eleven or fifteen and works under different rules according to the specific topic under discussion. Thus, even where the indisputable importance of the Union finally leads its negotiating partners to accept a deal allowing for its participation, this is generally perceived as a concession worthy of compensation from the European side. During the last century, the Ottoman Porte was probably confronted with similar problems when fighting for a place at the table where the self-styled civilized Christian powers deliberated about the fate and fortunes of the world.

No less importantly, even in those areas where the EU is the sole negotiator, any agreement must be subsequently approved—often by a unanimous vote of the Member States. This means that Member State representatives are not only

---

[32] See M. Feldstein, "EMU and International Conflict" (1997) November/December *Foreign Affairs*.

present (and seated in the second if not in the first row of the bargaining chamber), but are also able and willing to pursue an autonomous policy. I might perhaps add that our American friends are masters in the art of provoking and exploiting any internal divergence which they perceive among the Member States' positions with a view to prevailing over the Union's stance.

7. GLOBAL DEMOCRACY AND EUROPEAN FEDERALISM

Here, again, we are faced with an issue of democracy—not just European democracy, but global democracy. As everyone knows, nowadays more and more political decisions are only effective if taken at a world-wide level. In the same way that economic integration caused a progressive shift in decision-taking from the national to the European level, today's trends towards globalization imply that many crucial choices affecting everyday life must be made in such fora as the WTO, the IMF or, at the very least, the OECD. For the reasons just exposed, in its present shape the EU is unable to play a role commensurate to its weight in the global economy. As a result, its citizens are not afforded adequate representation when major choices are taken which may affect the world as a whole.

But there is more at stake than Europe's interests. This point has been recently made by André Fontaine, *Le Monde*'s former editor and a most respected French political writer. "The real raison d'être of the European Union" he wrote, "is to be distinct from the American colossus and able to weigh against it. And the Atlantic-liberal globalised world of the turn of the century is in great need of those 'checks and balances' which the founding fathers deemed indispensable for the United States".[33] Of course, one might object that a stronger Europe would essentially favour Europeans with the Union becoming another dominant player alongside the USA. But such an objection would ignore the fact that, not unlike economic markets, political systems are likely to function better when they are not kept under the thumb of a single actor. One might go further and suggest that the perspective of a Euro-American condominium seems more reassuring than a Sino-American duopoly?[34]

There is some truth in Weiler's remark that some of my arguments for a European State have little to do with democracy and everything to do with power. Yet, Weiler completely misses the point of global democracy—or is

---

[33] A. Fontaine, "Une Europe de la diversité", in *Le Monde* of 18 May 1998 (author's own translation).

[34] I fully subscribe to Roy Denman's remarks: "The next century will see a European federation become a world superpower, dealing with the United States as an equal partner. This change in the relationship will need much careful handling on both sides. Let us hope that the two superpowers will, as Carlyle wrote of the armies of Prussia and Britain in the Seven Years' War (1756–1763), 'march divided but fight united'—this time for peace, democracy and justice in the world" (see "Yes, America, a Single Currency for the Coming Superpower", in *International Herald Tribune* of 16 January 1998.

perhaps content to contemplate such an interesting creature as Europe's tentative democracy while sitting at the bow of the world's dominant ship.

In conclusion, a more incisive and uniform EU foreign policy would not only be in Europe's best interest but would greatly benefit international relations at large. By creating the Euro, we have managed to endow Europe with a currency able to rival, in due course, the US dollar[35]. After the *jus monetae*, there is a compelling case for fully transferring to the Union the *jus tractatus* and its bedmate, the *jus belli*. Since these prerogatives—currency, foreign policy, defence—traditionally define the minimal requirements of a statal body politic, the perspective of a European State shall emerge from the twilight where it has been lingering nervously for years. At that stage discussion of federalism, until recently discredited as retrograde or even ridiculed as outlandish, will become topical once again.

---

[35] See P. Pollard, "The Role of the Euro as an International Currency" (1998) 4 *Columbia Journal of European Law* 395; and E. Thiel, "The Euro: Should the U.S. Worry?", *ibid.*, at 447.

6

Safeguarding Human Rights: The Role of the European Court of Justice

1. THE ABSENCE OF A BILL OF RIGHTS IN THE EC TREATY

"THE DISCUSSION OF our problem", said a well-known student of International law in an essay of eighteen years ago, "has to start with the statement of a plain fact: the Constitution of the European Communities does not contain any provision relating to the protection of human rights".[1] On the other hand, the Solicitor General of England and Wales stated in a case in 1978 that it was beyond comprehension "why so many distinguished people [were] wasting so much time debating the need for a new Bill of Rights incorporating the provisions of the European Convention on Human Rights if we already [had] one in the Treaty of Rome".[2]

It is difficult to find in legal literature two more conflicting views than these. If it were to be admitted that both were true, it would be necessary to assume that the authors differ radically regarding the definition of what constitutes human rights. But since that is not the case, one must perforce conclude that either or both of those views are incorrect. I am of the opinion that both are incorrect and it seems to me that they are accounted for by a propensity—which is pronounced in all cases but particularly when the subject matter is a heated one, such as human rights—which the philosopher Alf Ross perceived among lawyers: a tendency to join the "untamed, the metaphysicists and the mystics in that residual category made up of those whose thinking is perturbed and emotional".

In reality, anyone who tries to look at the EC Treaty otherwise than through ideological glasses and without unavowed political intentions will find that it safeguards two important fundamental rights: the traditional liberal freedom of movement—with which, enriched with new content, Articles 48 to 60 endow employees, self-employed workers and providers of services—and the more modern right of freedom from discrimination based on nationality[3] and Article 119 on sex. The latter provision, it is true, merely prescribes equal pay for the

---

[1] P. Pescatore, "Fundamental Rights and Freedoms in the System of the European Communities" (1970) 18 *American Journal of Comparative Law* 343.

[2] *Allgemeine Gold- und Silberscheidenanstalt* v *Commissioners of Customs and Excise* (1978) II *Common Market Law Reports* 292.

[3] Articles 6, 40 (3), 48 (2) and (3) and 220 of the EC Treaty.

same work; but Council Directive 76/207 considerably extends its scope.[4] In other words, women are also guaranteed equality of treatment regarding access to employment and all aspects of the employment relationship.

However, that is all: unless—but this would be tantamount to setting foot upon quicksand—one wishes to take the view that fundamental rights are conferred by the provisions which are intended to improve the standard of living of Community citizens[5] or those in which reference is made to the Parliament's supervisory powers,[6] to observance of the law[7] and to the guarantees of independence required regarding the Members[8] of the Court of Justice.[9] With all respect to the Solicitor General, to say that the EC Treaty contains a Bill of Rights is, in short, absurd. On the contrary, it is not absurd to ask whether it might not have been appropriate for the Treaty to contain a Bill of Rights. One writer says that it should not, pointing out that, unlike the Member States, the Community does not have all-embracing powers and that its legal order is exclusively, or at least preponderantly, a means of economic integration.[10] But, it might be asked in reply, is it not a fact that the major legal discovery of the twentieth century is the danger which the economy represents to human rights?

The founding fathers of the EEC were of course aware of all this. What therefore accounts for the omission to which I have referred? Weiler puts forward a theory to explain this which is convincing.[11] Some of the States which were preparing to ratify the EC Treaty, he says, must have thought that a Bill of Rights represented a threat because it could, potentially, enable the powers vested in the new Community to be extended. It will be argued in reply that to grant Community citizens a *corpus* of fundamental rights would limit those powers; but, however logical it may be, that objection takes no account of history. History (I am thinking of the USA) shows that the listing of inviolable rights in a constitutional document sooner or later seems to constitute an invitation to extend the powers of the central authorities to the very limits of those rights. In other words, there is often inherent in a Bill of Rights a tendency towards the achievement of ends which were not being pursued by its introduc-

---

[4] Council Directive 76/207/EEC of 9 February 1976 on the implementation of the principle of equal treatment for men and women as regards access to employment, vocational training and promotion, and working conditions, OJ 1976 L 39, p. 40.

[5] Articles 2, 3, 39, 51, 117 and 123 EC.

[6] Articles 137, 138 and 144 EC.

[7] Articles 164, 173 and 179 EC.

[8] Article 167 EC.

[9] See J. Bridge, "Fundamental Rights in the European Community" in J. Bridge, D. Lasok, D. Ferret and R. Plender (eds.) *Fundamental Rights* (London, 1973), p. 291 *et seq.*; and L. Marcoux, "Le concept de droits fondamentaux dans le droit de la Communauté économique européenne" (1983) *Revue Internationale de Droit Comparé* 719.

[10] L. Dubois, "Le rôle de la Cour de justice des Communautés européennes. Objet et portée de la protection" (1981) *Revue internationale de droit comparé* 609.

[11] J.H.H. Weiler, *Il sistema comunitario: struttura legale e processo politico* (Bologna, 1985), p. 139 *et seq.*; and "Eurocracy and Distrust: Some Questions concerning the Role of the European Court of Justice in the Protection of Fundamental Human Rights within the Legal Order of the European Communities" (1986) 612 *Washington Law Reviews* 1112.

tion: rights created to protect individuals ultimately become closely associated with the powers acquired by or attached to the central authority and therefore reduce the prerogatives of the peripheral authorities. It is reasonable to presume that in 1957, when the European climate was already tinged with scepticism and in any event was no longer virginal, those peripheral authorities—that is to say the national States—were not prepared to become the victims of a similar process.[12]

2. THE EARLY DECISIONS OF THE COURT OF JUSTICE

If that view is correct, then the view adopted by the six original Member States evinced a considerable degree of short-sightedness. Their Constitutions in fact contain, in varying degrees, a significant number of fundamental rights or, as in the case of France, refer to the *Déclaration des droits de l'homme et du citoyen* of 1789; it was therefore unthinkable that their citizens, already enjoying those safeguards with respect to national measures, would not sooner or later claim the right to the same protection against measures adopted by the European institutions. In other words, having been halted at the doorway to the Community legal order, fundamental rights would have knocked on the windows until they were let in. It was the Court of Justice that opened the windows and the manner in which it did so is an example of judicial activism which has few parallels even in the country (the USA) where that expression was coined.[13]

The beginnings were anything but encouraging. Various ECSC and EEC measures were challenged by two German steel undertakings and a number of Italian farmers.[14] The applicants relied, on the one hand, upon the rules of the *Grundgesetz* (German Basic Law) which guarantee the freedom to choose one's occupation and the right of ownership, and, on the other, upon the principles governing the protection of fundamental rights in the Member States. The Court adopted a defensive posture: its task, it said in *Stork*, was "to ensure that in the interpretation and application of the Treaty the law is observed", and

---

[12] In the draft Treaty establishing the European Defence Community, it was nevertheless expressly provided in Article 3 that the Community was obliged to respect "les libertés publiques et les droits fondamentaux des individus". Similar provisions were also contained in Article 3 of the draft Treaty establishing the European Political Community together with provision for references by the Court of Justice of the Communities for a preliminary ruling by the European Court of Human Rights. The proposal to incorporate a provision of that kind in the Treaties of Rome was strongly contested (see M. Zuleeg, "Fundamental Rights and the Law of the European Communities" (1971) 8 *CMLRev* 446).

[13] See T. Koopmans, "The Roots of Judicial Activism" in Matscher, F. *et. al.* (eds.), *Protecting Human Rights: The European Dimension, Studies in Honour of G.I. Wiarda* (Cologne-Berlin-Bonn-Munich, 1988), p. 317 *et seq.*

[14] See Case 1/58 *Stork & Cie v High Authority* [1959] ECR 43; Joined Cases 36, 37, 38 and 40/59 *Comptoirs de vente du Charbon de la Ruhr, "Präsident", "Geitling", "Mausegatt", et Entreprise I. Nold KG v Haute Autorité de la CE du charbon et de l'acier,* ("Ruhrkohlen-Verkaufsgesellschaften") [1960] ECR 857; and Case 40/64 *Sgarlata v Commission* [1965] ECR 279.

therefore that it was not legitimate for it to examine the "ground of complaint . . . that . . . [the High Authority] had infringed principles of German constitutional law".

Similar observations were made by the Court in *Ruhrkohlen-Verkaufsgesellschaften*. The Court emphasized that it was not called upon "to ensure that rules of internal law, even constitutional rules, enforced in one or other of the Member States are respected", and it added that "Community law . . . does not contain any general principle, express or implicit, guaranteeing respect for acquired situations". The first statement is incontestable. It should however be noted that the Court had already recognized that the legal principles common to the Member States could be used in order to complement Community law; it could therefore have relied upon that dictum, adopting *inter alia* the proposal made by Advocate General Lagrange; and, at least in *Sgarlata*, the applicants explicitly referred to it. So what fear is reflected in the reply—it was described, by some,[15] as "brutal", and by others as tantamount to a veritable denial of justice[16]—which have just been quoted?

Identifying it does not pose too many difficulties. In those years, the Court's primary objective was to fight tooth and nail to defend the freedom of action of the newly-created European institutions as a precondition for an independent Community system of law. What would be left of that system, the Court doubtless asked itself, if the Council and the Commission were compelled to ensure that every measure adopted by them was in conformity with the constitutional guarantees of the six Member States or even—since the gap between the two legislative levels is not so very great—with any type of national provision?

The fact is, however, that if the Court feared such a possibility, the consequences of its preoccupation were exactly the opposite of what was hoped for.[17] The lack of any protection for fundamental rights within the Community actually led the German Constitutional Court at Karlsruhe to doubt whether the Community order had any lawful democratic basis and therefore to refuse to accord it independent status with respect to the national systems. Thus, it handed down a judgment on 18 October 1967 to the effect that the transfer of powers to the Community could not deprive German citizens of the protection accorded to them by the *Grundgesetz*; it followed that Community law had to be examined at national level to ensure that it was compatible with internal constitutional provisions.[18]

---

[15] P.H. Teitgen, "La protection des droits fondamentaux dans la jurisprudence de la Cour de Justice des Communautés européennes" in AA.VV. *L'adhésion des Communautés européennes à la Convention européenne des droits de l'homme* (Brussels, 1981), p. 24.

[16] G. Cohen-Jonathan, "Les droits de l'homme dans les Communautés européennes" in *Recueil d'études en hommage à Charles Eisenmann* (Paris, 1975), p. 100.

[17] G.L. Tosato, "La tutela dei diritti fondamentali nella giurisprudenza della Corte delle Comunità europee" in *Studi in onore di Giuseppe Sperduti* (Milan, 1984), p. 720 *et seq.*

[18] Bundesverfassungsgericht, judgment of 18 October 1967, in *BVerfGE*, 22, p. 293, reproduced in (1968) *CMLRev* 483.

3. THE NEW APPROACH

The Court was therefore obliged to adopt a new approach. Its first change of direction was, however, fairly modest, being no more than a mere *obiter dictum* in the judgment in *Stauder*:[19] when asked to give a preliminary ruling on the validity of a Commission measure, the Luxembourg Judges took the view that it contained "nothing capable of prejudicing . . . fundamental human rights" but went on to say—although this was not essential to the exposition of the grounds for their decision—that those rights were "enshrined in the general principles of Community law . . . protected by the Court".

More complex reasoning was expounded by the Court in the second judgment in which it adopted its new approach: *Internationale Handelsgesellschaft*.[20] The Verwaltungsgericht (Administrative Court) of Frankfurt had asked the Court of Justice to determine whether the rules on the lodging of deposits contained in a Regulation on cereal exports conflicted with the principles of economic liberty and proportionality safeguarded by the German Basic Law. In its reply the Court referred first of all to its judgments in *Stork* and *Ruhrkohlen-Verkaufsgesellschaften*: if, it said, the validity of measures adopted by the institutions were to be judged in the light of the constitutional provisions of one or more Member States rather than solely by reference to Community law, the unity of Community law would be called into question, as would "the legal basis of the Community itself". Having said that, however, the Court repeated its dictum in *Stauder* and added that the protection of fundamental rights, as general principles of the Community order, was "inspired by the constitutional traditions common to the Member States" and was to be ensured "within the framework of the structure and objectives of the Community".

To treat these judgments and those that followed as nothing more than a reaction to the German revolt referred to earlier would, however, be to go too far. The claimed entitlement to examine the validity of Community measures, referred to in the order of 18 October 1967 and in various other pronouncements of the Bundesverfassungsgericht and later the corresponding Italian judicial authority,[21] did not stem principally from the disappointment felt in Karlsruhe

---

[19] Case 29/69 *Stauder* v *City of Ulm* [1969] ECR 419.

[20] Case 11/70 [1970] ECR 1125.

[21] As regards the former, see Bundesverfassungsgericht, judgment of 25 July 1971, in *BVerfGE,* 31, p. 145, in which there reappears the idea that the decisions of the Court of Justice do not by themselves provide any certainty of protection of human rights "coinciding" with that provided by the Karlsruhe Court, and of 29 May 1974, known as the "*Solange-Beschluss*" case (*BVerfGE,* 37, p. 271, reproduced in (1974) 2, *Common Market Law Reports* 540 and 569) in which it is stated that in the event of a conflict between the provisions of secondary Community law and German constitutional provisions concerning fundamental rights, the latter must prevail until such time as the Community has a system of its own for the protection of human rights "conforming" to that of the Basic Law.

As regards Italy, see judgment of 27 December 1973, No 183, *Frontini,* in *Giurisprudenza costituzionale,* 1973, p. 2401, reproduced in (1974) *Common Market Law Reports* 381 and 397. The Italian court ruled that limitations on sovereignty favouring the powers of the Community could not

as a result of the first Luxembourg judgments; it was derived more from an unfavourable appraisal of the entire institutional structure of the Community and, in particular, the absence in Community legislation of a catalogue of fundamental rights approved by a democratically elected Parliament. The judgments in *Stauder* and *Internationale Handelsgesellschaft* are attributable to a similar finding, namely that a "democratic deficit" had become apparent in the management of the Community.

The time when the Court saw its primary task as that of ensuring the independence of the Community institutions had long passed. The insignificance of the Strasbourg Assembly, the development of authorities not subject to supervision, such as COREPER and the increasing bureaucratization of the Commission led to the result that the legislative output of the Community bore few similarities to that of a representative democratic process.[22] In view of the risk of government by national and European civil servants, it became the number one priority to define in precise terms a *higher law* on the basis of which their action could be monitored, even if to do so might raise the spectre of government by judges; or, rather, make that spectre more threatening insofar as the discovery of fundamental rights came shortly after the vindication of principles such as the direct effect of Community provisions and the primacy of Community law, which likewise were not written into the Treaties but were enshrined in a number of famous judgments.[23]

Let us examine therefore the successive stages involved in the development of this "higher law". Between 1969 and 1970 the Court based Community protection of human rights on values common to the Constitutions of the Member States, a source which was rich and flexible, perhaps even too flexible, that is to say providing insufficient "certainty" for the purposes of the control which the Court intended to exercise. In order to appease Karlsruhe and to put a brake on the bureaucrats, what was in fact needed was a firmer anchorage or, if you prefer, something closer to a written catalogue of rights.

Then in 1974 came the *Nold* judgment.[24] Called upon for a second time to protect the right of ownership and free enterprise against a Commission decision concerning the operation of the *Ruhrkohlen-Verkaufsgesellschaften*, the Court took two great steps forward: on the one hand it stated curtly that it was unable to "uphold measures which are incompatible with fundamental rights recognized by the Constitutions of the Member States"; on the other, it referred

---

"in any event allow the organs of the EEC an unacceptable power to infringe the fundamental provisions of our constitutional law or unalienable human rights. And it is obvious that if ever such an aberrant interpretation were to be given to Article 189 of the EEC Treaty, then in those circumstances a safeguard would always be provided by the review carried out by this court to ensure the enduring compatibility of the Treaty with those fundamental principles".

[22] Weiler, *supra* n. 11, p. 143 *et seq.*

[23] See, for example, Case C-26/62 *NV Algemene Transport- en Expeditie Onderneming Van Gend en Loos v Nederlandse Administratie der Belastingen* [1963] ECR 3; and Case 6/64 *Costa v ENEL* [1964] ECR 585.

[24] Case 4/73 *Nold, Kohlen- und Baustoffgrosshandlung v Commission* [1974] ECR 491.

to the "guidelines" provided by "international treaties for the protection of human rights on which the Member States have collaborated or of which they are signatories" and which therefore can provide "guidelines which should be followed within the framework of Community law".

Applying those principles, the Court stated that, although they are protected by the constitutional laws of the Member States, the right of ownership and the right to freely choose and practice a trade or profession are in general subject to limitations dictated by the public interest and do not therefore constitute "unfettered prerogatives"; it is therefore legitimate, within the Community legal order, for those rights to be subject to certain limits "justified by the overall objectives pursued by the Community, on condition that [their] substance . . . is left untouched".

4. THE PREVALENCE OF INTERNATIONAL AGREEMENTS ON HUMAN RIGHTS

Of the two types of rules thus taken as a reference point (comparative constitutional law and international agreements for the protection of human rights), it was the second which proved most immediately productive.

In 1975 the *Rutili* judgment was delivered.[25] An Italian immigrant in France, who was involved in a number of acrimonious trade-union and political conflicts, was, on grounds of public policy, prevented from entering four *départements*. The Court held that the limitations placed by secondary Community law on the powers of Member States regarding control of aliens reflected a higher principle: a principle—and this is where the progress was made—which did not derive, as in the *Nold* case, from "international treaties" in general but was enshrined in the provisions of a specific instrument, namely Articles 8 to 11 of the European Convention on the Protection of Human Rights (ECHR) and Article 2 of Protocol No 4 thereof. The Court pointed out that that Convention had been "ratified by all the Member States"[26] and that, by virtue of a clause common to the above-mentioned provisions, the rights protected by them (respect for privacy, freedom of thought, expression, association and residence) might be subjected to restrictions in the interests of public policy only to the extent to which such restrictions were permissible "in a democratic society".

Five years later it was Liselotte Hauer's turn. On the basis of a Community Regulation, Frau Hauer had been refused permission to plant a vineyard. On that occasion, the Court did not refer to the ECHR, which provides only summary guidelines regarding rights of ownership and free enterprise,[27] but based its decision on a comparison of the constitutional provisions of the Member States. An interesting feature of the judgment is its reference to the Declaration

---

[25] Case 36/75 *Rutili v Minister for the Interior* [1975] ECR 1219.
[26] France did not ratify the Convention until 3 May 1974.
[27] See Article 1 of Protocol No 1.

of 5 April 1977 whereby the political organs of the Community formally acknowledged that they were bound to respect fundamental rights.[28]

5. THE FUNDAMENTAL RIGHTS RECOGNIZED IN COURT OF JUSTICE DECISIONS

It may be said that in the *Rutili* and *Hauer* judgments the form of the new case law of the Court became stable, if not final; that is to say, at least in broad outline, it is based on principles which are no longer open to challenge. The fact remains, however, that although the Court held that all fundamental rights could be protected, it has only been able to uphold some of them.

More specifically (and, of course, disregarding the rights of an economic nature with respect to which reference should be made to *Valsabbia and others*[29] and *Hoogovens Groep*,[30] as well as to *Nold* and *Hauer*), the Court concerned itself with:

(a)   "due process", pointing out in *Pecastaing*,[31] that the safeguards provided by Community law are equivalent to those contained in Article 6 of the ECHR and stating in *Van Landewyck*[32] and *Musique Diffusion*[33] that the latter instrument does not apply to administrative procedure in competition matters, and that the Commission, which is the "overlord" of that procedure, cannot be regarded as a "tribunal";

(b)   the fact that criminal law provisions cannot be made retroactive,[34] stating that, as well as being enshrined in Article 7 of the ECHR, that principle is common to all the Member States;

(c)   respect for private life,[35] making a finding that, in the broad sense in which it is defined in Article 8(2) of the ECHR, that right is also upheld by Community law;

(d)   the principle of review by courts,[36] recognizing that it was in the nature of a general rule upheld by Articles 6 and 13 of the ECHR and adopted by the Constitutions of all the Member States; and

---

[28]   See Case 44/79 *Hauer* v *Land Rheinland-Pfalz* [1979] ECR 3727.

[29]   Joined Cases 154, 205, 206, 226–228, 263 and 264/78, 39, 31, 83 and 85/79 *SpA Ferriera Valsabbia and others* v *Commission* [1980] ECR 907.

[30]   Joined Cases 172 and 226/83 *Hoogovens Groep BV* v *Commission* [1985] ECR 2831.

[31]   Case 98/79 *Josette Pecastaing* v *Belgium* [1980] ECR 691.

[32]   Joined Cases 209–215 and 218/79 *Heinz van Landewyck SARL and others* v *Commission* [1980] ECR 3125.

[33]   Case 100/80 *SA Musique Diffusion Française and others* v *Commission* [1983] ECR 1825.

[34]   See Case 63/83 *Regina* v *Kent Kirk* [1984] ECR 2689.

[35]   See Case 136/79 *National Panasonic (UK) Ltd* v *Commission* [1980] ECR 2033 and Case 145/83 *Stanley Adams* v *Commission* [1985] ECR 3539.

[36]   Case 141/84 *Henri de Compte* v *European Parliament* [1985] ECR 1951; Case 222/84 *Marguerite Johnston* v *Chief Constable of the Royal Ulster Constabulary* [1986] ECR 1651; and Case 222/86 *Union nationale des entraîneurs et cadres techniques professionnels de football (Unectef)* v *Georges Heylens and others* [1987] ECR 4097.

(e)   business secrecy enjoyed by lawyers,[37] including that right in the list of fundamental rights by virtue of an approach common to the laws of the ten Member States.

On a more general level, the judgment in *Cinéthèque*[38] is deserving of mention, insofar as it referred to the rights upheld by the Human Rights Convention in order to mark the boundaries of the area within which the Court exercises its power of review. The French Law of 1982 on audio-visual communication provides *inter alia* that the distribution of films in the form of video-cassettes is permitted only after they have been shown for a specified period in cinemas. The Court was called upon to determine whether that provision was compatible with Community law and then, in the course of the proceedings, whether it conflicted with Article 10 of the ECHR, which safeguards freedom of expression; but the Court rejected the second claim, pointing out that "although it is true that it is the duty of this Court to ensure observance of fundamental rights in the field of Community law, it has no power to examine the compatibility with the European Convention of national legislation . . . which concerns . . . an area which falls within the jurisdiction of the national legislator".

A number of other judgments could also be cited (of interest, for example, is *Testa, Maggio and Vitale* v *Bundesanstalt für Arbeit*, a social-security case, which describes "solidarity" between the values upon which the protection of fundamental rights is based, or the now numerous pronouncements regarding the right to a fair hearing in administrative proceedings and disciplinary proceedings),[39] but that would not add much to what has already been said. It is perhaps more useful to devote attention to the two sets of rules upon which the Court has based its decisions. They are principles which raise problems of not insignificant importance and I intend to make brief reference to them before appraising, in terms of institutional policy, the contribution which the chapter of legal history which I have so far reviewed has made to the building of the Communities.

6. THE PRINCIPLES WHICH ARE UPHELD

In the first place let us analyse the phrase "constitutional traditions common to the Member States". Its remote origin lies in the second paragraph of Article 215 of the EC Treaty, which provides that any damage caused by the Community's institutions or servants is to be made good "in accordance with the general

---

[37] Case 155/79 *AM & S Europe Ltd* v *Commission* [1982] ECR 1575.

[38] Joined Cases 60 and 61/84 *Cinéthèque SA* v *Fédération nationale des cinémas français* [1985] ECR 2605. See, however, the subsequent developments mentioned *supra* in Chapter 2, Section 7.

[39] See Joined Cases 41/79, 121/79 and 796/79 [1980] ECR 1979. For a clear exposition of this case law, see J. Schwarze, "The Administrative Law of the Community and the Protection of Human Rights" (1986) 23 *CMLRev* 401; O. Due, "Le respect des droits de la défense dans le droit administratif communautaire" (1987) *Cahiers de droit européen* 383.

principles common to the laws of the Member States". The Court relied upon that provision almost immediately, going far beyond the limits of non-contractual liability; and having thus created a new source of Community law, the Court used it in the area of human rights. But what does the term "common" principles (or values or traditions) mean? If a right is to be upheld by Community law, does it have to be guaranteed by the laws of *all* the Member States? And what approach must be adopted where the degree of protection offered in respect of that right is *different* in every single Member State, a phenomenon which occurs above all in the case of economic and social rights? Must the Court adopt the principle in the form providing the *maximum* protection or the *minimum* protection or yet again, as it were, the arithmetical *mean* of the various forms?

The Judges did not find a solution to these problems immediately, but did so after a long and very indirect process; a process, indeed, so contorted that legal writers continue to express doubts about it which cannot easily be set aside; doubts not only as to whether it is well founded, but also as to whether it can actually be identified.

Disregarding the language—often ambiguous and sometimes contradictory—of the judgments cited above, I think, however, we can say that: (a) in order to be "common" a principle does not have to form part of the system of every Member State; (b) the Court does not have to go looking for maximum, minimum or average standards. The yardstick by which it measures the approaches adopted by the various systems derives from the spirit of the EC Treaty and from the requirements of a Community which is in the process of being built up: the form of protection to be chosen is therefore either one which *conforms to the greatest extent* with such criteria or else simply *conforms* with them if there is no need to make a comparison because the right invoked by a party, although not conflicting with the fundamental principles of the other systems, is guaranteed by only one system.

Problems of no lesser complexity are raised by the fact that the Court has ever more frequent recourse to the ECHR, either considering the provisions thereof and applying them directly or else using them as ancillary arguments in support of principles which it derives in the first place from the Treaties and from secondary Community law.[40] According to a view which is widespread in legal literature,[41] the Luxembourg Court considers it to be an integral part of

---

[40] P. Pescatore, "La Cour de justice des Communautés européennes et la Convention européenne des droits de l'homme" in Matscher *et al.* (eds.) *supra* n. 13, p. 441 *et seq.*

[41] Among the most recent studies, see in particular Pescatore, *ibid.*, p. 450 *et seq.*; F. Capotorti, "A propos de l'adhésion éventuelle des Communautés à la Convention européenne des droits de l'homme" in R. Bieber (ed.), *Das Europa der zweiten Generation, Gedächtnisschrift Sasse* (Nomos, Baden-Baden, 1981), Volume 11, p. 714 and also Advocate General Capotorti's Opinion in Case 98/79 *Pecastaing, supra* n. 31. In 1976 the Commission stated that it favoured that view (*European Communities Bulletin*, Suppl. 5/76); subsequently, however, it abandoned that view, preferring to promote the adhesion of the Community to the ECHR (*European Communities Bulletin*, Suppl. 2/79).

Community law, and the latter would therefore have ultimately assimilated that written Bill of Rights of which, if Weiler is to be believed, the authors of the EC Treaty chose to deprive it for fear of setting in motion a process likely to increase the powers of the European institutions. Other commentators, on the other hand, consider that the Convention remains technically separate from Community law. In other words, the Court confines itself to perceiving in the Convention a set of mere guidelines, a source of inspiration for identifying, for the purpose of minimum protection, the rights which are implicitly guaranteed by Community law.[42]

Personally, I find the first view more convincing, supported as it is by an argument of considerable force. Since, it is said, ratification of the Convention by the last Member State (France, 1974), the Community is required to observe its substantive provisions: this follows from the well-known principle of substitution, which the Court had already applied with respect to the General Agreement on Tariffs and Trade.[43] More precisely, the phenomenon may be seen as part of a process of succession, which is both functional and, at the same time, limited. Like the Member States, the Community cannot discharge its functions unless in doing so it observes the rights upheld by the ECHR: those functions, in fact, were transferred to it *cum onere et emolumento*.

The view which I find preferable is, moreover, specifically confirmed by the *Panasonic* judgment, in which the Court considered the right to privacy only in relation to Article 8 of the ECHR and stated plainly that, in the Community context, the observance of fundamental rights is guaranteed "in accordance with" international treaties. It is now therefore certain that the ECHR and GATT are binding upon the Community authorities with the same force and, accordingly, that the substantive provisions of the ECHR constitute a criterion against which other criteria should be evaluated.

7. A LEGAL AND POLITICAL OVERVIEW

Let us now endeavour rapidly to review from both the legal and political point of view the path followed by the Court in endowing Community law with an

[42] See G. Cohen-Jonathan, 'La problématique de l'adhésion des Communautés européennes à la Convention européenne des droits de l'homme' in *Mélanges Teitgen* (Paris, Pedone, 1984), pp. 92–93; H. Mendelson, "The European Court of Justice and Human Rights" (1981) *Yearbook of International Law* 156; S. Ghandi, "Interaction between the Protection of Fundamental Rights in the European Communities and under the European Convention on Human Rights" (1982) *Legal Issues of European Integration* 300; R. Lecourt, "Cour européenne des droits de l'homme et Cour de justice des Communautés européennes" in Matscher *et el.* (eds.), *supra* n. 13, p. 335 *et seq.* See also the Opinion of Advocate General Trabucchi in Case 118/75 *Lynne Watson and Alessandro Belmann* [1976] ECR 1185 and, years later, Opinion 2/94 (Accession to the European Convention on Human Rights) [1996] ECR I-1759.

[43] See the judgments in Joined Cases 21–24/72 *International Fruit Company NV v Produktschap voor Groenten en Fruit* [1972] ECR 1219; Case 9/73 *Schlüter v Hauptzollamt Lörrach* [1973] ECR 1135; and Case 38/75 *Douaneagent der NV Nederlandse Spoorwegen v Inspecteur der invoerrechten en accijnzen* [1975] ECR 1439.

unwritten Bill of Rights. As was pointed out earlier, such a development constituted an exceptional example of judicial activism. However, that assessment
must be clearly understood. That example is certainly not exceptional in the
sense that it reflects a particularly high degree of dynamic liberalism, revealing
a very great awareness on the part of the Court of the new needs of a world
which, like Europe between 1960 and 1980, was rapidly undergoing social and
cultural transformation. On the contrary, from that point of view, there is no
possible comparison between the judgments to which I have referred and, for
example, the decisions of the United States Supreme Court in the times of
Kennedy and Johnson or the pronouncements of the Italian Constitutional
Court in the early 1970s. The Luxembourg Court has created the wrappings but
has put very little, if anything, inside them. In most cases, in fact, the Court has
rejected the parties' claims and, quite apart from that, it cannot be said that the
Court has been called upon to consider the most significant of the social and cultural needs to which I have referred. The only dispute in which that has happened—or, if you prefer, in which the Court had to give a decision on values
which may be generically described as "progressive"—is, after all, that of the
trade unionist Rutili.

The word "exceptional" is used, therefore, to describe something else, namely
the extent to which the action taken by the Court has affected the pattern of the
relationships between the Communities and the Member States with regard to
their respective powers. It is well known that in a federal system the allocation
of powers as between the central and peripheral authorities laid down in the
constitution takes two main forms: one, which is (or rather was) specific to
Canada, where that arrangement is seen as an absolute, an end in itself which is
not therefore open to change; and another, the kind adopted in the USA, where
it is regarded merely as a useful instrument for the higher purposes of the Union,
so that it is susceptible to change if the pursuit of those purposes so requires. All
the information we have is conducive to the view that the founding fathers of
the EEC intended to adopt the first and more restrictive approach. Let us disregard the decline in European idealism between 1950, when Robert Schuman
gave the starting signal for the adoption of a supranational approach, and 1957.
What is more revealing regarding the option which the authors of the EC Treaty
favoured is the complexity of the procedures for amendment laid down in
Article 236; but even more eloquent is the fact that the Community was recognized as having specific purposes only in the sector of commerce and trade, and
its powers, which are described with a maximum of detail, are only those strictly
necessary for the attainment of those purposes.

However, circumstances have frustrated the intention of the founding
fathers. As in the USA, the borderline between central and peripheral powers
has proved to be movable, and the Court has been responsible for moving it,
almost as if it wished to offset by progress in the legal field the retreats from the
idea of supranationality which were imposed over the same period of years at
the decision-making level (consider, for example, the refusal to agree to major-

ity decisions in the Council of Ministers). There are innumerable examples of how that borderline has been moved. On the one hand, long before the Single European Act came into force, the Community had been endowed with new powers and had therefore penetrated areas—environmental protection, consumer protection and education—from which it was excluded by the EC Treaty or in which it was mentioned only in passing. On the other hand, the powers entrusted to it by the EC Treaty have been extended or enriched far beyond the limits laid down in the Treaty.

Whatever the reason for its inception—indirect pressure from the German and Italian Constitutional Courts or the intention to make amends for the insufficiently democratic nature of the Community system, the development of a higher law, superior rules for the protection of fundamental rights, constitutes the high point of the second kind of intervention, which may be less bold but is certainly safer. It is inherently so and, at times, it is so because of the specific form which it takes. Consider for example the judgment in *Casagrande*,[44] which attributed to Article 12 of Regulation 1612/68[45] not only the aim of helping to achieve freedom of movement but also the function of guaranteeing to the children of migrant workers the right to study; and there is also the more explicit statement contained in *Razzouk and Beydoun* v *Commission*.[46] The Court was called upon to consider the legality of the different schemes for survivors' pensions adopted by the Staff Regulations in respect of deceased Community officials on the basis of their sex and it upheld equality between the sexes as a right of a fundamental nature, from which it followed that "in relations between the Community institutions . . . and their employees [or] the dependents of employees . . . the requirements imposed by the principle of equal treatment are in no way limited to those resulting from Article 119 of the EEC Treaty".

It might be said that I too, like the English Solicitor General, am speaking in a "perturbed and emotional" fashion: because the extension of powers brought about by the creation of a higher law is indeed spectacular, but it has no effect, or has only an indirect effect, on the laws of the Member States and therefore does not encroach upon the powers available to them. However, such a criticism would perhaps be shortsighted. If one day the Court should happen to put some substantial content into the wrappings which so far it has merely been preparing, the governments of the Member States, acting through the Council of Ministers, might well discover that their powers have been considerably eroded. And matters could go further, as may be seen once again from the constitutional history of the USA. Until 1925, the limitations laid down in the American Bill of Rights were held to be applicable only to the Federal Government, but in that year a celebrated decision of the Supreme Court (*Gitlow* v *New York*)[47]

---

[44] Case 9/74 *Donato Casagrande* v *Landeshauptstadt München* [1974] ECR 773.

[45] Council Regulation (EEC) No 1612/68 of the Council of 15 October 1968 on freedom of movement for workers within the Community, OJ 1968 L 257, p. 2.

[46] Joined Cases 75 and 117/82 C. *Razzouk and A. Beydoun* v *Commission* [1984] ECR 1509.

[47] 268 U.S. 652 (1925).

extended them to the laws and administrative practices of the individual states. Is it conceivable that something like that could happen in Europe?

Some years ago, Weiler stated that the *Rutili* judgment—which, among the judgments on this subject delivered by the Court by that time, was without doubt the most advanced—had opened the door to such a development. The Judges, as has been seen, held that the Council Regulation limiting the power of the Member States to impose controls upon aliens gives voice to a principle adopted by the ECHR. Therefore, Weiler argued, that principle forms part of Community law and, as such, is binding upon the national authorities with the result that any measures conflicting with it are inoperative.[48] Some years later, however, the judgment in *Cinéthèque* appeared to confound Weiler's prediction, and Weiler has in fact courteously, but nevertheless strongly, criticized that decision.[49]

My opinion is that what Weiler read in *Rutili* was what *Rutili* intended to say, but he underestimated the exceptional political and human nature of the conflict which the Court had to consider in that case. I doubt therefore whether, unless it finds itself faced with a dispute similarly capable of inducing it to adopt "forceful", solutions, the Court will take up from where it left off at a time now long past. In the near future, the most that could be envisaged is that the Court might censure the violation of a fundamental right by a national authority if the right in question was associated with a legal situation governed by the EC Treaty;[50] and, of course, it may be expected that the legal systems of the Member States will, to use Frowein's term, be influenced by the case law of the Court by virtue of a "dialectical development". Because Community law penetrates national legal systems directly, it is in fact unlikely that, in interpreting the laws of their own States in the light of a fundamental freedom, the national courts will remain below the standards set by the Court of Justice.[51]

8. CONCLUSIONS

I could not conclude this Chapter without referring to the changes brought about in the relations between the Community order and the national courts by the decisions of the Court of Justice on human rights. I stated at the beginning that there were various preoccupations about the judgments of the early 1970s;

---

[48] Weiler, *supra* n. 11, p. 164 *et seq.*

[49] See J.H.H. Weiler, "The European Court at a Crossroads: Community Human Rights and Member State Actions" in *Du droit international au droit de l'intégration, Liber amicorum Pierre Pescatore* (Nomos, Baden-Baden, 1987), p. 821 *et seq.*

[50] See M. Waelbroek, "La protection des droits fondamentaux à l'égard des Etats membres dans le cadre communautaire" in *Mélanges Dehousse* (Paris-Brussels, 1979), Volume 11, p. 333 *et seq.* That view was put forward by Advocate General Trabucchi in Case 118/75 *Watson and Belmann, supra* n. 42.

[51] I.A. Frowein, "Fundamental Human Rights as a Vehicle of Legal Integration in Europe" in M. Cappelletti, M. Seccombe, J.H.H. Weiler (eds.), *Integration through Law, Europe and the American Federal Experience*, Volume 1, Book 3 (Berlin-New York, 1986), p. 302.

one of those—not one of major importance, but nevertheless one which cannot be ignored—was the fear that the independence and primacy of Community law might collapse under pressure from national interests and legal traditions as a result of the interpretation of it adopted by the judges of the Member States, principally in the constitutional courts.

However, the turnaround on the part of the Karlsruhe court when, by a judgment of 22 October 1986,[52] it declared inadmissible applications against the implementation in Germany of Community rules which were considered incompatible with human rights is attributable, as is indicated in the judgment itself, to the path taken by the Court of Justice. What the German Judges found decisive, in particular, was the way in which the Court confirmed that the protection of fundamental rights was a mandatory requirement and determined the scope of those rights by drawing upon the ECHR and the common traditions of constitutional law. Those factors, together with their conclusion that the Court of Justice observes the principle of legality, takes care to ensure that the principle *audi alteram partem* is observed, guarantees the right to a fair hearing and ensures proper legal assistance, brought the German Justices round to the view that the jurisprudence developed in Luxembourg had finally made up for the lack of a Community Bill of Rights, the document which, they said twelve years earlier, would have to be adopted by means of a democratic legislative process before they would abandon their practice of scrutinizing Community law for themselves.

The Court of Justice could not have hoped to receive any more solemn and welcome recognition than that. There is every reason to believe that it will continue to prove worthy of it.[53]

---

[52] *BVerfGE*, 77, p. 339. With respect to this judgment and the parallel evolution of the case law of the Italian Constitutional Court (judgments of 8 June 1984, No 170, and 23 April 1985, No 113), see P. Mengozzi, "La tutela dei diritti dell'uomo e il rapporto di coordinamento-integrazione funzionale tra ordinamento comunitario e ordinamenti degli Stati membri nei recenti sviluppi della giurisprudenza costituzionale italiana e tedesca" (1987) *Diritto comunitario e degli scambi internazionali* 479.

[53] See, however, the so-called Maastricht-*Urteil*, Bundesverfassungsgericht, judgment of 12 October 1993, *BVerfGE*, 89, pp. 155–213, discussed in Chapter 4 and reproduced in (1994) 1 *Common Market Law Reports* 57.

7

The Effect of Community Law on the Employment Law of the Member States

I. INTRODUCTION

"AT THE VERY centre of the capitalist system lies, disguised as a contract, an essentially coercive and highly asymmetrical relationship the parties to which are necessarily hostile to one another". Those words are taken from a monograph, dedicated to Max Weber, by a distinguished Italian sociologist, Gianfranco Poggi.[1] They are quoted here because they identify effectively, concisely and fully the phenomenon from and through which labour law has come into being in the West and, in particular, in the Member States of the European Communities. Indeed there is one point on which even the most radical legal writers must agree: irrespective of their era and of the *Weltanschauung*—Liberal, Catholic, Socialist and even, let it be said, Fascist—to which they have from time to time subscribed, legislatures in Europe have invariably sought to modify the phenomenon that Poggi has so neatly encapsulated: in other words, they have always operated with a view to ensuring that workers enjoy the greatest possible freedom when it comes to concluding contracts of employment, to tempering the coercion and asymmetry inherent in the employment relationship and to causing the innate mutual hostility between employee and employer to yield to a rational assessment of the costs and benefits deriving from it.

Have Western legal systems been successful in their pursuit of those ends? If we take the level of conflict in factories and offices as a yardstick of success, the answer fifteen years ago would have been in the negative; today, perhaps, it would be in the affirmative. But it is not this—whether we saw things in the correct light then or whether it is today that the truth is being uncovered—it is not this that this Chapter seeks to establish. What matters is that the legislatures of the capitalist countries have at least embarked upon the undertaking that was urged upon them by workers' protest or the uneasy consciences of the bourgeoisie, by the slow advance of the idea of equality or the wish to strengthen the state by procuring for it the allegiance of the working masses. In other words,

---

[1] G. Poggi, *Calvinismo e spirito del capitalismo* (Il Mulino, Bologna, 1984), p. 46.

what matters is that the parliaments and political classes in question reacted to pressure—motivated in one way or another—for reform, for it is precisely that aspect which most clearly distinguishes their actions from those of the Community legislature. The founding fathers of the Community—and the same applies to the Council and the Commission in Brussels—never sought, or at all events never sought as their first aim, to reform the lot of the man who sells his labour. EC labour law, the broad outlines of which were sketched into the EC Treaty, and which were subsequently developed in Brussels, is not the outcome of criticism of an unequal relationship which is the source of major conflicts at the heart of the capitalist system.

This difference between Community and national levels may perhaps disappoint those who expect Brussels to produce schemes which are more ambitious and effective than individual national states can manage. But there is a reason for the difference. One needs only to scrape away the rhetoric which inflates the preamble to the EC Treaty and finds its way into some of its provisions to realise that the man in the street was not wrong when he spoke of the "common market" rather than the "Community". Although they were conceived as stages on the way to more ambitious ends, the original Treaty and the amendments made to it by the Single European Act had only one real objective: the creation of a European market based on competition and characterized, on the one hand, by the liberalization of trade between the Member States and, on the other, by the establishment of a common custom tariff *vis-à-vis* the rest of the world. It is obvious that labour—and employed labour, in particular—is inextricably involved in that objective. It is therefore logical that the EC Treaty and Community secondary legislation should be concerned with labour. But it is also logical that they should be concerned with it only to the extent of that involvement and, above all, in the light of the potential impact of workers' material and legal position on the attainment of that objective.

Here are two examples which have the merit of taking us straight to the heart of the matter. A market intended to be a truly common market is inconceivable unless the supply of and demand for labour can dovetail in every respect. A market intended to enjoy genuine freedom of competition will not function if, in the regions to which it extends, employment is subject to excessively disparate rules. Hence it is necessary to give workers the right to move from one end of the Community to the other and to eradicate those regional differences in legislation which are liable to distort competition between undertakings. It is all the better if their abolition has beneficial social effects or, to put it another way, if it eliminates discrimination, pockets of low pay and archaic managerial prerogatives. But it is nothing more than that. The legislature did not have its sights set in principle on raising the level of welfare and the quality of life. The legislature had its sights set above all on those factors which are likely to obstruct the proper functioning of the market, in order to remove them or attenuate their impact.

It is understandable, then, that scholars in the field of Community labour law[2] should tend to present their subject as comprising two sets of rules; (a) those serving directly to establish a common labour market and (b) those calculated to define a Community social policy so that the common labour market, but also and primarily the common market itself, can function properly. This may seem odd to someone accustomed to distinguishing between the law relating to trade unions, collective bargaining and industrial conflict, on the one hand, and the law relating to the individual employment contract, on the other. Yet, in the Community law sphere, it is the only sensible distinction or, better, the only one which is both rigorous and worthwhile.[3]

The rules from which Community employment law stems—and it is better to establish this at the outset—do not constitute a homogeneous system, but derive from varied sources. They are contained: (a) in the Treaties establishing the Community; (b) in the provisions adopted by the Council, the Commission and, more recently, the European Parliament (in particular, regulations and directives); and (c) in the national measures for the implementation or reception of Community law.

As far as freedom of movement for workers is concerned, the Community legislature has had recourse to regulations in order to achieve standardization of the legislation on access to employment, equality of treatment and the possibility of workers' remaining within the territory of a Member State after having been employed there. In this way, the Community legislature has had a direct and immediate effect on the legislation of the Member States, which have been deprived of any margin of discretion in implementing the Community rules (with the exception, of course, of amending or supplementary provisions allowed by the regulations themselves). On the other hand, in those cases where standardized rules have not appeared necessary, in so far as specific rights did not have to be accorded to migrant workers or where standardization has been prevented by difficulties of a legislative or, more often, a political nature, the Community legislature has fallen back upon directives, which are more flexible instruments. In particular, directives have been issued both to eliminate obstacles to the transfer of workers from one country to another and to harmonize national laws on specific aspects of working conditions, such as equality of treatment as between male of female workers, collective dismissals, the rights of workers in cases of transfers of undertakings and insolvency of employers.[4]

---

[2] F. Pocar, *Diritto comunitario del lavoro, Enciclopedia giuridica del lavoro*, in G. Mazzoni (ed.) (Cedam, Padova, 1983), p. 6 *et seq*; G. and A. Lyon-Caen, *Droit social international et européen*, 6th edn. (Dalloz, Paris).

[3] See also an earlier version, G.F. Mancini, "Labour Law and Community Law" (1985) *The Irish Jurist* 1.

[4] The social security implications of the transfer of a worker from one territory to another have been excluded. The aggregation of periods of social security cover, wherever completed, tends of course to eliminate the obstacles to freedom of movement which might otherwise arise. The coordination of national legislation on social security for migrant workers has, however, been complicated by the fact that certain legislation allows for the existence of social security schemes which differ from each other within the same Member State.

2. "WORKERS", "EMPLOYED PERSONS" AND COMMUNITY LAW
ON FREE MOVEMENT

It should be pointed out in the first place that Community law did not purport to have an impact on internal rules governing individual employment relationships or trade union activity, except in so far as it was necessary to do so in order to eliminate the obstacles which hindered integration of workers coming from other Member States into the employment regime of the State concerned.

Freedom of movement for employed workers is guaranteed by Articles 48 to 51 of the EC Treaty and by a series of measure of the Council, most of which date back to the 1960s: for instance Regulation 1612/68, Directive 68/360 and Directive 64/221.[5] Charles Evans Hughes wrote that "The constitution is what the judges say it is". In other fields of legal knowledge that assertion is debatable, but in our sphere it has more than a tinge of truth. The reason is that Community law has merely reached its adolescence and is full of discontinuities and gaps, while, until the mid-1980s at least, the Court of Justice in Luxemburg was synonymous with judicial activism at full tilt. Admittedly, even in the field of labour law that activism was often driven by a desire to extend the jurisdiction of the Community, almost, as it were, to make up for the set-backs which, ever since the days of the Gaullist revolt, the Community has suffered at the decision-making level at the hands of the Member States.[6] But it is equally true that the Community Court has become fully aware of the enormous burden in human terms of the problems created by the movement of workers. What is said about the founding fathers' frigidity towards social issues does not apply to the Judges of the Court. If ours is not just a traders' Europe, and if it is good that this is so, it is the Judges of the Court whom we must thank.[7]

Consequently, the judgments of the Court of Justice must play a leading role in any remarks on the fundamental principles of Community law, starting with the first question which must be considered: what is the precise scope of Articles 48 to 51 and of the secondary legislation implementing the principles laid down in those articles? Employed workers are the beneficiaries of the rights guaranteed by both Articles 48 to 51 and the secondary legislation adopted in that respect. In addition, to qualify for those rights it is necessary to be a worker and to be in a relationship of employment in the Community sense of those two expressions. Indeed, it is clear that if the employment relationship had to be defined in the light of the legislation of the various Member States there would be as many definitions as there are national legal systems in the Community, and one would have to forego a common labour market or to see it reduced to a cipher.

---

[5] OJ (English Special Editions), 1968(II), p. 457, and 1963–1964, p. 117, respectively.

[6] As argued brillantly by J.H.H. Weiler, *Il sistema comunitario europeo* (Il Mulino, Bologna, 1985).

[7] See also Chapter 8.

That remark accords with the need to recognize that Community sources are in the nature of uniform substantive law and that they therefore have a far greater unifying capacity than would be the case were they regarded—as a student of international law would regard them instinctively—simply as conflict rules. In any event, backing for this view is provided by the decisions of the Court. As early as 1964, the Court held that by the very fact of its having established freedom of movement for workers the EC Treaty gave "Community scope" to that term.[8] However, its judgment in *Levin v Staatssecretaris van Justitie*[9] is even clearer and more valuable. In order to determine the meaning of the terms "worker" and "activity as an employed person" it is appropriate, according to that judgment, to have recourse to "the generally recognized principles of interpretation, beginning with the ordinary meaning to be attributed to those terms in their context and in the light of the objectives of the Treaty".

The lowest common denominator of the Member States' systems with regard to the concept of "activity as an employed person" is without doubt the subordination of the individual performing the work to the direction of the person who made the job available. Hence the addressees of Articles 48 to 51 are all those who share that characteristic. "All" in the context means absolutely everybody, from *au pair* girls to medium-distance pacemakers, from seasonal workers to professional footballers. Those examples are taken from decisions of which at least two (*Walrave* and *Donà*) have become famous.[10] However, the highwater mark in the protection of the parties to technically or socially peripheral relationships was reached in *Levin v Staatssecretaris van Justitie*, which has just been mentioned. Mrs Levin, a British national, applied for a residence permit in the Netherlands but her application was rejected by the Dutch authorities on the ground that she did not pursue a genuine occupation there and hence did not qualify for the protection of Article 48. A resolute English woman, Mrs Levin held firm; she appealed against the decision to an administrative court, which asked the Court of Justice whether Article 48 also applied to a Community citizen who pursued an activity in a Member State other than his or her own and earned less than the national subsistence minimum.

The Court answered the question in the affirmative: for the purposes of the right of free movement it held that the expression "employed person" also covered persons who pursued or wished to pursue an activity as an employed person on a part-time basis only and who, by virtue thereof, obtained or would obtain only remuneration lower than the minimum statutory or contractual remuneration in the sector under consideration. The only activities not covered were those which were "on such a small scale as to be regarded as purely marginal and ancillary". But those are not the only advances which make *Levin* an

---

[8] Case 75/63 *M.K.H. Unger, the wife of R. Hoekstra v Bestuur der Bedrijfsvereniging voor Detailhandel en Ambachten* [1964] ECR 177.

[9] Case 53/81 [1982] ECR 1035.

[10] See Case 36/74 *Gaetano Donà v Mario Mantero* [1974] ECR 1405; and Case 13/76 *B.N.O. Walrave, and L.J.N. Koch v Association Union cycliste internationale and others* [1976] ECR 1185.

important judgment. Its reference to the rights of persons *wishing* to work, that is to say, of workers seeking employment, is equally significant. Indeed there had previously been disagreement on the question. In the case of *Lynne Watson and Alessandro Belmann*,[11] Advocate General Trabucchi had argued that Article 1 of Regulation 1612/68 authorized a national of a Member State to enter another Member State in order to seek employment. But most authorities considered that the wording of Article 48 was decisive, since it guaranteed "the right . . .; (a) to accept offers of employment actually made; (b) to move freely within the territory of Member States for this purpose". It was considered that "for this purpose" meant that it was permissible to move only if there was an offer and only in order to accept it.[12]

However, the aforementioned sentence in *Levin* is an *obiter dictum*, and hence a degree of caution is required when assessing its background and drawing conclusions from it. But the Court, in the view of this author, intended to reject precisely the narrow definition of worker just mentioned. The judges must have said to themselves that Article 48, like any other primary or secondary provision of Community law, should be read in the light of the main objectives of the EC Treaty, which certainly include a free labour market and—with reference to Article 118—full employment. If job-seekers are forbidden to go to the areas in which they consider it probable that they will be able to find employment the market will be very much less free, the objective of employment will be frustrated and the EC Treaty will be observed in letter but not in spirit.

3. RIGHTS OF ENTRY AND RESIDENCE

Whilst the EC Treaty lays them down in general terms, the rules for the implementation of rights of entry and residence, part of the substance of the guarantee of free movement, are very detailed. Thus, Directives 68/360 and 73/148[13] require the Member States (a) to let workers intending to work in another Member State leave their territory and (b) to allow job-seekers from other Member States to enter their territory on production of an identity card, and to issue them with a (uniform) residence permit. Obviously, and in contrast with the experience of non-Community aliens, the residence permit does not "confer" the right to reside in the Member State of issue but has solely declaratory effects.[14]

Anyone who can call to mind the number and type of formalities which a migrant worker had to undergo a mere quarter of a century ago will surely

---

[11]   Case 118/75 [1976] ECR 1185.

[12]   For example, Lyon-Caen, *supra* n. 2, p. 215.

[13]   Council Directive 73/148/EEC of 21 May 1973 on the abolition of restrictions on movement and residence within the Community for nationals of Member States with regard to establishment and the provision of services, OJ 1973 L 172, p. 14.

[14]   See Pocar, *supra* n. 2, p. 104.

regard these rules as progress. What is more, the Court has interpreted them in such a way as to bring to light their full emancipatory scope. In the *Royer*[15] case, for example, failure by a national of a Member State to comply with entry and residence formalities was held not to justify his expulsion: since entry and residence are rights of Community origin, such conduct on the part of the migrant cannot be regarded as threatening public policy. The second judgment (*Watson and Belmann*) is less clear but more detailed and, on careful inspection, just as open-ended. Miss Watson, a British subject, went to Milan to work as an *au pair* at the home of Signor Belmann, an Italian. At the magistrate's court in Milan she was accused of not having notified her presence to the police (an offence for which the penalty is detention or a fine and deportation). In parallel proceedings, Belmann was charged with failing to notify particulars relating to Miss Watson. In the course of these criminal proceedings the national court asked the Court of Justice whether such national rules were compatible with Articles 48 of the EC Treaty.

The Court's answer was "Yes, but . . .", the "but" being unquestionably more important than the "Yes". It held that the Member State might impose on nationals of another Member State the requirement with which Miss Watson had failed to comply and might impose a penalty for failure to comply therewith. Furthermore, it held that the requirement was lawful even where there were no equivalent constraints on nationals of the country laying down the requirement. However—and this is the crux of the judgment—the penalty must not be so severe as to impede the free movement of workers. Deportation was just that, a penalty disproportionate to the slightness of the interest which it safeguarded and to the importance of the right which it injured.[16]

4. NATIONAL LAW AND THE RIGHTS OF NATIONALS TO TRAVEL ABROAD

With respect to the *right of citizens to travel abroad* (a right recognized by Article 2(2) of Directive 68/630 and the same provision of Directive 73/148), the laws of the Member States are substantially in line with the Community provisions: the only exception is the United Kingdom where the passport system does not appear to be in conformity with Community law, in so far as the issue of such documents is, at least formally, a matter of discretion. On the other hand, now that more than forty years have passed since the EC Treaty was signed, the

---

[15] Case 48/75 *Jean Noël Royer* [1976] ECR 497.

[16] The Court made substantially similar statements in its subsequent judgments in Case 8/77 *Concetta Sagulo, Gennaro Brenca and Addelmadjid Bakhouche* [1979] ECR 1495; and Case 157/79 *R v Stanislaus Pieck* [1979] ECR 2171. The dicta in *Watson and Belmann* were taken up in Italian decisions (Consiglio di Stato, judgment No 455 of 3 July 1986, Rassegna dell'avvocatura dello Stato 1986, I, V, p. 504.) on the basis that Community nationals should receive different treatment from that accorded to aliens; as a result, Community nationals cannot be expelled merely on grounds of convenience, on the basis of a minor infringement, such as the requirement that an alien must make a declaration of residence.

right of entry and the *right of residence* of Community workers and their right
to live with the members of their family on the territory of the Member States
are far from being fully guaranteed.[17] There are certainly examples of rigorous
compliance with the Community provisions.[18] But it is apparent from a detailed
analysis that, in general, there are considerable discrepancies between the
Community rules and the national implementation rules and, above all, a disturbing growth of administrative practices which are clearly incompatible with
the Community requirements.

Those irregularities are, in part, the result of national legislative methods.[19]
There are indeed Member States—for example Belgium and the United
Kingdom—which have not considered it appropriate expressly to transpose the
self-executing provisions of the Treaties and of regulations (and in such cases,
as is obvious, the immediate applicability and the primacy of Community law
entail the implicit abolition or, at least, the non-application of national provisions which are incompatible), whereas others—France, Greece and Spain—
have chosen to bring together in a single legislative corpus the provisions which
are directly applicable and those which require implementation at national
level. In more general terms, however, it must be recognized that the obstacles
placed in the way of aliens (from the Community and elsewhere) by the systems
prevailing in the Member States are attributable to factors which are at the same
time political, economic and social: thus, in particular, the activities of terrorist
groups, imbalances in population growth, high levels of unemployment and the
consequent wish to reserve the available jobs as far as possible for nationals.

A number of specific examples may be considered. In Belgium, for example,
the fact that the right of residence is granted to Community citizens "on the
terms and for the period determined by the King, in accordance with
Community regulations and directives" is in itself contrary to the principle
according to which that right derives directly from the EC Treaty and must not
therefore be subject to any national restrictions or interference. That is not all.
The rules concerning the validity of residence permits in cases in which a
migrant worker is called up for military service in his own country and those
which lay down the penalties which may be imposed for infringements of the

---

[17] Article 48 of the EC Treaty has of course, in its entirety, been held to be a "mandatory provision" and indeed to be one of those which "have direct effect in the legal orders of the Member States
and confer on individuals rights which national courts must protect" (Case 167/73 *Commission* v
France [1974] ECR 359; Case 13/76 *Donà, supra* n. 10; Case 1/78 *Patrick Christopher Kenny* v
Insurance Officer [1978] ECR 1489).

[18] A particularly clear statement to that effect is provided by the judgment of the Luxembourg
Conseil d'État of 19 December 1986 in the case of *Carli* v *Ministre de la Justice*. It is, however, worth
remembering the decisions of the United Kingdom courts favouring a restrictive interpretation of
the purpose and scope of the Community provision, which—having regard to the judgment in Case
175/78 *R* v *Vera Ann Saunders* [1979] ECR 1129—they do not regard as applicable to "purely internal situations".

[19] On this problem in general see G.F. Mancini, "The Incorporation of Community Law into the
Domestic Laws of the Member States", Third Unidroit International Congress *Uniform Law in
Practice*, Rome, September 1987, reproduced as Chapter 15.

rules on the movement of persons from one country to another also appear to be contrary to Community law. In the absence of specific rules for Community citizens, the possibility of any foreigner who enters or resides illegally in Belgium being arrested, whilst a Belgian national carrying an identity document is only liable to a moderate fine, conflicts with the principles upheld by the Court in the *Royer* and *Pieck* judgments. And as far as administrative practice is concerned, attention should be drawn to the conduct of certain municipalities in the Brussels region which, in flagrant disregard of national provisions which are in conformity with Community law, impose burdensome requirements for the issue of residence permits.[20]

But difficulties and infringements have occurred and persist in several other Member States. Thus, in the case of the United Kingdom—whose system was examined and censured in the *Pieck* judgment—situations have been noted which are incompatible with various provisions of Regulation 1612/68 (Article 10(1)(a)) and Regulation 1251/70[21] (Article 2(2) and (5)) concerning the rights of members of migrant workers' families.[22]

In the case of Germany, in addition to the situation highlighted in the *Sagulo* case, an action was brought by the Commission under Article 169 of the EC Treaty which was of the opinion that, by making the extension of a residence permit subject to the availability of "decent" housing, German law was incompatible with the combined provisions of Article 48 of the EC Treaty and Article 10(3) of Regulation 1612/68. The Court upheld its point of view.[23] Finally, in the case of French law, mention must be made of the existence of unlawful provisions regarding Spanish and Portuguese workers who did not establish themselves in France during the period prior to accessions: their right of entry is subject to possession of a long-stay visa and of a valid employment contract.

5. FREE MOVEMENT AND MIGRANTS' FAMILIES

Once, it is said, migrants and members of their family[24] are admitted to a country to work there, they must be treated in the same way as nationals of that country. That observation is correct. However, it is possible to speak of equal treatment in either a formal or a substantive sense. Can it be said that Community law also recognizes a substantive right to equal treatment, in the

---

[20] See the various actions brought against Belgium by the Commission under Article 169 EC: Case 321/87 *Commission v Belgium* [1989] ECR 997 and Case C-344/95 *Commission v Belgium* [1997] ECR I-1035.

[21] Regulation (EEC) No 1251/70 of the Commission of 29 June 1970 on the right of workers to remain in the territory of a Member State after having been employed in that State, OJ 1970 L 24, p. 402.

[22] As regards the extension of the right of residence to family members who do not necessarily have to reside with the migrant worker, see Case 267/83 *Aissatou Diatta v Land Berlin* [1985] ECR 567.

[23] Case 249/86 *Commission v Germany* [1989] ECR 1263.

[24] Case 131/85 *Emir Gül v Regierungspräsident Düsseldorf* [1986] ECR 1573.

sense that it makes it possible to discriminate in favour of persons in a weaker position and hence of aliens? It has been stated that, since Article 48 of the EC Treaty does no more than prohibit "discrimination based on conditions of work", it does not legitimize actions of such far-reaching significance.[25] In confirmation of what could be regarded as the EC Treaty's coldness towards anything which does not assist the functioning of the common market, the guarantee of free movement excludes any form of what the Americans term "affirmative action". Moreover, there is not the slightest indication of a transition from form to substance, not even in Regulation 1612/68, even though it gives expression to the Treaty stipulation in the form of much fuller and more incisive provisions. Nor can it be said that such a transition has been made by the Court.

As far as the judgments of the Court are concerned, those in *Reina* and *Casagrande*[26] come to mind as being particularly innovative. Regulation 1612/68 provides that a migrant is to enjoy "the same social and tax advantages" as those accorded to workers who are nationals of the host Member State (Article 7(2)) and that his or her children are to be entitled to be admitted to educational courses under the "same conditions" as those which apply to the children of national workers (Article 12). In *Reina* the Court took the view that the term "advantage" covered interest-free loans granted by a German bank with state assistance on the birth of a child with a view to stimulating the birthrate, and in *Casagrande* the Court stretched the concept of educational "conditions" to cover educational grants which the authorities of the Free State of Bavaria made to pupils with insufficient means. There can be no doubting the boldness of those decisions, especially the *Casagrande* decision, which, despite the absence of EC Treaty provisions and perhaps contrary to the intention of the Treaty, legitimized the inclusion of access to education in the matters which come within the competence of the Community.[27] But in the field of the labour law, the boldness of those decisions lies in their having squeezed the last egalitarian drop from the secondary legislation. Furthermore, in *Commission* v *France*[28] the Court stressed the importance of the objectives of Article 117 and pointed out that the equality of treatment guaranteed to Community workers operates also for the benefit of nationals: the latter run no risk of being placed at a disadvantage by the possibility that Community workers might be offered conditions of work or remuneration inferior to those laid down in domestic law.

---

[25] Pocar, *supra* n. 2, p. 38.
[26] Case 65/81 *Francesco and Letizia Reina* v *Landeskreditbank Baden-Württemberg* [1982] ECR 33; and Case 9/74 *Donato Casagrande* v *Landeshauptstadt München* [1974] ECR 773.
[27] See Weiler, *supra* n. 6, p. 38.
[28] Case 167/73 [1974] ECR 359.

6. THE PRINCIPLE OF EQUAL TREATMENT

How have the national legislatures reacted to those stimuli?[29] As a rule the laws of the Member States treat Community workers in precisely the same way as national workers and in so doing render unlawful any difference of treatment based exclusively on nationality. However, close examination of their provisions reveals numerous irregularities, particularly as regards granting to migrant workers social and tax advantages which are available to nationals.[30]

Although frequently criticized in the decisions of the Court,[31] national legislation often contains clauses which are unlawful, including in particular the requirement of residence for a given period as a precondition for entitlement to social benefits. As is obvious, such a requirement entails indirect discrimination no different from that which the Court has held to be incompatible with Article 9 of Regulation 1612/68.[32]

The problem has become particularly acute with respect to the right of migrant workers to receive *vocational training* and to pay a registration fee for such training which is no higher than that demanded of nationals. In this area, there have been several cases in which the national provisions have been declared incompatible with Community law.[33]

No less serious infringements are to be found in the field of trade union activity. On the one hand, certain Member States tend to classify it as political activity and to treat it in the same way; on the other, there is legislation such as that in force in Greece, where the Civil Code itself (Article 107) requires that the

---

[29] At the direction of the Hanover summit (27 and 28 June 1988) the Commission was instructed to prepare a comparative study of the legislation of the Member States regarding working conditions, as a basis for the preparation of new instruments harmonizing national law.

[30] With respect to the availability to Community workers of subsidised housing, see Case 63/86 *Commission v Italy* [1988] ECR 29; and Case 305/87 *Commission v Greece* [1989] ECR 1461.

[31] Case 261/83 *Carmela Castelli v Office national des pensions pour travailleurs salariés (ONPTS)* [1984] ECR 3199; Case 249/83 *Vera Hoeckx v Centre public d'aide sociale de Kalmthout* [1985] ECR 973; Case 76/72 *Michel S. v Fonds national de reclassement social des handicapés* [1973] ECR 457; Case 122/84 *Kenneth Scrivner and Carol Cole v Centre public d'aide sociale de Chastre* [1985] ECR 1027; Case 68/74 *M. Angelo Alaimo v Préfet du Rhône* [1975] ECR 109; Case 32/75 *Anita Cristini v Société nationale des chemins de fer français* [1975] ECR 1085; Case 63/76 *Vito Inzirillo v Caisse d'allocations familiales de l'arrondissement de Lyon* [1976] ECR 2057; Case 157/85 *L. Brugnoni e R. Ruffinengo v Cassa di Risparmio di Genova e Imperia* [1985] ECR 1739; Case 94/84 *Office national de l'emploi v Joszef Deak* [1985] ECR 1873; and Case 59/85 *The Netherlands v Ann Florence Reed* [1986] ECR 1283.

[32] Case 152/73 *Giovanni Maria Sotgiu v Deutsche Bundespost* [1974] ECR 153; and Case 15/69 *Württembergische Milchverwertung-Südmilch AG v Salvatore Ugliola* [1969] ECR 363.

[33] See Case 293/83 *François Gravier v Ville de Liège* [1985] ECR 593; Case 309/85 *Bruno Barra v Etat belge and Ville de Liège* [1988] ECR 355; Case 24/86 *Vincent Blaizot v Université de Liège and others* [1988] ECR 379; Case 39/86 *Sylvie Lair v Universität Hannover* [1988] ECR 3161; Case 197/86 *Stephen Malcom Brown v The Secretary of State for Scotland* [1988] ECR 3205; Case 263/86 *Belgium v René Humbel and Marie-Thérèse Edel* [1988] ECR 5365; Case 42/87 *Commission v Belgium* [1988] ECR 5445; and Case 235/87 *Annunziata Matteucci v Communauté française de Belgique et commissariat général aux relations internationales de la Communauté française de Belgique* [1988] ECR 5589.

most senior posts in trade unions must be occupied by Greek nationals. In order to uphold Community law and to safeguard the equality of treatment which it proclaims in that respect too (Article 8 of Regulation 1612/68), there then remains the remedy of review by the courts which is always available with respect to any restrictive measure.

In an area which for some time remained largely unexplored, tax measures also conceal indirect discrimination in some Member States. Thus, in Belgium (although the problem arises in similar terms in other countries as well) supplementary insurance premiums can only be deducted from professional income if they have been paid in Belgium, a condition which thus operates to the detriment of aliens who work there but are insured in another Member State.[34]

Associated with the question of access to employment is the principle of Community preference with respect to nationals of non-member countries. The information available regarding this delicate problem[35] is not sufficient to allow an overall judgement to be formed. That principle is, however, expressly upheld in the recent Italian legislation on the employment and treatment of migrant workers from outside the Community. For the latter, provision is made both for different job lists and, as a precondition for their being recruited and authorized to work, for prior proof that no Italian or Community workers with equivalent qualifications are available to take up the posts offered. What is more, the Italian legislature did not avail itself of the possibility of derogating from the principle of Community preference which Regulation 1612/68 allows in favour of the nationals of non-member countries in the case of offers of employment to named persons by virtue of reasons of a professional nature, the "confidential nature of the post offered" and family ties between the employer and the worker, or in cases in which the reasons given by the employers appear justified.[36]

A few more words are called for on the question of access to employment in sports activities. According to the Court, they are economic activities for the purposes of Article 2 of the EC Treaty and, in so far as they constitute activities as employed persons, they fall within the scope of the provisions on freedom of movement for workers. The exclusion of foreign sportsmen is thus lawful only in those sporting events—such as matches between teams representing countries—whose economic importance is non-existent or is surpassed by other values.[37]

---

[34] See, however, the response of the Court in Case C-204/90 *Hanns-Martin Bachmann* v *Belgium* [1992] ECR I-249; and Case C-300/90 *Commission* v *Belgium* [1992] ECR I-305.

[35] The Commission's initiative intended to coordinate national migration policies concerning non-Community aliens, embodied in Decision 83/381 (OJ 1985 L 217, p. 25) is well known; it was annulled by the Court in Joined Cases 281, 283, 285 and 297/85 *Germany* v *Commission* [1987] ECR 3203.

[36] Even though there are no specific legislative provisions in the Netherlands either, the policy of the authorities, which has been approved by court decisions, is to interpret the rules regarding access to the labour market so as to guarantee priority for nationals and persons from other Member States.

[37] See Cases 36/74 and 13/76 *Donà* and *Walrave*, *supra* n. 10.

Prior to the *Bosman*[38] ruling, the problem of the compatibility with Community law of the rules by which the sports federations of the Member States limit the number of foreign sportsmen (including Community nationals which an affiliated association can take on) had been the subject of heated debate in Italy in the case of footballers. There was no national decision specifically dealing with football but principles had been laid down in previous national decisions enabling the problem, when it arose, to be resolved. In particular, it was held, on the one hand, that provisions adopted by federations cannot derogate from Member State provisions[39] and, *a fortiori*, from Community provisions or those of Community origin, and, on the other, that any sportsman (and likewise any sports association) can appeal against such measures to the administrative courts. In fact, the powers of federations come within the area of public law and decisions adopted by them constitute administrative measures in the strict sense of the term.[40]

Over the years there have of course been changes. As from 1 January 1988 new "charters" entered into force for sports federations and, according to the first commentators to concern themselves with them, they redefined the legal conditions applicable to federations and remove their status as public bodies. This innovation necessarily had repercussions on employment contracts between sportsmen and sports associations; although they continued to be modelled on standard forms drawn up by the sports federations, it appears that they were to be governed exclusively by private law, with the result that any disputes to which they gave rise would have to be brought before the ordinary courts.

Is that position compatible with Article 48 of the EC Treaty? Intrinsically, there is no doubt that it is. On the other hand, there are considerable doubts as to whether, by virtue of the private nature of the contract, it can be inferred that the federations have a legitimate right to limit the recruitment of footballers from other Member States. Indeed, if that interpretation were adopted, the consequences of the new legislation would be not dissimilar to those of an express prohibition contained in legislation or rules of a lesser status. It might therefore be concluded that the Member State is under an obligation to repeal the new rules, in so far as they constitute distorted or improper protection of the freedom of action of private bodies, and that for that purpose the intervention of the judicial authorities—sporadic and belated as it would inevitably be—does not appear to be sufficient.

---

[38] Case C-415/93 *Union royale belge des sociétés de football association ASBL and others v Jean-Marc Bosman* [1995] ECR I-4921.
[39] Combined divisions of the Court of Cassation, 5 September 1986, No 5430, (1986) *Massimario del Foro Italiano*, 954.
[40] Combined divisions of the Court of Cassation, 9 May 1986, No 3091, (1986) *Foro Italiano*, I, 1257.

7. PUBLIC POLICY, SECURITY AND HEALTH EXCEPTIONS TO
THE RIGHT OF FREE MOVEMENT

Let us now turn from the substantive aspect to the limitations. Freedom of movement is brought to a standstill every time the shield of public interest is raised, since it may be denied on "grounds of *public* policy, *public* security or *public* health", and does not extend to employment in the *public* service or to activities involving participation in the exercise of *public* powers.

Considering, first of all, the exception based on *public policy*, the phrase quoted above is taken from Article 48(3) of the EC Treaty (and from Article 56 as regards the self-employed, who are subject to identical rules), but to interpret it one should refer to Directive 64/221. Article 3 of that Directive made a remarkable contribution to the content of that phrase by providing that national measures taken on grounds of public policy must be based on "the personal conduct of the individual concerned". A measure with general preventive objectives or designed to be exemplary would therefore be unlawful. An excellent rule but a very demanding one. It is not easy to justify the threat posed by particular conduct in purely individual terms when, as almost invariably occurs, it is part of a joint activity or is the result of imitation or is likely, in turn, to be imitated.

That, and the other difficulties which everyone can imagine (few concepts are as closely linked to the political history and customs of a nation, and the Community is made up of fifteen Member States), explain why, at the outset, the Court swayed between liberal initiatives and conservative back-slidings. *Bonsignore*[41] should be mentioned as one of the less conformist judgments of the Court. Bonsignore, an Italian national resident in Germany, was found guilty of causing death by negligence and of unlawful possession of firearms. Upon his being convicted, the federal authorities ordered that he should be deported; that is to say, they applied a measure which is regarded in German law itself as a deterrent and so was not justified on the ground of the specific conduct of the person subject to the deportation order. The Court held that such a measure was not compatible with Community law. The derogation set out in Article 48(3) had to be strictly construed and "personal conduct" signified that a deportation order might only be made for an actual, specific offence against public policy.

The philosophy underlying the *Van Duyn* judgment is wholly different.[42] It is worth setting out the facts of that case at some length. Miss Van Duyn, a Dutch national, travelled to the United Kingdom to take up employment with a bizarre religious sect, the very unchurchlike Church of Scientology, whereupon the United Kingdom authorities refused her leave to enter on the ground that the activities of the sect were socially harmful. Compelled to return to the Netherlands, Miss Van Duyn challenged the refusal of leave to enter on the

---

[41] Case 67/74 *Carmelo Angelo Bonsignore* v *Oberstadtdirektor der Stadt Köln* [1975] ECR 297.
[42] Case 41/74 *Yvonne Van Duyn* v *Home Office* [1974] ECR 1337.

ground that it was contrary to Article 48 of the EC Treaty. Thereupon the High Court asked the Court of Justice whether the mere association of a Community national with a given organization was capable of constituting "personal conduct" such as to justify restrictions on free movement.

The Court answered the question in the affirmative: participation in the activities of an organization and identification with its designs constituted a voluntary act of the person concerned and fulfilled the condition laid down in the Directive. Obviously we are a long way from *Bonsignore*, and that impression is strengthened by a later and highly dubious assertion made in the judgment. Although the activities of the Church of Scientology were viewed as antisocial, they were not prohibited under English law. Yet the Court considered that paradox to be irrelevant for the purposes of Community law, perhaps without realizing that such a decision exposed it to a charge of failing to observe the principle of non-discrimination. However, that aspect of English law plainly discriminated between British nationals, for whom the derogation on grounds of public policy had no consequences, and other Community citizens wishing to work in the United Kingdom, to whom the derogation might apply.

At any rate the Court swiftly recovered from that lapse to take an increasingly unwavering course. Take the case of *Rutili*.[43] Rutili, who worked and resided in France and, as is often the case with Italians, was a staunch upholder of the cause of the class struggle, was the subject of an order prohibiting him from setting foot in four French departments. As well as laying down many other (and decisive) principles, the Court's judgment established that, since the measure in question could not be applied to French nationals on account of their trade union activities, it could not be regarded as legitimate. Then there is the case of *Adoui and Cornuaille*,[44] where the Court held that Belgium was not entitled to expel waitresses-cum-prostitutes who were nationals of another Member State if it did not impose equivalent sanctions on prostitutes of Belgian nationality. In other words, the Member States are entitled to suppress prostitution, but that right is limited by the prohibition of discrimination. Hence it is not permissible to purge "a bar which was suspect from the point of view of morals" of their foreign staff only.

But the highest point of the trajectory which I have sought to trace is the judgment in *Bouchereau*.[45] *Bonsignore* established that the public policy proviso, as a derogation from the rule of free movement, must be construed narrowly. The judgment in *Rutili* consolidated that principle, stating that the scope of the proviso "cannot be determined unilaterally by each Member State without being subject to control by the institutions of the Community" (taking a less circumspect approach, it may be stated that the Court may also verify the importance of the interest that the measure based on public policy is designed to safeguard).

[43] Case 36/75 *Roland Rutili* v *Ministre de l'intérieur* [1975] ECR 1219.
[44] Joined Cases 115 and 116/81 *Rezguia Adoui and Dominique Cornuaille* v *Belgium* [1982] ECR 1665.
[45] Case 30/77 *R* v *Pierre Bouchereau* [1977] ECR 1999.

Bouchereau identified the interest that is to be regarded as eligible for protection. It was not sufficient, according to the Court, that the measure constituted a reaction to the "perturbation to the social order which any infringement of the law involved", public policy was infringed solely by a "genuine and sufficiently serious threat affecting one of the fundamental interests of society". So, the time when it was sufficient to belong to a marginal sect to have an entry permit refused is worlds away.

In order to ensure that the application of restrictive measures against aliens does not lead to abuse, even though the substantive criteria laid down by Directive 64/221 may in fact be observed, that Directive requires the Member States:

(a)   to decide whether or not to grant the first residence permit within a period of six months, during which time the person concerned is authorized to remain temporarily on their territory;

(b)   to make the adoption of such a measure conditional upon an opinion being obtained from an authority independent from the administrative authority before which the person concerned must have an opportunity to defend himself and be represented in accordance with the national procedure;

(c)   to notify any expulsion order to the person concerned; and

(d)   to allow him to challenge the restrictive measure, with the benefit of the same safeguards as are available to nationals of the host Member State with respect to administrative measures.

In this area, the contribution made by the Court has been of fundamental importance. In the first place, it held that the provisions laying down those obligations have direct effect in domestic law.[46] It then stated that a precise and detailed statement of the reasons for the expulsion measure or refusal of a residence permit was essential, in order to enable the person concerned to protect his interests (*Rutili* and *Adoui and Cornuaille*). The Court then went on to make it clear that, save in cases of urgency which have been properly "justified", an alien cannot be expelled before he has had an opportunity to lodge an appeal (*Royer*) and may be expelled subsequently only on condition that he has been able to present his defence in full.[47]

Finally, the Court has laid down the criteria for assessing the independence of the authority called upon to give its opinion on restrictive measures and the procedures to be followed in that connection, even where the body concerned is not a judicial authority (*Adoui and Cornuaille*). In particular, it was stated that the opinion of that authority must be given shortly before the expulsion measure, to ensure that there are no new factors to be taken into consideration. In so far as it must be assessed with reference to the personal conduct of the person concerned, the social danger resulting from the alien's presence in the territory may

---

[46]   Case 131/79 *R* v *Secretary of State for Home Affairs, ex parte Mario Santillo* [1980] ECR 1585.
[47]   Case 98/79 *Josette Pecastaing* v *Belgium* [1980] ECR 691.

change in the course of time and must therefore be assessed at the time when the decision ordering expulsion is taken (*Santillo*).

These decisions have had a profound effect on national law. Two examples will suffice. In the first place, in France, the *Rutili* judgment produced a veritable earthquake shaking the foundations of the system of administrative measures and making a decisive contribution to the preparation of the law which requires that all individual unfavourable measures should contain a statement of reasons on which they are based. Secondly, in Denmark, in the parliamentary debates concerning the transposition of Directive 64/221 there were long discussions about the conformity of the national measures with the principles upheld by the Court. The Minister of Justice succeeded in making his view prevail to the effect that, in the event of a conflict, Community legislation takes precedence; and there is no doubt that that was the correct solution. As was stated in the *Santillo* judgment, the provisions of the Directive are sufficiently well defined and specific to enable them to be relied upon by any person and applied by any court.

By contrast, it is very doubtful whether the procedural guarantees available to Community nationals under the United Kingdom system satisfy the requirements laid down in *Adoui and Cornuaille*.[48]

8. EMPLOYMENT IN THE PUBLIC SERVICE

As is well known, Article 48(4) of the EC Treaty provides a derogation from freedom of movement and extends it to employment in the public service. However, that provision does not define public service; nor is any further clarification to be gleaned from Article 55, which excludes from the freedom to provide services activities which are connected, even occasionally, with the exercise of official authority.[49] It therefore fell to the Court to expound the concept. In Community law, the Court stated, a post is to be considered public if the activities involved entail participation, direct or indirect, in the exercise of public authority and duties which are concerned with safeguarding the general interests of the state and other administrative units.[50]

Those decisions, which were motivated by the fact that the public authorities in the Member States have assumed ever greater responsibilities of an economic and social character and carry on activities falling within the scope of the EC Treaty, have nevertheless not succeeded in eroding the resistance to the entry of

---

[48] See, in more recent years, Case C-175/94 *R* v *Secretary of State for the Home Department, ex parte John Gallagher* [1995] ECR I-4253.

[49] But see the clarifications made of this point by the judgment in Case 2/74 *Jean Reyners* v *Belgium* [1974] ECR 631.

[50] Case 152/73 *Giovanni Maria Sotgiu* v *Deutsche Bundespost* [1974] ECR 153; Case 149/79 *Commission* v *Belgium* [1980] ECR 3881 and [1982] ECR 1845; Case 307/84 *Commission* v *France* [1986] ECR 1734; Case 66/85 *Deborah Lawrie-Blum* v *Land Baden-Württemberg* [1986] ECR 2139; Case 225/85 *Commission* v *Italy* [1987] ECR 2625.

aliens into the civil services of the Member States. Imposed as it is in certain cases by the constitution itself (Belgium, France, Italy and the Netherlands) and inspired sometimes by feelings of xenophobia or merely by protectionism in times of soaring unemployment, the practice of reserving posts in the public service only for nationals goes well beyond the derogation (which is of limited scope and must be interpreted strictly) that the Court recognises in Article 48(4). Nor can it be said that the measures taken by the Member States to comply with the principles upheld in Luxemburg are always satisfactory. It may perhaps be said the legislative initiatives undertaken in the Netherlands and in Italy are in fact satisfactory, in so far as their purpose is to identify the posts for which possession of the nationality of the state concerned remains an absolute requirement (it should not be forgotten, however, that in those countries, and also in Greece, there are requirements which conflict with Community law regarding employment in public bodies with economic functions, para-state bodies and universities as well); but they are certainly not satisfactory in Denmark, where Community citizens are only offered posts on a contractual basis.[51]

In the 1980s, work was in progress on a Community initiative designed to combat the resistance of Member States (vividly illustrated by the declaration made on 11 June 1987 by the French Minister with responsibility for the Civil Service to the National Assembly and on 31 March 1988 by the Luxembourg Minister of Employment to the Parliament of the Grand Duchy). The Commission proposed to review the compatibility with Community law of the conditions as to nationality laid down by the Member States for employment in bodies engaged in commercial activities (public transport, gas and electricity supply, posts and telecommunications, radio and television and shipping) and for employment in health services, public teaching and research institutes.[52]

9. COMMUNITY LABOUR LAW AND SOCIAL POLICY

It is notorious that, for the lawyer, liberties are a bottomless well. The guarantee established by Article 48 of the EC Treaty could be examined still further but Community labour law has two strands and it is time that the second is considered. The second strand concerns all those working in the Community, the non-migrant as well as the migrant worker. Accordingly it is that strand which affects us most closely and has a more direct impact on the established equilibria of our various systems, often disturbing or upsetting them. What we are concerned with here is a battery of instruments with which the Community has

---

[51] The discrimination arising from this was noted in the judgment in Case 225/85 *Commission v Italy*, *supra* n. 50; and Case 33/88 *Pilar Allué and Carmel Mary Coonan v Università degli Studi di Venezia* [1989] ECR 1591.

[52] For subsequent developments in France see the French Laws of 25 July 1991 and 16 December 1996. See also Conseil Constitutionnel, decision of 23 July 1991, *Recueil des décisions du Conseil Constitutionnel*. Regarding Luxembourg see Case C-473/93 *Commission v Luxembourg* [1996] ECR I-3207.

been equipped for the purposes of implementing a social policy. Here the most important of those instruments shall be considered: the rules designed to harmonize the Member States' labour law and, in particular, their laws on employment.

The EC Treaty, once again, if not disappointing, makes promises which in its own context *desinent in piscem*. Thus Article 117 opens the subject of harmonization with a flourish of trumpets: "Member States agree upon the need to promote improved working conditions and an improved standard of living for workers, so as to make possible their harmonization while the improvement is being maintained". But those words were written by men in whose system of values competition was pre-eminent—competition that was to be both free and fair. Now, what factors, by diversifying terms of employment from one country to another (and, within a given country, from region to region), are most likely to threaten that particular value? Obviously, differences in pay and in particular differences based on sex, if it is admitted that nothing has such a great impact on the cost of such a large number of products as the employment in jobs open to either sex of underpaid female labour. Now we can see the fishy tail of Horace's witticism come into view: the conditions whose harmonization and improvement are promised boil down in practice to the pay of those women who perform work which men also perform, since the Single European Act (Article 118A) has added only the minimum requirements concerning health and safety of workers. Indeed, Article 119 of the EC Treaty, passing from the trumpet to the penny whistle, provides that "each Member State shall . . . ensure . . . the application of the principle that men and women should receive equal pay for equal work".[53]

Earlier on this Chapter spoke of the founding fathers' "frigidity". Well, it would appear that the thread linking the two articles is characterized by more than coldness, it is intellectually clumsy and even a little suicidal. Let us assume that the only differential whose abolition is worth promoting is that which is based on sex. It is true that to eliminate sex discrimination with regard solely to jobs that can be performed by either sex still leaves sex discrimination with a considerable capacity for distortion. But, then, how is it possible not to perceive the potential impact on relations between undertakings in the Community of the existence of regimes which differentiate also in fields other than that of pay—as regards access to employment and the numerous rights and obligations situations surrounding the duties attaching to work and remuneration? There are, in short, too many gaps and too many threats to the very aims of the EC Treaty. It is therefore understandable that the no less "cold" but certainly more modern and sophisticated legislature in Brussels finally took action to tackle the situation. Thus, in the mid 1970s two directives were adopted, first Directive 75/117, which required non-discriminatory systems of classification to be introduced and extended the principle of equal pay to cover not just the same

---

[53] See, however, the Social Agreement reached at Maastricht by 11 of the then 12 Member States and the subsequent amendments agreed by the 15 Member States in the Amsterdam Treaty.

work but work of equal value, and, secondly, Directive 76/207, whereby the Member States were obliged to abolish everything—laws, individual contracts, practices—contrary to the principle of equal treatment in the field of training and the substance of employment contracts and dismissal.[54]

Let us consider some of the Court's decisions relating to those Directives. A distinction can usefully be made between the Court's response to actions brought by the Commission against the Member States and its answers, by way of preliminary rulings, to questions put to it by national courts. The first case may well leave one perplexed. Of the Member States which the Community's "public prosecutor" charged with having failed to comply with Directive 75/117 or Directive 76/207, or both, Luxembourg, Denmark and France lost whilst Italy, the United Kingdom and Germany were acquitted or escaped with a few bruises.[55] Timidity in the face of the "big" countries? Probably not. In fields such as restrictions on the movement of goods (take for example the judgments on beer and pasta)[56] or, say, aid for certain industries, the big countries number their defeats at the Court in dozens a year; in any event, they lose no less frequently than the small countries. There must therefore be other reasons for the phenomenon just described.

The most significant reason springs from an—admittedly debatable but also legitimate—analysis of the reality of the situations which the Court's judgments affect. "The only genuine revolution of our time", as the Italian philosopher Norberto Bobbio[57] wrote, women's progress towards equality mobilizes interests and sentiments for and against which are too strong, too deeply rooted in the cultures and in the psyche of the various societies for it to be fully governed from the centre. Persuade the periphery to assist its progress by all means; but do not force it with Jacobin severity to quicken its pace more than the states desire. In practical terms it is one thing to invoke consumers' interests in support of a prohibition of the importation of margarine not packed in cubes and another to justify the lack of rules specifically designed to combat discrimination in posts in the public service on the ground that equality in that sphere is already guaranteed by the constitution.[58] In the first case the centre may strike

---

[54] Council Directive 75/117/EEC of 10 February 1975 on the approximation of the laws of the Member States relating to the application of the principle of equal pay for men and women, OJ 1975 L 45, p. 19; and Council Directive 76/207/EEC of 9 February 1976 on the implementation of the principle of equal treatment for men and women as regards access to employment, vocational training and promotion, and working conditions, OJ 1976 L 39, p. 40.

[55] Case 58/81 *Commission v Luxembourg* [1982] ECR 2175; Case 143/83 *Commission v Denmark* [1985] ECR 427; Case 61/81 *Commission v United Kingdom* [1982] ECR 2601 and 165/82 *Commission v United Kingdom* [1983] ECR 3431; Case 163/82 *Commission v Italy* [1983] ECR 3273; Case 248/83 *Commission v Germany* [1985] ECR 1474. See also Case 312/86 *Commission v France* [1988] ECR 6315 and 318/86 *Commission v France* [1988] ECR 3559.

[56] See, for example, Case 178/74 *Commission v Germany* [1987] ECR 1227; and Case 202/82 *Commission v France* [1984] ECR 933.

[57] N. Bobbio, *Pro e contro un'etica laica* (Il Mulino, Bologna, 1964), p. 162.

[58] The first example is taken from Case 340/82 *Commission v France* (subsequently removed from the register by Order of 6 March 1985), and the second from Case 180/83 *Moser v Land Baden-Württemberg* [1984] ECR 2539.

hard, even if it is probable the consumers are genuinely used to recognizing margarine from its square packaging; it cannot do so in the second because the greater protection promised by an *ad hoc* law is liable to be outweighed by the tensions (and later, perhaps, the disappointments) that the adoption of such a law would cause.

The other reason lies in the difficulty in rebutting arguments of the kind sometimes heard in the Member States ("we have a democratic constitution and we do not need anything else"). Such arguments are technically weak. A Judge at the Court knows that none of the Member States is on a par with Khomeini's Iran; he knows that all the Member States (and not without reason) are proud of the guarantees which their citizens enjoy; he also knows that the most dangerous challenges to the primacy of Community law have come from none other than the national constitutional courts and are rooted in fear lest Brussels produce rules which might damage their respective Bills of Rights. Is it easy for that Judge to say to one of the Member States that he does not believe in the effectiveness of its highest-ranking provisions of law and in particular in their ability directly to bind the administration? No, it is not; it is not easy above all in view of the fact that the Member State could respond by treating, more or less overtly, that expression of no confidence as inadmissible. In the fragile system that the Community remains today there is one mistake more than any other that the Court may not allow itself to make: that of forgetting that it must be both a fox and a lion. It is the fox that diverts the lion away from the conflicts which may detract from its prestige and hence from its authority.

In contrast, requests for preliminary rulings afford the Court more scope for activism, again for a variety of reasons. First of all, since the national court may do no more than ask the Court to interpret Community law, the Court knows that it has to rule on the contested measure only indirectly. In addition, any ruling of incompatibility which only it may make will not have effect *erga omnes* but will serve as a precedent (but not as the common law lawyers understand that term). Lastly, there is the crucial factor that the Court is not being asked to intervene by Brussels, the reasons for whose actions before the Court are often indecipherable, but by a national official of the Member State in question who, being an expert in legal matters, is eminently credible, watchful as to the social "fall-out" of his decisions and, by definition, impartial.

That surely explains the incisiveness of judgments such as that in (a) the *Defrenne II* case, holding that Article 119 of the EC Treaty was directly applicable;[59] (b) in *Garland*,[60] in which it was held that a number of facilities granted to employees after retirement were covered by the principle of equal pay both in the public service and in relation between individuals, whether or not based on a collective contract; (c) the judgments which have clarified the concept of

---

[59] Case 43/75 *Defrenne v Société anonyme belge de navigation aérienne Sabena* [1976] ECR 455.

[60] Case 12/81 *Eileen Garland v British Rail Engineering Ltd.* [1982] ECR 359.

remuneration;[61] (d) those which have laid down the criteria for comparing working conditions of women and men,[62] in which the principle of equality of remuneration laid down in Article 119 is applied even where a worker carries out tasks which are of greater value than those of the person whose remuneration is taken as a basis for a comparison, and (e) that in the *von Colson* case.[63]

Dwelling briefly on *von Colson*, since it is unquestionably the most important of those judgments as far as equal treatment is concerned, it is well known that directives leave the Member States free to choose the means by which they give effect to the model proposed by the Community, provided, of course, that they do not drain it of its substance or betray its spirit. Germany had availed itself of that facility when, for the purpose of putting an end to discrimination in access to posts in the public service, it required the administration to reimburse expenses incurred by unsuccessful job applicants. The Court at Hamm, a small town in Westphalia, asked the Court of Justice whether such a provision was compatible with Community law. The answer was in the negative. The Member State, it was held, may choose not to impose a real remedy, such as the conclusion of a contract for the employment of the candidate discriminated against, but if it opts for the obligatory solution it must make provision for a sanction which has a real deterrent effect. So, after it had been victorious in the conflict imposed upon it by the Commission—and in the very field of employment in the public service—Germany suffered defeat at the hands of a provincial court.

One could not wish for more eloquent confirmation of the greater effectiveness in this field of the request for a preliminary ruling; and that continues to be the case even if one shares the view that the declining number of references for preliminary rulings by the United Kingdom courts was prompted by the disappointment caused by the negative reply given in *Marshall*[64] on the horizontal effects of directives.[65]

---

[61] Case 80/70 *Gabrielle Defrenne* v *Belgium* ("*Defrenne I*") [1971] ECR 445; Case 69/80 *Susan Jane Worringham and Margaret Humphreys* v *Lloyds Bank Ltd* [1981] ECR 767; and Case 23/83 *W.G.M. Liefting and others* v *Directie van het Academisch Ziekenhuis bij de Universiteit van Amsterdam and others* [1984] ECR 1275.

[62] Case 129/79 *Macarthys Ltd* v *Wendy Smith* [1980] ECR 1275; and, in particular, Case 157/86 *Murphy and others* v *An Bord Telecom Eireann* [1988] ECR 673.

[63] Case 14/83 [1984] ECR 1891. Among the judgments delivered in proceedings under Article 169 EC, particularly noteworthy is Case 143/83 *Commission* v *Denmark, supra* n. 55, which upheld the possibility of implementing the principle of equality of treatment by means of collective agreements. That possibility was opposed—or, more specifically, the fact that collective contracts cannot serve as a vehicle for the transposition of Community directives was stressed—by Advocates General Verloren van Themaat in Case 91/81 *Commission* v *Italy* [1982] ECR 2133 and Sir Gordon Slynn in Case 235/84 *Commission* v *Italy* [1986] ECR 229.

[64] Case 152/84 *M.H. Marshall* v *Southampton and South-West Hampshire Area Health Authority (Teaching)* [1986] ECR 723.

[65] The area in which the Court has applied the principle of sex equality with the greatest incisiveness is, however, that of the Community public service. For the relevant case law, which is peripheral to the subject matter of this discussion and little known, albeit of considerable interest, see the fine article by P. Gori, "Il principio della parità di trattamento dell'uomo e della donna nella giurisprudenza della Corte di giustizia delle Comunità europee" (1985) *Rivista di diritto europeo* 7 et seq.

To what extent has Community legislation on equality had an impact on internal legal systems? And what has been the Court's contribution to that process? The answers which are to be found from an analysis of the laws of the various Member States do not leave much room for enthusiasm. Although in nearly all of them both Directives 75/117 and 76/207 have been transposed by means of laws or by collective bargaining and their courts have often upheld the direct effect of Article 119 of the EC Treaty,[66] extensive grey areas and arduous problems of interpretation nevertheless remain. This is evidenced, on the one hand, by the frequency with which the Commission brings actions under Article 169 of the EC Treaty and, on the other, by the ever more complex questions which the national courts refer to the Court of Justice.

It seems that inequalities in remuneration continue to exist, aggravated by the devastating effects which the technological revolution of the last decade has had on the employment of women. It has been rightly said that the weakness of the Community rules is one of the problems at the root of this phenomenon. In the absence of a clearly defined basis for the requisite criteria of assessment, the concept of work of equal value is nothing if not elusive. The very concept of indirect discrimination is often left without any real substance and its transposition into national law (Spain, the Netherlands and the United Kingdom are the most noteworthy cases) has been rendered more difficult by the complex statistical evaluations which are called for. Furthermore, it is well known that the Court of Justice itself defined the limits of that concept with great circumspection.[67]

Moving on from the question of remuneration to that of working conditions and, in particular, access to employment, we cannot fail to observe that progress towards equality is hindered in numerous legal systems by the vitality of the principle—which has always been of crucial importance in the West—of freedom of contract, by the lack of any penalties for defaulting employers and, above all, by the absence of any rules which place the burden of proof upon employers.

10. COMMUNITY LABOUR LAW AND FURTHER HARMONIZATION

The Council issued three Directives between 1975 and 1980: the national rules which are required to conform to a predetermined Community model now extend to staff redundancies, the right to the preservation of jobs in the event of a transfer of a business, and employees' pecuniary claims *vis-à-vis* an insolvent employer.[68] There is no need in the context of this Chapter to dwell on their

---

[66] See, for example, the clearly expounded decision (No 348/1985) of the combined divisions of the Greek Court of Cassation.

[67] Case 96/80 *J.P. Jenkins* v *Kingsgate (Clothing Productions) Ltd* [1981] ECR 911.

[68] Council Directive 75/129/EEC of 17 February 1975 on the approximation of the laws of the Member States relating to collective redundancies, OJ 1975 L 48, p. 29; Council Directive 77/187/EEC of 14 February 1977 on the approximation of the laws of the Member States relating to the safeguarding of employees' rights in the event of transfers of undertakings, businesses or parts

content; it is of more interest to ask whether those Directives are to be regarded as a departure from or at least a breach in the fidelity which, albeit without ruling out adjustments, modernization and some modicum of reform, Brussels has always shown towards the ideological testament of which it is the executor.

The answer to such a question must fall somewhere between hesitancy and a plain no. There is some novelty in the most recent legislation. For instance, whatever vantage point is taken to examine the Directive on insolvency it cannot be explained in terms of the proper functioning of the market. However, it is true that (a) it protects rather marginal interests; (b) the model put forward for the Member States is very weak; and (c) when it comes to the transposition of its precepts into national law the Member States have left too many loopholes for it to be possible to expect truly uniform European rules.[69] The other two Directives are, in contrast, more robust, but in their case the logic of the EC Treaty reigns, once again, supreme. Thus the Directive on transfers of undertakings merely supplements an instrument on the approximation of national law on mergers of limited companies, and the Directive on redundancies fully reflects the philosophy which, as we have seen, underlies Article 117 of the EC Treaty. Admittedly, reductions in staff are a terrible thing, and to stand idly by in the face of unemployment which "no longer smells of gunpowder but of decay"[70] would be unworthy of our Europe, which is the heir of the enlightenment and suffused with the notion of welfare. Yet like it or not, upstream from enlightenment and welfare there is no getting away from the conditions of competition. If a country can authorize redundancies on less stringent conditions than other countries its industry will be given an incalculable advantage. And it is against that advantage that war is being declared.

On the other hand, it has always been a matter of debate at Community level whether it is in fact appropriate to harmonize the rules governing employment relationships and working conditions. There is no doubt that uniformity may contribute to the strengthening of economic and social cohesion; but—some point out—it is also true that those advantages represent only a marginal interest in advanced economies and complex societies which, like those of the Member States, are similar in their political inspiration.

The second opinion is substantially correct and this is confirmed *inter alia* by the sparse and hardly memorable decisions of the Court which have so far been evoked by the directives concerned with matters other than equality. Interpreting Directive 75/129, the Court held that it was not applicable to cases such as voluntary collective resignations by workers following non-payment of their wages as a result of their employer's insolvency or failure to carry out a col-

---

of businesses, OJ 1977 L 61, p. 26; Council Directive 80/987/EEC of 20 October 1980 on the approximation of the laws of the Member States relating to the protection of employees in the event of the insolvency of their employer, OJ 1980 L 283, p. 23.

[69] Pocar, *supra* n. 2, p. 252 *et seq.*
[70] V.M. Albert, *Un pari pour l'Europe* (Seuil, Paris, 1983), p. 130.

lective dismissal in cases where this was compulsory.[71] Dealing with Directive 77/187, on the other hand, the Court ruled that it does not apply to a case where the transferor has been declared insolvent.[72]

As regards the national systems, of particular interest are the difficulties which certain Member States have encountered in transposing the Directive on collective dismissals.[73] It is also doubtful whether the Portuguese rules governing the role played by workers' representative organizations are compatible with Article 2 of Directive 75/129. As regards the Directive on the insolvency of employers certain deficiencies have been noted in the French legislation, particularly as regards the period for which the payment of remuneration is guaranteed.

Of greater importance has been the contribution made towards the development of internal systems of law by the Directive on the transfer of undertakings, in particular because some of them (as in the case of Belgium[74]) did not contain specific machinery which could serve as a basis for rules on the transfer of employment contracts.[75] In the same context the results obtained by several Member States in their implementation of the Directive are noteworthy, even if sometimes bizarre: for example, the Danish legislature took advantage of this opportunity to make it more difficult for workers to exercise influence on management decisions regarding transfers.

---

[71] Case 284/83 *Dansk Metalarbejderforbund and Specialarbejderforbundet i Danmark* v *H. Nielsen & Sn, Maskinfabrik A/S* [1985] ECR 553.

[72] Case 135/83 *H.B.N. Abels* v *Direction de la Bedrijfsvereniging voor de Metalindustrie en de Electrotechnische Industrie* [1984] ECR 4097.

[73] Case 91/81 *Commission* v *Italy, supra* n. 63; Case 131/84 *Commission* v *Italy* [1985] ECR 3531; and Case 215/83 *Commission* v *Belgium* [1985] ECR 1039.

[74] Case 237/84 *Commission* v *Belgium* [1986] ECR 1251. See, however, Convention Collective No. 32*bis* of 7 June 1985.

[75] See also the judgment in Case 235/84 *Commission* v *Italy, supra* n. 63; and Case 53/88 *Commission* v *Greece* [1990] ECR I-3917, concerning the incomplete implementation of Directive 80/987.

8

The Free Movement of Workers in the Case Law of the European Court of Justice

ACCORDING TO CHARLES Evans Hughes, the celebrated American scholar and judge, "the Constitution is what the judges say it is". If the word "Constitution" is replaced by "EC Treaty", the phrase retains its relevance. This is so because the document which established the European Economic Community suffers from numerous lacunae and also because until recently Luxembourg was a byword for unrestrained judicial activism. It is true that in the field of labour-related matters, such activism has frequently been motivated by a desire to consolidate the jurisdiction of the Court and at the same time to ensure the full and effective functioning of the common market. It is, however, also true that the Judges of the Court have approached the human problems associated with the free movement of workers in a very sensitive manner. If it can be said to be a good thing that our Europe is not merely a Europe of commercial interests, it is the Judges who must take much of the credit.

Since the foundation of the EEC the free movement of workers has given rise to an extensive body of case law. The movement within the common market of workers from Member States is now slowing down. However, immigration from the Third World and Eastern Europe is on the increase, and this is a matter which has given rise to serious problems for Member States amid the Community as a whole. Nonetheless, these developments have not led to a reduction in the number of cases referred to Luxembourg for preliminary rulings. It has to be added that the four accessions to the Community have also increased the potential for conflict, if only because of the peculiarities of the common law systems and the transitional measures applicable to Greece, Spain and Portugal.

The Court has shown that it pursues a two-fold aim when dealing with the free movement of workers. Its first aim is to derive directly effective subjective rights from the principle of free movement of workers, rights upon which the migrant worker can rely against the authorities in proceedings before the courts of the Member State in which he works. Secondly, the Court aims to guarantee uniform application of Community law, thereby abolishing the many forms of

direct and indirect discrimination which existed within the legal and administrative procedures of Member States even before the EC Treaty was signed and
which continue to be applied in even more subtle ways today.

As subsequent sections reveal, in order to realize its first objective, the
European Court recognized the direct effect of Article 48 of the EC Treaty and
subsequently of numerous provisions of the two Directives covering this subject.
This bold approach met, at least initially, with stubborn resistance from certain
major national legal systems and also provoked harsh criticism in political circles.[1] Moreover, the Court conferred on itself what we might describe as a
hermeneutic monopoly for the purpose of counteracting the unequal and discriminatory application of the rules on freedom of movement. Thus, it decided
that it was not a matter for national legislation to define key concepts such as
employed persons, social advantage, public policy etc. These definitions would
have to be elaborated at Community level.[2]

The remainder of this Chapter is divided into three sections. In Section 2, the
ambit of the practical and material application of the rules relating to the
movement of workers is identified. The content of such provisions is then examined in Section 3 and, finally, the two restrictions which the EC Treaty imposes
on the freedom of movement are analysed in Section 4. The treatment of primary and secondary law is kept to a minimum so as to avoid the theoretical
debates to which their interpretation has given rise.

2. THE SCOPE OF THE RULES RELATING TO THE FREE MOVEMENT OF WORKERS

Although the free movement of workers is established by Article 48 of the EC
Treaty, neither that article nor the regulations and directives detailing its content and governing its application expressly define the term "worker". From the
elements mentioned in Article 48(2) ("employment", "remuneration" and
"other conditions of work and employment") one can, by contrasting them with
the terms used in Article 52 ("activities as self-employed persons") and in Article
59 ("freedom to provide services"), deduce that a "worker" is any Community
national who carries out an "activity as an employed person". However, the
true scope of these terms remains unspecified.

The Court did not formally answer this question until 1986. As was stated in
the judgment in *Lawrie-Blum*,[3] a worker is "any person performing for remuneration work the nature of which is not determined by himself for and under
the control of another, regardless of the legal nature of the employment relationship". However, this definition is not complete. In 1982, in its judgment in

---

[1] As Chapter 1 already mentioned, the former French Prime Minister Michel Debré declared that
the Court in Luxemburg was suffering from "morbid megalomania".

[2] As was done, for example, in Case 75/63 *M.K.H. Unger, the wife of R. Hoekstra v Bestuur der
Bedrijfsvereniging voor Detailhandel en Ambachten* [1964] ECR 177.

[3] Case 66/85 *Deborah Lawrie-Blum v Land Baden-Württemberg* [1986] ECR 2121.

Levin,[4] the Court had stated that the work also had to be an "effective and genuine economic activity". The Court, therefore, had limited itself by drawing conclusions based upon the particular facts of the case, as it has done previously. In 1974, for example, in *Sotgiu*,[5] the Court had ruled that factors such as the professional title of the worker (wage-earner, white collar employee, manager) and the public or private nature of the contractual relationship were irrelevant. Other judgments also delimited the scope of the employment relationship in a series of more or less problematic situations, such as in the case of the *au pair* girls.[6] The same occurred in the cases of the middle-distance cycle pacemakers[7] and the professional footballers.[8]

Having stressed the importance of a precise definition, one should then look at how the Court has clarified a few of the elements of this definition before and after the judgment in *Lawrie-Blum*. First, according to the Court, the extent and duration of the work done and the legal nature of the employment relationship are irrelevant. In line with the judgment given in *Levin*, in particular, a worker can be someone who engages or intends to engage in a part-time activity and consequently is or will be paid less than the minimum wage guaranteed by law and under the contracts of employment applicable to that particular activity. Accordingly, both a teacher employed for only 12 hours a week who supplements his income with social security benefits[9] and a university student who briefly takes on employment connected with his studies in order to finance the latter[10] may benefit from the rules on freedom of movement.

Consequently, it is not necessary that the work be continuous or full-time. However, the Court has gone beyond this conclusion, significant though it is, by ruling that a national of a Member State need not be working at the material time in order for him to be entitled to rely on Article 48 of the EC Treaty. It is sufficient that a person is in the course of preparing to be a worker (as was the plaintiff Lawrie-Blum, who had moved from England to Germany in order to work as a trainee teacher) or that he had been a worker and remained in the country in which he worked in order to pursue studies related to his previous experience.[11] More significantly, the judgments in *Levin* and *Adoui and Cornuaille*[12] refer to the rights of those who "intend to carry out work" or "wish to seek work". This was given clear expression in *Antonissen*.[13] In holding that

---

[4] Case 53/81 *D.M. Levin v Staatssecretaris van Justitie* [1982] ECR 1035.

[5] Case 152/73 *Giovanni Maria Sotgiu v Deutsche Bundespost* [1974] ECR 153.

[6] Case 118/75 *Lynne Watson and Alessandro Belmann* [1976] ECR 1185.

[7] Case 36/74 *B.N.O. Walrave and L.J.N. Koch v Association Union cycliste internationale and others* [1974] ECR 1405.

[8] Case 13/76 *Gaetano Donà v Mario Mantero* [1976] ECR 1333.

[9] Case 139/85 *R.H. Kempf v Staatssecretaris van Justitie* [1986] ECR 1741.

[10] Case 197/86 *Steven Malcolm Brown v Secretary of State for Scotland* [1988] ECR 3205.

[11] Case 39/86 *Sylvie Lair v Universität Hannover* [1988] ECR 3161.

[12] Joined Cases 115 and 116/81 *Rezguia Adoui and Dominique Cornuaille v Belgium* [1982] ECR 1665.

[13] Case C-292/89 *R v Immigration Appeal Tribunal, ex parte Gustaff Desiderius Antonissen* [1991] ECR I-745.

it was not contrary to the provisions governing the free movement of workers for a Member State to provide that a non-national may be required to leave its territory if he has not found employment there after six months, unless he can show he is continuing to seek work and has a genuine chance of being employed, the Court held that Article 48(3) must be interpreted as enumerating, in a non-exhaustive way, certain rights benefitting nationals of Member States in the context of the free movement of workers. That freedom includes the right for nationals of Member States to move freely and stay within the territory of other Member States for the purposes of seeking employment.

The apparent broadening of the principle in the judgments cited above may appear to be at variance with the requirement that the work should have an economic relevance, as stipulated in *Levin*. This discrepancy, however, is only apparent when one considers that, as stated in Article 2 of the EC Treaty, the founding fathers of the Community attributed to the Treaty the material objectives of progress (a harmonious development of economic activities, a continuous and balanced expansion, an increase in stability and an accelerated raising of the standard of living). Moreover, the Court has done all within its powers to dilute the concept of "economic activity". It has even applied it to cases where the work was carried out in the context of activities like prayer and meditation. In *Steymann*,[14] for example, the Court ruled that the support given by a religious or philosophical community to its members may be regarded as the indirect *quid pro quo* for genuine and effective work.

On the other hand, the Judges in *Bettray*[15] reached a different conclusion. A German drug addict worked for a Dutch undertaking under a public programme designed to re-educate and re-integrate such people into society. In line with its previous case law, the Court did not consider the low productivity of the worker or the public source of his remuneration. However, it took the view that the purpose of the scheme and the reason why the plaintiff had been employed made it impossible to describe his work as an "economic activity". Accordingly, this activity did not allow the Court to guarantee the rights inherent in the free movement of workers.

Bettray, however, is an extreme case. Apart from it, the only cases where the Court systematically excludes the applicability of Article 48 are those which are known as "domestic" cases. The judgment in *Saunders*[16] is a good example. Mrs Saunders, a UK national, was prosecuted before an English court for refusing to obey an order to move to Northern Ireland and not return to England or Wales for a period of three years. The question whether Mrs Saunders was protected by the rules on free movement of workers was referred to the Court of Justice. The Court replied in the negative. According to the judgment, rights laid down in the EC Treaty cannot be applied to circumstances where there is no factor connecting them to any of the situations envisaged by Community law. A sen-

---

[14] Case 196/87 *Udo Steymann v Staatssecretaris van Justitie* [1988] ECR 6159.
[15] Case 344/87 *I. Bettray v Staatssecretaris van Justitie* [1989] ECR 1621.
[16] Case 175/78 *R v Vera Ann Saunders* [1979] ECR 1129.

tence or penalty for an act committed within the territory of a Member State, which deprives or restricts the freedom of movement of such a national, is a "wholly domestic situation" and Community law cannot interfere in its application.

Saunders was followed by many similar judgments. In *Morson*,[17] the government of the Netherlands was found to have acted lawfully in refusing entry into its territory to nationals of a non-member country. These nationals of a non-member country were relatives of Dutch nationals, but they had never worked in any other Member State. The *Iorio*[18] judgment was to the effect that Community law did not prohibit the Italian railway authorities from limiting access to certain trains to passengers holding tickets for a minimum number of kilometres, provided that this restriction was applied without discrimination on grounds of nationality.

3. THE SUBSTANCE OF THE GUARANTEE OF FREE MOVEMENT OF WORKERS

This Section deals with the contents of the guarantee of free movement of workers, beginning with the rights which it enshrines: entry and residence. The EC Treaty sets them out in a general manner, while the secondary legislation which regulates their application is very detailed. Directives 68/360[19] and 73/148[20] respectively oblige Member States to grant to nationals of those States the right to leave their territory in order to take up activities as employed persons in another Member State and to allow entry into their territory to nationals of other Member States on production of a valid identity card or passport, and to issue them with a residence permit. If one looks back a little more than thirty years and recalls the many formalities that a migrant worker had then to go through, one will undoubtedly appreciate the valuable progress which these new rules represent. Moreover, the Court has interpreted them in such a way as to highlight their emancipatory scope.

The basis of this jurisprudence is the case of *Commission v France*,[21] in which the Court ruled that Article 48 of the EC Treaty and Regulation 1612/68[22] had direct effect. From this the Court was to draw a very important inference. As

---

[17] Joined Cases 35 and 36/82 *Elestina Esselina Christina Morson v Staat der Nederlanden and Hoofd van de Plaatselijke Politie in de zin van de Vreemdelingenwet and Sewradjie Jhanjan* [1982] ECR 3723.

[18] Case 298/84 *Iorio v Azienda Autonoma delle Ferrovie dello Stato* [1986] ECR 247.

[19] Council Directive 68/360/EEC of 15 October 1968 on the abolition of restrictions on movement and residence within the Community for workers of Member States and their families, OJ 1968 L 257, p. 13.

[20] Council Directive 73/148/EEC of 21 May 1973 on the abolition of restrictions on movement and residence within the Community for nationals of Member States with regard to establishment and the provision of services, OJ 1973 L 172, p. 14.

[21] Case 167/73 *Commission v France* [1974] ECR 359.

[22] Regulation (EEC) No 1612/68 of the Council of 15 October 1968 on freedom of movement for workers within the Community, OJ 1968 L 257, p. 2.

stated in *Royer*,[23] the right of residence does not flow from the issue of a residence permit. It is a right which is vested in migrant workers by virtue of Community law. The issue of a permit is thus reduced to a mere formality. The worker who neither applies nor is in possession of one may be penalized, but any such penalty must not be disproportionate to the aim or interest to be protected and cannot therefore jeopardize his freedom of movement. In other words, a worker cannot be deported nor, it seems, imprisoned on these grounds.

The subject of entry and residence also has an important social aspect. According to Article 48, these rights belong only to the worker. Article 10 of Regulation 1612/68, however, extends the benefits to relatives of the worker; more precisely, to the spouse and descendants who are under the age of 21 or are dependants thereon, and to dependent relatives in the ascending line of the worker and his spouse. The nationality of the relatives is irrelevant. Nevertheless, in order for family members to obtain residence permits, the worker must have available for them "housing considered as normal" for national workers in the region where he is employed. It is obvious that we are dealing here with progressive rules, not to say generous ones. The Court's interpretation of these rules is equally commendable. In *Commission* v *Germany*,[24] it ruled that the requirement of normal housing applied only to the time at which the relatives join the worker in the Member State in which he is employed. Consequently, it is incompatible with Community law for the national authorities of a Member State to refuse to renew a residence permit on the ground that the housing is no longer suitable for reasons such as an increase in the number of family members.

Even more interesting, in view of the light which they shed on the moral-political stance of the Court, are the judgments which define the term "spouse". In *Diatta*[25] it was held that a woman separated from a migrant worker had a right of residence even if both parties had demonstrated an intention to divorce. This was so because until a competent authority had made an official announcement the marital relationship could not be regarded as dissolved. The existence of such a relationship, however, is essential. It implies, as the Court affirmed in *Reed*,[26] that the right cannot be guaranteed to the unmarried partner of a worker, at least not until such time as social evolution has brought about the legal recognition in all Member States of cohabitation *more uxorio*. In a multinational community in which the electorate of one of the Member States, Ireland, had expressly demonstrated at one stage its opposition to the legalization of divorce, this reservation constitutes proof of liberalism in the strongest sense of the word.

It has been said that once migrant workers have been allowed to enter into a Member State for the purpose of working, they—and, since the judgment in

---

[23] Case 48/75 *Jean Noël Royer* [1976] ECR 497.
[24] Case 249/86 *Commission* v *Germany* [1989] ECR 1263.
[25] Case 267/83 *Aissatou Diatta* v *Land Berlin* [1985] ECR 567.
[26] Case 59/85 *Netherlands* v *Ann Florence Reed* [1986] ECR 1283.

Gül,[27] their relatives—must be treated in the same way as nationals of that Member State.

This observation is correct. Yet, one can speak of equality in two senses: formal and substantive. Is it possible to say that Community law recognizes the second meaning of equality, that is to allow for discrimination in favour of the weak and consequently in favour of the foreigner? Some writers correctly point out that, by limiting the prohibition of discrimination to "nationality . . .", as regards employment, remuneration and other conditions of work and employment", Article 48 of the EC Treaty does not go far enough. The guarantee of free movement excludes any form of affirmative action, as the American courts call it. On the other hand, there is no sign of a move from formal to substantive protection, not even in Regulation 1612/68, which expands the provisions of the EC Treaty by means of sharper and more robust arrangements.

Neither has the Court of Justice made this move. On the contrary, it has declared that the equality of treatment guaranteed to migrant workers may also benefit national workers in that it protects them against the risk that wages or working conditions inferior to those guaranteed under national law may be offered to migrant workers. Nevertheless, one must not underestimate the contribution of the Court's case law to this area. Whilst not taking the "affirmative action" route, the Court has attempted to distil as much equality as possible from the EC Treaty and secondary legislation. This is shown by two lines of judgments.

The first group consists of those judgments which have recognized the rules on equality of treatment as being directly effective, with the result that they can be invoked before national courts in the Member State of employment. Those rules, therefore, also take precedence over any national provisions to the contrary, be they legislative, administrative or contractual.[28] The second group includes those judgments which have given a wide interpretation to the concept of "working conditions". In particular, the Court has declared that, when nationals of the host State enjoy similar guarantees, the migrant worker has the right:

(a)   to have the periods of his military service taken into account in the calculation of his seniority in the undertaking in which he works;[29]

(b)   to have special protection against dismissal if he is disabled;[30]

(c)   to receive compensation if assigned to work in an area different from that in which he resides;[31] and,

(d)   to receive aid granted for the acquisition and use of immovable property.[32]

---

[27]   Case 131/85 *Emir Gül v Regierungspräsident Düsseldorf* [1986] ECR 1573.

[28]   Case 9/74 *Donato Casagrande v Landeshauptstadt München* [1974] ECR 773.

[29]   Case 15/69 *Württembergische Milchvertretung-Südmilch AG v Salvatore Ugliola* [1969] ECR 363.

[30]   Case 44/72 *Pieter Marsman v M. Rosskamp* [1972] ECR 1243.

[31]   Case 152/73 *Sotgiu, supra* n. 5.

[32]   Case 305/87 *Commission v Greece* [1989] ECR 1461.

More problematic is the position taken by the Court with regard to the discrimination against foreign workers on linguistic grounds. The final subparagraph of Article 3(1) of Regulation 1612/68 refers to the possibility that national rules requiring a linguistic ability may be imposed on the migrant worker, when such knowledge is required by reason of the nature of the post to be filled. Ireland requires teaching staff in public vocational education institutions to hold a certificate providing adequate knowledge of the Irish language, defined in the Constitution as the "national language" and "first official language" of the State. It is a fact, however, that the vast majority of Irish people do not use Irish and that even teaching in the Republic is normally carried out through the medium of English.

The case of *Groener*[33] falls within this context. Mrs Groener, a Dutch national, was an art teacher in a third-level education institution in Dublin and possessed a high level of fluency in English. She was refused a permanent position because she did not have the above-mentioned certificate. She took her case to the Irish High Court, and it in turn referred to Luxembourg the question whether the relevant legislation was compatible with Community law. In what was evidently a very difficult case, the Court of Justice replied in the affirmative. The Court held that in Ireland there is a policy to promote the use of Irish, which has special historical roots, and this policy cannot be questioned from the point of view of Community law. Consequently, it is not unreasonable to require that teachers should have a knowledge of the language, given the obvious importance of their role in the education of each new generation. However, this policy cannot be applied in a manner disproportionate in relation to the aim pursued nor can it give rise to discrimination. For example, it would not be legitimate to require, as Irish law does, that the linguistic knowledge must have been acquired within the national territory.

It is a truism that "welfare state" legislation which is found to a greater or lesser extent in all Member States, guarantees to its workers a series of social and tax advantages. Regulation 1612/68 provides that the principle of equal treatment also applies to these advantages. The credit must go to the Court for having defined the ambit of these rules in general terms—all those rights "which, whether or not linked to a contract of employment, are generally granted to national workers . . . and the extension of which to workers who are nationals of other Member States therefore seems suitable to facilitate their mobility"[34]—and for having included in such terms rights with or without an economic content, which in any event have a very tenuous link with the situation of a migrant worker. In this way, as the judgment in *Reed*, cited above, demonstrates, the Court overcame the problem of not being able to equate the partner in cohabitation *more uxorio* with a spouse, for the purpose of granting

---

[33] Case C-379/87 *Anita Groener v Minister for Education and the City of Dublin Vocational Education Committee* [1989] ECR 3967.
[34] Case 207/78 *Ministère Public v Gilbert Even et Office National des pensions pour travailleurs salariés (ONPTS)* [1979] ECR 2019.

a residence permit, by proceeding on the basis of a "social advantage" for the worker.

If *Reed* can be regarded, so to speak, as an exercise in judicial acrobatics, other judgments confine themselves to demonstrating the strong social sensibility so characteristic of the case law of the Luxembourg Court. Citing a few examples at random: the right to a minimum income for dependent relatives in the ascending line of the worker has been treated as a social advantage[35] as have university grants for the benefit of one's own child;[36] the payment of reduced rail fares by large families;[37] interest-free, state-assisted, long-term loans by a German bank for the purpose of stimulating the birth rate;[38] the opportunity to use one's native tongue in legal proceedings if the law of the host Member State grants this right to nationals living in different areas of the country.[39]

4. RESTRICTIONS IMPOSED ON THE FREE MOVEMENT OF WORKERS

Having discussed the content, let us now examine the restrictions. The right to free movement disappears each time public interest rears its head. The right may be limited "on grounds of *public* policy, *public* security or *public* health" and does not apply to "employment in the *public* service" or to activities connected with the exercise of official authority.

First, as regards the exception based on public policy, the formula set out above is contained in Article 48(3) of the EC Treaty, but to interpret it one should look at Directive 64/221.[40] In effect, Article 3 of the Directive has extensively enhanced the EC Treaty formula by providing that the national measures adopted in the name of public order must be based on the "personal conduct of the individual" to whom they are to apply. Therefore, a measure adopted with the general purpose of prevention or as an example to others will be unlawful. This is not only a commendable rule, but also one which is extremely difficult to implement. It is far from easy to justify the danger of certain behaviour in purely personal terms when, as is almost always the case, the danger in view is the risk of imitation by others and the fact that the actions in question are repugnant to society as a whole.

This difficulty explains why the Court may have initially hesitated between a liberal and conservative position on this matter. Few notions are so closely

---

[35] Case 261/83 *Carmela Castelli* v *Office national des pensions pour travailleurs salariés (ONPTS)* [1984] ECR 3199.

[36] Joined Cases 389 and 390/87 *G.B.C. Echternach and A. Moritz* v *Netherlands Minister for Education and Science* [1989] ECR 723.

[37] Case 32/75 *Anita Cristini* v *Société nationale des chemins de fer (SNCF)* [1975] ECR 1085.

[38] Case 65/81 *Francesco Reina and Letizia Reina* v *Landeskreditbank Baden-Württemberg* [1982] ECR 33.

[39] Case 137/84 *Ministère Public* v *Robert Heinrich Maria Mutsch* [1985] ECR 2681.

[40] Council Directive 64/221/EEC of 25 February 1964 on the coordination of special measures concerning the movement and residence of foreign nationals which are justified on grounds of public policy, public security or public health, OJ 1964 L 56, p. 850.

linked as public policy to the political history and customs of the Member States. This confirms, as the English judge Lord Burrough commented last century, that public policy is "an unruly horse to ride". *Bonsignore*[41] is among the least conservative of the Court's judgments. Bonsignore was an Italian national resident in Germany, where he was found guilty of manslaughter and the illegal possession of firearms. After passing sentence, the German authorities deported him. In so doing they applied a national measure which was regarded by German law as a deterrent, and which therefore excluded the necessary link with the personal conduct of the person in question. The Court held that the measure was incompatible with Community law. The reservation contained in Article 48(3), it declared, was an exception which had to be strictly construed. The concept of "personal conduct" implied that deportation could only be allowed if the accused person had specifically and directly breached public order and security.

The *Van Duyn*[42] judgment was inspired by a different philosophy. It is worth looking at the case in detail. A Dutch national moved to the United Kingdom to work as a secretary for the Church of Scientology, a bizarre pseudo-religious movement. The authorities in England refused her entry, claiming that the activities of the sect were harmful to society. Miss Van Duyn alleged that the decision forcing her to return to the Netherlands constituted an infringement of Article 48 of the EC Treaty. The High Court in London referred to the Court of Justice the question whether membership by a Community national of a particular group could in itself constitute "personal conduct" capable of justifying measures restricting the right to free movement.

The Court answered that question in the affirmative. Participation in the activities of an organized group, as well as identification with its aims and designs, was, the Court said, a voluntary act on the part of the person concerned. Consequently, it fulfilled the requirement of Directive 64/221 with regard to the issue of personal conduct. This reply is highly questionable and merits the criticism to which it has been subjected. Although the English courts regarded this religion as antisocial, there was in fact no legislation which actually prohibited the activities of the Church of Scientology. The Court of Justice considered such an anomaly to be irrelevant for the purposes of Community law. Perhaps it did not appreciate that such a decision exposed the Court to the accusation that it had disregarded the principle of equality. It is clear that this aspect of English law discriminates between British citizens, upon whom the provision has no effect, and all other Community nationals wishing to work in the United Kingdom, to whom the provision applies.

The Court of Justice quickly recovered from this slip by adopting a more open approach, as may be seen in the case of *Rutili*.[43] Rutili was a worker resident in France and, as one often finds in the case of Italians, a standard bearer

---

[41] Case 67/74 *Carmelo Angelo Bonsignore v Oberstadtdirektor der Stadt Köln* [1975] ECR 297.
[42] Case 41/74 *Yvonne Van Duyn v Home Office* [1974] ECR 1337.
[43] Case 36/75 *Roland Rutili v Minister for the Interior* [1975] ECR 1219.

in the class struggle. He was refused entry into four departments, among them the one in which he lived with his wife. The Court found that, since the measure in question did not equally apply to French nationals in respect of trade union matters, it had to be considered as unlawful. So, Rutili was able to return home, where he was euphorically welcomed by his friends and received, rumour has it, a more guarded reception from his wife.

The principle established in *Adoui and Cornuaille*, is similar to the above. It was there held that Belgium was not entitled to deport waitress-prostitutes who were nationals of another Member State, if it did not apply an equally severe sanction to Belgian prostitutes. In other words, the Belgian authorities had the right to suppress the oldest profession in the world, but this right was limited by the prohibition of discrimination. Consequently, it was unlawful to expel foreign workers from, as the somewhat Victorian language of the Court put it, "a bar which was suspect from the point of view of morals".

However, the culmination of this development is the judgment in *Bouchereau*.[44] In *Bonsignore* it was established that in order to justify a restrictive measure, there had to be a real threat to public order. *Rutili* and *Adoui* developed this principle by requiring that the values detrimentally affected by the conduct of a foreign worker had to be universally held. *Bouchereau* identified in very narrow terms the values which merit protection. It was not enough, the Court held, that the measure had been adopted in reaction to the "perturbation of the social order which any infringement of the law involves". Public policy is infringed only by "a sufficiently serious threat . . . affecting one of the fundamental interests of society". Long gone are the days when membership of a marginal sect was enough to justify refusal of entry to a Member State.

In order to avoid abuse in the application of these measures to the migrant worker, and in order to ensure respect for the substantive restrictions already mentioned, Directive 64/221 obliges Member States:

(a) to grant or refuse a first residence permit not later than six months from the date of application, during which time the person concerned shall be allowed to remain in the territory pending the decision;

(b) not to permit a restrictive decision to be taken by the administrative authority until an opinion has been obtained from a competent authority of the host country before which the person concerned enjoys such rights of defence and of assistance and representation as the domestic law of that country provides for; and

(c) to notify the person concerned of the decision and allow the same legal remedies in respect of that decision as are available to nationals of the State in question.

With regard to these obligations, the Court's contribution reflects once again a high degree of liberalism. In effect, the Court has:

---

[44] Case 30/77 *R v Pierre Bouchereau* [1977] ECR 1999.

(i)   declared that the relevant provisions have direct effect in the domestic arena;[45]

(ii) ruled that decisions to deport or refuse a residence permit must provide adequate and precise details (*Rutili, Adoui and Cornuaille*);

(iii) held that a foreign national may not in general be deported before he has had an opportunity to lodge an appeal (*Royer*) and that deportation may subsequently be carried out only on condition that the person concerned is in a position, despite his absence, to obtain a fair hearing and to present his defence in full.[46]

The Judges have set out the criteria against which the independence of the body taking the decision on the restrictive action must be measured. They have stated that this decision must be taken immediately before deportation is carried out. Since the decision must be based on personal conduct, the threat to society posed by the foreigner can change in the course of time. That is why it must be assessed at that point in time which reduces the possibility that new factors may be taken into consideration to a minimum, thus leading to an unjustified expulsion (*Santillo*).

Finally, as regards the second exception to the freedom of movement, Article 48(4) of the EC Treaty provides that such freedom does not apply to employment in the public service. This provision, however, does not define the concept of public service. Neither does Article 55 of the EC Treaty, which excludes activities connected with the exercise of official authority. Consequently, the Court has been obliged to use the "hermeneutic monopoly" to which reference was made earlier in order to affirm that, in Community law, employment in the public service consists in the direct or indirect participation in the exercise of public policy, or the carrying out of tasks with the aim of protecting the general interests of the state (*Sotgiu* and various other judgments, among them *Lawrie-Blum*).

There is not much to say about the first requirement, namely that set out in Article 55, and it is probably more interesting to examine the implications of the second. Why is it necessary that the activities of the worker be in defence or promotion of the general interest? It is not difficult to answer that question. The public authorities in many Member States have taken on broader economic and social responsibilities and tasks which correspond less and less to the traditional functions of public administration. If, consequently, the exception contained in Article 48 were extended to all employment where such responsibilities are assumed and such tasks carried out, the EC Treaty would cease to be applied to a large number of workers. Worse still, significant differences in treatment would emerge as between Member States, given that all intervene in different ways and to varying degrees in their respective economics.

---

[45] Case 131/79 *R v Secretary of State for Home Affairs, ex parte Mario Santillo* [1980] ECR 1585.
[46] Case 98/79 *Josette Pecastaing v Belgium* [1980] ECR 691.

That said, it should be stressed that the case law of the Court has been unable to overcome, except to a modest extent and only in relation to the lower and middle levels of employment (nursing staff, railway workers, university researchers, secondary level teachers etc.), the resistance on the part of Member States to the employment of foreigners in public administration. This resistance, however, is hardly surprising if one takes account of the widespread view that the functioning of the public service is an exercise of full state sovereignty, and if one bears in mind the importance, particularly in times of high unemployment, of maintaining an adequate reserve of places. Moreover, the practice of reserving public administration posts for nationals is imposed in some Member States (Belgium, France, Italy, the Netherlands) by the constitution. More generally, this has its roots in xenophobic sentiments which may not be evident on the surface but undoubtedly exist at all levels of national bureaucracy.

The above factors explain why the Commission proposed some years ago to develop Article 48(4) by means of a directive. There was serious doubt about such a proposal, including the view that Member States would take advantage of it to restrict the right of movement and deprive the decided case law of its full effect. The principal danger in a possible legislative intervention is different, namely the ossification of a process which, since it is linked to the objective of political union of the Member States, should be allowed to continue in as unrestricted a manner as possible. Thus, it is preferable that the matter should be entrusted to the Court of Justice and that the political organs of the Community strive towards the creation of a "citizens Europe" by establishing an area free of borders in which all Community nationals, and not only workers and providers of services, may be able to circulate freely.

9

The New Frontiers of Sex Equality
Law in the European Union

I. INTRODUCTION

IT WAS A commonplace in the past to observe that the tasks and activities which the EEC had set for itself in recitals 2, 3 and 5 of the Preamble, Articles 2, 3 and Title VIII of the EC Treaty,[1] lacked any autonomy with regard to the dominant object of that Treaty, namely the economic integration of the Member States through the establishment of a common market based on the free movement of the factors of production and undistorted competition. True, the principles of equality and social justice, at least in the shallow form in which they appeared in those provisions, displayed a certain potential for normative and judicial use, but they both appeared encompassed in, and functional to, this economic end.

The background to the inclusion of Article 119, establishing the principle that men and women should receive equal pay for equal work, provides a particularly good example of the subordinate status of the original EC Treaty's social provisions. Drafted "with an eye toward preventing the exploitation of lower paid female labour by competing nations",[2] Article 119 was clearly intended to avoid the sort of distortions of competition between the participating Member States which might have resulted from their widely divergent wage differentials.[3] Nevertheless, although the economic rationale for the hastily cobbled

---

[1] *Inter alia*, securing a high level of employment and social protection, raising the standard of living and quality of life of the peoples of Europe and ensuring equal pay without discrimination based on sex.

[2] C.L. Claussen, "Incorporating Women's Reality into Legal Neutrality in the EC: The Sex Segregation of Labor and the Work-Family Nexus" (1991) 82 *Law and Policy in International Business* 787–813, at 787.

[3] The Spaak report of the Intergovernmental Committee created by the Messina Conference published on 21 April 1956, identified working conditions, including the relation between the wages of men and women, as a factor capable of distorting certain branches of economic activity. See further Ohlin, "Social Aspects of European Economic Co-operation: Report by a Group of Experts" (1956) 102 *International Labour Review* 99–123, discussed in detail in C. Barnard, "The Economic Objectives of Article 119" in T. Hervey and D. O'Keeffe, (eds.), *Sex Equality Law in the European Union* (John Wiley & Sons, 1996), pp. 321–334, at p. 322; R.A. Elman, "The EU and Women: Virtual Equality" in P.-H. Laurent and M. Maresceau (eds.), *The State of the European Union. Deepening and Widening*, Volume 4 (Lynne Rienner Publishers, 1998), pp. 225–239, at p. 226; G. De Búrca, "The Role of Equality in EC Law" in A. Dashwood and S. O'Leary (eds.), *The Principle of Equal Treatment in European Community Law* (Sweet & Maxwell, London, 1997), pp. 13–34, at p. 27; and C. Hoskyns, *Integrating Gender. Women, Law and Politics in the European Union* (Verso,

together Franco-German compromise which culminated in the adoption of Article 119 of the EC Treaty was unmistakable, the exact nature of the legal obligation which that provision entailed remained unclear.[4]

Over forty years later, few if any would argue that Article 119 remains ancillary to the predominantly economic objectives of the European Community. Quite apart from the judicial transformation which that provision and its legislative progeny[5] have experienced, the progressive acquisition of new competences by the Community, the increasing powers attributed to its Parliament and its consequent evolution into a political entity endowed with at least some of the features of democratic constitutionalism,[6] has meant that a significant measure of conceptual and operational autonomy has been conferred on the values of equality and social justice. The European Union is still far from being inspired principally by the aim of promoting tolerance, diversity and multiculturalism; but it has arguably turned its back on the days when it was fair to describe its predecessor, the EEC, as being basically about securing market freedoms, the prohibitions of discrimination which it enacted as "largely market-integrating provisions"[7] and its citizens as "market citizens"[8] or, more bluntly, as simple "units of a production factor".[9]

The cases which have come before the Court, in the main via Article 177 references from national courts, have proved the essential vehicles in the transformation of Article 119 from a modestly conceived provision designed to prevent competitive disadvantage and social dumping to an integral part of one of the most fundamental principles of the EU's constitutional code.[10] The purpose of

1996), pp. 52–57. Barnard reports that at the time the EC Treaty was signed, the French had a wage differential of just 7 per cent compared to between 20–40 per cent in the Netherlands and Italy.

[4] Barnard (1996), *supra* n. 3, at pp. 323–325. The French and German governments of the day had disagreed about the extent to which the new Treaty should intervene in matters governed by national labour and social legislation. This disagreement has resurfaced at regular intervals between different Member States throughout the course of the integration project.

[5] See, in particular, Council Directive 75/117/EEC of 10 February 1975 on the approximation of the laws of the Member States on the principle of equal pay for men and women, OJ 1975 L 45, p. 19; Council Directive 76/207/EEC of 9 February 1976 on the implementation of the principle of equal treatment for men and women as regards access to employment, vocational training and promotion, and working conditions, OJ 1976 L 39, p. 40; and Council Directive 79/7/EEC of 19 December 1978 on the progressive implementation of the principles of equal treatment for men and women in matters of social security, OJ 1979 L 6, p. 24.

[6] See further G.F. Mancini, "Europe: the Case for Statehood" (1998) 4 *European Law Journal* 29–42 and Chapter 4.

[7] De Búrca, *supra* n. 3, at p. 27.

[8] See generally M. Everson, "The Legacy of the Market Citizen" in J. Shaw and G. More (eds.), *New Legal Dynamics of European Union* (Clarendon Press, 1995), pp. 73–90.

[9] G.F. Mancini, "The Making of a Constitution for Europe" (1989) 26 *Common Market Law Review* 595, at 596 and Chapter 1. See also the decisions of the Court of Justice in Case C-85/96 *Martínez Sala v Freistaat Bayern* [1998] ECR I-2691 and Case C-274/96 *Criminal Proceedings against Horst Otto Bickel and Ulrich Franz* [1998] ECR I-7637, which reveal the extent of the rights that Member State nationals can derive from Articles 8 and 8a EC.

[10] Elman, *supra* n. 3, at p. 227, argues that the Court's enlightened position concerning sex discrimination owes itself both to the mobilization of women in favour of equal rights and to a realization by the Court that a more interventionist posture would enhance its own prestige. Regarding

this Chapter is to chart some of the more recent ups and downs in the jurisprudence of the Court of Justice on the scope, meaning and consequences of EC sex equality law. Particular attention is paid to three of the most controversial issues discussed by the Court this decade—the rights, benefits and protection afforded pregnant workers, the compatibility of national affirmative action programmes with Community law and the extension of the prohibition of discrimination on grounds of sex to transsexuals and homosexuals.

While the Court has done much to breathe life into Article 119 and EC sex discrimination legislation generally, there seems to be a growing perception of the Court's recent decisions as a desertion of its early courageous stance.[11] In this as in other fields of Community law, traces of the economic mantle which enveloped the original EC Treaty are often detected in its decisions, as are tensions between the dual economic/social purposes of Article 119 first identified by the Court in *Defrenne II*.[12] The temporal limitation in *Barber*, the distinction between pregnancy and pregnancy-related illnesses or indeed the endorsement of national procedural limitations in sex discrimination claims are viewed as examples of the Court seeking to reconcile the economic interests of employers and society at large and the rights of disadvantaged groups.

Yet it is arguable that the criticisms levelled at the Court sometimes overlook the constraints which stem from use of the principle of equal treatment/nondiscrimination itself. The latter can undoubtedly act as both an indispensable shield and sword in the hands of those litigants who seek to vindicate rights which Community law has conferred on them; but it can also prove either an unwieldy and inappropriate instrument in those cases where no straightforward comparator exists,[13] or an insufficient basis for an applicant to succeed in other cases where an additional leap of faith from the Court is required regarding the scope of Community law.[14] In more recent and novel cases in which applicants

the latter see also H. Rasmussen, "Anti-Sex Discrimination and the Court", *The European Court of Justice* (Gadjura, 1997/8), ch. 7, pp. 205–236, at pp. 234–235.

[11] See, for example, E. Ellis, "Recent Developments in EC Sex Equality Law" (1998) 35 *CMLRev*. 379–408, at 379, where she states that the Court has lost sight of the objectives of the legislation and is operating as a drag on the system; and G. More, "Equality of Treatment in EC Law: the Limits of Market Equality" in A. Bottomley (ed.), *Feminist Perspectives on the Foundational Subjects of Law* (Cavendish, 1996), pp. 261–278, at pp. 274–275.

[12] Case 43/75 *Gabrielle Defrenne v Société anonyme belge de navigation aérienne Sabena* [1976] ECR 455.

[13] See L.M. Finley, "Transcending Equality Theory: A Way Out of the Maternity and the Workplace Debate" (1986) 86 *Columbia Law Review* 1118–1182, at 1181: "equality analysis . . . is fundamentally flawed as a means for dealing with the systemic and more subtle gender subordination that we must confront now that the easy cases have been won . . . [Equality] is particularly illsuited for issues of gender differences that appear biologically based, such as childbearing, because it is predicated on a search for sameness".

[14] See also C. Barnard, "The Principle of Equality in the Community Context: *P, Grant, Kalanke* and *Marschall*: Four Uneasy Bedfellows?" (1998) 57 *Cambridge Law Journal* 352–373, at 361, where she suggests that the structure of Community law—a non-discrimination model with a short exhaustive list of prohibited grounds—has meant that the Court has been reluctant to embrace some of the broader principles of equality developed in other jurisdictions; and H. Fenwick, "From Formal to Substantive Equality: the Place of Affirmative Action in EU Sex Equality Law" (1998) 4

have sought protection or asserted rights on the basis of Article 119 and the relevant Directives, the Court has been confronted with what is essentially a conflict between equality and difference.[15] When the Court has resorted to alternative means to vindicate the rights of complainants, most notably with reference to the general principles of law and fundamental rights which it is bound to protect, the results have sometimes been spectacular. Expecting the Court always to rule with reference to this technique and in a fashion which could be regarded as an expansion of the frontiers of EC law is, however, unrealistic. Since the principle of non-discrimination or equal treatment alone has failed to fulfil the expectations which many designed for it, the time has therefore come to think of other means to protect disadvantaged groups, while avoiding the marginalization which those opposed to special protection most fear.[16]

2. FORMAL VERSUS SUBSTANTIVE EQUALITY

The merits and weaknesses of substantive as distinct from formal equality are generally at the heart of the discussion in academic literature on sexual inequality and its redress. The European Union has proved to be no exception in this regard.[17] The Court of Justice is seen by most commentators, not without regret or criticism, as having favoured a formal understanding of the principle of equality whereby like is treated strictly as like, with the resulting assumption that women must in all relevant respects be like men in order to be equally treated.[18] One of the results of this approach is said to be that, whereas a few women may gain access to the preconditions necessary to assert equality on male terms, the majority do not. In addition, it has been observed that, by focusing on formal equality, the Court may be depriving women of their "traditional" roles while not actually ensuring effective equal treatment.[19] In the same vein, judgments of the Court have been criticized for permitting the removal of a

European Public Law 507–516, at 510, who deals with the constraints imposed by the objectives of the internal market project.

[15] See, in the specific context of pregnancy, S. Fredman, "A Difference with Distinction: Pregnancy and Parenthood Reassessed" (1994) 110 *Law Quarterly Review* 106–123.

[16] For discussion of this debate in the specific context of pregnancy rights see J. Sohrab, "Avoiding the 'Exquisite Trap': A Critical Look at the Equal Treatment/Special Treatment Debate in Law" (1993) 1 *Feminist Legal Studies* 141–162, where the author argues at 159 that: "The perceived necessity of making a choice between equal or special treatment is a false choice. In some areas equal rights are necessary, while in others it is gender-specific rights that are necessary, for instance in pregnancy. Neither approach is, nor should be, the exclusive 'answer' or strategy or claim, and arguing over substantive equality by opposing equal with special and vice-versa is at best redundant and at worst a costly distraction".

[17] See, for example, in the particular context of affirmative action, C. Barnard and T. Hervey, "Softening the approach to quotas: positive action after *Marschall*" (1998) 20 *Journal of Social Welfare and Family Law* 333–352; or Fenwick, *supra* n. 14.

[18] See, for example, T. Hervey and J. Shaw, "Women, Work and Care: Women's Dual Role and Double Burden in EC Sex Equality Law" (1998) 8 *Journal of European Social Policy* 43–63, at 48; and Fenwick, *supra* n. 14.

[19] See Sohrab, *supra* n. 16, at 148.

number of the privileges enjoyed by women in the name of equality—the age at which women may receive their pensions, for example, has been moved from 60 to 65, leading to a levelling down of standards rather than to an improvement of the position of female employees.[20]

It is undoubtedly true that a purely formalistic approach to equality and a reliance on male comparators in an employment market which has been structured by and, in modern times at least, for men, will not succeed in many if not most cases in neutralizing those factors which have traditionally led to the disadvantaging of women. Nevertheless, there is a certain degree of inconsistency involved in criticisms of this sort of levelling down. After all, maintaining women's retirement privileges could also be regarded as, on the one hand, inconsistent with their greater life expectancy and, on the other, the result of stereotypes about the "weaker" sex and the source of competitive disadvantage.[21] Indeed, at the origin of one of the many important jurisprudential developments in EC law was precisely the refusal by a female worker who had reached the age set for female retirement to accept that she could not work as long as her male colleagues.[22]

Furthermore, although intense competition and long and rigid working hours may have been largely male creations,[23] it seems short-sighted to view the demands which employers place on the modern workplace as purely male-orientated.[24] As one commentator has remarked, "[T]he expectation that the incorporation of women within capitalist labour markets, replete with intrinsic economic and social disparities, facilitates sexual equality is riddled with irony".[25] The male norm—in Weberian terms an "Idealtypus"—who is conceived as independent, unconnected to others and abstracted from the messy realities of family responsibilities etc., also sits uneasily with the increasingly large sections of the population, male and female, either out of work or in precarious employment relationships and therefore excluded from the benefits

[20] See, for example, Barnard, *supra* n. 14, at 373, where she discusses Case C-408/92 *Constance Christina Ellen Smith* v *Avdel Systems Ltd*. [1994] ECR I-4435.

[21] In the former respect see Case C-9/91 *R* v *Secretary of State for Social Security, ex parte Equal Opportunities Commission* [1992] ECR I-4297; and in the latter, A. Peters, "The Many Meanings of Equality and Positive Action in Favour of Women Under EC Law—A Conceptual Analysis" (1996) 2 *European Law Journal* 177–196, at 180 and 187.

[22] See Case 152/84 *M.H. Marshall* v *Southampton and South-West Hampshire Area Health Authority* [1986] ECR 723.

[23] See in this respect K. Abrams, "Gender Discrimination and the Transformation of Workplace Norms" (1989) 42 *Vanderbilt Law Review* 1183, at 1222, who argues that the demarcation of work and family exists because the workplace was built by and around men and men's lack of child-rearing responsibilities meant that employers could structure jobs to demand extensive, uncompromised commitment. Fredman (1994), *supra* n. 15, at 107, traces the widespread acceptance in the United Kingdom of the ideology of maternity and domesticity to the end of the nineteenth century. Although the man's wage was rarely truly sufficient to support a family, with the result that most working class women had to find some form of paid work, the effect of the ideology was that the workplace was not required to accomodate pregnancy or childcare.

[24] See Hervey and Shaw, *supra* n. 18, at 48.

[25] See Elman, *supra* n. 3, at p. 234.

which it is in the free market's financial interests to bestow on those willing or forced to accept exacting and inflexible working patterns.[26]

This is not to suggest that courts should ignore either the realities or causes of typically lower paid female work, women's often a-typical employment status or the segregated nature of the labour markets into which they are frequently forced. In the absence of legislation, litigants will be eager to challenge judicially the notion of a natural or pre-ordained line dividing work and family and the effects which this demarcation has on the organisation of the workplace and working time.[27] However, these are not only gender issues; *mutatis mutandis*, they are also, if not more so, ones that concern race, class and the effects of mature capitalism.[28] It is difficult and indeed controversial for any Court to engage in social engineering; for a Court whose "domestic" nature is still challenged[29] and whose jurisprudence has at times been the subject of threats and limitations it must be accepted as doubly so.

In contrast to formal equality, substantive equality (referred to as the "anti-subjugation" or "antisubordination" principle by some American constitutional lawyers)[30] rejects the male norm and seeks to situate notions of equality in the context of women's historically inferior status and position of disadvantage.[31] It was to a substantive notion of equality that the Court was aspiring in *Hellmut Marschall* v *Land Nordrhein-Westfalen* when it accepted that "even where male and female candidates are equally qualified, male candidates tend to be promoted in preference to female candidates particularly because of prejudices and stereotypes concerning the role and capacities of women in working life and the

---

[26] See also Sohrab, *supra* n. 16, at 159: "The male standard may in fact hide a liberal capitalist economic standard, and so whichever strategy feminists pursue, if capitalist concerns dominate the policy process then capitalist needs are likely to win out". Note, however, that Eurostat's seasonally adjusted unemployment rates regularly reveal that more women than men are unemployed. See further S. Vousden, "Gender, exclusion and governance by guideline" (1998) 4 *Journal of Social Welfare and Family Law* 468–479 on the adoption of measures to combat women's exclusion from the labour market.

[27] Claussen, *supra* n. 2, at 800, argues that popular conception of gender roles, social responsibilities and family life affect the dynamics of the workplace influencing the hierarchies and power relations which develop within it. Thus, in Case 184/83 *Ulrich Hofmann* v *Barmer Ersatzkasse* [1984] ECR 3047, having recognized that Directive 76/207 is designed to implement the principle of equal treatment for men and women as regards *inter alia* working conditions, the Court emphasized at para. 24 that "the directive is not designed to settle questions concerned with the organisation of the family or to alter the division of responsibility between parents". The Court's narrow appraisal of the objectives of Directive 76/207 meant that it was seen as perpetuating a "separate spheres" approach to work and care, with women falling within the category of care-givers. See Hervey and Shaw, *supra* n. 18, at 50. See also Case C-218/98 *Oumar Dabo Abdoulaye and others* v *Régie nationale des usines Renault SA*, judgment of the Court of 16 September 1999, where the applicants unsuccessfully challenged as discriminatory and contrary to Article 119 EC the granting of a benefit to female workers on maternity leave to the exclusion of fathers.

[28] Claussen, *supra* n. 2, at 801.

[29] See G.F. Mancini, "A Case Study of the Court of Justice of the European Communities" in P. Yessiou-Faltsi, (ed.), *The Role of the Supreme Courts at the National and International Level* (Sakkoulas Publications, 1998), pp. 421–452, at p. 422 and Chapter 12.

[30] See O. Fiss, "The Immigrant as Pariah" (1998) 23 *Boston Review* 4–7, at 5–6.

[31] See generally C.A. MacKinnon, "Reflections on Sex Equality Under Law" (1991) 100 *Yale Law Journal* 1281–1328; and, in the specific context of the EU, Hervey and Shaw, *supra* n. 18, at 48.

fear, for example, that women will interrupt their careers more frequently, that owing to household and family duties they will be less flexible in their working hours, or that they will be absent from work more frequently because of pregnancy, childbirth and breastfeeding".[32] Thus women's different situation—the differences being a result of biological, social, economic, cultural and historic factors which do not affect men in the same way, if at all—is taken into consideration.

According to Hervey and Shaw, a substantive approach to equality is also context-specific, meaning that the notion of what is required in a particular case is modifiable depending upon the current structures which may operate to women's detriment.[33] But as *Marschall* demonstrates, if the Court is criticized for its overly formal approach, the Court Reports are not without examples of such a substantive approach to equal treatment either. The Court's case law on indirect discrimination bespeaks a substantive approach,[34] as does the kernel of its pregnancy jurisprudence. In one of its most recent decisions in the latter field, for example, not only did the Court hold that the exercise of the rights conferred on women in conformity with Article 2(3) of Directive 76/207 cannot be the object of unfavourable treatment regarding access to employment or their working conditions, but it candidly added that "the result pursued by the Directive is substantive, not formal, equality".[35]

3. PREGNANCY AND THE WORKPLACE

Much of the criticism levelled at the formal approach to equality concerns the preponderant role given the male norm; a comparator which fails to take account of the considerations which often disadvantage female workers *vis-à-vis* their male colleagues—first and foremost their role as child-bearers, thereafter traditional divisions of responsibility in child-rearing and the partition of household duties[36] and even preconceptions about the capabilities of female workers. It is a norm, in other words, which overlooks women's difference, whether physiological or social. Thus, "[I]n an employment market arranged around the assumption of constant availability for work of employees, with no career breaks, or parental duties, women employees who have children (only the

---

[32] Case C-409/95 [1997] ECR I-6363, para. 29. More argues, however, that the Court's shift to a substantive conception of equality in this case is only partial, see G. More, annotation of Case C-409/95 *Hellmut Marschall v Land Nordrhein-Westfalen*, forthcoming *CMLRev*.

[33] Hervey and Shaw, *supra* n. 18, at 49.

[34] See also L. Senden, "Positive Action in the European Union Put to the Test. A Negative Score?" (1996) 3 *Maastricht Journal of International and Comparative Law* 146, at 158–159.

[35] Case C-136/95 *Caisse nationale d'assurance vieillesse des travailleurs salariés* v *Evelyne Thibault* [1998] ECR I-2011, para. 26. See also Directive 79/7, which allows Member States to adopt specific provisions for women to remove existing instances of unequal treatment.

[36] Not surprisingly Hervey and Shaw, *supra* n. 18, at 50, see the work/care divide as the inescapable subtext or backdrop to the vexed issue of sex equality in the labour market.

women, not the men) are perceived as more costly employees since, first, the woman will be unavailable for work during maternity leave, and, second, there is no guarantee for the employer that the woman will return to work after the child is born".[37]

Unlike the United States Supreme Court, a jurisdiction often lauded for its record in equal protection, the Court of Justice chose, at the first opportunity, not to apply a comparator or seek a male norm when determining whether the dismissal or refusal to employ pregnant employees was discriminatory. Whereas the Supreme Court had originally held that distinctions concerning pregnancy are not based on sex because the group of non-pregnant persons consists of members of both sexes,[38] the European Court in *Dekker* decided that since only women can be refused employment on grounds of pregnancy, such a refusal constitutes direct discrimination on grounds of sex.[39] In reaching this conclusion the Court emphasized that such discrimination cannot be justified in terms of the financial loss which an employer might suffer during the maternity leave and held that the fact that there were no male candidates for the job (with the result that there was no male comparator in the instant case) did not affect its answer.[40] This conclusion was confirmed in *Webb* v *EMO Air Cargo (UK) Ltd*,[41] a case in which a female employee absent from work due to a pregnancy-related illness had been dismissed. In concluding that this dismissal constituted direct discrimination under EC law, the Court held that "there can be no question of comparing the situation of a woman who finds herself incapable, by reason of pregnancy discovered shortly after the conclusion of the employment contract, of performing the task for which she was recruited with that of a man similarly incapable for medical or other reasons". In other words, "pregnancy is not in any way comparable with a pathological condition".[42]

While the Court's jettisoning of the need for a pregnant complainant to point to a comparator has been praised by some for having "eschewed the minefield

---

[37] See in this respect H. Fenwick and T. Hervey, "Sex Equality in the Single Market: new directions for the European Court of Justice" (1995) 32 *CMLRev.* 443–470, at 443–447; and para. 29 of the decision in Case C-409/95 *Marschall*, cited *supra* n. 32.

[38] See *Geduldig* v *Aiello*, 417 US 484 (1974) and *General Electric Co.* v *Gilbert*, 429 US 125 (1976). See also *Bliss* [1978] 6 WWR 711, a decision of the Supreme Court of Canada prior to the adoption of the Charter of Rights and Freedoms. In the United Kingdom the Industrial Tribunal in *Turley* v *Allders Stores* [1980] IRLR 4 held that dismissal by reason of pregnancy was incapable, as a matter of law, of amounting to sex discrimination because a man can never be dismissed on the same ground.

[39] Case C-177/88 *Elisabeth Johanna Pacifica Dekker* v *Stichting Vormingscentrum voor Jong Volwassenen (VJV-Centrum) Plus* [1990] ECR I-3941, para. 12.

[40] *Ibid.*, paras 12 and 17. Note that the American and Canadian precedents which held that there was no sex discrimination in these circumstances have since been overridden: see s. 701(k) of the Civil Rights Act, added by way of amendment in 1978 and *Brooks* v *Canada Safeway Ltd* [1989] 1 SCR 1219. The approach of courts in the United Kingdom seemed to change in *Hayes* v *Malleable* [1985] IRLR 367, where the Employment Appeal Tribunal reasoned that it was not the pregnancy as such which gave rise to dismissal but the consequences of pregnancy and it therefore compared a pregnant employee with a male employee suffering a long-term illness.

[41] Case C-32/93 [1994] ECR I-3567.

[42] *Ibid.*, at paras 24–25.

of the comparative approach to pregnancy" and adopted a substantive test of equality,[43] it has been the object of considerable criticism in other quarters. Ellis, for example, argues that "an element of comparability is important to the component of adverse impact" which is at the heart of anti-discrimination law. If direct discrimination were defined simply as "nasty treatment" on the ground of sex, enormous discretion would be left in the hands of persistently male courts and tribunals to decide what is to the detriment or advantage of complainants, the majority of whom are female.[44] While the same author recognizes that pregnancy is the one truly exceptional situation affecting women and not men, she urges the Court to measure the treatment received by pregnant complainants by means of a comparison with the treatment received or receivable by a member of the opposite sex, placed in broadly the same circumstances as the complainant. Yet it is difficult to see where a Court would begin to find such a comparator. If the female sex's unique biological capacity to bear children and society's traditional assumption that women are more apt to rear them are at the heart of much of the less advantageous treatment which women receive in the labour market, surely no Court should ignore this fact by searching for comparable situations affecting men which do not in reality exist. Perhaps we should not lose sight of the fact that admitting that men and women are different is not tantamount to legitimating discriminatory treatment.[45]

A more difficult aspect of the Court's jurisprudence in this field is that some of the consequences of pregnancy, in particular illnesses leading to absences from work or medical advice requiring the same, have been separated from the pregnancy itself and a male comparator has been reintroduced in order to assess how a man in a similar situation would have been treated. The comparator becomes relevant again—it seems—because it is the effects of pregnancy rather than the pregnancy itself which are at issue.

Thus, in *Hertz*,[46] a case decided on the same day as *Dekker*, the Court held that beyond the period of maternity leave, any illness, even if it is a consequence of the pregnancy, is to be treated as sex-neutral, since both men and women could become ill in the ordinary course of events. The Opinion of Advocate General Darmon in that case is particularly instructive as regards the difficulties facing the Court. He confessed to having been "tempted to propose a solution whereby medical conditions which were directly, definitely and preponderantly due to pregnancy or confinement would enjoy a sort of 'immunity', in the sense that the principle of equality of treatment would restrain the employer from

---

[43] See, for example, Hervey and Shaw, *supra* n. 18, at 51.

[44] See E. Ellis, "The Definition of Discrimination in European Community Sex Equality Law" (1994) 19 *ELRev.* 563–580, at 571; and R. Wintemute, "When is Pregnancy Discrimination Indirect Sex Discrimination?" (1998) 27 *Industrial Law Journal* 23–36.

[45] Although the Court's decision in Case C-342/93 *Gillespie v Northern Health and Social Services Board* [1996] ECR I-475 and its case law on pregnancy-related illnesses will no doubt have given rise to cause for concern.

[46] Case C-179/88 *Handels- og Kontorfunktionærernes Forbund i Danmark v Dansk Arbejdsgiverforening ("Hertz")* [1990] ECR I-3979.

dismissing his employee for a reasonable period after the event in question".[47] However, he resisted this temptation on the grounds that Community law as it stands does not envisage such a requirement[48] and that this ostensibly attractive expedient would be sure to produce a number of negative effects which it would be hard to remedy: namely an obligation on employers to maintain a female employee unable to work for several years after pregnancy while contributing towards the social security benefits payable to her, the difficulties which national courts and employers would face in defining the circumstances meriting protection and the risk that a device protecting a few women affected by severe post-natal problems might jeopardize the chances of all women wishing to enter the labour market.[49] Thus, once a female worker has exhausted her entitlement to the various types of maternity leave, her periods of absence for reasons of sickness, even if those reasons can be traced back to pregnancy or confinement, cannot be attributed to the normal risks of maternity and must accordingly be viewed in the same light as the absences of any other worker, unless the national legislature provides special protection.[50]

The Court has therefore chosen to apply a substantive test as regards pregnancy itself and a comparative test as regards those consequences of pregnancy leading to illness and absence from work which continue after the protected period. In its decision in *Brown*, however, the Court introduced a variation to this dual approach, holding that the principle of non-discrimination requires protection of pregnant workers throughout the period of pregnancy.[51] Those confused by what could be regarded as the Court's "multi-speed" approach to pregnant workers are to be forgiven. Dismissal for absences due to pregnancy-related illnesses which manifest themselves or continue after the maternity leave comes to an end is not discriminatory since sick male workers can be discharged in similar circumstances (*Hertz*), while dismissal for absences due to pregnancy-related illnesses which manifest themselves during the pregnancy itself is "linked to the occurrence of risks inherent in pregnancy and must therefore be regarded as essentially based on the fact of pregnancy" (*Brown*). The upshot of this jurisprudence—admittedly a questionable one—is that only the latter type of dismissal is regarded as constituting direct discrimination on grounds of sex,

---

[47] See his joint Opinion in Cases C-177/88 *Dekker, supra* n. 39 and C-179/88 *Hertz, supra* n. 46, para. 43.

[48] Article 2(3) of the Equal Treatment Directive 76/207 leaves to the Member States the task of adopting appropriate provisions concerning the protection of women, particularly, as regards pregnancy and maternity.

[49] Opinion of Advocate General Darmon, paras. 45–47.

[50] Case C-179/88 *Hertz, supra* n. 46, para. 48 of the Opinion and para. 16 of the decision.

[51] Case C-394/96 *Mary Brown v Rentokil Ltd.* [1998] ECR I-4185, para. 24. In reaching this conclusion the Court expressly departed from a previous decision of its sixth chamber (at para. 27) which, in the light of Case C-179/88 *Hertz*, had not differentiated between pre and post-confinement illnesses, see Case C-400/95 *Handels- og Kontorfunktionærernes Forbund i Danmark v Dansk Handel & Service ("Larsson")* [1997] ECR I-2757, para. 23. For an excellent commentary on the pitfalls involved in the use of the principle of non-discrimination in pregnancy cases see E. Ellis, annotation of Case C-394/96 *Brown v Rentokil Ltd* (1999) 36 *CMLRev.* 625–633.

despite the fact that the absence from work in both cases is attributable to pregnancy.

Since it is difficult to imagine male workers suffering from the numerous complications to which pregnancy may give rise and which the Court's Reports most genteelly decline to discuss, the distinction drawn in *Hertz* and *Brown* between pre and post-confinement pregnancy-related illnesses should probably be attributed to the utilitarian concerns which Advocate General Darmon vocalized some years before in *Hertz*. Yet the Court has been quick on other occasions to reject economic justifications for the treatment of pregnant workers. In *Pedersen*,[52] for example, the pregnant applicants were deprived, before the beginning of their maternity leave, of their full pay when their incapacity for work was the result of a pathological condition connected with pregnancy. The Court explicitly stated that this discrimination cannot be justified by the aim of sharing the risks and economic costs connected with pregnancy between the pregnant worker, the employer and society as a whole. That goal, in the view of the Court, cannot be regarded as an objective factor unrelated to any discrimination based on sex within the meaning of the Court's case law.

This complex, differentiated judicial approach to the protection of pregnant workers was perhaps to be expected: determining how the workplace is to deal with pregnancy and home-care is highly problematic and relying on the principle of equal treatment as a means to distribute the burden was always likely to prove insufficient. On the one hand, as Fredman argues, formal or symmetrical equal treatment simply requires consistency of treatment between men and women, with the result that women's rights are entirely dependent on the extent to which comparable rights are afforded to comparable men. On the other, equal treatment tends to place the social cost of pregnancy and child-bearing on individual employers or, in the alternative, if and when the action of employers is found to be justified, on those female workers who bear children. Nowhere is the State factored into the equation as a third, yet implicated party to which costs can be spread.[53]

Whether or not Directive 92/85 on the introduction of measures to encourage improvements in the safety and health at work of pregnant workers and workers who have recently given birth or are breastfeeding[54] acknowledges the social value of pregnancy and parenthood, it certainly represents a departure from the equality-difference rationale which has pervaded much of the Court's case law.

---

[52] See Case C-66/96 *Handels- og Kontorfunktionærernes Forbund i Danmark v Fællesforeningen for Danmarks Brugsforeninger and Dansk Tandlægeforening and Kristelig Funktionær-Organisation v Dansk Handel & Service* ("*Pedersen*") [1998] ECR I-7327, paras 35 and 40.

[53] See Fredman, *supra* n. 15, at 110–111. See also Finley, *supra* n. 13; and Hervey and Shaw, *supra* n. 18, at 61, who argue that, as EC law stands, care-giving work is conceived as some form of privatized activity, the burden of which falls primarily on women. Note that in tort law, the extension of negligence is often presented as a loss-spreading device given that manufacturers either insure themselves or raise prices, thereby passing on costs to society at large (thanks are due to Leo Flynn for this comment).

[54] OJ L 348, p. 1.

Articles 3–6 of the same Directive deal with the hazards (chemical, physical, biological) which may be encountered by pregnant workers or those who have recently given birth, while Article 7 covers night work. Pursuant to Article 8, all pregnant workers are entitled to a continuous period of maternity leave of at least fourteen weeks. Article 10, codifying the jurisprudence of the Court in *Dekker*, provides that it is unlawful to dismiss a pregnant worker from the beginning of pregnancy until the end of their statutory maternity leave.[55] Thus, the Community legislator has finally opted for a special protection regime of sorts, thereby taking some pressure off the Court and relieving it of the need to wrestle with equal treatment/non-discrimination tools which are at its disposal in an area where comparisons of male and female are often, if not always, untenable.

It remains to be seen, of course, whether Directive 92/85 is any more successful than the principle of equal treatment in protecting pregnant workers before and after the birth of their children. The legislative history of the Directive reveals to what extent more stringent protection had to be sacrificed on the altar of compromise in order for its adoption to be secured.[56] Rights being only as good as their content[57] and the remedies available to enforce them, the circumscribed nature of the provisions in the final version of the Directive as compared to the original Commission and Parliament proposals underline the obstacles involved in reaching agreement at Community level on what amounts to a considerable alteration in responsibility for social and employment policies. Furthermore, even this special protection instrument is not free from the difficulties which dogged the Court's jurisprudence on this subject in the past. Thus, only mothers benefit from maternity leave pursuant to the Directive and they are entitled during this period to income amounting to no less than the rate of sick pay benefit. Clearly the Directive has not signalled the end of assumptions about the division of employment and child-care responsibilities and use of the sick male employee comparator.

4. GRAPPLING WITH AFFIRMATIVE ACTION

Pursuant to a Bremen statute requiring that, in promotion procedures administered by a public body, women must be given priority if they constitute less than

---

[55] Save in exceptional cases, unconnected with the pregnancy, provided for in the national legislation. Note that Directive 92/85 is not applicable to the type of situation which was at issue in Case C-179/88 *Hertz*, *supra* n. 46. In Case C-400/95 *Larsson*, *supra* n. 51, para. 25, the Court pointed out that Article 10 of Directive 92/85 provided for special protection for women by prohibiting dismissal during the period from the beginning of their pregnancy to the end of their maternity leave, save in exceptional cases unconnected with their condition. In addition, it held that it was clear from the objective of that provision that absence during the protected period, other than for reasons unconnected with the employee's condition, can no longer be taken into account as grounds for subsequent dismissal.

[56] See E. Ellis, "Protection of Pregnancy and Maternity" (1993) 22 *Industrial Law Journal* 63–67.

[57] See Fredman, *supra* n. 15, at 119.

half of the workforce and possess qualifications equal to those of their male competitors, a female candidate with the same qualifications as a male colleague was promoted. Unhappy with this decision, the process which that male candidate, Kalanke, set in motion led to the Court of Justice's first direct shot at affirmative action programmes.[58] He claimed that the promotion decision was contrary to the principle of equality enshrined in the *Grundgesetz* and, on appeal, Germany's Supreme Labour Court, the Bundesarbeitsgericht, although convinced that the Bremen statute did not violate the Basic Law, referred a number of questions to the Court of Justice as regards the compatibility of that statute with the Equal Treatment Directive.

In its decision in *Kalanke*[59]—a ruling which was regarded as embarassingly laconic even by commentators versed in legal cultures for which judicial conciseness is a virtue—the Court of Justice declared that the tie-break provision of the Bremen statute was incompatible with European Community law. It recognized that Article 2(4) of the Equal Treatment Directive permits the enactment of measures which, although discriminatory in appearance, are designed to eliminate or reduce actual instances of inequality which may exist in the reality of social life and hence improve women's ability to compete on the labour market and to pursue a career on an equal footing with men. As a derogation from an individual right laid down in the Directive, however, that provision must be strictly interpreted: it could not therefore be understood as legitimizing national rules which guarantee women absolute and unconditional priority for appointment or promotion, since such measures go beyond the furtherance of equal opportunities and overstep the limits of Article 2(4). In other words, while the legislator may licitly act in their favour by affording them equality of opportunity, it cannot provide female workers with equality of result without unlawfully discriminating against their male competitors. Equality of result—this seemed to be the Court's underlying assumption—is not a goal which can be regulated; rather it is to be achieved in the thick of social relations by exploiting the equal starting points which the law may provide.

The *Kalanke* decision elicited a huge response throughout the Community and indeed beyond, which was for the most part negative, with the Court's performance being subjected to a scathing appraisal in some cases.[60] The most

---

[58] In Case 312/86 *Commission v France* [1998] ECR 6315, the Court simply held, para. 15, that the exception provided for in Article 2(4) of Directive 76/207 is specifically and exclusively designed to allow measures which, although discriminatory in appearance, are in fact intended to eliminate or reduce actual instances of inequality which may result in the reality of social life. Nothing in the papers of that case made it possible, however, to conclude that a general preservation of special rights for women in collective agreements may correspond to the situation envisaged in Article 2(4).

[59] Case C-450/93 *Eckhard Kalanke v Freie Hansestadt Bremen* [1995] ECR I-3051, paras 18–19.

[60] See variously, Peters, *supra* n. 21; S. Moore, "Nothing Positive from the Court" (1996) 21 *ELRev.* 156–161; E. Szyszczak, "Positive Action After *Kalanke*" (1996) 59 *Modern Law Review* 876–883; T. Loenen and A. Veldman, "Preferential Treatment in the Labour Market After *Kalanke*: Some Comparative Perspectives" (1996) *International Journal of Comparative Labour Law and Industrial Relations* 43–53; S. Fredman, "Reversing Discrimination" (1996) 113 *Law Quarterly Review* 575–600; S. Prechal, annotation of Case C-450/93 (1996) 33 *CMLRev.* 1245–1259;

powerful criticisms levelled at the ruling were of a twofold nature. In the first place, the position of the Court was regarded as being at odds with its previous jurisprudence. By proscribing indirect discrimination the Court had already penetrated into the province of substantive equality. Thus, when it had to deal with seemingly sex-neutral classifications between part-time and full-time workers pursuant to which the former, who were preponderantly women, were paid at a lower hourly rate than their full-time colleagues or were excluded from pension schemes or additional pension benefits, its rulings clearly relied on a view of equality as a *collective right* since the unequal treatment is defined by a measure's impact on *groups* and is essentially proved by *statistics*.[61] Having ventured so far, it is arguable that the Court could have easily covered the not too large conceptual distance separating indirect discrimination from the form of discrimination which affirmative action programmes seek to overcome. Quotas for female workers are a case in point. Whether rigid or soft, they are, like the provision impugned in *Kalanke*, "linked" to group membership and they constitute legally differentiated treatment intended to redress factual inequalities and to arrive at equality in fact.[62]

The second line of criticism pointed to the Court's inability to discriminate between discriminations, as it were. One ought perhaps to make allowances for the uneasiness which judges who have delivered dozens of rulings based on notions such as the irrelevance of sex and the invidiousness of its use in the allocation of benefits might feel when admitting that the same use may serve remedial objectives and could on this ground be legitimated.[63] Yet it takes a highly

Senden, *supra* n. 34; L. Charpentier, "L'arrêt *Kalanke*. Expression du discours dualiste de l'égalité" (1996) *Revue trimestrielle de droit européen* 281–303; S. Scarponi, "Pari opportunità e 'Frauenquote' davanti alla Corte di Giustizia" (1995) *Rivista di diritto europeo* 717–737; and L. Calafà, "Le 'quote condizionate' a favore delle donne al vaglio della Corte del Lussemburgo" (1998) Pt.II *Rivista italiana di diritto del lavoro* 214–225. It is interesting to note that, with few exceptions (see, for example, J. Shaw, "Positive Action for Women in Germany: The Use of Legally Binding Quota Systems" in B. Hepple and E. Szyszczak (eds.), *Discrimination: Limits of the Law* (1992) ch. 20, pp. 386–411, at p. 394 and p. 406, although this piece was written prior to *Kalanke*), the literature does not discuss whether affirmative action programmes in Europe or elsewhere have been successful. Furthermore, at least part of the criticism levelled at reliance on a formal and meritocratic approach to equality is due to the fact that it favours the few women who have gained or can gain access to the preconditions necessary to assert equality on male terms (education presumably being one of these factors). It is somewhat ironic, however, that one of the objectives of positive discrimination is precisely to put women in high profile management, professional and public positions in order to encourage other women to persevere and to combat many of the prejudices that have slowed women's progress in the employment market to date. One of the principal goals of positive discrimination has little to do, therefore, with the employment prospects of the low paid, part-time or a-typical female labour whose situation formal equality standards fail to address.

[61] See, *inter alia*, Case 96/80 *J.P. Jenkins* v *Kingsgate (Clothing Productions) Ltd* [1981] ECR 911 or Case 170/84 *Bilka-Kaufhaus GmbH* v *Karin Weber von Hartz* [1986] ECR 1607, discussed in Peters, *supra* n. 21, at 188.

[62] Peters, *supra* n. 21, at 188.

[63] See also in this respect L. Betten and V. Shrubsall, "The Concept of Positive Sex Discrimination in Community Law. Before and After the Treaty of Amsterdam" (1998) *International Journal of Comparative Labour Law* 63–77, at 69, who comment on the disincentive effect which positive discrimination measures may have on an equally qualified male candidate and, indeed, on all who are committed to genuine equal opportunity; and Peters, *supra* n. 21, at 193, who lists efficiency losses,

aseptic view of justice as a value independent of the socio-political context in which it is administered or, more likely, a strong ideological bias (such as, for example, primacy of the individual[64] and of merit or blindness of the state to the disparities between its citizens) not to appreciate the simple fact that what really matters is the purpose of discrimination.[65]

Whatever history assesses the contribution of the Court to have been in this respect, there seems to be little doubt that women are increasingly enjoying important aspects of equality of opportunity in the European Union. As Peters points out, only very few rules which unduly classify according to sex persist in the Member States.[66] However, while national legislation and, at Community level, the Equality Directives, have been useful in combatting individual cases of sex discrimination, some commentators call attention to the fact that they have had no significant impact on the sex segregated labour market or on the promotion of women in professional and public life.[67] In addition, it is notorious that many women continue to earn less than their male counterparts in identical or similar posts and that they still fail to attain senior management positions, the factors (whether projected: stereotypes, role models as exemplified by the unambitious homemaker/ambitious breadwinner polarity—or real: unequal divisions of family responsibilities) which preclude them from piercing the "glass ceiling" being well known.

With this in mind, it could be argued that neutralizing those factors and thus opening the upper career echelons to women, as the Bremen tie-break rule proposed to do, is not invidious. As Ronald Dworkin has argued, a practice or

resentment, reinforcement of the idea that women cannot compete, damage to self-esteem, the danger of tokenism and the assimilation of women into a male world as possible negative effects of positive discrimination.

[64] Regarded by many as characterizing the Court's approach in *Kalanke*, see, for example, Barnard and Hervey, *supra* n. 17, at 335; and Fenwick, *supra* n. 14, at 508–509. See also S. Fredman, "After *Kalanke* and *Marschall*: Affirming Affirmative Action", forthcoming *Cambridge Yearbook of European Legal Studies*, where she argues that a "symmetrical" approach to equality rests on three basic propositions—abstract justice, individualism and state neutrality.

[65] For discussion of the various ideologies vying for position when symmetrical and substantive approaches to equality are applied see Fredman, *supra* n. 60, at 576 *et seq.* and 596 in particular. See also Loenen and Veldman, *supra* n. 60, at 50: "when discussing the legitimacy of preferential treatment, the crucial question is not *whether* the equality clause protects individuals, but *against what* does it protect them".

[66] Peters, *supra* n. 21, at 180. Of the equal treatment cases coming before the Court of Justice nowadays, many concern not whether discrimination (or at least direct discrimination) exists but whether complainants are able to enforce their rights effectively given national procedural rules and limitations: see, for example, Case C-246/96 *Mary Teresa Magorrian and Irene Patricia Cunningham* v *Eastern Health and Social Services Board* [1997] ECR I-7153, or Case C-326/96 B.S. *Levez* v *T.H. Jennings (Harlow Pools) Ltd* [1998] ECR I-7835.

[67] See S. Mazey, "EC Action on Behalf of Women: The Limits of Legislation" (1988) XXVII *Journal of Common Market Studies* 63–84, at 63; Peters, *supra* n. 21, at 180; and Betten and Shrubsall, *supra* n. 63, who point out that although women are now achieving more in key areas of higher education than men, they still are behind in the competition for jobs and even in professions where there is a similar proportion of male and female employees, the top positions are predominantly held by men. This is not, of course, a purely European phenomenon; for an analysis of gender equality in a totally different context see A. Marfording, "Gender Equality Under the Japanese Constitution" (1996) *Verfassung und Recht Übersee* 324–346.

norm is insulting if it makes race or sex a criterion with which to exclude ethnic or female candidates, because it was generated by and signalled contempt. When race or sex are used to bring about a more just or equal society, however, the discrimination, far from being invidious, is benign.[68] Levelling the two forms of the unequal treatment—malign and benign—and inferring from the rejection of the former a duty to condemn the latter, is tantamount, as Justice Stevens put it in his famous dissent in *Adarand* v *Peña*,[69] to disregarding the difference between a "No Trespassing" sign and a welcome mat.

Despite the vehement reaction to the Court's decision in *Kalanke* from a wide range of sources—with a number of feminist groups, national and European parliamentarians, and even some effervescent clergymen, sharing, sometimes with excessive acerbity, the gist of the censures coming from Academe—it would be wrong to suggest that the ruling was out of step with developments elsewhere in the Community and beyond. The Member State governments, including those of Germany and the United Kingdom, which traditionally have made no bones about criticizing the Court's jurisprudence in labour and social matters,[70] held themselves reassuringly aloof. What is more, a few months after *Kalanke*, the United States Supreme Court delivered its widely reported judgment in *Adarand* v *Peña* in which it held that affirmative action schemes must be subject to strict (that is, in practice, fatal) scrutiny. Similarly, the Italian Constitutional Court had set aside a provision which reserved a quota for women on the lists of candidates for municipal and provincial elections and the same fate greeted the attempts by New Labour in the United Kingdom to ensure that more women appeared on the ballot in the 1997 elections.[71] *Kalanke*, in other words, could have been convincingly presented as just one more episode in a world-wide judicial rebellion against the notion that there are "creditor or debtor" races and sexes[72] or, more generally, as further evidence of an eclipse

---

[68] *Taking Rights Seriously* (1987), ch. 9, pp. 223–239. See also Mackinnon, *supra* n. 31, at 1325; and S. Douglas Scott, "Ruling Out Affirmative Action" (1995) *New Law Journal* 1586–1587, at 1587.

[69] *Adarand Constructors Inc.* v *Federico Peña* 515 U.S. 200 (1995).

[70] For example, the response of the German government to the decision of the Court in Case C-120/95 *Nicolas Decker* v *Caisse de maladie des employés privés* and Case C-158/96 *Raymond Kohll* v *Union des caisses de maladie* [1998] ECR I-1831 and I-1931 or the attempt by the United Kingdom to annul the Working Time Directive, Case C-84/94 *United Kingdom* v *Council* [1996] ECR I-5755.

[71] See the decision of the Italian Corte Costituzionale of 12 September 1995, No. 422, *Giurisprudenza costituzionale* 1995, p. 3255 *et seq.*; G. Brunelli, "L'alterazione del concetto di rappresentanza politica: leggi elettorali e 'quote' riservate alle donne" (1994) *Diritto e Società* 545–593; and *Jepson and Dyas-Elliot* v *The Labour Party* [1996] Industrial Relations Law Reports 116, where the Industrial Tribunal held that the refusal of the Labour Party to allow the applicant men to be considered for selection as candidates because the constituencies to which they applied were required to have all-women shortlists was contrary to the Sex Discrimination Act 1986. Any possible justification of the positive discrimination involved on the basis of Article 2(4) of the Equal Treatment Directive 76/207 was excluded since, in accordance with the decision of the Court of Justice in *Kalanke*, that provision could not have intended a total block on one sex. See also decision No. 82–146 DC of the French Conseil Constitutionnel of 18 November 1982, OJ 1982 p. 3475, where a law establishing electoral quotas was deemed to be unconstitutional.

[72] See the concurring opinion of Scalia J in *Adarand*, *supra* n. 69.

being endured by the substantive approach to the issue of positive discrimination.

The Court, however, seized the first opportunity which presented itself to clarify and indeed modify its stance. The opportunity came in the *Marschall* case in the form of a reference from a German administrative court concerning another regional statute whose rules coincided with those of Bremen but for one point: a clause by virtue of which equally qualified female candidates are granted priority in appointment and promotion procedures unless reasons specific to an individual male candidate tilt the balance in his favour. Such a proviso, the Court held, makes all the difference: a tie-break rule mitigated by it is compatible with European Community law.[73]

What should one make of this decision, so close in time and yet so different in outcome to the Court's ruling in *Kalanke*? It will be remembered that in *Kalanke* the Court had disapproved of national provisions conferring on women "absolute and unconditional" priority for appointment or promotion. Several commentators refused to pay any attention whatsoever to these words, while others,[74] in particular the European Commission,[75] saw in them the sterling keystone of the judgment and, possibly, the basis for a different decision if the Court ever happened to scrutinize a quota system which did not preclude the assessment of the particular circumstances of an individual case.[76]

It is suggested that neither of these views is entirely correct. On the one hand, passing over two adjectives as incisive as "absolute" and "unconditional" in a judgment all skin and bone and given by a Court whose reluctance to indulge in *obiter dicta* is proverbial, seems rather careless. On the other, it is impossible not to see that the exclusion of these characteristics in the law of the Land Nordrhein-Westphalen is not enough to explain such an apparent change in the judicial position in less than two years. The decision in *Kalanke* focused almost entirely on the difference between equality of opportunity and equality of result, the former being lawfully pursuable by legislatures and the latter looming on the horizon as a possible issue of societal evolution. Just like the scheme envisaged by the Bremen statute, the quota system anticipated by those who hoped for a different decision in future would have aimed at equality of result. How then could a cryptic and conceptually slender exception, such as the possibility of particular circumstances of an individual case being taken into account, affect their essential affinity?

In view of these considerations, many commentators have assumed that the Court which drafted *Kalanke* was deeply divided, with the result that much soul-searching continued in Kirchberg after that decision was pronounced about the compatibility with Community law of national affirmative action

---

[73] Case C-409/95 *Marschall* v *Land Nordrhein-Westfalen* [1997] ECR I-6363.

[74] See, for example, Schiek, D., "Positive Action in Community Law" (1996) 25 *Industrial Law Journal* 239–246, at 243–244; and Prechal, *supra* n. 60, at 1258.

[75] See the Commission Communication on the *Kalanke* judgment, COM (96) 88.

[76] See Szyszczak, *supra* n. 60, at 882.

programmes.[77] Whether favourably or unfavourably, the tremendous role which interest groups, specifically the women's movement, played in the 1960s and 1970s in putting equal treatment of men and women on the Community agenda has been the subject of considerable comment.[78] It does not seem, therefore, beyond the bounds of possibility that, two or three decades later, the widespread hostile reaction to the *Kalanke* judgment did not pass unnoticed and that close attention was paid to the arguments of those academics, women's groups, Member States and Community institutions which felt that the Court could have ruled, consistently with its previous jurisprudence and the spirit of Community law, to the contrary.

Be that as it may, *Kalanke* was not reversed, which poses the problem of making some sense out of its coexistence, however strident, with *Marschall*, not to mention the rest of the Court's jurisprudence as regards gender equality. In other words, what *is* the doctrine of the Court in this crucial area? Resorting to American conceptual categories, its doctrine might be defined as follows: the Court strictly scrutinizes measures which entail direct discrimination while a more lenient test is applied to indirect discrimination and those forms of affirmative action which provide a tie-break rule in recruitment and promotion procedures. It is impossible to squeeze more than this succinct formula from the case law. The diverse quality of the two criteria which it displays is, however, sufficient evidence that affirmative action programmes are not, after all, undergoing a global eclipse. The eclipse is confined to the USA and is probably rooted in a venerable ideological ground—a mix of egalitarianism and rugged individualism—which the progressive upsurge of the 1960s and the 1970s may have shattered, but which has remained fertile enough to yield new and vigorous crops. In Europe, that ground is much thinner and the crops which it yields seem stunted.[79]

---

[77] See variously Moore, *supra* n. 60, at 161; Senden, *supra* n. 34, at 151; and Betten and Shrubsall, *supra* n. 63, at 64. More, *supra* n. 32, speculates about the effect of the different composition of the Court in *Kalanke* and *Marschall*.

[78] See, for example, Rasmussen, *supra* n. 10, at pp. 208 and 211; Elman, *supra* n. 3, at pp. 227–227; and Hoskyns, *supra* n. 3, at pp. 60–75.

[79] Electoral quotas may prove to be an exception, see *supra* n. 71. Attempts are being made in at least one Member State—France—to make constitutional provision for such quotas. See the debate in the French Senate of 26 January 1999 on the adoption of a draft constitutional law to this effect, OJ 1999 No 4, p. 240, débats parlementaires, Sénat. The survival of Member State positive action programmes is confirmed by the amendment of Article 119 EC by the Amsterdam Treaty. Paragraph 4 now provides that: "With a view to ensuring full equality in practice between men and women in working life, the principle of equal treatment shall not prevent any Member State from maintaining or adopting measures providing for specific advantages in order to make it easier for the underrepresented sex to pursue a vocational activity, or to prevent or compensate for disadvantages in professional careers". It remains to be seen what approach the Court will adopt in further and more detailed preliminary references on the subject of positive discrimination, see Cases C-158/97 *Badeck and others*, OJ 1997 C 199, p. 10; Opinion of the Advocate General of 10 July 1999 on C-407/98 *Abrahamsson and Anderson*, OJ 1999 C 1, p. 10.

5. THE LIMITS OF "SEX" IN EC SEX EQUALITY LAW

Perhaps the most vivid testimony to the Court's contribution to the quest for equality between the sexes has been the eagerness with which the intellectual and political leaders of Europe's other disadvantaged groups, not least lesbians and gay men, have seized the principle of equality as a means to do away with the range of traditional social, cultural and economic rules and notions which affect their constituents. On the hard climb towards greater equality which confronts them, the Union may, as Clapham and Weiler recognized, represent a shortcut, since a legislative or judicial victory within its context has a direct and legally binding effect in all of the Member States, thus making specific campaigns in each of them unnecessary.[80]

To what extent has the Union measured up to these hopes? As far as the Treaties are concerned, steps forward have been taken. Thus, in the wake of pressures brought to bear by the European Parliament, the Commission, numerous non-governmental organizations and, possibly, the delegations of some Member States,[81] the authors of the Amsterdam Treaty inserted Article 6a, which lists "sexual orientation", as distinguished from "sex", among the potentially discriminatory factors which the Council, acting unanimously, is empowered to combat.[82] This is far from being a second-rate success, especially because account is being taken at the Community's constitutional level of the discrimination which lesbians and gay men suffer, as has occurred in South Africa and Canada.[83]

---

[80] See A. Clapham and K. Waldijk (eds.), *Homosexuality: A European Community Issue. Essays on Lesbian and Gay Rights in European Law and Policy*, International Studies in Human Rights, No 26 (Martinus Nijhoff, 1993), at p. 11. See also P. Skidmore, "Sex, Gender and Comparators in Employment and Discrimination" (1997) 26 *Industrial Law Journal* 51–61, at 61.

[81] Certainly the introduction of a general non-discrimination clause received the support of the Reflection Group set up prior to the 1996 IGC.

[82] Article 6a provides that "Without prejudice to the other provisions of this Treaty and within the limits of the powers conferred by it upon the Community, the Council, acting unanimously on a proposal from the Commission and after consulting the European Parliament, may take appropriate action to combat discrimination based on sex, racial or ethnic origin, religion or belief, disability, age or sexual orientation".

[83] Section 15(1) of the Canadian Charter provides that "[E]very individual is equal before and under the law and has the right to equal protection and equal benefit of the law without discrimination and, in particular, without discrimination based on race, national or ethnic origin, color, religion, sex, age or mental or physical ability". The Canadian Supreme Court has held that sexual orientation is an analogous ground of discrimination to those specifically enumerated in s.15(1): see *Egan* v *Canada* [1995] 2 SCR 513 and *Vriend* v *Canada*, decision of the same Court of 2 April 1998. Section 9(3) of the Bill of Rights in the South African Constitution of 1996 provides that "the State may not unfairly discriminate against anyone on one or more grounds, including . . . sexual orientation". In a recent decision in the *M*. case, the Supreme Court of Ontario held that Ontario must extend the definition of "spouse" to include same-sex partners. The Court pointed out that homosexual couples will often form long, lasting, loving and intimate relationships that create financial dependence: "To deny full access to spousal benefits promotes the view that M. and individuals in same-sex relationships generally are less worthy of recognition and protection": reported in the *Financial Times*, 23 May 1999.

In *National Coalition of Gay and Lesbian Equality* v *Minister for Justice*, decision of the South African Supreme Court of 9 October 1998, that Court struck down as unconstitutional certain

It is, however, a success patently marred by the requirement of a unanimous vote in Council for legislation to be adopted to combat discrimination in the fields mentioned. If one recalls the legislative stalling which has accompanied the adoption of much of the Community's legislation on equal treatment, it would be surprising if Member States which until recently differed markedly in their treatment of homosexuals were to agree unanimously on a single Community text prohibiting discrimination, if only because of the economic costs which such a measure might entail for Member States,[84] or the opposition likely to be brought to bear by religious groups.

As for judicial developments, homosexuals, who had been greatly encouraged by the Court's ruling in *P. v S.*,[85] must have been deeply disappointed by its subsequent decision in *Lisa Grant* v *South West Trains*.[86] In *P.*, the Court had broken ground when it held that employment discrimination against transsexuals constitutes direct discrimination incompatible with Article 119 of the EC Treaty. The forceful language of the Court, which stated that "[T]o tolerate such discrimination would be tantamount . . . to a failure to respect the dignity and the freedom to which [transsexuals are] entitled and which the Court has a duty to safeguard" clearly indicated that the decision went beyond a purely economic rationale.[87] In terms of the principle of equal treatment, *P. v S.* is def-

---

legislative provisions establishing a sodomy offence and providing for the consequences of conviction for such an offence. In his concluding remarks, Justice Sachs argued that "[A]lthough the Constitution itself cannot destroy homophobic prejudice it can require the elimination of public institutions which are based on and perpetuate such prejudice. From today a section of the community can feel the equal concern and regard of the Constitution and enjoy lives less threatened, less lonely and more dignified. The law catches up with an evolving social reality". It is interesting to note that both the Canadian and South African decisions concentrated on the issue of equality as fundamental to human dignity which held such sway with the European Court of Justice in a discrimination claim by a transsexual, see *infra* n. 85. Note also that in *Euan Sutherland* v *United Kingdom*, Appln. No 25186/94, the European Commission on Human Rights held in its report of 1 July 1997 that, in the light of developments in social and medical thinking on homosexuality, the law concerning the age of consent should also evolve.

[84] See Skidmore, *supra* n. 80, at 61.

[85] Case C-13/94 *P. v S. and Cornwall County Council* [1996] ECR I-2143.

[86] C-249/96 [1998] ECR I-621.

[87] At para. 24 of his Opinion, Advocate General Tesauro had urged the Court to grasp the opportunity of leaving a mark of undeniable civil substance, by taking a decision which was bold but fair and legally correct, inasmuch as it was undeniably based on and consonant with the great value of equality. Parallels could be drawn between the approach of the Court in *P.* and that of Advocate General Jacobs in his much cited but not followed argument in Case C-168/91 *Christos Konstantinidis* v *Stadt Altensteig* [1993] ECR I-1191. According to Advocate General Jacobs, Member State nationals who availed of their free movement rights (thereby bringing themselves within the scope of Community law) should be entitled to expect that their fundamental rights would be respected. Similarly, in Case C-13/94 *P.*, *supra* n. 85, the Court ensured that the fundamental rights of a Member State national in employment were not infringed by his or her employer. See also L. Flynn, annotation of Case C-13/94 (1997) 34 *CMLRev*. 367–387, at 384, who notes that the Court stated that fundamental human rights include the principle of equality, that this principle extends to transsexuals and that, on this basis, the Equal Treatment Directive must be read in the light of the principle of equality. The traditional approach would have been to look first at the scope of the Directive and then to ask whether that principle of equality applied within its scope.

initely not, as one commentator both hoped and doubted, an authority comparable with *Van Gend en Loos*, *Costa v Enel* or *Internationale Handelsgesellschaft*, were it only for the reason that, unlike those judgments, it does not constitute an *unprecedented* step in the Court's "voyage to establish a new Community legal order".[88] It is simply one more—although admittedly very telling—product of a philosophy which the Court has followed, with inevitable high and low points, since the days of *Defrenne II*. What the Court (in terms of the outcome) and the Advocate General (in terms of the reasoning which he employed) had succeeded in doing in *P. v S.* was to attack "a rigid insistence that members of one sex should behave only in conformity with the gendered expectations which are associated with that sex".[89] Furthermore, it appeared from its ruling in *P. v S.* that the Court was willing to determine the scope of application of Community law with reference to its duty to protect fundamental rights.

At issue in *Grant* were travel concessions made available by South West Trains Ltd to the spouses and unmarried partners of its employees. This same concession was refused the female partner of one of their female employees, Lisa Grant. Ms Grant complained about this discrimination to an Industrial Tribunal which asked the Court of Justice whether the employer's refusal was in breach of Article 119 of the EC Treaty and the Equal Pay Directive 75/117 and whether discrimination based on sex includes discrimination based on the employee's sexual orientation. On the first point, Ms Grant argued that, had it not been for her sex, she would have received the benefit for her partner and Article 119 of the EC Treaty, which mandates equal pay for men and women, was therefore violated. On the second point, she relied on the ever more favourable treatment of same-sex couples by the legislation of the Member States and certain international instruments. These breakthroughs, she submitted, prove that sexual orientation is increasingly regarded as being entitled to the same protection as sex.

The Court rejected both arguments. The "but for" test is flawed, it held, because, comparing like with like, the correct comparator of Ms Grant is not a man having a female partner, but a male employee who has a partner of the same sex. A male employee in that comparable situation would no doubt have been treated as she had been. As to the second argument, a survey of Member States' laws and practices was said to demonstrate that "while in some [Member States] cohabitation by two persons of the same sex is treated as equivalent to marriage, although not completely, . . . in most of them it is treated as equivalent to a stable heterosexual relationship outside marriage only with respect to

---

[88] C. Barnard, "Kite Flying or a New Constitutional Approach" in Dashwood and O'Leary, *supra* n. 3, pp. 59–79, at p. 75.

[89] Flynn, *supra* n. 87, at 382. Thus Advocate General Tesauro noted that discrimination against women is more often due to what is perceived as their appropriate role rather than their physical characteristics. For a similar approach in the USA see *Oncale v Sundowner*, U.S. Sup. Ct., 4 March 1998, where the Supreme Court accepted that same sex sexual harassment was contrary to Title VI of the Civil Rights Act.

a limited number of rights, or else is not recognised in any particular way".[90] The Court conceded that in the case of *Toonen*, involving the right to privacy of a homosexual man in Tasmania, the Human Rights Committee of the International Covenant on Civil and Political Rights had held that the reference to sex in Articles 17(1) and 2(1) of the Covenant included sexual orientation.[91] However, it pointed out that the Committee is not a court of law and it delivers "viewpoints", not judgments. In any event, this particular viewpoint could not have an impact on the scope of Article 119, which may only be appreciated in the light of the EC Treaty framework.[92]

Surprisingly, the *Grant* decision was not, in general, greeted with a hostile reaction in the media. However, it is unlikely that the same quiet acceptance of what will be perceived by some as unnecessary judicial reluctance to engage in a legitimate cause will pervade academic literature, much of which had forecast or hoped for an extension of *P.* were a case concerning discrimination against homosexuals to arise.[93] Clearly, the Court's conclusion that since the condition imposed by the undertaking's regulations applied in the same way to female and male workers, there was no direct sex discrimination, was crucial to the failure

[90] Case C-249/96, para. 31. In this paragraph of the *Grant* decision the Court distinguishes between Member States where there is legal recognition of same-sex partnerships and Member States which confer equivalent rights on heterosexual relationships outside marriage and homosexual ones. It does not, however, take account of those Member States (or their number) which prohibit discrimination on grounds of sexual orientation. Note that same-sex partnerships are given legal recognition in Denmark (Danish Registered Partnership Act 1989) Sweden (Swedish Partnership Act 1994) and the Netherlands (Law No.324 of 5 July 1997). The Dutch Council of State is also examining proposed legislation which would allow same-sex couples to marry. Catalunya has a law affording some rights to stable partnerships, as does Belgium. Proposed legislation on cohabitation (*pacte civil de solidarité*) is presently before the French Senate and other proposals on partnership seem to have been mooted in Germany, Finland and Luxembourg. Discrimination on grounds of sexual orientation is directly or implicitly prohibited to varying degrees with regard to employment and the provision of services in a number of EU Member States (Denmark, Finland, France, Netherlands, Spain, Sweden—which, since 1 May 1999, has an Ombudsman against discrimination on grounds of sexual orientation—Ireland, Italy and Luxembourg) See generally, R. Wintemute, *Sexual Orientation and Human Rights* (Clarendon Press, 1997), 265–267, x–xi and 136. See also L.R. Helfer, "Lesbian and Gay Rights as Human Rights: Strategies for a United Europe" (1992) 32 *Virginia Journal of International Law* 157–212; Spackman, P.L., "*Grant v. South West Trains*: Equality for Same-Sex Partners in the EC" (1997) 12 *American Journal of International Law and Policy* 1063–1120, at 1093 *et seq.*

[91] *Toonen* v *Australia* (1994) 1 IHRR 97. Mr Toonen, an activist for the promotion of homosexual rights in Tasmania, challenged sections of the Tasmanian penal code which criminalized various forms of sexual contact between consenting male adults in private, claiming that they were an unlawful or arbitrary interference with his right to privacy under the International Covenant on Civil and Political Rights.

[92] Which is somewhat different to the scope and effect given the principles of equality and respect for human dignity in *P.* The Court in Case C-249/96 *Grant*, *supra* n.86, also set much store by the fact that the new Article 6a TEU, inserted by the Amsterdam Treaty (which, at the time, was signed but not ratified in all Member States) mentioned sex and sexual orientation expressly and distinctly; an approach regarded by some as high-handed, since this legal recognition given the new Treaty provisions prior to ratification seemed to suggest that the Member States' approval was regarded as a "trifling triviality": see K.A. Armstrong, "Tales of the Community: Sexual Orientation Discrimination and EC law" (1998) 20 *Journal of Social Welfare and Family Law* 455–479, at 461.

[93] See, for example, Flynn, *supra* n. 87.

of Grant's case. This approach is problematic, however, for reasons which go to the heart of the questions facing courts when the principle of non-discrimination on grounds of sex is used by litigants in situations which are not easily amenable to the application of a straightforward male/female comparator.[94] Applying an "asymmetric" approach to equal treatment in *Grant* would have enabled the Court to compare the treatment by an employer of a lesbian employee *vis-à-vis* her female partner with that received by a heterosexual employee *vis-à-vis* his female partner. Whereas the latter is entitled to the travel concessions, the former is not. However, to conclude, as in *P.*, that the discrimination was based essentially if not exclusively on sex meant that the Court still had to take that leap forward which would bring sexual orientation within the notion of sex in the Community's sex equality provisions. The Court chose not to do so, its choice being based on what it regarded as the absence in the laws of the Member States, in the decisions of the Court and Commission of Human Rights, in other international instruments and in Community law itself,[95] of evidence that sexual orientation came within the notion of sex in Article 119 of the EC Treaty and the Equality Directives.

Some commentators will perhaps be tempted to draw an unflattering comparison between the Court's response to the applicant's argument founded on fundamental rights and the decision of the Human Rights Committee in *Toonen*. Of course, it could be argued that the provisions of the Tasmanian Penal Code which Mr Toonen challenged were definitely more injurious to human dignity and freedom (the values protected by the Court in *P. v S.*) than the policy of South West Trains on travel concessions, morally disputable as it was.[96] However, such a distinction becomes less convincing when one remembers that what was at issue in *Grant* was an applicant's claim that a fundamental principle of EC law was being disregarded.[97] Nevertheless, the passing

---

[94] See R. Wintemute, "Recognising New Kinds of Direct Sex Discrimination: Transsexualism, Sexual Orientation and Dress Codes" (1997) 69 *Modern Law Review* 334–359, at 350; and Armstrong, *supra* n. 92, at 459. In the context of pregnancy and pregnancy-related issues, see also *supra* Section 3. More argues that the use of a "similarly situated test" obscures the fact that a court can achieve any result it chooses by simply changing the measure it uses. The measure of whether one is "like" or "unlike" is left undetermined with the result that this indeterminacy permits judges to apply the mandate of equality according to whichever measure they choose, usually according to preexisting gender stereotypes. See G. More, "'Equal Treatment' of the Sexes in European Community Law: What Does 'Equal' Mean?" (1993) 1 *Feminist Legal Studies* 45–74, at 51 and 63–64.

[95] According to the Court, "in the present state of the law within the Community" persons who have a stable relationship with a partner of the same sex could not be regarded as being in the same situation as those who are married or who have a stable relationship outside marriage with a partner of the opposite sex.

[96] Skidmore, *supra* n. 80, at 59, remarks that the vehemence of the Court's condemnation of the discrimination suffered by P. can be interpreted as revealing the naked prejudice in the employer's decision to dismiss.

[97] In Case C-180/95 *Nils Draehmpaehl v Urania Immobilienservice OHG* [1997] ECR I-2195, the Court's decision was predicated on the need for employers and Member States to respect the *principle* of non-discrimination; even those job applicants who had no chance of being appointed to the post advertised were regarded as being entitled to compensation (albeit limited) when sex discrimination had affected the appointments procedure.

acceptance, without discussion or support, in *Toonen*, that sexual orientation could be considered part of sex was not a strong precedent on which to rely.[98]

What might be open to greater criticism by commentators of the *Grant* decision is the absence of concrete comparative references by a Court whose fundamental rights jurisprudence was developed and is now based by virtue of a Treaty provision on the common constitutional traditions of the Member States. Given that, with respect to both the issue of the equivalence of homosexual and heterosexual couples and the question whether discrimination on grounds of sex covered that on grounds of sexual orientation, the Court was basing its decision on a perceived lack of evolution in national, Community and international law to support such conclusions, it will perhaps be regretted that further and more detailed evidence of this lack of evolution was not adduced.

In terms of the quest by individuals and gay rights campaigners to force an extension of the protection afforded by EC sex discrimination law to them and to their members, the ruling in *Grant* did not signal the end. A further reference for a preliminary ruling concerning a homosexual medical assistant who challenged his dismissal from the Royal Navy on the grounds of his homosexuality under the Equal Treatment Directive was subsequently withdrawn. In the light of the decision in *Grant*, the referring judge in the *Perkins* case could see no realistic prospect of any change of mind on the part of the Court.[99]

In another case, this time before the Court of First Instance, a Swedish official of the Council of Ministers claimed that the Community should grant him and his male companion the benefits which Sweden attaches to partnership contracts entered into by same-sex couples.[100] D., however, did not succeed where *Grant* had already failed. Transposing the reasoning of the Court in *Grant* to the discrimination complaint of a Community official whose employment clearly comes within the scope of application of Community law, the Court of First Instance held that at the present stage of development of law in the European Community, stable relationships between people of the same sex are not assimilated to relationships between married persons. As a result, employers are not obliged to extend to same sex partners, even ones whose relationship has been officially recognized by national authorities, the effects of traditional marriage. The Council, in its capacity as the applicant's employer, was under no obligation to treat his registered partnership as a marriage within the meaning of the

---

[98] Wintemute, *supra* n. 90, at p. 146, notes that the Committee's failure to give a reason for including sexual orientation within the notion of sex has been criticized.

[99] See the decision of Lightman J. in *R v Secretary of State for Defence, ex parte Terence Perkins*, judgment of 13 July 1998, and the Order of the Court of 16 September 1998 removing the case from the register of the Court of Justice: a withdrawal which may have confirmed some commentators' fears that the risk inherent in the approach of Stonewall, the gay rights group backing these cases, was paralysis were the outcome in Case C-249/96 *Grant* not to go in their favour: see Armstrong, *supra* n. 92, at 464.

[100] See Case T-264/97 *D. v Council*, judgment of the Court of First Instance of 24 January 1999. The *Lag* (1994: 1117) *om registrerat partnerskap* of 23 June 1994 allows two persons of the same sex to register their partner with the Swedish authorities. Such registered partnerships are assimilated to marriage in Sweden and have, by and large, the same legal effects as a marriage.

statutory provisions governing the rights of Community officials. Like the Court of Justice in *Grant*, the Court of First Instance in *D.* held that it was for the Council, as legislature, to bring about the changes necessary to allow Community officials who found themselves in the same position as the applicant to benefit from household allowances for their partners. This decision has been appealed before the Court of Justice both by D. and by the Swedish government which argues that the definition of marriage in the EC Staff Regulations is for the Member States to decide and since the applicant is regarded as married under Swedish law the benefits which he has applied for should be granted.[101]

Grant in particular was an excellent example of applicants seeking judicially what their national parliament had failed to give them by legislative means, namely equal treatment as regards employment, pension and social security benefits.[102] *D.*, in contrast, involves reliance by an applicant on the decision by the legislature in his Member State of origin to grant legal recognition and registration to same-sex partnerships. Clearly difficulties remain for homosexuals' judicial strategy. This is certainly due to objective reasons, such as the inspiration and the language of the rules that the Court of Justice is called upon to interpret in Article 119 and the Equality Directives. As Clapham and Weiler pointed out with farsight, while the Equal Treatment Directive clearly applies to transsexuals, there was no ground for being "sanguine" about the possibility of applying it to anti-homosexual discrimination.[103] Some commentators, however, will probably also explain it in terms of other factors, namely a certain reluctance on the part of the Court to embrace scabrous social causes without any assurance of support by a substantial segment of public opinion and with the almost certain hostility of at least some Member States.[104]

[101] See *Financial Times*, 29 March 1999 and Joined Cases C-122/99 P and C-125/99 P *D. and Sweden* v *Council*.

[102] Indeed the applicant was very clear in her press statement after the announcement of the decision that this was the intention: "we set out to raise awareness that there is discrimination in the workplace and we have done what we have set out to do": *The Guardian*, 18 February 1998. See also Armstrong, *supra* n. 92, at 464, on the use of law as an instrument of social change and the limitations of litigation strategies in this particular context.

[103] See A. Clapham and J.H.H. Weiler, "Lesbians and Gay Men in the EC Legal Order" in Clapham and Waldijk, *supra* n. 80, pp. 7–69, at p. 21; and Flynn, *supra* n. 87, at 381. Cf. A. Byre, "Equality and Non-Discrimination" in Clapham and Waldijk, *supra* n. 80, at p. 216.

[104] The contrast between this attitude and that of the American judiciary could not be more striking. As is well known, for example, in a referendum held in Colorado, the majority of voters adopted an amendment to the state constitution which would have prohibited all legislative, executive or judicial action at any level of state or local government designed to protect lesbian, gay and bisexual persons against discrimination. The United States Supreme Court, however, did not hesitate to strike down that piece of legislation in *Romer* v *Evans* 134 L. Ed. 2d 855 (1996); and in *Baehr* v *Lewin* 852 P. 2d 44 (Haw. 1993), neither did the Supreme Court of Hawaii demur at holding, in the face of vehement protests by political and religious groups, that excluding same-sex couples from civil marriage is *prima facie* sex discrimination.

6. CONCLUSIONS

By virtue of Article 164 of the EC Treaty, the Court, as it has when necessary reminded itself and others, is bound to ensure that, in the interpretation and application of the Treaty, the law is observed. Even before the Member States had inserted an article referring to the Union's respect for fundamental rights, it was in this provision that the Court located its competence, indeed its duty, to vindicate and protect those rights. In *P. v S.* the Court did not hesitate to rise to the challenge which its Advocate General had identified "by taking a decision which is bold but fair and legally correct, inasmuch as it is undeniably based on and consonant with the great value of equality".[105] Reliance by applicants on *P.* in subsequent cases has not produced similar dramatic advances in the protection of the fundamental right to equality.

In the past the case law of the Court of Justice is said to have been "ever alert and to the fore in ensuring that disadvantaged persons are protected".[106] Perhaps the heightened expectation to which this case law gave rise amongst some explains the extent of the disappointment which has greeted its more recent decisions. The Court itself may be struggling to deal with the constraints imposed by Article 119 and the Equality Directives while attempting to live up to the standards of rights protection which it has set for itself. Of course, courts cannot be held solely responsible for bringing about the economic, social and cultural changes which pursuance of meaningful equality dictates; but neither can they ignore those voices of civil society, whether resonant or faint, hostile or friendly, which exhort them to do more or reason differently in line with their own jurisprudence and the spirit of the laws which they enforce, nor can they shy away from their duty to keep abreast of evolving social realities.

---

[105] See the Opinion of Advocate General Tesauro in Case C-13/94, *supra* n. 85, para. 24.
[106] *Ibid.*

10

The United States Supreme Court and the European Court of Justice

THE TASK OF comparing and contrasting the roles of the United States Supreme Court and the Court of Justice of the European Communities is a daunting one. It is rendered acutely difficult by the obvious fact that the two political entities in question—namely, the USA and the European Community/Union—were born in vastly different circumstances. The USA came into being as a result of a revolutionary, anti-colonial war. Few circumstances can be so propitious to the fostering of a sense of common destiny as the need to unite in order to throw off the shackles of colonialism and to remain united in order to prevent their reimposition. One need only recall Benjamin Franklin's famous dictum—"We must indeed all hang together, or, most assuredly, we shall all hang separately"—in order to realize that the union between the newly-independent American states was condemned to succeed.

The founding fathers of the European Community were denied such a compelling argument to further their cause. But all successful unions between states are born of necessity, either political or economic. In the case of Europe the driving forces of union were the dread of descending again into the horrors of the Second World War and the spectre of the seemingly relentless march of Soviet-inspired Communism, coupled with the more mundane need to build a strong, integrated economy capable of competing with larger, more powerful rivals, notably of course the USA. Again it is Benjamin Franklin who provides the pithy quotation: "No nation was ever ruined by trade". Similarly no union between nations or states was ever ruined by trade. Thus it is hardly surprising that the authors of both the American Constitution and the EC Treaty understood the need for unfettered commerce between the several states of the unions thereby created and the need to confer on the central organs of those unions the power to regulate commerce, both internal and external. No comparison between the roles of the two courts would be complete without at least a cursory examination of the American court's case law on the commerce clause of the Constitution and the European Court's jurisprudence on Article 30 of the EC Treaty.

But before approaching such specific issues, the comparison should perhaps focus at a more general level by looking at the two courts from a structural and organizational point of view. Sections 2, 3 and 4 will examine, first, the composition of the courts and the manner in which their members are appointed and, secondly, their respective working methods,[1] together with their case load problems and the ways in which they have attempted to solve them.

2. THE COMPOSITION OF THE TWO COURTS

The first topic might seem prosaic to some but it is in fact of the utmost importance. The rules governing the appointment and tenure of judges, especially judges of a supreme or constitutional court, play a vital role in determining whether a court has the moral and political authority which only democratic legitimacy can confer and which only a judiciary whose independence is beyond doubt can hope to retain.

The two systems could hardly be more different. As regards the number of justices, in Europe the number is laid down in the EC Treaty but may be increased (not reduced) by the Council of Ministers if the Court so requests. So far the one political imperative that prevails in this area has required that there should be as many Judges as there are Member States (plus one, if that number is even, in order to prevent a stalemate), since it is felt that each Member State should have the right to nominate one Judge. The larger States also have the right to nominate an Advocate General, for whom there is of course no equivalent in the USA.

The American Constitution does not specify the number of Justices but leaves the task to Congress. The number varied over the years between a maximum of ten and a minimum of five. The composition was fixed at nine in 1869 and has remained constant ever since. The fluctuations seem to have been determined partly by the westward expansion of the nation and partly by politics, in the most sordid sense of the term. For example, the increase to ten Justices was motivated by the need to secure a majority favourable to President Lincoln's war policies. The most notorious example of this phenomenon (though one that never came to fruition) was the court-packing plan developed by President Franklin Roosevelt as a result of his understandable frustration with the resistance to his New Deal legislation on the part of the conservative majority on the Supreme Court. Happily, the spectre of court-packing is one evil that has not so far threatened the European Court, though other, perhaps more insidious forms of political pressure have sometimes been brought to bear on the Judges in Luxembourg.

As to the systems of appointment and tenure, the differences are great and are of immense significance from the point of view of democratic legitimacy and judicial independence. The Judges of the American court are nominated by the President and are appointed by him "by and with the Advice and Consent of the

---

[1] See further in this respect Chapter 12.

Senate". Their European counterparts are appointed "by common accord of the governments of the Member States". The Judges of the Supreme Court, like other federal judges, hold office "during good behaviour" and may be removed only by death or impeachment. Thus, only the Almighty or the Senate may dismiss a federal judge in the USA. Less fortunate are their European brethren, who hold office for a six-year, renewable term.

What does all this mean in terms of democratic legitimacy and judicial independence? And what does it mean in terms of representativity? Some conclusions are easy to draw: for example, that the American Judges have an undoubted aura of democratic legitimacy since their appointment is dependent on the positive assent of both the elected branches of government; or that the independence of the federal judiciary is as solidly entrenched as it conceivably could be, notwithstanding the view of Gerald Ford, who as leader of the House Minority attempted in 1970 to set in motion the impeachment of Justice William O. Douglas and observed that an impeachable offence was whatever the House and Senate wanted it to be. It is equally obvious that the European Court is sadly lacking in democratic legitimacy and that whatever independence it possesses— and it has shown not a little over the years—is due to the robustness of its Members rather than to security of tenure.

In terms of representativity, slightly less obvious consequences flow from the differing systems of appointment. Nominations to the Supreme Court emanate from a single source—the United States President. Presidents, who may anticipate a new Supreme Court appointment every twenty-two months, according to an analysis completed in the late 1950s by Robert Dahl, are guided by who knows what criteria. Doubtless the desirability of elevating competent jurists to the bench plays some part. But perhaps more important is the political imperative of ensuring that both sexes and various ethnic groups are represented, as well as the desire to appoint persons who share the President's ideological convictions. As a system of checks and balances it is less than perfect: Jimmy Carter, a Democrat, had the remarkable distinction of being the only President to serve a full term without being able to make a single nomination, whereas the Republicans who preceded and followed him (Presidents Nixon, Ford, Reagan and Bush) were able to secure the appointment of 11 Justices between them. The result is of course a rather conservative Supreme Court which does not necessarily reflect the breadth and variety of political thought in Main Street, USA.

How does the practice in Europe compare? The EC Treaty says that the Members of the European Court are appointed by the governments of the Member States acting by common accord. The unwritten rules say that each government nominates its candidate and the others acquiesce. The absence of any equivalent of confirmation hearings before the Senate means that the appointments take place without the glare of publicity and without of course the intrusive scrutiny of Europe's elected law-makers. In one sense the composition of the Court reflects Europe's ethnic diversity with great precision, since each nationality is represented. The system also guarantees a less monochrome, more politically balanced Court. Because each Judge's term of office expires after six years and because governments change with equal or greater regularity in most Member States, it is likely that at any given time roughly half the Members of the Court will have been nominated by a conservative administration and roughly half by a socialist or liberal administration. In another sense, however, the Court is extremely unrepresentative: until 1999, with the appointment of the first female Judge at the Court of Justice, the fifteen judges and nine Advocates General had included only one woman among their ranks, the French Advocate General Simone Rozès.

3. THE COURT'S WORKING METHODS, CASE LOAD AND DOCKET

Turning to the question of working methods and the related issue of case load and docket control, again the differences are vast. The Supreme Court has a docket of over 6,000 cases. The Court of Justice has three or four hundred. Most of the American Court's cases come to it by way of the discretionary appeal procedure known as *certiorari* and over 95 per cent of those cases are dismissed without any review of the merits on the ground that they are "uncertworthy"— a concept which is somewhat puzzling to European lawyers but which must mean that the case raises no issue of general importance and leads to no major injustice. Thus the Washington justices have the inestimable privilege, denied to their brethren in Luxembourg, of being able to decide what to decide.

At the Court of Justice jurisdiction is mandatory (as was most of the Supreme Court's jurisdiction until 1925). Not all of the cases raise issues of major constitutional significance. In 1993, for example, the Court was asked by a German court to interpret a provision in the Common Customs Tariff in order to enable that court to determine the rate of customs duty applicable to a consignment of ladies' pyjamas. The question asked was whether a garment must be wholly and exclusively suitable for wearing in bed in order to be classified as pyjamas or whether it is sufficient if that is the garment's primary purpose.[2] Of course, ensuring the uniform application of Community law is one of the Court of Justice's most important functions and it is vital that goods imported into the Community should be subject to the same rate of duty, regardless of the point of entry; but presumably if the Court of Justice ever acquires the power to indulge in agenda-setting, the customs classification of ladies' pyjamas will not be high on the agenda.

Having whittled its docket down to manageable proportions, the American Court is able to hear the chosen cases in plenary session. The European Court, on the other hand, refers most of its cases to chambers of three or five Judges; only cases raising novel or important issues are decided by the full Court (which may mean as few as nine Judges). The Supreme Court somehow manages with-

---

[2] Case C-395/93 *Neckermann Versand AG v Hauptzollamt Frankfurt/Main-Ost* [1994] ECR I-4027.

out the institutions of Reporting Judge and Advocate General. At the European Court each case is assigned to a Reporting Judge soon after it is registered; his task is to steer the case through the various stages of the procedure and to draft the judgment of the Court. Each case is also assigned to one of the nine Advocates General, whose task is to present an independent Opinion setting out his personal view of how the case should be adjudicated.

Perhaps the greatest difference between the two courts is that in Washington a Judge who disagrees with the majority is free to enter a dissenting opinion, whereas in Luxembourg all he can do is grit his teeth and sign the ostensibly unanimous, collegiate judgment. If he is Reporting Judge his fate is even worse, for the practice is that he must still draft the judgment in spite of his dissent. In Washington an altogether healthier practice has developed, whereby a member of the majority is designated to write the Court's "opinion".

It is sometimes suggested that the Court in Luxembourg should permit dissenting opinions or set forth separately the Judges' personal reasons for supporting a decision of the Court. No doubt every Judge at the European Court has on some occasion regretted the absence of such a faculty; it is probably just as certain that very few of the Judges would be willing to compromise the authority of the Court's rulings by openly revealing that it is divided on some issues. Here it must be remembered that the Community legal order is still an infant, whereas American federalism has grown to maturity. Looked at in the proper historical perspective, the European Court's practice is perhaps not radically different from that of the Supreme Court under Chief Justice Marshall, who well understood that a young court administering and helping to create a new legal order must suppress disagreement in order to enhance its authority by a show of unanimity. His great rival for supreme authority, President Thomas Jefferson, also understood that point. For in a letter written in 1820 he railed against the Marshall court for producing opinions "huddled up in a conclave, perhaps by a majority of one, delivered as if unanimous, and with the silent acquiescence of lazy or timid associates, by a crafty chief Judge, who sophisticates the law to his mind by the turn of his own reasoning". This is not of course to suggest that Jefferson's image of the Supreme Court in the early nineteenth century corresponds in any way to life at the European Court in the 1990s; none the less there is much truth in Jefferson's perception that a court, especially a young court at the apex of a new legal order, may enhance its prestige and authority by concealing internal dissension with a display of artificial unanimity.

4. DRAFTING

Desirable though unanimity is, it must be conceded that it has done nothing to improve the style and readability of the European Court's judicial utterances. The judgments emanating from Luxembourg purport to be the work of a college of judges; they are drafted in French, usually by a non-francophone, and employ a terse, impersonal and arid style that has no pretensions to literary elegance. Moreover, the need to produce a judgment that is acceptable to all the signatories means that compromises have to be made, the price of which is often a loss of clarity and coherence. Sometimes it is easy to concur as to the result but difficult to agree on the reasons for the result, which may lead to elliptical judgments, with a slightly oracular tone, as contentious passages are jettisoned one by one, until all that remains is the bare minimum of legal reasoning needed to support the outcome.[3] Of course if that means shorter judgments, not everyone would disapprove. It might even be said that the Court of Justice has shown a tendency in recent years to abide by the advice of Oliver Wendell Holmes, one of the great stylists of the Supreme Court, who said: "the eternal effort of art, even the writing of legal decisions, is to omit all but the essentials".

Holmes' secret weapon was a high drafting table at which he worked in a standing position—"Nothing conduces to brevity like the caving in of the knees", he once said. Many commentators regret that his method is apparently eschewed by the present-day Justices, for prolixity and verbosity are the sins most frequently imputed to the Supreme Court in the latter half of the twentieth century. Long opinions, overloaded with footnotes and cross-references, are the product of a relentless quest for perfect justice and academic thoroughness. In the half century from 1936 to 1986 the average opinion doubled in length, though not apparently in stylistic accomplishment. "A great literary wasteland" was one author's description of the United States Reports. There are, however, notable exceptions. An editorial in the *Washington Post* once praised an opinion of the Supreme Court in a case concerning copyright in the Roy Orbison song "Pretty Woman". Not only did Justice Souter, the author of the opinion, display great knowledge of contemporary musical culture; he also produced an opinion that was "fun to read", according to the *Post*. The author has yet to see an editorial in *Le Monde*, *La Stampa* or *The Times*, suggesting that a judgment of the Court of Justice was fun to read.

5. COMPARING JURISPRUDENCE

Turning to the jurisprudence of the two tribunals, is it possible and worthwhile to compare the philosophies that have inspired their work, the techniques they have employed and the results they have reached? The answer must be affirmative, but only on condition that we do not forget the great differences that exist between the contexts in which the two Courts have operated and continue to operate. The first difference concerns their respective jurisdictions. The scope of judicial scrutiny in Luxembourg is far more limited than in Washington, though it is steadily extending to areas certainly unforeseen by the founding fathers (for

---

[3] See also Chapter 11.

example, in 1991 the European Court had to deal with an Irish measure concerning abortion);[4] on the other hand, the untidy and constantly changing relations between the Community organs of government are at the root of an acrid interinstitutional litigation which our American brethren are happily spared.

Far more important is the second difference. Unlike the USA the European Community was born as a peculiar form of international organization. Its peculiarity resided in the unique institutional structure and the unprecedented law-making and judicial powers it was given. But those features—admittedly reminiscent of a federal state—should not overshadow two essential facts. In the first place, whereas the American Declaration of Independence speaks of "*one people*" dissolving the bonds that connected them with "another people", the preamble of the EC Treaty recites that the contracting parties are "determined to lay the foundations of an ever closer union among the *peoples* of Europe" (an expression, by the way, which reappears thirty-six years later in the preamble of the Maastricht Treaty, thus evoking the image of a platonic betrothal destined never to end in wedlock or some other form of carnal connection). In the second place, the instrument giving rise to the Community was a traditional multilateral treaty.

Now, treaties are basically different from constitutions. In many countries (and "many" includes even some of the founding states of the EC) they do not enjoy the status of higher law; their interpretation is subject to canons unlike all others, such as, for example, the presumption that states do not lose their sovereignty; and, as a rule, they devise systems of checks and balances whose main function is to keep at bay the powers of the organization they set up. True enough, the EC Treaty has undergone a process of constitutionalization which started in the early 1960s when the Court read into it a clause giving Community law pre-eminence *vis-à-vis* Member State law and decided that Treaty provisions may in certain circumstances be relied upon by private individuals. Yet, defining the Treaty as the European Constitution is still to a very large extent tantamount to indulging in a wishful metaphor. Much as they would like to do it, in other words, the Luxembourg judges are not yet in a position to exclaim like Chief Justice Marshall in *McCulloch* v *Maryland*: "we must never forget that it is a constitution we are expounding".[5]

6. THE COMMERCE CLAUSE AND ARTICLE 30 EC

Having entered these caveats, it is impossible to deny that the conflicts of a similar nature which knock at the door of both Courts are manifold. Beginning with the vast body of case law related to the building and the development of a common market, there is no doubt that in this area both experiences are relevant to

---

[4] Case C-159/90 *The Society for the Protection of Unborn Children Ireland Ltd* v *Stephen Grogan and others* [1991] ECR I-4685.
[5] U.S. (1 Cranch) 137 (1803).

each other and it is equally clear that their mutual relevance is almost exclusively due to the contribution of the respective judiciaries. Since *Gibbons v Ogden*,[6] the American Court has played a central role in the integration of a once balkanized economy by broadly construing the federal power written in the commerce clause: "Congress shall have power to regulate commerce with foreign nations, . . . among the several states and with Indian tribes". In the famous words of Justice Cardozo, the clause "was framed on the theory that the people of the several states must sink or swim together"; but the Tenth Amendment conferred on those very states the power to provide for the general welfare of their inhabitants. The interpretation of the commerce clause has therefore imposed on the Court a most delicate task: balancing the national interest in the establishment of a common or single market with a bewildering variety of local needs and traditions.

The European Judges had to cope with the same sort of problem. They could not spin their case law from the implications of a laconic constitutional precept, since the EC Treaty is quite specific both in requiring the Member States to dismantle trade barriers and in defining the policy goals which permit their authorities to enact measures with restrictive effects on commerce. But the language of the respective Articles (30 and 36) is broad. Thus the Court of Justice was likewise granted a leeway for interpretation sufficiently large to stimulate its ingenuity in umpiring, as an American lawyer would say, the European federal system: namely, in furthering integration without impinging on the vital interests of the Member States.

Nor is that all. As regards the techniques of integration adopted by the two Courts, it is usually admitted that their jurisprudence has evolved in strikingly similar ways. Yet, differences are to be found in the manner in which the balancing exercise is performed, the Court of Justice placing in general a heavier thumb on the Community side of the scale than the Supreme Court does on the federal side.

Why is that so? In response to this fascinating query, it has been conjectured that the stiffer jurisprudence moulded by the Court of Justice is a function of the political and institutional weakness of the Community. In other words, while the Supreme Court can afford to be tolerant of state legislation which has potentially restrictive effects when it is justified by a *prima facie* valid reason, the Luxembourg Judges are bound to take a rigid stance as regards the powers of the Member States lest the achievements of forty years be swept away by a tide of resurgent protectionism. Path-breaking judgments such as *Cassis de Dijon*[7] which invalidated restrictive measures, reasonable in themselves and even-handed, but simply not justified by overriding requirements, should therefore be understood as props and stays of a wobbly polity or, in a different perspective, as stages in the above-mentioned process tending to endow the Community with a genuine constitution.

---

[6] 9 Wheat. 1, 189–190 (1824).

[7] Case 120/78 *Rewe-Zentral AG* v *Bundesmonopolverwaltung für Branntwein* [1979] ECR 649.

Let me dwell for a minute on this all-important point. The contribution which the Court has made to the process of constitutionalization by discovering a supremacy clause and by enabling individuals to invoke certain provisions of the EC Treaty has been widely studied.[8] On the other hand, little has been said about the role of the Court as a centralizing agency in the realm of the economy and an even scantier consideration has been devoted to a more general, but closely related subject: the threads connecting free trade, judicial review of state legislation and the creation of federal systems.

Obviously, comparison between the American and the European experiences is crucial here. As Kommers has shown, a good starting-point would be Alexander Hamilton's essays in *The Federalist*. Hamilton was indeed the first to realize that a truly national economy was a precondition of the USA's political existence as a Nation: "Under a vigorous government" he wrote, "the natural strength and resources of the country, directed to a common interest, would baffle all the combinations of European jealousy to restrain our growth". And it was also Hamilton who first understood how decisive the weight of the judicial power would be in the march towards a unified economy. For several years, he foretold, Congress would be unlikely to have recourse to its power over commerce; but the judiciary could be trusted to set aside all sorts of state measures if incompatible with an open market.

These intuitions proved prophetic both in the USA and in Europe. The American Court did exactly what Hamilton had predicted it would do; and the Court of Justice trod in the steps of its American counterpart, though under conditions at times so unpropitious, so untoward, as to make its case law appear an even more telling demonstration of Hamilton's farsightedness. After all, it is not preposterous to regard *Cassis de Dijon* or, subsequently, *Gouda*[9] as reactions to the failure of the Community's political organs to make use of their power over commerce or, in the language of the EC Treaty, to harmonize Member States' standards in the production of goods and the provisions of services.

7. PROTECTING FUNDAMENTAL RIGHTS

So much as far as commerce is concerned; fundamental rights is the second area of substantive law which should be considered.[10] With the exception of equality in working conditions irrespective of nationality and gender, the framers of the EC Treaty did not envisage the need to protect such rights. Presumably, they knew that bills of rights are in the long run a powerful vehicle of integration and in 1957, when the European climate was already tinged with scepticism and in any event no longer virginal, they were not eager to see the integration process

---

[8] See further Chapters 1 to 3.
[9] Case C-288/89 *Stichting Collectieve Antennevoorziening Gouda and others* v *Commissariaat voor de Media* [1991] ECR I-4007.
[10] See also Chapters 1, 3 and 6.

speeded up by a central authority empowered to safeguard the civil liberties of the Community citizens first in Brussels and later, perhaps, in the six countries concerned.

But there is a further possibility. The founding fathers may have thought that the scope of Community law was essentially limited to economic issues and, as such, did not involve human rights problems. If this is the reason why they omitted to guarantee those rights, no American observer should be shocked by their attitude. In arguing for the ratification of the Constitution despite the absence of a Bill of Rights, Alexander Hamilton and James Madison took the view that the limited powers bestowed on the federal government made such a bill unnecessary. Indeed, it is well known that the Supreme Court did not issue any important opinion in the area of free speech until well into this century.

In Europe, however, time seems to have run faster. As Community law came to govern diverse and sometimes unforeseen facets of human activity, it encroached upon a whole gamut of old and new rights with an economic and a strictly "civil" content. Thus a problem that in 1957 might have appeared of practical insignificance turned ten years later into one of the most controversial questions of Community law, so much so that it ended up taking on the character of a major judicial conflict. On October 1967, the German Constitutional Court indicated, albeit in a hypothetical fashion, that the Community legal order, lacking any protection for human rights, had no lawful democratic basis.[11] The transfer of powers from Germany to the Community could therefore not deprive German citizens of the protection accorded to them by their own constitution; it followed that Community law had to be scrutinized at the national level to ensure that it was compatible with internal constitutional provisions.

It was brutal blow, jeopardizing not only the supremacy but the very independence of Community law. Something had to be done, and the Court did it, both for fear that its hard-won conquests might vanish and because of its own growing awareness that a "democratic deficit" had become apparent in the management of the Community. Thus, initially in dicta and finally in *Nold*,[12] the Luxembourg Judges declared that "fundamental rights form an integral part of the general principles of law", the observance of which they are called upon to ensure. In the years following *Nold*, the Court drew on the common constitutional traditions of the Member States and on the European Human Rights Convention in order to identify whatever elements could contribute to the preservation of minimum civilized standards in the legislative output and the administrative practice of Brussels. More specifically, and disregarding rights of a purely economic nature, the Court concerned itself with procedural due process,[13]

---

[11] *Bundesverfassungsgericht*, judgment of 18 October 1967, in *BVerfGE*, 22, p. 293, reproduced in (1968) *CMLRev* 483.

[12] Case 4/73 *J. Nold, Kohlen- und Baustoffgrosshandlung* v *Commission* [1974] ECR 491.

[13] See, *inter alia*, Case 98/79 *Josette Pecastaing* v *Belgium* [1980] ECR 691.

respect for private life,[14] legal professional privilege,[15] the non-retroactivity of criminal law provisions,[16] the principle of review of administrative measures by courts,[17] the inviolability of domicile,[18] the right not to incriminate oneself[19] and so forth.

How should one assess this case law? If it is compared with the torpid, parsimonious and contradictory use which the Supreme Court made for more than a century of the Bill of Rights, born in April 1789, it is difficult not to share the opinion of Cappelletti, who said of the judges at the European Court that, by claiming "for themselves the capacity to do what the framers did not even think of doing and what the political branches of the Community do not even try to undertake, those thirteen little men unknown to most of the 320 million Community citizens, devoid of political power, charisma and popular legitimation", have written a unique page in the history of law.[20] But—it should be added at once—that page is not yet complete; and, in contrast to what has happened in the USA, it is doubtful whether it can be completed in the foreseeable future.

8. FUNDAMENTAL RIGHTS REVIEW AND MEMBER STATE LEGISLATION

This section addresses the greatest of the problems which, in a federal or quasi-federal system, a charter of fundamental rights poses for the organ entrusted with the task of umpiring that system: namely, the question whether the limitations imposed by such a charter apply only to the acts of the central authorities or whether they extend to acts adopted by the states, provinces or nations of which the federation or quasi-federation is composed.

After having powerfully contributed to the framing of the Bill of Rights, James Madison came to believe that, as the law of the land, it ought to be applied against the states as well as against the national government. But in *Barron* v *Baltimore*[21] his view was emphatically rejected by Chief Justice Marshall speaking for an unanimous tribunal; and the Supreme Court remained faithful to that ruling for almost a century. It was not until 1925, in the case of *Gitlow* v *New York*,[22] that freedom of speech and freedom of the press were held to be protected against state action under the due process and the equal

---

[14] Case C-404/92 P *X* v *Commission* [1994] ECR I-4737.

[15] Case 155/79 *AM & S Europe Limited* v *Commission* [1982] ECR 1575.

[16] Case 63/83 *R* v *Kent Kirk* [1984] ECR 2689.

[17] Case 222/86 *Union nationale des entraîneurs et cadres techniques professionnels du football (Unectef)* v *Georges Heylens and others* [1987] ECR 4097.

[18] See, *inter alia*, Joined Cases 46/87 and 227/88 *Hoechst AG* v *Commission* [1989] ECR 2859.

[19] Case 374/87 *Orkem* v *Commission* [1989] ECR 3283.

[20] See M. Cappelletti, *The Judicial Process in Comparative Perspective* (Clarendon Press, Oxford, 1989), and for a further discussion of the protection of fundamental rights by the Court of Justice, in particular, see Chapter 6.

[21] 32 U.S. (7 Pet.) 243 (1833).

[22] 268 U.S. 652 (1925).

protection clauses of the Fourteenth Amendment; and only in the 1940s, 1950s and 1960s was Justice Hugo L. Black able to steer the Court into applying to the fifty states the other major Bill of Rights' safeguards. Nowadays, the accepted doctrine is that states may provide additional guarantees for their citizens, but have no authority to reduce rights and liberties from the minimum standard required by the federal constitution.

In Europe, as I have said, we are a long way from such a result. In *Cinéthèque*[23] the Court of Justice made it clear that it had "no power to examine the compatibility" with the European Human Rights Convention of laws concerning areas which fall "within the jurisdiction of the national legislature". More recently, the Court has refined that sweeping ruling by holding that national measures implementing Community provisions must not disregard fundamental rights protected in Community law and that national measures which restrict the free movement of goods and services, but which contribute to one of the overriding interests recognized by Community law, are only permissible if they comply with fundamental rights.[24] But let us be realistic: however much the Court or Community pride themselves on these achievements, they are hardly impressive in comparison with the progress made in the USA.

Of course, the difference between the achievements of the Supreme Court in the field of fundamental rights, and those of the Court of Justice, is readily explained. In Strasbourg there exists a court whose specific task is to ensure compliance with the European Human Rights Convention by forty-something states, including all the Member States of the European Union; and notwithstanding the slowness of its procedures and the tiny number of judgments that it pronounces, that court performs its task with great authority. Moreover, as Chapter 6 points out, it cannot be denied that, in terms of respect for fundamental rights, no Member State of the European Union is comparable with Huey Long's Louisiana or George Wallace's Alabama. But quite apart from such factors, the true reason why the Court of Justice has been unable to follow in the footsteps of the Supreme Court, that is from testing Member State laws against the unwritten charter of rights it has read into Community law, is very different: it has to do with the gulf which separates the two polities: the American Union, shaped in the course of two centuries, well established and nearly unlimited in its reach and substantive jurisdiction; the Community, a relatively recent and hybrid organism combining some supranational and many intergovernmental elements.

As regards the construction of a common market, that gulf has not had significant effects; on the contrary, it has induced the Court of Justice to develop a

---

[23] Joined Cases 60 and 61/84 *Cinéthèque SA and others v Fédération nationale des cinémas français* [1985] ECR 2605.

[24] See further Case C-260/89 *Elliniki Radiophonia Tiléorassi AE v Dimotiki Etairia Pliroforissis and others* ("*ERT*") [1991] ECR I-2925; and Case C-368/95 *Vereinigte Familiapress Zeitungsverlags- und vertriebs GmbH v Heinrich Bauer Verlag* [1997] ECR I-3689.

case law that is even more incisive than that of the Supreme Court. The fact is, however, that in this field there is no basic divergence among the Member States: a Europe conceived as a giant Heathrow duty-free shop, as a consumers' union with goods, services and capital flowing unhindered, is a goal accepted by all, even by politicians to whom federalism is anathema. Matters stand very differently as regards the subject of fundamental rights, which is far more emotion-loaded and far closer to the core of national sovereignty. Here it is highly probable that a judgment of the Court of Justice comparable to *Gitlow* v *New York*, let alone *Roe* v *Wade*,[25] would not be obeyed. The Court is aware of the danger and eschews a conflict that would be fatal for an organ almost devoid, as it is, of powers that are not traceable to its institutional standing and the persuasiveness of its judgments. All that it can do, therefore, is to contemplate the gulf between the American union and the more limited achievements of Europe in chagrin, if not in hopelessness, and seek to whittle it down day after day with patience and determination.

---

[25] 410 U.S. 113 (1973).

11

Language, Culture and Politics in the Life of the European Court of Justice

1. INTRODUCTION

A MONGST THE JUDICIAL organs presently in operation in the Western world the Court of Justice of the European Communities is unique in many respects: the native tongues of its fifteen Judges are eleven in number; of the Member States from which they originate seven are monarchies and eight are republics; ten have a unitary structure, while five are divided into regions with varying degrees of autonomy; eight have some form of judicial review of legislation, while in seven of them such a concept is alien or downright blasphemous; two possess a legal culture moulded by centuries of judge-made law, whereas lawyers in the other thirteen have been brought up to believe that law-making is strictly the function of the legislature.[1] No less importantly, the polity which has its judicial branch in Luxembourg has grown into something more than an international organization, but it has not yet become a state. Moreover, its foundations are in a state of constant flux. Suffice it to remember that during its forty-seven years of life it has undergone three major constitutional reforms and that, whereas it initially had a single source of legitimacy—the will of the Member States—it has since acquired a second one, in the shape of the election by direct universal suffrage of a Parliament now endowed with significant budgetary and legislative powers.

One could develop further the list of characteristics that make the European Court of Justice an unprecedented and unparalleled institution; but those already referred to are sufficient to demonstrate the daunting nature of the exercise which we are to undertake: identifying and appraising the language problems, the cultural influences, the political pressures and the institutional constraints which affect the jurisprudence of the Court.

2. THE LANGUAGE PROBLEM

Let us begin with the least powerful of those factors: the multilingual nature of

---

[1] For an extreme example of the reluctance to recognize the creative role of judges, see article 5 of the *Code Civil* (French Civil Code), which prohibits courts from making general pronouncements about the law.

the Court. Advocate General Jacobs, echoing George Bernard Shaw, has recently written that "unlike the English and the Americans, who are divided by a common language, language differences in Europe do not prevent a common way of thinking".[2] The irony of that remark cloaks an undoubted truth, at least to the extent that when, for example, an Italian judge talks in French or English with his Greek or Danish colleagues they are not on different wavelengths. Yet the fact of having to speak French, which has been the Court's working language since 1952, in the deliberation room and having to draft judgments in French, puts the non-francophones at a definite disadvantage *vis-à-vis* their brethren from France, Belgium and Luxembourg. Being of course accomplished gentlemen, they would never consciously take advantage of their colleagues' handicap; but the full mastery of a language—especially of so noble and captivating a language—is an irresistible weapon; and the owner of that weapon will not be likely to refrain from using it.

In spite of this inconvenience, a strong case can be made for the obligation to deliberate and draft in only one language. Some of its positive effects are of a practical nature and are obvious: a decision-making process devoid of interpreters and translators is clearly more efficient or, in any event, less cumbersome, than one which must rely on them. Other effects are less obvious, but probably more important. In a microcosm whose inhabitants have such diverse roots the use of the same language, bringing with it shared access to the culture which finds expression in that language, facilitates the formation of an *esprit de corps*: in short, it promotes that sense of togetherness without which an institution which is obliged to take several new members on board every three years and which acquires detractors in direct proportion to its increasing visibility could not function effectively or even survive.

Moreover, French is not only charming; it is also a rigorous and terse language which puts a penalty on the florid and the twisted. Translated into French, certain judgments of the German Constitutional Court and even certain opinions of the American Justices appear exceedingly verbose, hopelessly convoluted and sometimes slightly preposterous. The case law produced in Luxembourg is rightly criticized for its often stunted reasoning and its frequently oracular tone; but such shortcomings must be attributed much more to the need to render judgments that are acceptable to all the signatories than to the language in which they are conceived and drafted. By contrast, the language (and the underlying culture) are to a large extent responsible for their normal concision and clarity: a clarity which is all the more indispensable as a good half of those judgments are given in answer to references coming from national judges whose knowledge of Community law and its bewildering intricacies is inevitably summary.

---

[2] F.G. Jacobs, "The European Court of Justice: Some Thoughts on its Past and its Future" (1994–95) *The European Advocate* 2, at 7.

3. THE INPUT FROM DIVERSE LEGAL CULTURES

"La lengua es compañera del imperio" (language is the companion of Empire), said the Spanish grammarian Antonio de Nebrija in 1492. The monopoly of French in the deliberation room of the Court of Justice is indeed a consequence of the hegemony which France as a political power (and hence French legal thinking) exerted in the framing and the early application of the Treaties that gave rise to the European Community. Article 177 of the EC Treaty, which governs the procedure under which national courts seek preliminary rulings from the European Court on questions of Community law, was partly modelled on the system regulating constitutional litigation in Italy; but the first paragraph of Article 173, which empowers the Court to review the legislative and administrative acts of the Council and the Commission,[3] is an obvious tributary of French administrative law.[4] In fact, the very structure of the Court shows deep traces of the French influence. Just consider the rule (Article 166) dealing with the Advocates General: the term is borrowed from French criminal procedure where the *avocat général* plays the role of prosecuting counsel; the functions (delivering, with complete impartiality, Opinions on cases brought before the Court) are entirely equivalent to those of the *Commissaire du gouvernement* at the *tribunaux administratifs* and the Conseil d'Etat, the supreme administrative Court of France.[5]

Thus it is hardly surprising that throughout the 1950s and early 1960s the judgments of the European Court looked like a carbon copy of the judgments of the great French courts: same conceptual frames of reference (a strict notion of misuse of powers is a case in point),[6] same idiosyncrasies (such as a reluctance to use general principles of law), same method of exposition (for example, the opening of each paragraph with "*attendu que . . .*" ("considering that . . .").[7] But this subserviency was bound to recede if not to disappear entirely. Germany had too important and proud a legal tradition for the German Judges in Luxembourg to accommodate themselves to a backwater role in the development of the Community case law. As a consequence, and perhaps in the wake of the growing prestige won by the Federal Republic as an impeccable *Rechtsstaat*, a certain German approach to the study and the use of the law began to work its way into the judgments of the Court.

---

[3] Article 173 of the EC Treaty also empowers the Court to review the legislative and administrative acts of certain other institutions, although these powers were restricted by the changes made in the Maastricht Treaty to a limited number of circumstances.

[4] J. Rivero, "Le problème de l'influence des droits internes sur la Cour de justice de la CECA" (1958) *Annuaire français de droit international* 295, at 303.

[5] K. Borgsmidt, "The Advocate General at the European Court: A Comparative Study" (1988) 13 *ELRev* 106.

[6] Rivero, *supra* n. 4, at 304.

[7] See generally M. Lasser, "Autoportraits judiciaires: le discours interne et externe de la Cour de cassation"; F. Ranieri, "Styles judiciaires dans l'histoire européenne: modèles divergents ou traditions communes?", unpublished papers delivered at a conference on "Langages de justice" at the Ecole Nationale de la Magistrature, 3–4 June 1994, Paris.

Unlike their Latin and English brethren, the German Judges have a partiality for what they call "general clauses". To Lord Burrough, an eminent judge of the nineteenth century, public policy was "an unruly horse to ride";[8] to his present-day counterparts between the Rhine and the Oder that notion and, together with it, those of good faith, good morals, proportionality, legitimate expectation etc., are "the ethical lungs of positive law" and should be fully exploited in assessing the legality of any act, be it made by individuals or by a public authority. In due course, this conception gained the upper hand over the French aversion for all that is hazy or flexible, and it flooded Community law. Proportionality is the greatest beneficiary of that flood. A notion unknown to the EC Treaty, it means that a public authority may impose on citizens, for the benefit of the public interest, only such obligations, restrictions and penalties as are strictly necessary for the attainment of the purposes pursued; and it has become a crucial test in deciding whether the legislative and administrative output of the Community institutions and the Member States is in violation of the EC Treaty.

If partiality for the *Generalklauseln* is rooted in German legal thinking (in fact, its high-water mark was reached during the agony of the Weimar Republic),[9] the exceptional importance that the German legal community attaches to the subject of fundamental rights constitutes an obvious reaction to the totalitarian experience of the Third Reich and the establishment of a Communist regime in the very heart of the Nation. Now, it is well known that the framers of the EC Treaty did not envisage the need to protect those rights; and it is equally well known that, in its early times, the Court dismissed on this ground a number of complaints lodged by German businessmen against Community regulations which they accused of violating the right to own private property and the freedom of enterprise. In 1969, however, this case law began to crack at the edges; in a famous *obiter dictum* in the *Stauder* judgment the Court recognized that respect for fundamental rights forms part of the general principles of law which it is required to uphold,[10] and from that moment onwards it applied fundamental rights more and more forcefully as a standard for testing the validity of the legislation and the administrative measures emanating from Brussels. Today, it is commonly held that the Luxembourg Judges have read into the EC Treaty an open-ended and constantly growing charter of fundamental rights.[11]

To what extent were the German Members of the Court responsible for this remarkable example of judicial activism? In a system under which all judgments

---

[8] *Richardson* v *Mellish* 2 Bing 252.

[9] W.J. Hedeman, *Die Flucht in die Generalklauseln: eine Gefahr für Recht und Staat* (Mohr, Tübingen, 1933).

[10] Case 29/69 *Stauder* v *City of Ulm* [1969] ECR 419, at para. 7.

[11] See G.F. Mancini and V. Di Bucci, "Le développement des droits fondamentaux en tant que partie du droit communautaire", in Academy of European Law (ed.), *Collected Courses of the Academy of European Law*, Volume I, Book I (Kluwer, 1991), pp. 27–52; and see Chapters 1, 3 and 6.

are ostensibly unanimous, their contribution is bound to remain unknown; although, those who have met one of them (the late President Hans Kutscher), might be inclined to believe that they participated with particular enthusiasm. But even if that assumption were wrong, the powerful role that German legal culture played in the evolution of the Court's case law could not be underestimated. On 29 May 1974 the Constitutional Court in Karlsruhe decided that the protection of fundamental rights in the Community framework was inadequate and reserved for itself a power to review Community legislation in the light of the catalogue of rights enshrined in the German constitution.[12] Thus faced by an ominous threat to the Community-wide validity of Council and Commission acts, the Court of Justice was forced to quicken its pace on the road it had taken with *Stauder* and the subsequent judgments. Whether directly or indirectly, therefore, at the basis of its most spectacular accomplishment—the birth of a fully-fledged Community Bill of Rights—there was a German thrust.

1973: enter the British and Irish Judges. What did their culture bring to the Court? Their most conspicuous contribution concerns the style and the format of the hearings. The typical advocate in continental Europe is accustomed to put on his robe, make his submissions—would-be Cartesian in France, ornate in Italy, ponderous in Germany, entangled in the Netherlands, artful in Greece— and bid adieu. If a member of the bench dares to question, let alone interrupt him, he is at a loss, coughs, stares at the ceiling and grumbles out a usually irrelevant answer. Some go so far as to resent these judicial interferences, as they would call them, and make no effort to conceal their annoyance. The advent of the two insular Judges put an end to such habits. Their colleagues loved their refusal to accept listlessly the kind of assistance which the lawyers were prepared to give them and started to act accordingly. As a result, interruptions are now frequent and a question period has become a permanent feature of the hearings, much to their advantage in terms of usefulness and liveliness.

But this is only part of the picture. The British and Irish Judges enriched the conceptual patrimony of the Court with rules and notions drawn from the common law, sometimes with surprisingly positive results. A judgment of 1974 (*Van Duyn*) held that, under certain circumstances, provisions of directives not yet implemented may be relied upon by private individuals;[13] this decision, which perhaps goes beyond the letter of Article 189 of the EC Treaty, was accepted by the legal community in the Member States five years later (in *Ratti*), when the Court justified it in terms reminiscent of the doctrine of estoppel: it would be inequitable to allow a Member State which has failed to implement a directive within the prescribed period to profit from its own failure at the expense of a citizen on whom the directive is intended to confer rights.[14]

An even more significant contribution was the refined case law technique of the common law, which caused the Court to become more, as it were,

---

[12] BVerfGE, 37, p. 271, reproduced in (1974) 2 *Common Market Law Reports* 540 and 569.
[13] Case 41/74 *Yvonne Van Duyn* v *Home Office* [1974] ECR 1337.
[14] Case 148/78 *Pubblico Ministero* v *Tullio Ratti* [1979] ECR 1629.

precedent-conscious and therefore more skilful in distinguishing cases or in correcting itself when it felt that a case had been wrongly decided. Civil law jurisdictions have never been quite as cavalier in their attitude towards precedent as is sometimes imagined in England and the USA, but it is true that the sophisticated case law apparatus developed by the common law (subtle distinctions between binding and persuasive authority, or between *ratio decidendi* and *obiter dicta*, and fastidious (sometimes spurious) attempts to distinguish cases on the facts) has never held much appeal for lawyers on the European mainland. As the former Dutch Member of the Court, Thijmen Koopmans, has pointed out,[15] it is a myth that the Court never cited its previous decisions before the advent of Judges trained in the jurisprudential techniques of the common law. However, it would be wrong to believe that the comparative rarity of references to earlier case law in the 1960s and early 1970s was due entirely to the fact that there were fewer cases to cite; it was also due in part to a typically continental preference for vague allusions to the "settled case law of the Court" and for disguised quotations from previous judgments. Moreover, during that period, it would have been considered positively indecent expressly to overrule a precedent or to acknowledge the existence of a conflict in the case law. In the following decades the practice of citing previous judgments becomes increasingly common and there is evidence of a conscious attempt to build up a coherent body of case law. While opinions may differ as to whether the common law influence was responsible for that change of approach, it is perhaps not without significance that when in 1990 the Court finally took the bold step of expressly overruling a previous judgment it did so at the instigation of a British Advocate General.[16]

But old habits die hard. It is well known that in the late 1980s and early 1990s the Court gave a series of deeply irreconcilable judgments on the scope of Article 30 of the EC Treaty, which prohibits quantitative restrictions on imports in trade between Member States and measures having equivalent effect.[17] When the Court finally resolved to clear up the confusion in *Keck and Mithouard*[18] the resulting judgment appears to reflect a remarkable amalgam of the common law and civil law approaches to precedent: the Court indicated expressly that it intended to overrule some of its earlier decisions but did not state which ones were no longer to be considered good law and, as a result the judgment has been subjected to scathing criticism. Certainly, English lawyers must find such an approach perplexing. Perhaps the truth of the matter is that the collegiate nature of the judgments, which have to be presented as unanimous, with no provision

---

[15] T. Koopmans, "*Stare Decisis* in European Law" in D. O'Keeffe and H.G. Schermers (eds.), *Essays in European Law and Integration* (Kluwer, Deventer, 1982), p. 11, at p. 17.

[16] Case C-10/89 *SA CNL Sucal v HAG GF AG (HAG II)* [1990] ECR I-3711.

[17] See D.T. Keeling, "The Free Movement of Goods in EEC Law: Basic Principles and Recent Developments in the Case Law of the Court of Justice of the European Communities" (1992) *The International Lawyer* 467–483.

[18] Joined Cases C-267/91 and C-268/91 *Criminal Proceedings against Bernard Keck and Daniel Mithouard* [1993] ECR I-6097.

for dissenting opinions, does not lend itself to the sort of rigorous case law technique practised by common law judges. Consequently, it is to the Opinions of the Advocates General that one must turn for a detailed review of the case law. The Advocate General, like a common law judge, has the luxury of expressing an individual view of the law, unencumbered by the need to accommodate the conflicting views of his colleagues. He is thus in a better position to identify the different strains in the case law and to state which should be lovingly nurtured and which should be allowed to wither on the vine. The point is illustrated by a comparison of Advocate General Tesauro's exhaustive review of the case law on Article 30 of the EC Treaty in his Opinion in *Hünermund*[19] and the Court's laconic judgments in that case and in *Keck and Mithouard*.

4. *UNE CERTAINE IDÉE DE L'EUROPE*

Important though the cultural factors referred to above may be, it is none the less true that the most significant—the one that left the greatest impression on the Court's case law in the most exciting years of its history (the 1960s)—is internal to the Court; internal in the sense that it arose from the synergy produced by the coming together of jurists who, though steeped in different cultures and legal traditions, shared a common set of values. The Luxembourger Pierre Pescatore, who was appointed to the Court in 1967 and is undoubtedly the most influential jurist the Court can boast, defined it as *une certaine idée de l'Europe*.[20]

It is a definition both cold and vague; nonetheless, richer and more precise than others, such as "religion of integration" or "European mysticism", which have come into fashion, with more than a touch of mockery, among recent court-watchers. Its richness will be appreciated by those who remember that *une certaine idée de la France* was the phrase by which General De Gaulle summarized the universalistic vocation and the consequent role in world affairs that he attributed to his country. As for its greater precision, it will suffice to point out that the political outlook and the actual work of Judge Pescatore and his brethren showed no trace of fundamentalist temptations and no propensity to day-dreaming. They may have been federalists at heart, but their pragmatism made them reticent to declare themselves as such; in any event they regarded the European federation as a possible end-product of a process about the length and the difficulties of which they had no delusions. Their basic interest was precisely the development of that process and of the role which the Court could play both in preventing its foundations from collapsing and in fostering, if only in fits and starts, its march forward.

---

[19] Case C-292/92 *Ruth Hünermund v Landesapothekerkammer Baden-Württemberg* [1993] ECR I-6787.

[20] P. Pescatore, "The Doctrine of Direct Effect: An Infant Disease of Community Law" (1983) 8 *ELRev* 155, at 157.

The two landmark judgments of the 1960s, *Van Gend en Loos*[21] and *Costa* v *ENEL*,[22] are perfect examples of the real motives determining the choices of the Court in that seminal period. The EC Treaty, while including some hortatory provisions to this effect (for example, Article 5), fails to state squarely whether Community law is pre-eminent *vis-à-vis* the domestic legislation of Member States. It is self-evident, however, that if its pre-eminence had not been openly declared, the Community would have faced a rapid process of dilution and would soon have been transformed into one of the many international organizations which rub along more or less effectively according to the changing interests of the contracting states. *Costa* v *ENEL*, which read a supremacy clause into the EC Treaty, was clearly founded on this assumption, even if it did not fully spell it out; and the substantial acceptance that it won in the judiciaries and the administrations of both the original and the new Member States proved its timeliness and soundness. Pescatore rightly describes the principle of the primacy of Community law as a *"condition existentielle"* of the Community.[23]

Being about the survival of the Community as a supranational body, *Costa* v *ENEL* can be described as a defensive judgment. *Van Gend en Loos* was instead essentially offensive. By holding that EC Treaty rules may be invoked directly in national courts if they confer rights on individuals and impose on the Member States an obligation so clear-cut that it can be fulfilled without the necessity of further measures, the Court proved that it cared also for the progression of the Community in terms of both supranationality and democracy.

As the EC Treaty clearly shows, the Community was not conceived as a democratic entity. On the one hand, its decision-making machinery and its daily management were exclusively entrusted to the leading members of the national executives (the Council), a technocratic élite (the Commission) and a college of ambassadors (COREPER); on the other hand, the ordinary citizen had—and still has, since the procedural rules of the EC Treaty have not changed—limited ways of vindicating his rights under Community law against the encroachments of the powers that be, especially at the national level. All he can do when any such right is infringed is to invoke it before a national court; which in turn may—or, if its judgment is not subject to appeal, must—refer the matter to the Court of Justice under Article 177 of the EC Treaty, requesting it to give a preliminary ruling on the interpretation of the relevant Community provision.[24]

Scrutinised against this background, the scope of *Van Gend en Loos* appears truly emancipating. If a number of EC Treaty rules had not been made invocable by individuals, the "relevant Community provisions" to be interpreted by

---

[21] Case 26/62 NV *Algemene Transport- en Expeditie Onderneming Van Gend en Loos* v *Nederlandse Administratie der Belastingen* [1963] ECR 3.

[22] Case 6/64 *Costa* v *ENEL* [1964] ECR 585.

[23] P. Pescatore, "Aspects judiciaires de l'*acquis communautaire*" (1981) *Revue trimestrielle de droit européen* 617, at 623.

[24] For a discussion of the inherent weaknesses in the system of remedies established by the EC Treaty, see G.F. Mancini and D.T. Keeling, "Democracy and the European Court of Justice", (1994) 57 *Modern Law Review* 175–190, reproduced as Chapter 3.

the Court could have been found only in the legislative acts by which the Council implements the Treaty; that is in measures whose adoption is entirely dependent on the will of the Member States, with their perennially resurfacing protectionist tendencies and their inborn resistance to any surrender of sovereignty. Suppose that, in order to become enforceable, Articles 30, 48 and 59, which proclaim the free movement of goods, workers and services, had to wait for some sort of enabling legislation: would French brewers have been able to market their beer in Germany? Would Italian coal-miners have shared, on a par with local employees, the social advantages available in Belgium? Would British businessmen advertizing on satellite TV have had their publicity broadcast in the Netherlands? It is thanks to *Van Gend en Loos* that such persons have become the direct beneficiaries of the Community legal order.

That *certaine idée de l'Europe* which constituted in the 1960s the home-made philosophy of the Court contained various elements: in particular, realism and passion. Passion is not a judicial virtue, even though there have been numerous examples of it in the initial phases of great institutional and political enterprises, such as the construction or renewal of a State (even Judge Bork made allowances for the boldness of the Marshall Court).[25] In the case of the European Judges, however, one always has the impression that their passion was kept at bay by their realism; or, rather, that realism channelled passion towards goals not quite envisaged by the framers of the EC Treaty and therefore capable of creating imbalances in their scheme, but digestible in the long run by the political actors and apt to evoke a positive reaction on the part of the national judiciaries.

A happy and fruitful combination of values, as one can see; so fruitful, indeed, that it contaminated the Judges of the following generation. In the 1960s, wrote Thijmen Koopmans, "the Europeans discovered the importance of law and legal institutions"; in the 1970s they "found out how many interesting things you could *do* with the law".[26] *Cassis de Dijon*[27] is the judgment which best epitomizes those interesting things. Prior to it, while nobody doubted that all discriminatory obstacles to the free movement of goods were prohibited by Article 30 of the EC Treaty, the status of non-discriminatory restrictions was uncertain. Some Member States claimed that their national standards of production and marketing could only be displaced by harmonized rules which, under Article 100 of the EC Treaty, the Council was empowered to adopt unanimously. In *Cassis de Dijon* the Court swept away this theory by ruling that any goods legally produced and marketed in a Member State could be freely traded

---

[25] "Although he [Marshall] may have deliberately misread the statutes, he did not misread the Constitution. His constitutional rulings, often argued brilliantly, are faithful to the document. Marshall's tactic may perhaps be understood, for the survival of the Union was probably in some part due to the centralizing and unifying force of Marshall and his Court": R. Bork, *The Tempting of America: The Political Seduction of the Law* (The Free Press, 1990), p. 21.

[26] T. Koopmans, "The Role of Law in the Next Stage of European Integration" (1986) 35 *International and Comparative Law Quarterly* 925, at 928.

[27] Case 120/78 *Rewe-Zentrale* v *Bundesmonopolverwaltung für Branntwein* [1979] ECR 649.

throughout the Community unless they failed to comply with national rules founded on certain overriding requirements such as fair trading and consumer protection. In short, the Court imposed on the Member States a mutual recognition of their respective standards; which practically amounted to rendering the enactment of harmonizing directives unnecessary or, in blunter words, to deriving the existence of the common market directly from the EC Treaty.

5. THE RETREAT FROM ACTIVISM

Cassis de Dijon was probably the swan song of the activist Court of old. The 1980s did not record any judgment of a comparable calibre. At the beginning of the 1990s the Court seemed to rouse itself again. A few controversial judgments (*Chernobyl*,[28] *Factortame*,[29] *Francovich*[30]) and the first Opinion on the judicial aspects of the Treaty establishing the European Economic Area[31] led several observers to think that a new activist season was in the offing. It was, however, little more than a blaze which soon burnt out making room for a case law not only inspired by restraint, but increasingly revisionist, that is to say, not averse to blunting the conquests made in the previous decades. Much as generalizations are dangerous in dealing with changes of culture and mood, one is tempted to conclude that the Court has undergone a process of secularization. Realism is no longer a balance to passion; it has superseded passion and has become a synonym of minimalism.

What factors caused this apparent withering of the Court's European faith? In Chapter 1, I tried to account for the ebbing of the Court's case law during the 1980s in terms of the outburst of energy which the political institutions of the Community, now including a stronger and more buoyant Parliament, experienced in the aftermath of the Single European Act. Judicial creativeness, said that Chapter, is justifiable in periods of legislative stagnation or in defence of society's democratic values; but "when democracy advances and politics asserts its claims, judges are bound to take a pace back".[32] This view, however, was falsified by subsequent events. As a matter of fact, the flare of activism which warmed the early 1990s took place precisely while the feverish atmosphere brought about by the completion of the single market was reaching its climax; and today's revisionist tendencies began to manifest themselves as soon as the gloom spread throughout Europe by the painful ratification of the Maastricht Treaty put a curb on the commitment of the Council and the Commission.

---

[28] Case C-70/88 *European Parliament v Council ("Chernobyl")* [1990] ECR I-2041.

[29] Case C-213/89 *R v Secretary of State for Transport, ex parte Factortame Ltd* [1990] ECR I-2433.

[30] Joined Cases C-6/90 and C-9/90 *Francovich and Bonifaci and others v Italian Republic* [1990] ECR I-5357.

[31] Opinion 1/91 [1991] ECR I-6079.

[32] G.F. Mancini, "The Making of a Constitution for Europe" (1989) 26 *CMLRev* 595, at 613, reproduced as Chapter 1.

The explanation must therefore be sought at a deeper level. Its background is essentially cultural and has to do with the decay, stretching well beyond the Community's experience, of the idealistic thinking which prevailed among lawyers between the end of the Second World War and the beginning of the 1980s. Judge Koopmans calls it "the loss of legal optimism".[33] True enough, the judiciaries of Italy, France and Spain have been involved for the past few years in a trial of strength with the respective political élites and are determined to reform them or even, as an Italian prosecutor put it, to "straighten the moral spine of the nation"; but these expressions of faith in the redeeming properties of the law sound so outdated and strident as to erode the popular support which the same judges won when they exposed the venality of the politicians. In fact, faced by intractable economic and social problems (the fiscal crisis of the welfare state in the first place, but also the growing demands of environmentalist and consumer groups, the mass migrations from the third world etc.), a vast number of lawyers on both sides of the Atlantic have ceased to believe that the law should aim at realizing policy ends and no longer identify themselves as social engineers.

The minimalist approach of the European Court's recent case law may well have its remote cause in the form which this disenchantment was bound to take in the particular context of the European Community. For all their political poise and the high technical quality of their legal arguments, the early Judges had seriously hoped that they could, if not achieve integration by themselves, set in motion a dialectical process which would eventually oblige the political actors to achieve it. But this expectation proved exaggerated. For almost thirty years, their successors must have thought, European politics made little progress and experienced more than one episode of dismal capitulation. When it finally blossomed, as was the case in the late 1980s, it produced some admittedly important but overdue reforms culminating in the dubious blessings of the Maastricht Treaty, and was followed by another period of sclerosis. Are such ups and downs not enough to impart a lesson of humility even to the firmest believer in the justiciability of integration?

They are, of course. However, in order for humility to shape, as it did, a low-profile jurisprudence, more specific factors were necessary. Those factors were provided both by the conditions in which the Maastricht Treaty was ratified and by certain provisions of that Treaty itself. The hostility which the Treaty elicited among the more nationalist-minded political circles and interest groups of some Member States is well known; less known is the fact that the Court was a favourite target of that hostility in the campaigns preceding the Danish and French referenda and, with particularly nasty tones, in the debates which took place in the British House of Commons. The disappointing outcome of these battles (the Maastricht Treaty was rejected in the first Danish referendum and approved by a thin majority of the French electorate and the British Parliament)

---

[33] Koopmans, *supra* n. 26.

obviously impressed the Judges in Luxembourg; for, as Mr Dooley, the clear-thinking saloon-keeper created by Finley Peter Dunne, said in his rich Irish brogue, "th' Supreme Coort follows th' iliction returns". But an even deeper mark was left on the Judges by their discovery of the antagonism, however une-ducated, which the Court's case law had provoked; and that mark became indelible when Germany entered the field.

It is no secret that, among the governments of the Member States, the German one has been since 1957 the staunchest supporter of European unity and, with the possible exception of Belgium, the only one which never disguised its pref-erence for an evolution of the Community in a federal direction. It is therefore easy to visualize the dismay of the Court, first, when the German press began, in the autumn of 1992, to criticize vehemently some judgments benefiting Italian and non-Community migrant workers and, later, when it learnt that those protests were inspired or shared by the Minister of Social Affairs, Norbert Blüm, and even by Chancellor Kohl. The last straw, however, was the news that Germany might propose, at the Intergovernmental Conference due to take place in 1996, to delete the second paragraph of Article 177 of the EC Treaty.[34] The provision in question, which empowers the lower-ranking national courts to refer questions of Community law to Luxembourg, was indeed at the root of the decisions that the German Government had found so unpalatable; but Germany should have known that the whole of Community law owes the better part of its development precisely to the mechanism set up by that rule. After all, *Costa v ENEL* and *Cassis de Dijon* were decided in answer to questions coming from a small claims court in Milan and a fiscal court in Hesse.

Was it then at preventing a further development of Community law that the Germans were aiming? Perhaps. In any event, one thing is clear: Germany was trying to cow the Court into a greater deference to her interests or, less crudely, to the interests of the Member States whenever they are perceived as clashing with those of the Community. The value at stake, therefore, was the indepen-dence of the Court—and this was all the more alarming as a serious attempt on that value had already been made by the framers of the Maastricht Treaty.

6. THE ASSAULT ON THE *ACQUIS COMMUNAUTAIRE*

It should be pointed out right away that the Maastricht Treaty did not deserve the wholesale vilification to which it was subjected, even by politicians and scholars of unshakable European faith. For instance, it is undeniable that the creation, although in stages, of a monetary union, the recognition of a Union cit-izenship, even if the rights attached to it are limited, and the co-decision powers bestowed on the Parliament, were all important gains as far as the proponents

---

[34] The suggestion that only courts against whose decision there is no appeal should be allowed to seek a preliminary ruling has been advanced by a senior German civil servant. See P. Clever, "Grundsätzliche Bemerkungen zur Rechtsprechung des EuGH", *Die Angestelltenversicherung* 2/93.

of greater integration are concerned. However, once rendered unto Caesar that which is Caesar's, it must be admitted that the Maastricht Treaty included more than one rule eating into the ground conquered in the course of four decades by the Community legislature and the case law of the Court of Justice. In the jargon of the trade this ground is called the *acquis communautaire* and the preservation of the *acquis* has evolved into something akin to a constitutional principle. Paradoxically, the Maastricht Treaty ratified (in Article B) and at the same time nullified that evolution.

As far as the Court's case law is concerned, the "hijacking" of the *acquis*, as Curtin[35] has called it, was perpetrated by three protocols annexed to the Maastricht Treaty, amongst which the so-called Barber Protocol is the most notorious. On 17 May 1990 the Court held in the *Barber* case that Article 119 of the EC Treaty, which proclaims the right for men and women to receive equal pay for equal work, applied to benefits paid under private pension schemes in the United Kingdom.[36] The financial consequences of this ruling being potentially considerable for the pension funds, the Court limited its retroactive effect, but failed to define clearly the extent of the limitation: should equal treatment— this is the question which it left open—apply to all pension payments made after 17 May 1990 or should it extend only to payments corresponding to pension contributions made in respect of periods of employment subsequent to that date? Considering that the latter hypothesis would have postponed the advantages of equality for many years, four national courts immediately asked the Court of Justice to clarify what it had meant; but before the Court could answer, the Protocol intervened like a bolt from the blue. For the purposes of Article 119 of the EC Treaty, it reads, benefits under occupational social security schemes shall not be considered as remuneration if they are attributable to periods of employment prior to 17 May 1990.

In commenting on the scope of this Protocol, Curtin wrote that, by purporting to "interpret" the meaning of an existing EC Treaty article, the Member States sought to present the Court with a *fait accompli*. Other writers have observed that the Protocol demonstrates an intention on the part of the Member States to re-assert their prerogative as "masters of the Treaties".

The Treaties founding the European Communities are not of course writ in stone and they do themselves, like any constitutional document, contain articles expressly providing for their amendment. Any such amendment enters into force after being ratified by all the Member States in accordance with their respective constitutional requirements. If the spectre of a *gouvernement des juges* is to be avoided, there can be no objection in principle to a Treaty amendment—duly sanctified by referenda and votes in national parliaments—which reverses a judgment of the Court of Justice or restricts the Court's freedom to interpret one of its earlier decisions.

---

[35] D. Curtin, "The Constitutional Structure of the Union: A Europe of Bits and Pieces", (1993) 30 *CMLRev* 17.

[36] Case C-262/88 *Barber* v *Guardian Royal Exchange Assurance Group* [1990] ECR I-1889.

It is true that some might think it a case of legislative bad manners when the governments of the Member States, meeting at an Intergovernmental Conference, propose a Treaty amendment that deprives the Court of the power freely to interpret one of its earlier rulings at the very time when it is being requested to do so by a number of national courts under a constitutional provision as important as Article 177 of the EC Treaty. Some might go so far as to regard it as an outright assault on the separation of powers.[37] But even there it must be conceded that if the governments of the Member States, which are after all endowed with greater democratic legitimacy than the Court of Justice, are firmly persuaded that a particular view as to the correct interpretation of a Treaty article must prevail, on grounds of economic and social necessity, they are entitled to incorporate that view in a proposed amendment of the Treaty, notwithstanding the pendency of litigation concerning the point in issue.

None the less, no one who cares about the prestige of the Court can feel happy about the manner in which the Barber Protocol was adopted. The painful lesson for the Court is that nothing that it does cannot be undone and that no aspect of the *acquis communautaire* is safe from abrogation if it proves unpalatable to the Court's political masters.

This unfortunate impression was confirmed by a further Protocol adopted at Maastricht which allows Denmark to retain its "existing legislation on the acquisition of second homes". The legislation in question prohibits non-Danish nationals from acquiring second homes in Denmark and was apparently motivated by resentment among a section of the Danish population over the fact that large numbers of Germans acquire holiday homes in certain parts of the country. The Danish Second Homes Protocol may be seen as a direct response to a judgment of 1989 in which the Court of Justice held that Greek legislation prohibiting foreigners from owning immovable property in border regions was contrary to the fundamental freedoms enshrined in the EC Treaty.[38]

The right of nationals of a Member State to own immovable property in another Member State had formed part of the *acquis communautaire* since the earliest days of the Community. It may be traced back to Article 54(3)(e) of the original EEC Treaty and was confirmed by the Council of Ministers in 1961 in two General Programmes on the abolition of restrictions on freedom of establishment[39] and freedom to provide services.[40] It is surely ironic that the statesmen in Maastricht who gave birth to the noble concept of European Union citizenship (Article 8 EC) and proclaimed the right of every citizen of the Union to move and reside freely within the territory of the Member States (Article 8a EC) should by the very same act have sanctioned national legislation which deprives Union citizens of one of the essential aspects of the right of residence,

---

[37] G.C. Rodríguez Iglesias, "Der Gerichtshof der Europäischen Gemeinschaften als Verfassungsgericht" (1992) 27 *Europarecht* 225, at 244.

[38] Case 305/87 *Commission v Greece* [1989] ECR 1461.

[39] Official Journal, English Special Edition, Second Series IX, 7.

[40] Official Journal, English Special Edition, Second Series IX, 3 [or 9].

and which does so moreover in deference to a latent xenophobia that is inconsistent with the whole philosophy of the EC Treaty.

Faced with the contradiction between Articles 8 and 8a of the EC Treaty, on the one hand, and the Danish Second Homes Protocol on the other, it is difficult to avoid concluding that the authors of the Maastricht Treaty were engaged in a massive exercise in schizophrenia. That attitude is nowhere more apparent than in their treatment of the Court of Justice. In some respects they maintained the faith in law and the justiciability of integration that led the authors of the Rome and Paris Treaties to create the Court of Justice in the first place. For example, the representatives of the Member States incorporated into the Maastricht Treaty, almost verbatim, the Court's judgments in the *Les Verts*[41] and *Chernobyl* cases concerning the capacity of the European Parliament to sue and be sued under Article 173 of the EC Treaty. More significantly perhaps, in Article 171 of the EC Treaty, they entrusted to the Court the power to impose pecuniary sanctions on a Member State which fails to comply with a judgment establishing that the State is in breach of its obligations.

The latter provision is a remarkable testament of faith in the Court of Justice. That makes it all the more surprising that the Member States did not feel able to rely on the wisdom of the Court to find an appropriate way of resolving the uncertainty created by the *Barber* judgment. An even greater source of disquiet is that Article L of the Maastricht Treaty excluded the jurisdiction of the Court to interpret whole sections of that Treaty, including its so-called Second and Third Pillars (Titles V and VI), dealing respectively with the common foreign and security policy and cooperation in the fields of justice and home affairs.

That governments should wish to conduct their foreign and security policy away from the troublesome scrutiny of judges is perhaps understandable, and most judges would in any case be reluctant to charge headlong into the thorns and brambles of the foreign affairs political thicket. But to exclude cooperation in the field of justice and home affairs from the jurisdiction of the Court of Justice was surely anomalous. Moreover, if it is borne in mind that the cooperation envisaged extended to matters such as asylum policy, immigration policy in relation to nationals of non-member countries, judicial cooperation in civil and criminal matters and customs cooperation, the implications are alarming. The very principle that the Community is founded on the rule of law is endangered. By virtue of the "coordination" between Member States envisaged under the Third Pillar, decisions affecting the legal situation of individuals may be taken; and yet those individuals, instead of acquiring rights under Community law which they can invoke directly in the courts, were to be dependent on the goodwill and grace of their national governments. If the effect of *Van Gend en Loos* was to take Community law out of the hands of the politicians and bureaucrats and to give it to the people, there was a real danger that the effect of Maastricht's Third Pillar would be to reverse that process in certain important areas.[42]

---

[41] Case 294/83 *Parti écologiste "Les Verts" v European Parliament* [1986] ECR 1339.
[42] Mancini and Keeling, *supra* n. 24, at 183.

There was, moreover, a second fundamental principle that was in jeopardy: namely, the principle of the uniform application of Community law.[43] If the Court is not empowered to interpret agreements made between the Member States in the field of justice and home affairs, there is no means of ensuring that those agreements produce the same effects throughout the Community. It was to be hoped therefore that the Council would make use of the faculty, provided for in Article K.3(2) of the Maastricht Treaty, of conferring jurisdiction on the Court of Justice to interpret conventions adopted in the field of justice and home affairs.[44]

7. CONCLUDING REMARKS

The Member States acting collectively at Maastricht were, with Germany in the van, more committed to pursuing the goal of European unity than the Member States sitting on the Community Council of the 1960s and the 1970s. Yet they sharply penalized a Court of Justice which the intellectual climate prevailing in the 1980s had already made circumspect, while their predecessors had evinced *vis-à-vis* a more aggressive Court a fundamentally benign neglect. The reasons accounting for this strange paradox will have to be explored by political historians. Some will perhaps find in it a confirmation of a truth the hard core of which Alexander Hamilton was the first to discover:[45] courts are indeed very fragile bodies if an identity crisis or simply a phase of soul-searching on their part attracts on them the malevolent attention of the other powers in the form of political pressures and institutional constraints; and if such attention is sufficient to turn, as happened in the case of the Court of Justice, the soul-searching into a significant departure from the philosophy which guided them before they started to search their souls, the consequences can be far-reaching.

What does the future hold in store for the Court of Justice? The answer to this question will perhaps emerge from the intense debates that are likely to develop as each future Intergovernmental Conference approaches. We can only hope that those debates are as broad-based as possible and that, whichever direction Europe chooses, it does so with the whole-hearted consent of the peoples of Europe. Perhaps, as the Court of Justice becomes increasingly visible, in spite of

---

[43] On the importance of that principle, see G.F. Mancini and D.T. Keeling, "From *CILFIT* to *ERT*: the Constitutional Challenge Facing the European Court of Justice" (1991) *Yearbook of European Law* 1, at 2 and see Chapter 2.

[44] Note that limited jurisdiction with respect to certain matters which fall within the third pillar was subsequently granted to the Court pursuant to the Amsterdam Treaty. Moreover, several areas, in particular those provisions relating to immigration and asylum, have been transferred to the first pillar, with the result that the usual rules concerning the Court's jurisdiction apply, subject to certain limitations as regards the preliminary reference procedure.

[45] "[T]he judiciary is beyond comparison the weakest of the three departments of power; . . . it can never attack with success either of the other two; and all possible care is requisite to enable it to defend itself against their attacks": A. Hamilton, The Federalist No 78, reproduced in *The Federalist Papers by Alexander Hamilton, James Madison and John Jay* (Bantam Books).

its apparent desire for a low profile and a quiet life, and as more and more people become aware of its ability to impinge positively on their lives, the politicians of Europe will realize that a further emasculation of the Court does not necessarily provide a vote-winning platform in elections or referenda. Perhaps they will also realize that, as one commentator put it, law is the raw material of integration. And before our political masters decide to tamper even more radically with the powers of the institution that has, over the years, made such vigorous use of that raw material, they will do well to look closely at the Court's case law and remember how many of Europe's citizens have benefited directly as a result of the Court's rulings.

They will, for example, remember the Belgian air hostess who claimed the right to the same rate of pay as her male colleagues,[46] the British nurse who objected to being compelled to retire several years earlier than a man,[47] the German woman who was prevented from getting a job as a canteen assistant at Cagliari University by a practice discriminating against non-Italians,[48] the French student who wanted to study cartoon-drawing at an academy of fine arts in Belgium and was required to pay a fee not imposed on Belgian students,[49] the Greek hydrotherapist who asked only that his name should not be distorted beyond recognition when transliterated by an over-zealous German registrar of marriages,[50] and above all the millions of consumers who are the direct beneficiaries of a common market founded on the principles of free trade and undistorted competition.

What citizen of Europe has not been assisted in some way by the rulings of the European Court in Luxembourg? As long as the Court goes on handing down judgments that enable ordinary men and women to savour the fruits of integration, it will continue to demonstrate its usefulness. And the Member States, whose systems of government are—as Article F of the Maastricht Treaty reminds us—founded on the principles of democracy, will surely hesitate before embarking on an incisive whittling down of its powers.

---

[46] Case 43/75 *Defrenne* v *Société anonyme belge de navigation aérienne Sabena* [1976] ECR 455.
[47] Case 152/84 *M.H. Marshall* v *Southampton and South-West Hampshire Area Health Authority* [1986] ECR 723 and Case C-271/91 *M.H. Marshall* v *Southampton and South-West Hampshire Area Health Authority* [1993] ECR I-4367.
[48] Case C-419/92 *Scholz* v *Opera Universitaria di Cagliari e Cinzia Porcedda* [1994] ECR I-505.
[49] Case 293/83 *Gravier* v *City of Liège* [1985] ECR 593.
[50] Case C-168/91 *Konstantinidis* v *Stadt Altensteig* [1993] ECR I-1191.

12

Practice, Procedure and Forms of Action at the European Court of Justice

I. INTRODUCTION

As the previous Chapter has already pointed out, amongst the judicial organs presently in operation in the Western world the Court of Justice of the European Communities[1] is unique in many respects: the native tongues of its fifteen Judges are eleven in number; of the Member States from which they originate seven are monarchies and eight are republics; ten have a unitary structure, while five are divided into regions with substantial although varying degrees of autonomy; eight have some form of judicial review of legislation, while in seven of them such a concept is alien or downright blasphemous; two possess a legal culture moulded by centuries of judge-made law, whereas lawyers in the other thirteen have been brought up to believe that law-making is strictly the function of the legislature.[2] Whatever else may be said about the Court of Justice, and much is said, the nature of the Court and the execution of its functions are clearly influenced, if not determined, by this diversity.

Given the absence of recourse to any higher judicial authority against its decisions, this Chapter analyses the Court of Justice in its capacity as a "supreme court". Section 2 focuses on the issue of supranationalism and discusses whether "supranational" is still an apt description of the Court. In the light of the evolution which the EC/EU has so far witnessed and is expected to undergo in the near future, it is indeed arguable that the Court of Justice has become the "domestic" court of a polity which has its own independent decision-making processes and is characterized by some of the traits of statehood. Devoting more than passing attention to the topic of "supranationalism" may appear unnecessary—a self-indulgent, semi-political aside in an otherwise technical context. Nevertheless, if the purposes of the Court of Justice as a supreme court are to

---

[1] It is worth noting, first of all, that when the Court of Justice is referred to as one of the institutions of the European Community, it includes the Court of First Instance. For the purpose of the bulk of this Chapter, however, reference is made to the Court as a judicial body.

[2] See also G.F. Mancini and D. Keeling, "Language, Culture and Politics in the Life of the European Court of Justice" (1995) 1 *Columbia Journal of European Law* 397, at 397 and see Chapter 11.

be understood, it is agreed that viewing the Court in its institutional context is an essential preliminary, and perhaps the foundation, of all that follows.

Section 3 concentrates primarily on the tasks allotted to the Court by the text of the EC Treaty. Attention is also drawn to the overall goal of the European integration process as stated in the opening words of the Treaty's Preamble and reiterated in the TEU, namely an "ever closer union among the peoples of Europe". The Court's awareness of this goal has undoubtedly exerted a profound influence on its perception of the purposes which it is intended to serve. This fact has led some legal and political commentators to criticize what they regard as the unbridled activism exhibited by the jurisprudence produced in Luxembourg and, in particular, its bias against the interests of the Member States whenever they clash with those of the Community. It is suggested that such charges and the ensuing calls for a curtailment of the Court's powers can partly be attributed to incomprehension of both the nature and consequences of the EC Treaty text and the role which supreme courts have traditionally played during their early experiments in judicial review.

Section 3 also assesses the nature of the Court's functions in the Community legal order, pointing out that its varied jurisdiction encompasses aspects of law which customarily fall to administrative, penal, international, (federal) constitutional courts and to industrial tribunals. This variety is also illustrated when the conditions for recourse to the Court are discussed. Although the Court has developed a restrictive approach to the standing and the substantive rights of private litigants under some EC Treaty provisions, they still have access to the Court via the Article 177 mechanism provided in the EC Treaty. This Section concludes with a survey of the Court's public and private purposes. With reference to the distinction debated in the USA between situations where courts are involved in "dispute resolution" and those where "public action" is in evidence, it is suggested that, although clearly a useful categorization when applied in theory to the Court of Justice, this distinction is not a watertight one when examined in the light of the Court's jurisprudence.

Finally, the organization, composition and working methods of the Court are outlined in Section 4. Much of this Section is descriptive and covers areas already dealt with in detail by a number of authors.[3] However, an attempt is made to examine, as concisely as possible, the workings of the Court for those unfamiliar with these aspects.

---

[3] See, for example, D. Edward, "The Nature of the Community Judicial Process. How the Court of Justice works as a judicial body" in *Festskrift til Ole Due* (Gad, 1994), p. 31; L. Neville Brown and T. Kennedy (eds.), *The Court of Justice of the European Communities* 4th edn (Sweet and Maxwell, London, 1994); and K.P.E. Lasok, *The European Court of Justice. Practice and Procedure* (Butterworths, London, 1994).

2. THE NATURE OF THE EC/EU AND ITS INSTITUTIONS

Coined in 1853 by Friedrich Nietzsche, the word "supranational" has a long history, but its application to the European Communities and their institutions was the work of Robert Schuman and dates back to 1953.[4] The great success with which his definition met proves that Schuman had indeed identified a reality not only unprecedented but, in addition, one unable to fit into the classic models of international and constitutional law without straining some of its features. In more recent times, however, the heuristic value of "supranational" has been impaired by a variety of factors: in the first place, its increasingly frequent application to regional organizations and bodies whose international nature cannot be seriously questioned or whose political substance is wholly inconsistent with their supranational label;[5] secondly, the coming into fashion of other expressions—"transnational" is a case in point—not clearly distinguishable from it;[6] and, thirdly, the widespread usage of "federalism" or "federal" with a meaning so loose as to make them applicable to practically all political structures in which power is shared by its constituent parts.[7]

But the obsolescence of Schuman's definition has been brought about by more than semantic incidents. Its paramount cause lies in the evolution of the EC. To be sure, the EC is not yet a federal state in the strict sense: for example, despite growing pressure at European Council meetings it does not yet have a defence

[4] According to Schuman the term "supranational" is situated at an equal distance from, on the one hand, international individualism which regards national sovereignty as intangible and which only accepts as limitations of sovereignty obligations which are contractual, occasional and revocable; and, on the other hand, the federalism of states which subordinate themselves to a super-state endowed with its own territorial sovereignty. See further Schuman's preface to P. Reuter, *La Communauté européenne du charbon et de l'acier* (LGDJ, 1953), at p. 7; K. Lindeiner-Wildau, *La Supranationalité en tant que principe de droit* (Sijthoff, 1970); and F. Capotorti, "Supranational Organizations" in *Encyclopedia of Public International Law* (North-Holland, 1983), Volume V, p. 262.

[5] Instances of the former are provided by the Council of Europe, NAFTA and Mercosur, while the latter is exemplified by the Cartagena Treaty and its institutions, including the Court in Quito (throughout 1995, Peru and Ecuador, both signatories to that Treaty, were involved in a number of military exchanges), and the organizations, also endowed with courts modelled on the Court of Justice, which are mushrooming in Africa, Central America and the Middle East. On the latter see P. von Chris Maina Peter, "European Integration and its Influence on Africa: A Comparison between the Maastricht Union Treaty and the African Economic Community Treaty" in M. Henssler *et al.* (eds.), *Europäische Integration und globaler Wettbewerb* (Recht und Wirtschaft, 1993), p. 141.

[6] See, for example, E. Stein, "Lawyers, Judges and the Making of a Transnational Constitution" (1981) 75 *American Journal of International Law* 1. See also B. Ackerman, *The Future of Liberal Revolution* (1992), at p. 39 *et seq.*; and Gibson and Caldeira, *Legitimacy, Judicial Power and the Emergence of Transnational Legal Institutions*, report presented at the conference of the Research Committee on Comparative Judicial Studies of the International Political Science Association, held at Forlì from 14 to 17 June 1992, under the aegis of the University of Bologna.

[7] See S.J. Boom, "The EU After the *Maastricht* Decision. Is Germany the 'Virginia' of Europe?" (1995) 43 *American Journal of Comparative Law* 177, at n.8. See further K. Lenaerts, "Is the European Union Federal?" in Fleerackers, F. *et al.* (eds), *Festschrift for Jan M. Broekman* (1996), at p. 418 *et seq.*

policy (since the WEU remains an independent organization), its foreign and security policies are carried out at an intergovernmental level, its central authorities are not empowered to levy taxes and, according to most commentators, cannot award themselves additional competences. Furthermore, its basic law is not the fruit of a constitutional convention, but is found in treaties of which, as the Bundesverfassungsgericht (BVerfG) claims, the Member States remain "masters".[8] Yet, if it is indisputable that treaties are inherently different from constitutions, history has surely taught us that treaties may be converted into constitutions or constitutions into treaties[9] and that in the course of these processes there comes a time when deciding which is which is a thorny and sometimes dramatic problem. It should not be forgotten, for example, that till the end of the Civil War (some would go so far as saying till the ratification of the Fourteenth Amendment in 1868),[10] the nature of the document produced by the Philadelphia Convention was controversial. A host of American statesmen and scholars regarded it, in the words of the Second Kentucky Resolution,[11] as "a compact under the style and title of a Constitution" and hence susceptible of being altered or denounced by the states which had acceded to it.

In the history of European integration the time has surely come when the balance may be said to have shifted towards a constitution-like document. The acquiescence, even if sometimes grudging, of all Member States to the primacy of EC law, the progressive extension of majority voting in the Council of Ministers,[12] the election by universal suffrage of the European Parliament and its growing participation in the legislative process,[13] the proclamation of Union citizenship,[14] and the forthcoming monetary union are all clues indicating that a

---

[8] Judgment of 12 October 1993, in *BVerfGE*, 89, p. 155 (the so-called Maastricht-*Urteil*), reproduced in (1994) *Common Market Law Reports* 57, where, at para. 55, the BVerfG maintained that Germany was one of the *"Herren der Verträge"*.

[9] In an article entitled "The Rise of World Constitutionalism" (1997) 83 *University of Virginia Law Review* 771–797, Ackerman provides a clear-sighted analysis of the conversion of treaties into constitutions and vice versa.

An example of the latter type of conversion is provided by Belgium, originally a unitary, then a regional and now a federal state risking dismemberment. Its Constitution of 5 May 1993 is evolving into a treaty between two communities, the Flemish and the Francophones, on the march towards "une indépendance qui ne dit pas son nom", see Delgrange, "Le fédéralisme belge: la protection des minorités linguistiques et idéologiques" (1994) *Revue de droit public et de la science politique en France et à l'étranger* 1170; S. Mancini, *Minoranze autoctone e stato. Tra composizione dei conflitti e secessione* (Giuffré, 1996), p. 128 *et seq.*

[10] See Ackerman, *ibid.*

[11] 16 November 1798.

[12] See, for example, P. Raworth, *The Legislative Process in the EC* (Kluwer, 1993).

[13] See variously R. Gosalbo Bono, "Co-decision: an appraisal of the experience of the European Parliament as a Co-legislator" (1994) 14 *Yearbook of European Law* 21; G.R.G. Ress, "Democratic Decision-making in the EU and the Role of the European Parliament" in T. Henkels *et al.* (eds), *Institutional Dynamics of European Integration: Essays in Honour of Henry G. Schermers*, Volume II (1994), p. 153; and J. Lodge, "The European Parliament After Direct Elections: Talking-Shop or Putative Legislature?" (1982) 5 *Revue d'intégration européenne* 259.

[14] See S. O'Leary, *The Evolving Concept of Community Citizenship* (Kluwer, Deverter, 1996), in particular ch. 1; and S. Hall, *Nationality, Migration Rights and Citizenship of the Union* (Kluwer, Deverter, 1996).

major change has occurred or, to say the least, is in the offing. The EC/EU seems to be leaping beyond the stage when it could be regarded as an international organization endowed with institutions and decision-making mechanisms so singular as to justify the rediscovery of "supranational" in order to grasp its essence. Moreover, a clear reflection of this new situation is detectable in the jurisprudence of the Court of Justice. While its path-breaking *Van Gend en Loos* ruling of 1963 still described the Community legal system as a branch of international law, albeit characterized by features of its own,[15] a judgment of 1986, *Les Verts*, referred to the EC Treaty as "the basic constitutional charter" of the EC.[16] Indeed, this reference reappeared five years later in terms even more significant when the Court inverted the language of the Kentucky Resolution as follows: "the Treaty, albeit concluded in the form of an international agreement, none the less constitutes the constitutional charter of a Community based on the rule of law".[17]

It may of course be argued that the Court has been indulging in a series of metaphors; nobody could deny, however, that these metaphors were used with the clear awareness that, particularly in the civil law tradition, the word "constitution" postulates statehood[18]—not necessarily a full-blown statehood, but at least an embryonic or dawning one. Is it worthwhile then to follow in the footsteps of Schuman and crystallize this phase in the evolution of the EC/EU by means of some new neologism? Though less sanguine about the scope of this evolution, the BVerfG believed that it is indeed worthwhile and held that today's EC is a *Staatenverbund*, namely a compound both qualitatively different from a *Bundesstaat*, or federation, and more closely-knit than an orthodox *Staatenbund*, or confederacy. But the failure of this exertion (a mere "play on words", was Everling's wise comment)[19] proves that taking a snapshot of what

---

[15] See Case 26/62 NV *Algemene Transport- en Expeditie Onderneming Van Gend en Loos* v *Nederlandse Administratie der Belastingen* [1963] ECR 3, 12: "the Community constitutes a new legal order of international law for the benefit of which the states have limited their sovereign rights, albeit within limited fields, and the subjects of which comprise not only Member States but also their nationals".

[16] See Case 294/83 *Parti écologiste "Les Verts"* v *European Parliament* [1986] ECR 1339, para. 23.

[17] See Opinion 1/91 [1991] ECR I-6079, para. 21; Case C-2/88 Imm. *J.J. Zwartveld and others* [1990] ECR I-3365, para. 16 and Case C-314/91 *Beate Weber* v *European Parliament* [1993] ECR I-1093, para. 8. In contrast to the BVerfG's assertion that the Member States are the "masters" of the EC Treaty, the Court in Opinion 1/91 seemed to recognize the existence of a hardcore of principles and essential values characterizing the Community legal system which may not be modified nor abrogated. Thus, at para. 71 it held that: "Article 238 of the EEC Treaty does not provide any basis for setting up a system of courts which conflicts with Article 164 of the EEC Treaty and, more generally, with the very foundations of the Community". See also C. Curti Gialdino, "Some Reflections on the *Acquis Communautaire*" (1995) 32 *CMLRev* 1089, at 1109 *et seq.*

[18] See, for example, Boom, *supra* n. 7, at 209: "A constitution by definition establishes the basic principles and laws of a *nation* or *state*".

[19] U. Everling, "The Maastricht Judgment of the German Federal Constitutional Court and its Significance for the Development of the EU" (1994) 14 *Yearbook of European Law* 1, at 7. See also Messen, "Hedging European Integration: The Maastricht Judgment of the Federal Constitutional Court of Germany" (1994) 17 *Fordham International Law Journal* 511, at 526, where the author points out that combining "'*Staaten-*' with '*-verbund*' instead of '*-bund*', has the charm of novelty but is burdened with connotations of former usage that are less than inspiring, such as networks of public utilities or of suburban train services".

can only be filmed is a waste of time. Reverting to the point of departure, it will therefore suffice to say that the germ of statehood characterizing the present fabric of the EC/EU, though not conferring on the Judges in Luxembourg the same legitimacy and self-assurance enjoyed by their brethren in states such as the USA, Australia or Switzerland, entitles them to feel and act as members of a domestic or municipal court. In any event, to borrow from John Locke, "so the thing be understood, I am indifferent as to the name".

3. THE PURPOSES OF THE COURT OF JUSTICE

(a) The EC Treaty definition of the purpose of the Court

As Section 1 signalled, the Court of Justice is sometimes accused of having been—and, to a more limited degree, of still being—exceedingly activist. It is, according to a recent critic, a Court with a "mission" and hence "unorthodox".[20] More crudely, other critics described it in the 1970s and 1980s as a Court portraying signs of a "morbid megalomania",[21] running "wild" and indulging in "revolting judicial behaviour".[22] Some of these charges are dictated by sheer Europhobia or by raw domestic interests; others, coming from politicians and scholars educated in countries where the legislature reigns supreme, reflect more or less consciously an understandable misgiving about the "countermajoritarian" nature of a judicial body wielding the power to review legislation.[23]

Whatever their motives may be, the Court's censors do not err when they point to the creativeness of its jurisprudence. Their weakness lies in their failure to recognize that the seeds of such creativeness and the soil necessary for it to flourish were contained in the EC Treaty. First and foremost in this respect is Article 164 of the EC Treaty which provides that "The Court of Justice shall ensure that in the interpretation and application of the Treaty the law is observed". In other and less "beguilingly simple" words,[24] this provision lays down a principle which signals a radical break from the theory and practice of

---

[20] P. Neill, "A Case Study in Judicial Activism", evidence submitted to the House of Lords Select Committee on the European Communities, 1996 Intergovernmental Conference, Session 1994–95, 18th Report, 218, at p. 245. The author draws this conclusion *inter alia* from the English version of my Opinion as Advocate General in Case 294/83 *Les Verts*, *supra* n. 16, where the Italian word *missione*, which also means task or assignment (Article 2 EC), has been heedlessly translated as "mission".

[21] See also G.F. Mancini, "The Making of a Constitution for Europe" (1989) 26 *CMLRev* 595, at 595 and see Chapter 1.

[22] See H. Rasmussen, *On Law and Policy in the European Court of Justice: A Comparative Study in Judicial Policy-making* (Nijhoff, 1986), at p. 12.

[23] See, for example, M. Cappelletti, *The Judicial Process in Comparative Perspective* (Clarendon Press, 1989), at p. 40 *et seq.* with reference to British critics of judicial law-making such as Lord Devlin.

[24] According to Neill's assessment of Article 164 EC.

international organizations and one which is teeming with far-reaching implications: the Community is founded on the rule of law[25] and the Court must see that this rule is enforced. What the Court did was to bring to light those implications; in fact, it took this task so seriously as to retouch or update the EC Treaty itself (which in any case had not been devised as a static instrument),[26] whenever the evolution of the Community threatened the central position held by the rule of law in its system of values.

Thus, when secondary legislation began to jeopardize certain fundamental rights of European citizens, the Court of Justice concluded, after a long period of soul-searching, that the nature of the Community as a *Communauté de droit* would be impaired if those rights were not protected and an open-ended catalogue thereof read into the EC Treaty.[27] In the same vein, when the European Parliament ceased being a debating forum and was vested with some tangible powers, the Court considered that the most (or perhaps only) democratic institution[28] of a Community based on the rule of law should be granted *locus standi* in order both to protect the individuals from an illegal exercise of those powers[29] and to have the latter protected from any onslaught by the Council and the Commission.[30]

In its seminal decisions of the 1960s and 1970s the importance attached by the Court to the notion of *Communauté de droit* plays perhaps a less crucial, but still quite visible, role. This certainly was the case in the *Van Gend en Loos* and *Van Duyn*[31] rulings. As Article 189 of the EC Treaty clearly shows, the possibility for Member States' citizens to rely on European law was an inherent and fundamental aspect of the Community legal order from the outset. The two judgments mentioned above applied this principle to EC Treaty rules and provisions of directives conferring rights on individuals in so clear-cut a form as to make enabling measures unnecessary. The citizens of the Member States were thus raised to the rank of "guardians" of the Treaty—a function until then performed by the Commission alone—with the result that the demand for

---

[25] The expression used by the Court—*Communauté de droit*—is modelled on *Etat de droit*, which is the French version of the German *Rechtsstaat*.

[26] See, for example, P. Eleftheriadis, "Aspects of European Constitutionalism" (1996) 2 *ELRev* 32; see also G.F. Mancini and D. Keeling, "From *CILFIT* to *ERT*: the Constitutional Challenge facing the European Court" (1991) 11 *Yearbook of European Law* 1, at 7 and see Chapter 2.

[27] For an analysis of this process see G.F. Mancini and V. Di Bucci, "Le développement des droits fondamentaux en tant que partie du droit communautaire" in Academy of European Law (ed.), *Collected Courses of the Academy of European Law*, Volume I, Book 1 (Kluwer, 1991), p. 27.

[28] Case 138/79 *SA Roquette Frères* v *Council* [1980] ECR 3333, para. 33, where the Court stated that the need to consult the European Parliament "represents an essential factor in the institutional balance intended by the Treaty. Although limited, it reflects at Community level the fundamental democratic principle that the people should take part in the exercise of power through the intermediary of a representative assembly".

[29] See Case 294/83 *Les Verts*, *supra* n. 16.

[30] See Case C-70/88 *European Parliament* v *Council* ("*Chernobyl*") [1990] ECR I-2041.

[31] Case 41/74 *Yvonne Van Duyn* v *Home Office* [1974] ECR 1337.

"observance of the law" and therefore the thrust of the rule of law itself were increased enormously via the mechanism of Article 177 of the EC Treaty.[32]

No less telling, however, are the examples of the decisions in *Costa v ENEL*[33] and *Simmenthal*.[34] In proclaiming, as it did in those judgments, that Community law takes precedence over national legislation, including constitutions, the Court was chiefly motivated by the need to hold in check the powerful centrifugal forces already at work in the new polity. There is no doubt, however, that it was also driven by the prospect of the discrimination to which European citizens would fall victim in the event that European law, if devoid of primacy, were not uniformly enforced throughout the Community. In a *Communauté de droit* such a possibility would indeed be intolerable.

Underrating the pregnancy of the language used in Article 164 of the EC Treaty and its decisive impact on the philosophy of the Court is, in conclusion, a serious mistake. It must be admitted, however, that all of the decisions cited above were influenced by a further element: the Court's acute awareness that the EC Treaty was but the foundation stone, as affirmed in the opening words of its Preamble, of "an ever closer union between the peoples of Europe". To the best of my knowledge, the Court has never quoted these precise words; but its members certainly bore them in mind when they defined the object of their duty "to secure observance of a particular legal order and to foster its development with a view . . . to achieving the objectives set out in . . . the EEC Treaty and to attaining a European Union among the Member States"[35] or when they asserted that "les traités européens ne sont rien d'autre que la mise en oeuvre partielle d'un grand programme général dominé par l'idée de l'intégration complète des États européens".[36] Nor should it be forgotten that in *Van Gend en Loos* the Court drew attention to the Preamble's reference not only to States but also to peoples.[37]

Could, or rather *should*, it have been otherwise? I do not believe so. Technically the bulk of the Preamble to the EC Treaty has no prescriptive character, but all of the recitals of which it is comprised embody the general design of the framers as it had coalesced when the Treaty was drafted, signed and ratified. As all authorities agree, the essentially optative nature of this design does not make it legally irrelevant; a judicial body intended to ensure observance of

---

[32] In the case of the *Van Duyn* doctrine, it has been submitted that the Court's devotion to the rule of law weighed in a further sense. Non-compliance with directives is the most typical and most frequent Member State infraction and the Community authorities often turned a blind eye to it. This gave directives a dangerously elastic quality. If the Court had condoned that quality, thus frustrating the legitimate expectations of the European citizens on whom directives confer rights, the latter "could no longer be termed law"; and nobody will deny that "directives are intended to have the force of law under the Treaty": see M. Cappelletti, M. Seccombe and J.H.H. Weiler, "A General Introduction " in M. Cappelletti *et al.* (eds.), *Integration Through Law* (de Gruyter, 1986), Volume I, Book 1, at p. 39.

[33] Case 6/64 [1964] ECR 1141.

[34] Case 106/77 *Amministrazione delle finanze dello Stato v SA Simmenthal* [1978] ECR 629.

[35] See Opinion 1/91, *supra* n. 17, para. 50.

[36] See the Opinion of Advocate General Römer in Joined Cases 27 and 39/59 *Alberto Campolongo v Haute Autorité* [1960] ECR 391.

[37] Case 26/62, *supra* n. 15, para. 12.

the provisions following the Preamble *must* take it into account if not as the ubiquitous compass needle of its interpretive operations, then as one, and surely not the least important, of the parameters which govern them.[38]

This obligation is at the root of the preference for Europe or, more prosaically, for the Community's interests, which characterizes such a large portion of the Court's case law.[39] The Court has been hauled over the coals[40] (and threatened with the deprivation or curtailment of some of its powers)[41] for this sin more than any other; but, once again, essentially because of its critics' disregard for the normative context within which it had been called on to act.

Of course, this is not always the case. Not all of the reprimands addressed to the Court were and are unjustified. Some observers have rightly pointed out the contradiction existing between the Court's emphasis on the rule of law and its restrictive interpretation of Article 173(4) of the EC Treaty, which empowers legal and natural persons to challenge Community decisions and regulations.[42] Others have effectively exposed the idle European rhetoric burdening certain judgments. By and large, however, even the most level-headed critics seem to forget that supreme courts have generally played a unifying role in the formative years of the states whose constitutions they were required to uphold and that their contemporary foes have not gone down in history for bashing them. Thomas Jefferson and James Madison did not conceal their intense dislike of Marshall's Court.[43] Today, Robert Bork, the most outspoken advocate of "strict constructionism" in America, acknowledges that *Marbury* v *Madison*[44] and *McCulloch* v *Maryland*[45] were indispensable for the survival and the development of the Union.[46] But the same could be said of a host of other federal

[38] S. Schepers, "The Legal Force of the Preamble to the EEC Treaty" (1981) 6 *ELRev* 356.

[39] See also G.F. Mancini and D. Keeling, "Democracy and the European Court of Justice" (1994) 57 *Modern Law Review* 175, at 186: "The preference for Europe is determined by the genetic code transmitted to the Court by the founding fathers, who entrusted to it the task of ensuring that the law is observed in the application of a Treaty whose primary objective is an 'ever closer union among the peoples of Europe'" and see Chapter 3.

[40] For examples of such criticism see, for example, T. Hartley, "The European Court, Judicial Objectivity and the Constitution of the European Union" (1996) 112 *LQR* 95; Neill, *supra* n. 20, at pp. 218 and 245.

[41] See, for example P. Clever, "Grundsätzliche Bemerkungen zur Rechtsprechung des EuGH" *Die Angestelltenversicherung* 2/93, or some of the British proposals for the 1996 IGC reflected in that government's White Paper, *A Partnership of Nations. The British Approach to the 1996 IGC* (CM 3181, 1996).

[42] On the restrictive nature of the Court's jurisprudence and proposals for reform see, *inter alia*, A. Arnull, "Private Applicants and the Action for Annulment under Article 173 of the EC Treaty" (1995) 32 *CMLRev* 7–49; A. Dashwood (ed.), *Reviewing Maastricht. Issues for the 1996 IGC* (Sweet and Maxwell, 1996), at pp. 301–303; and *infra* Section 3(c) "Conditions for Recourse to the Court of Justice".

[43] See Ketcham, *James Madison. A Biography* (1995), at p. 632.

[44] 5 U.S. (1 Cranch) 137 (1803).

[45] 17 U.S. (4 Wheat.) 316 (1819).

[46] See R. Bork, *The Tempting of America: the Political Seduction of the Law* (The Free Press, 1990), at p. 21: "Although he [Marshall] may have deliberately misread the statutes, he did not misread the Constitution. His constitutional rulings, often argued brilliantly, are faithful to the document. Marshall's tactic may perhaps be understood, for the survival of the Union was probably in some part due to the centralizing and unifying force of Marshall and his Court".

constitutional courts, which were scolded for their early "centralist" or "nationalist" inclinations, only to see their work vindicated by commentators endowed with the privilege of hindsight. Perhaps a similar destiny is in store for the Court of Justice.

(b) The jurisdiction of the Court

The scope of the Court's jurisdiction is wide and multi-faceted. Civil lawyers not conversant with EC law, used as they are in their own countries to see the powers embodying that jurisdiction shared among different specialized courts, find this fact particularly baffling.

The review of national legislation which the Court exercises at the request of the Commission (Article 169 EC) or a Member State (Article 170 EC) reflects in its procedural weakness the origins of the Community as a variation, however novel, on the type of international organizations then in existence. If at issue is a measure enacted or kept in force by a Member State and the Court finds it incompatible with the EC Treaty, that measure cannot be annulled. If the Member State is accused of failing to comply with a Treaty obligation (the implementation of a Community directive, for instance) and the charge is substantiated, no means are available to force the Member State into compliance. All that the Court can do is to declare it in breach of the EC Treaty and only if the Member State ignores this judgment will it be liable to a fine (Article 171 EC).[47] In the light of such provisions, among which only the last has some muscle, but which has seldom been used,[48] the Court's powers can be equated with those of a constitutional court only in a rudimentary sense.

By contrast, the Court can be said to exercise the functions of a full-blown constitutional court on the basis of Article 177 of the EC Treaty. As a consequence of the doctrine of direct effect, this preliminary reference procedure, which requires the Court to interpret Community law while leaving to the national court the task of applying that interpretation to the facts of the case, has evolved, for all practical purposes, into a powerful instrument for reviewing the compatibility with the EC Treaty of Member State legislation. Indeed, as Joseph Weiler points out, the inborn frailty of this instrument—its relying almost entirely on the goodwill of the national judiciaries[49]—has proved to be its strength, since the very fact that "their own" courts make the reference to the Court of Justice forces governments to juridify their arguments against the claims of the Community and shift to the judicial arena in which the Court is pre-eminent. Moreover, when the referring court accepts the ruling, which hap-

---

[47] As a result of an amendment introduced by the Maastricht Treaty, which marked a powerful step in the evolution of the EC.

[48] See, for the first case in which Article 171 EC has been used, Case C-387/97 *Commission* v *Greece*, pending, and the Opinion of Advocate General Ruiz Jarabo of 28 September 1999.

[49] See also Mancini and Keeling (1991), *supra* n. 26, at 1 *et seq* and see Chapter 2.

pens most of the time, the compliance pull of Community law becomes irresistible.[50]

The Court also controls the conformity of Community secondary legislation with the EC Treaty by means of the annulment procedure in Article 173, the preliminary reference procedure under Article 177, if its object is the validity of a Community measure, and the general remedy (*exception d'illégalité*) provided for in Article 184.[51] This review is explicitly regarded by the Court as having a constitutional character. In *Les Verts*, for example, the Court held that Article 173, whose original version in the EEC Treaty only mentioned control of the legality of the acts of the Council and Commission, also extended to the acts of the European Parliament which produce legal effects with regard to third parties. As mentioned above, this decision was grounded on the consideration that "the EEC is a Community based on the rule of law, inasmuch as neither its Member States nor its institutions can avoid a review of the question whether the measures adopted by them are in conformity with the basic constitutional charter, the Treaty".[52] If, the Court added, Article 173 of the EC Treaty were interpreted as excluding acts of the European Parliament from those which can be contested, the result would be contrary to both the spirit of the Treaty as expressed in Article 164 and to its general "system".[53] The Court also acts as a constitutional court when it gives binding Opinions on the compatibility of international agreements to be concluded by the Community with the provisions of the Treaty[54] and when it resolves disputes between the Community institutions involving their competences.[55]

Prior to 1989 and 1993, the Court acted as an "industrial tribunal" for the resolution of staff cases and as an administrative court along the lines of the French Conseil d'Etat when hearing actions for annulment and damages introduced by individuals on the basis of Articles 173, 178 and 215 of the EC Treaty. These fields now come within the jurisdiction of the Court of First Instance, but the Court still deals with them on appeal, albeit solely with regard to points of law.[56]

---

[50] See J.H.H. Weiler, "Journey to an Unknown Destination: A Retrospective and Prospective of the European Court of Justice in the Arena of Political Integration" (1993) 31 *Journal of Common Market Studies* 416, at 422.

[51] This remedy is derived from French administrative law, but a variation thereof exists also in English law where a challenge is raised collaterally to the validity of a statutory instrument or by-law in a prosecution for its infringement. See further Neville Brown and Kennedy, *supra* n. 3, at p. 151.

[52] See Case 294/83, *supra* n. 16, para. 23.

[53] *Ibid.*, para. 25.

[54] Article 228(6) EC.

[55] Articles 173 and 175 EC.

[56] See *infra* Section 4. Mention should also be made of Article 181 EC which provides that the Court of Justice has jurisdiction "to give judgment pursuant to an arbitration clause contained in a contract concluded by or on behalf of the Community, whether that contract be governed by private or public law". Only the parties to the arbitration clause can be parties to the action before the Court and the Court may only adjudicate upon claims arising from, or directly connected with, the contract. In addition, Article 182 EC provides for the Court's jurisdiction over disputes between Member States which relate to the subject matter of the Treaty and which are referred to it under a

(c) Conditions for recourse to the Court of Justice

The very nature of Article 169 of the EC Treaty implies that the persons affected by a national measure, or the absence thereof, which they deem to be in breach of Community law may ask the Commission to bring an action, but may not rely on it doing so. Article 169 facilitates the exercise by the Commission of its function as guardian of the Treaties and the Court has accordingly bestowed on the Commissioners, the final arbiters in this respect, complete discretion in deciding whether or not to initiate proceedings against a defaulting Member State.[57]

On the other hand, in actions before national courts, private litigants may request that a preliminary reference be made to the Court of Justice; but unless the court or tribunal hearing the case is one against whose decision no judicial remedy is available under national law, there is no obligation to bring the matter before the Court of Justice.[58] In fact, the whole Article 177 edifice relies on the utmost cooperation from the national courts—a condition which has so far been largely complied with in terms both of quantity and quality.[59] It is almost gospel that the better part of Community law has resulted from rulings given by the Court of Justice in answer to references from lower national courts.[60]

On its face, Article 173(4) of the EC Treaty appears to be the means of judicial recourse *par excellence* for individuals wronged by Community measures. It provides that "Any natural or legal person may . . . institute proceedings against a decision addressed to that person or against a decision which, although in the form of a regulation or a decision addressed to another person, is of direct and individual concern to the former". However, before cases brought by private litigants were transferred to the Court of First Instance, this provision was interpreted by the Court in an extremely restrictive way: a regulation, the Court held, must single the applicant out and affect him or her more seriously than others in a similar position if his or her action is to be deemed admissible.[61] As a consequence of such a construction, a regulation may be patently and outrageously unlawful, breach the principles of non-discrimination and proportionality, violate fundamental rights, inflict huge financial losses on a large number of persons

---

special agreement between the parties. While Article 181 has occasionally been used, no cases have yet been brought before the Court on the basis of Article 182. Both provisions play a very marginal role as regards the jurisdiction of the Court.

[57] See, for example, Case 247/87 *Star Fruit Company SA v Commission* [1989] ECR 291, para. 11: "[I]t is clear from the scheme of Article 169 of the Treaty that the Commission is not bound to commence proceedings provided for in that provision but in this regard has a discretion which excludes the right for individuals to require that institution to adopt a specific position".

[58] Article 177 EC, paras 2 and 3.

[59] Mancini and Keeling (1991), *supra* n. 26, and see Chapter 2.

[60] See in a similar vein Weiler, *supra* n. 50, at 423.

[61] See, for example, Case 25/62 *Plaumann & Co.* v *Commission* [1963] ECR 95, or Joined Cases 789 and 790/79 *Calpak SpA and Società Emiliana Lavorazione Frutta SpA v Commission* [1980] ECR 1949.

and yet be unamenable to direct challenges. All that a person injured by the act can do is to defy it and wait till an attempt is made to enforce it against him or her in the national courts, where he or she may contest its validity and succeed in having the issue referred to the Court under Article 177.[62]

As it will be remembered, the case law in question, which was probably devised as a floodgate with the aim, in the absence of *certiorari* or similar mechanisms, of avoiding an otherwise unmanageable tide of proceedings, has been sharply criticized. Two among the last judgments preceding the transfer of jurisdiction seemed to take cognizance of this opposition,[63] but the Court of First Instance has to date shown no willingness to cultivate those revisionist seeds. It remains to be seen whether they will be developed by the Court of Justice in its appellate capacity.

Much of what has been said about the Court's jurisprudence on the restrictive notion of standing for private litigants can be extended to its no less restrictive approach to the award of damages to individuals who claim loss or injury pursuant to Article 215 of the EC Treaty as a result of unlawful Community legislative or administrative measures. Article 215, which is now initially the concern of the Court of First Instance, provides that "[I]n the case of non-contractual liability, the Community shall, in accordance with the general principles common to the laws of the Member States, make good any damage caused by its institutions or servants in the performance of their duties". However, the Court of Justice would only have awarded compensation for damage caused by normative acts if the victim of the illegality could prove that the institutions have committed a sufficiently serious breach of a "superior rule of law" for the protection of the individual. In other words, it was not enough for their conduct to be knowingly unlawful, although this would suffice no doubt in the majority of the Member States; instead it must verge on the arbitrary or capricious.[64] The effect of such a construction was to deter individuals from recourse to this remedy; probably the result that the Court wished to attain, thereby avoiding the flood of cases with which it feared it would be unable to cope.

To conclude this survey of the various conditions for recourse to the Court, mention must be made of Article 175 of the EC Treaty. The latter provides a remedy against an institution which has infringed the Treaty by failing to act where it is *obliged* to do so. The Member States and the other institutions may bring an action before the Court of Justice to have the infringement established (Article 175(1)). In contrast, natural or legal persons may only challenge a failure to address to them any act other than a recommendation or opinion; in other words, only binding acts (Article 175(3)). Before any such action can be lodged, the institution in question must be called upon to define its position within the

---

[62] See Mancini and Keeling (1994), *supra* n. 39, at 188–189 and see Chapter 3.

[63] See Case C-358/89 *Extramet Industrie SA v Council* [1991] ECR I-2501; and Case C-309/89 *Codorniu SA v Council* [1994] ECR I-1853.

[64] See, for example, Joined Cases 116 and 124/77 *G.R. Amylum NV and Tunnel Refineries Limited v Council and Commission* [1979] ECR 3497.

space of two months. If it remains in default, an Article 175 action may be initiated within a further two months. If it defines its position refusing to act as the applicant wishes, the latter may seek to annul this refusal under Article 173. In practice, as evidenced by the fact that very few Article 175 actions have succeeded, this provision is too intricate and burdensome to be of real use for private litigants.

(d) The distinction between the Court's public and private purposes

Turning now to the question whether the Court's purposes are public or private: private purposes consist in the achievement of procedural and substantive justice for the parties to the litigation, while public purposes focus, *inter alia*, on the clarification, development and uniform interpretation of the law, the maintenance of public faith in the legal system, the assurance of correct procedure and the elimination of abuse, the protection of general public interests which may be affected by the outcome of a case and the maintenance of a balance between the interests of the state on the one hand, and those of the private sector or of individuals, on the other.

In attempting to apply this distinction to the purposes, both in law and fact, of the Court of Justice, it may prove useful to draw on a long-running American debate on the distinction between "cases" and "controversies". This debate has more recently been updated in terms of a distinction between the "dispute resolution" and "public action" models of litigation. The former model refers to the "traditional" judicial role of the courts as the authorities endowed with the power to determine particular, ongoing disputes between identified litigants. In other words, the court is viewed as a mere settler of conflicts. By contrast, the "public action" model regards courts as institutions "with a distinctive capacity to declare and explicate public values—norms that transcend individual controversies and that are concerned with the conditions of social and political life".[65] Can echoes of these models be detected in the purposes of the Court of Justice as established in the EC Treaty?

Clearly, Article 173(4) of the EC Treaty could be said to require the Court of First Instance to act as a dispute-settler. This provision, as we have seen, states that natural and legal persons may institute proceedings against an act addressed to them or which affects them directly and individually. Consider, for example, a situation in which company A complains to the EC Commission that the distribution system operated by company B is in breach of Article 85 of the EC Treaty, one of the basic provisions intended to guarantee undistorted competition. Its claim having been rejected by the Commission, company A resorts

---

[65] See Bator, Meltzer, Mishkin and Shapiro, *Hart and Wechsler's Federal Courts and Federal System*, 3rd edn (1988), at p. 79 *et seq*. See also Damaska, *The Faces of Justice and State Authority* (1986), who deals with the relationship between what he calls the "conflict solving" and "policy implementing" approaches to adjudication.

to Article 173 of the EC Treaty in an attempt to have this decision annulled. Similarly, when the Court of First Instance acts in staff cases, it is resolving a dispute or controversy between a Community civil servant and a Community institution. A further example is Article 215, paragraph 2 which, as we saw, governs the Community's non-contractual liability. Here again, when damages are sought by a farmer for losses he or she claims to have suffered as a result of the implementation of the Common Agricultural Policy (CAP), the purpose of the same Court is simply to achieve substantive justice according to the law for the parties concerned.[66]

By contrast, the "public action" model is inherent in the system of preliminary references under Article 177. According to the EC Treaty, the purpose of the Court of Justice in this context is simply to provide a preliminary ruling which interprets Community law in order to aid the national court in its resolution of a particular case. Any meddling on its part with the situation preceding or following the reference is excluded. Indeed, as the Court emphasized in *Costa* v *ENEL*, Article 177 "is based on a clear separation of functions between national courts and the Court of Justice" and the latter does not have the power to "investigate the facts of the case or to criticise the grounds and purpose of the request for interpretation".[67] Thus, in the *Van Gend en Loos* case, the Court was requested to interpret the notion of customs duties existing before the coming into force of the EC Treaty, which it did, its interpretation being subsequently applied to resolve the dispute pending before the national court on the reimbursement of duties imposed by the Dutch authorities. Yet, on spotting large Van Gend en Loos lorries on the high-speed motorways of Europe, few students of Community law remember or are concerned with the actual outcome of the case when it returned to the Netherlands. Rather, they remember *Van Gend en Loos* for the principle which, in accordance with the abovementioned definition of the public action model, transcended the individual controversy and which was concerned with the direct effect of Treaty rules, namely with a public value of supreme importance for the constitutional architecture of the EC.

Likewise, when the Commission seeks to establish on the basis of Article 169 of the EC Treaty that a Member State has failed to fulfil its Treaty obligations, the Court of Justice is not being called on to operate as a dispute-settler. This remark may appear to be in substantial, if not formal, contrast with the fact that the bulk of Article 169 actions originate in private complaints, or in private complaints transformed into European parliamentary questions or petitions.[68] Nevertheless, once it has filed its application with the Registrar, the

---

[66] When the Court acts as an arbitrator pursuant to Article 181 EC it could also be said to be involved in dispute resolution.

[67] Case 6/64, *supra* n. 33, at 593.

[68] The other category of Article 169 EC actions—against Member States which have failed to implement directives within the prescribed time-limit—are initiated automatically when the Commission notices that this time limit has expired without action being taken at the national level.

Commission does not stand proxy for the individual who spurred it into action, nor does it have an interest of its own in the outcome of the case; it simply acts in its capacity as guardian of the Treaties and the decision of the Court relates accordingly to the uniform application of EC law, the protection of Community and national interests and the prevention of abuse. Even more clearly, when adjudicating interinstitutional disputes concerning, for example, use of the appropriate legal basis for a regulation or a directive, the Court does not aim to achieve justice between the parties (indeed, how could *substantive* justice be achieved in such cases), but to secure, through the correct interpretation and application of EC law, a proper functioning of the Community's legislative process. Finally, it is self-evident that the very language of Article 164 (the Court must see that "in the interpretation and application of the Treaty the law is observed"), implies that the Court's concern with public purposes—the clarification, development and uniform enforcement of the law—is intended by the EC Treaty to be overarching if not paramount.

It must be observed, however, that, as the editors of Hart and Wechsler point out, the American distinction between dispute resolution and public action models does not involve watertight compartments;[69] in fact its application to particular cases reveals that the two models may intertwine.[70] This is no less true of the distinction between the private and public purposes of the Court of Justice as they flow from the EC Treaty: the jurisprudence of the Court itself clearly demonstrates its often fluid nature.

Thus, although Article 173(4) and 215(2) of the EC Treaty may appear to be carriers of controversies from civil society to the Court of Justice, some authors suggest that in its development of restrictive doctrines on the standing of private litigants and the conditions for the award of damages, the Court has had certain public interests in mind, such as the need to stem a flood of litigation which it regarded as capable of disrupting a balanced performance of its tasks. Similarly, in staff cases, when resolving disputes between two parties the Court has had occasion to apply to the Community civil service certain general principles which inspire its case law in other areas. In *Razzouk and Beydoun*,[71] for example, the Court held for the first time in the context of staff cases that the principle of equal treatment between men and women forms part of the fundamental rights the observance of which it has a duty to ensure. This breakdown of what on paper looks like a fairly safe application of the distinction between private and public purposes is not surprising, however, if one considers that the French notion of *contentieux administratif*, on which many Community "forms of action" are based, was not conceived as a system of dispute resolution, but was designed instead as a means of controlling the administration.

Theory and practice also diverge as regards the public action model of the Court's role. Although it is charged by Article 177 of the EC Treaty with the task

---

[69] See Bator *et al.*, *supra* n. 65, at p. 80.
[70] See A. Amar, "Law Story" (1988–1989) 102 *Harvard Law Review* 688, at n.138.
[71] Joined Cases 75 and 117/82 [1984] ECR 1509.

of interpreting EC law and not with applying it to the facts of individual cases, in recent years the Court has vigorously insisted on a detailed presentation by the national court of such facts, with the obvious consequence of getting objectively closer to participating in dispute resolution.[72] Apart from this striking development, the jurisprudence of the Court teems with judgments drawing heavily on the facts of the case. Consider, for instance, *Anita Cristini* v *SNCF*.[73] The widow of an Italian migrant, who had worked and resided in France, sought to avail herself and her large family of the type of fare reductions offered by the national railway company to French citizens in similar circumstances. In deciding that reductions of this type constitute a "social advantage" for migrant workers within the meaning of Article 7(2) of Regulation 1612/68 and that their widows should benefit therefrom, the Court could be said to have determined the actual dispute pending at national level. Although it may have been reaffirming the fundamental principle of free movement and non-discrimination and clarifying Community law in this respect, it was clearly willing, in both a real and literal sense, to defend, as the French say, *"la veuve et l'orphelin"*.

By way of conclusion, it seems evident that as regards the jurisdiction of the Court of Justice, again viewed as an institution, public purposes outweigh private ones, both in law and in fact. However, in the strategic area of preliminary references where, in principle, the public action model is pre-eminent, a gradual but clear shift towards dispute resolution is discernible. Is it conceivable that this movement signals the Court's progressive awareness of its own conversion into a fully "domestic" supreme court? If this were the case, the upshot of Section 2 of this Chapter could be said to be empirically verifiable.

4. THE ORGANIZATION, COMPOSITION AND WORKING METHODS OF THE COURT OF JUSTICE

(a) The judiciary

The composition of the Court of Justice is governed by Articles 165 to 168A of the EC Treaty.[74] A Protocol on the Statute of the Court of Justice is attached to all three Treaties and sets out its organization and procedure. In addition, the provisions of the Statute are developed in the Court's Rules of Procedure. The

---

[72] Indeed in Joined Cases C-320/90, C-321/90 and C-322/90 *Telemarsicabruzzo S.p.A* v *Circostel and Ministero delle Poste e Telecomunicazioni and Ministero della Difesa* [1993] ECR I-393, the Court considered this practice as a code of conduct which referring courts would do well to follow if their references are to be deemed admissible, at para. 6: "the need [it held] to provide an interpretation of Community law which will be of use to the national court makes it necessary that the national court define the factual and legislative context of the questions it is asking or, at the very least, explain the factual circumstances on which those questions are based".

[73] Case 32/75 [1975] ECR 1085.

[74] See also Articles 32 to 32d of the European Coal and Steel Community (ECSC) Treaty and Articles 137 to 140a of the Euratom Treaty.

latter are adopted by the Court itself on the basis of Article 188 of the EC Treaty, but require the unanimous approval of the Council of Ministers.[75]

Prior to the accession of Austria, Finland and Sweden in 1995, the Court consisted of thirteen Judges, twelve of whom were selected by their respective Member States, and one chosen on a rotational basis by the five large States—France, Germany, Italy, Spain and the United Kingdom. In 1993 this practice was confirmed by the European Council. In the event that an odd number of States acceded, thus rendering the number of Judges even, the additional Judge could be allowed to become an Advocate General.[76] The EC Treaty now provides for fifteen Judges, a number which can be increased by the Council of Ministers if the Court so requests, but which cannot be reduced.

The appointment of the Judges of the Court is required by Article 167 of the EC Treaty to be made "by common accord of the Governments of the Member States". In practice, Judges are nominated by their national governments and an unwritten rule, which to date has been scrupulously observed, dictates that the other Member States acquiesce. Judges are appointed for a six-year term of office, which is renewable. The appointment of new Judges and the reappointment of existing Judges are staggered so that there is a partial replacement of Judges every three years. This is to ensure that the work of the Court is disrupted as little as possible.

In conformity with the same Article 167, Judges of the Court must be "persons whose independence is beyond doubt and who possess the qualifications required for appointment to the highest judicial offices in their respective countries or who are jurisconsults of recognized competence".[77] This means that the Court is comprised of members who have served in their Member States as judges, prosecutors or senior government officials, but also of members who have worked as leading practising advocates and academics. In today's Court all of these professions are evenly represented.

Although it is quite clear from the EC Treaty text that appointees must be of the highest quality, the standing of the Court of Justice is prejudiced by its scant legitimacy and the weak security of tenure which its members enjoy. Indeed, few supreme courts in the Western world are so lacking in links, direct or indirect, with the symbols of democratic government and in few countries is the judiciary so bereft of formal guarantees of its independence.[78] The distinct independence demonstrated by the Court in the course of its life and the moral authority which it has acquired over the years are therefore essentially due to the robustness of the jurists who have sat on its benches and to the persuasiveness of their jurisprudence.

---

[75] See the Rules of Procedure of the Court of Justice, OJ 1981 L 176, p. 7 and OJ 1992 L 383, p. 117.

[76] Bull. EC 12–1993, 1.18. See also the new version of Article 166(1) EC.

[77] Article 167 EC.

[78] See Mancini and Keeling (1994), *supra* n. 39, at 176 and see Chapter 3; and generally, Gibson and Caldeira, *supra* n. 6, at p. 10.

The Court is nevertheless aware of the deficiencies of the rules governing the appointment and the tenure of its members. Thus, in a document prepared in view of the 1996–1997 Intergovernmental Conference, it suggested that a longer and unrenewable term of office would strengthen the independence of the Judges and Advocates General.[79] On the other hand, while not ruling out an involvement of the European Parliament in the appointment procedure,[80] the document clearly opposes the proposal that the nominees be heard by a Parliamentary Committee, since they would be unable adequately to answer the questions put to them without prejudging positions which they might have to adopt once appointed.

A related issue is that of the Court's representativeness. In one sense the Court is highly representative. Its composition reflects Europe's diversity with great precision[81] and the appointment of its members by the common accord of the governments contributes to making it politically balanced. Because each Judge's term of office expires after six years and because governments change with equal or greater regularity in most Member States, it is in fact likely that at any given time roughly half the members of the Court will have been nominated by a conservative administration and roughly half by a socialist or liberal one. In another sense, however, the Court is extremely unrepresentative, for the first forty-seven years of its life, of all its members, both Judges and Advocates General, only one, the French Advocate General Simone Rozès, was a woman.[82] The first female Judge at the Court of Justice, Fidelma Macken, was appointed in 1999.

It is well known that the fabric of the Community judiciary was strongly affected by French legal thinking. This influence is particularly evident as regards the office of Advocate General.[83] Its denomination is borrowed from French criminal procedure where the *avocat général* plays the role of prosecuting counsel and its functions are equivalent to those of the *Commissaire du gouvernement*[84] at the Conseil d'État and the *tribunaux administratifs*.[85] The method of appointment and the conditions of office of the Advocates General

[79] See *Report of the Court of Justice on Certain Aspects of the Application of the TEU* (May 1995), at p. 10.

[80] For proposals to this effect see the Resolution of the European Parliament of 6 July 1982, wherein it expressed the view that it should be involved in the appointment of the members. See also the Rothley Report for the European Parliament's Committee on Institutional Affairs, Doc. A3—0228/93. E.-U. Petersmann has suggested that members of the Court be drawn from the ranks of national constitutional courts, "How Can the European Union be Constitutionalised? The European Parliament's 1994 Proposal for a Constitution for the European Union" (1995) 50 *Aussenwirtschaft* 171, at 175.

[81] Although, as the Court itself underlined in its *Report on Certain Aspects of the Application of the TEU, supra* n. 79, it is conceivable that not all Member States will be able to appoint a Judge in the event of a wide enlargement. If this were the case, the representativeness of the Court, if only viewed from an ethnic angle, would be impaired.

[82] Following the accession of three new Member States in 1995, the Court of First Instance had two female members, Judge Tiili and Judge Lindh.

[83] Article 166 EC.

[84] In spite of its name, the *Commissaire* is entirely independent from the government.

[85] See K. Borgsmidt, "The Advocate General at the European Court: A Comparative Study" (1988) 13 *ELRev* 106.

are the same as those applicable to the Judges, although they do not take part in the election of the Court's President.

The number, national origins and system of rotation of Advocates General are slightly complicated. Essentially each of the five large Member States has one permanent member, while three posts are filled by the remaining ten States on a rotational basis. Thus, Germany, France, Italy, the United Kingdom and Spain may always count on putting forward one Advocate General. Italy, however, until 2000 had two, on the grounds that the non-accession of Norway evened the number of Judges, thus obliging the additional Judge, who was then Italian, to occupy the extra Advocate General's post offered by the provision mentioned at the outset of Section 4. The remaining Advocates General are from Denmark, Ireland, Greece and Luxembourg and their posts will become available to other Member States in 2000 and 2003, respectively.

In accordance with Article 166 of the EC Treaty, an Advocate General is entrusted "to make, in open court, reasoned submissions on cases brought before the Court of Justice" with complete impartiality and independence. There is no doubt that the Opinions of the Advocates General, which are followed by the Judges in the vast majority of cases, have proved both useful and influential. They tend to provide an exhaustive account of the law governing the issues in the case, sometimes enriching it with comparative surveys,[86] and are often a welcome explanation of what are otherwise, as some would say, excessively concise judgments.

The jurisdiction of the Court is mandatory. In order to ensure that its docket is handled as speedily as possible, the Court refers most of its cases to chambers of three or five Judges. The chambers number six in all and none of them is specialized in any particular kind of case. Judges who have dealt previously with certain specific issues may find, however, that they are called on to act as *rapporteur* in a case involving similar or related issues. As a result of this practice, one of the Court's Judges has become intimate with the intricacies of the European wine market, while others hold sway in their knowledge of milk quotas or the protection of wild birds.

Only cases raising novel or important issues are decided in plenary session, which may involve eleven (*petit plenum*) or fifteen (*grand plenum*) Judges.[87] Cases allotted to the *grand* and *petit plenum* have ranged from the ongoing dispute about the seat of the European Parliament,[88] which is regarded as a matter of great political sensitivity, to questions never previously addressed by the Court, such as the role of the Benelux Court in the context of Article 177 pre-

---

[86] See, for example, the treatment of American sources on positive discrimination in Advocate General Tesauro's Opinion in Case C-450/93 *Eckhard Kalanke v Freie Hansestadt Bremen* [1995] ECR I-3051.

[87] The expressions *grand* and *petit plenum* have been coined by the Court itself and are not to be found in any text.

[88] Case C-345/95 *France v European Parliament* [1997] ECR I-5215.

liminary reference procedures,[89] or the power of the Member States to adopt legislative measures contrary to an EC directive during the time limit in which the directive must be implemented at national level.[90]

(b) Appeals from the Court of First Instance

The Single European Act, which inserted Article 168A of the EC Treaty, empowered the Council to create a new Court of First Instance which was designed to be "attached to the Court of Justice with jurisdiction to hear and determine at first instance, subject to a right of appeal to the Court of Justice on points of law only and in accordance with the conditions laid down by the Statute, certain classes of action or proceeding".[91] The Statute of the Court has been amended accordingly.

Jurisdiction was initially only conferred on the new Court in staff, competition and ECSC cases, a decision on the transfer of dumping cases having been postponed. In response to a request made by the Court of Justice, however, the Council decided in 1993 to transfer to the Court of First Instance all proceedings instituted by natural or legal persons with the exception of cases involving antidumping measures,[92] which were handed over in 1994.[93] The Court of First Instance is expressly prevented by the terms of Article 168A from determining questions referred for a preliminary ruling.

As in the case of a normal judicial hierarchy, the Court of First Instance is uncontestably subordinate to the Court of Justice. Nevertheless, the jurisdiction of the two Courts may sometimes overlap, as when parallel cases on the same or connected issues are before them, one having been instituted by a Member State, the other by a natural or legal person.[94] Article 168A also specifies one of the most significant aspects of the relationship between the two Courts, namely that an appeal, as occurs in the case of continental courts of cassation, only lies

---

[89] Case C-337/95 *Parfums Christian Dior SA and Parfums Christian Dior BV v Evora BV* [1997] ECR I-6013.

[90] See Case C-129/96 *Inter-Environnement Wallonie asbl v Région Wallonne* [1997] ECR I-7411.

[91] See also Council Decision 88/591 (ECSC, EEC, Euratom) establishing a Court of First Instance of the European Communities, OJ 1988 L 319, p. 1 and Council Decision 93/550 (ECSC, EEC, Euratom) modifying that Decision, OJ 1993 L 144, p. 21.

[92] OJ 1993 L 144, p. 21.

[93] OJ 1994 L 66, p. 29. The Court of First Instance now also has competence to hear trade mark cases pursuant to Council Regulation (EC) No 40/94 of 20 December 1993 on the Community Trade Mark, OJ 1993 L 11, p. 1.

[94] See, for example, the cases provoked by the ban adopted by the Commission in 1996 against the export of beef from the United Kingdom: Case C-180/96 R *United Kingdom v Commission* [1996] ECR I-3903; Case T-76/96 R *National Farmers' Union International Traders Ferry Ltd, UK Genetics, RS & EM Wright Ltd and Prosper De Mulder Ltd v Commission* [1996] ECR II-815 and Case C-157/96 R v *Ministry of Agriculture, Fisheries and Food, Commissioners of Customs & Excise, ex parte National Farmers' Union, David Burnett and Sons Ltd, R.S. and E. Wright Ltd, Anglo Beef Processors Ltd, United Kingdom Genetics, Wyjac Calves Ltd, Internatinal Traders Ferry Ltd, MFP International Ltd, Interstate Truck Rental Ltd and Vian Exports Ltd* [1998] ECR I-2211.

to the Court of Justice on a point of law.[95] The Court has narrowly defined this notion and, as a rule, has so far exercised great restraint on appeal.[96]

(c) The working methods of the Court

A distinction should be drawn in this respect between direct actions and references for preliminary rulings. The references, as we have seen, are made by a national court pursuant to Article 177 of the EC Treaty and aim at obtaining a decision from the Court of Justice on a point of Community law necessary for the resolution of the case pending before the former. Direct actions, on the other hand, are brought before the Court by Member States or Community institutions and aim at the annulment of a Community act or at a judgment declaring that the Member State is in violation of the Treaty. By and large, however, the respective procedures are similar. What follows is a brief description of how references from national courts and direct actions are dealt with when they arrive at the Court.

Preliminary reference proceedings are commenced when the order for reference is lodged at the Court. As soon as proceedings have begun, the Court must notify this and all other procedural steps to the parties and to the national referring court. In addition, it must translate the text of the reference into the eleven official languages of the Community for notification to each Member State, to the Commission and, in certain cases, to the Council and the European Parliament. Once the reference is notified, the addressees have two months in which to lodge observations.

A direct action, in contrast, commences with the filing of an application (*requête*) with the Registrar, setting out the subject of the dispute, the grounds for the application and the form of the decision being sought.[97] The importance of the application lies in the fact that it contains, for all intents and purposes, the whole of the applicant's case and that it circumscribes the subsequent scope of the action. If the application is in a satisfactory form, it is served on the defendant who has one month to file his defence. The applicant can follow this with a reply and the defendant with a rejoinder which signals the end of the written procedure. All documents produced in the course of this procedure are translated into French, the Court's working language.

---

[95] See further Article 51 of the Protocol which specifies the grounds for an appeal—lack of competence of the Court of First Instance, a breach of procedure before it which adversely affects the interests of the appellant or the infringement of EC law by the Court of First Instance.

Pursuant to Article 54 of the Protocol on the Statute of the Court of Justice, the Court may choose to give final judgment in an appeal or refer the issue back to the Court of First Instance, which must then rehear the case in the light of the findings of the Court.

[96] See Case C-53/92 P *Hilti AG v Commission* [1994] ECR I-667, para. 42: "It should be pointed out that the appraisal by the Court of First Instance of the evidence put before it does not constitute (save where the clear sense of that evidence has been distorted) a point of law which is subject, as such, to review by the Court of Justice".

[97] For a more detailed analysis see Brown and Kennedy, *supra* n. 3, at p. 250.

Each case, whether a preliminary reference or a direct action, is assigned by the President to a Reporting Judge or *juge rapporteur* soon after the order for reference or the application are lodged. The task of the *juge rapporteur* is to steer the case through the various stages of the procedure and to draft the judgment of the Court. Each case is also assigned by the first Advocate General to one of his colleagues, whose task, as we have seen, is to present an independent opinion setting out his personal view of how the case should be resolved. The *juge rapporteur* prepares and presents to the Court and the parties a "report for the hearing" summarizing the facts of the case and the arguments of the parties. He also submits a preliminary report or *rapport préalable* to a general meeting of the Court's members on the basis of which the case is allocated to a particular chamber or to the *petit* or *grand plenum*. The preliminary report also indicates if and what additional questions should be posed to the parties, what issues of fact need to be proved or whether other measures of inquiry such as the production of documents, the supply of information or the commissioning of an expert's report are necessary. The parties may request a hearing which is followed, within a period of variable length, by the Opinion of the Advocate General.

There are no dissenting or concurring opinions in the judgments of the Court. If a Judge, even when holding the office of *juge rapporteur*, disagrees with the majority decision, or with its reasoning, he must still sign the ostensibly unanimous, collegiate judgment. The absence of a dissenting or concurring faculty is regretted by several court-watchers; but it is suggested that few of the Judges would be willing to compromise the authority of the Court's rulings by openly revealing that it is divided on some issues. EC law is still in its adolescence and as Chief Justice Marshall recognized in the early days of the United States Supreme Court, a young court administering and helping to create a new legal order has much to gain from cloaking any disagreement within its ranks.[98] It should be noted, however, that when the Court is split on a highly contentious issue, the minority will often be able to bring their opinions to bear on the language of the judgment. When controversial passages are jettisoned so that only the bare minimum of a draft more or less acceptable to all is retained, the result is at best a terse and dry judgment; at worst a decision ambiguous on matters of importance or based on an intellectually dissatisfying reasoning.

The curt language of the Court, however, should be attributed in the first place to the powerful influence of its early models, the French Conseil d'Etat and Cour de cassation.[99] This factor also accounts for the Court's inclination to steer clear of *obiter dicta* and to refrain, as far as possible, from ruling on questions wider than those necessary in the case.

---

[98] G.F. Mancini, "The U.S. Supreme Court and the European Court of Justice" in Versluys (ed.), *The Insular Dream* (1995), p. 113, at p. 117 and see Chapter 10.

[99] See further J. Rivero, "Le problème de l'influence des droits internes sur la Cour de justice de la CECA" (1958) *Annuaire français de droit international* 295, at 304.

13

Access to Justice: Individual Undertakings and EC Antitrust Law: Problems and Pitfalls

O N 31 DECEMBER 1992, the European Economic Community adopted the measures necessary finally to establish a single, large market within its territory. This was the commitment that the Member States had undertaken when they signed the so-called Single European Act on 17 February 1986.[1] Europe is no longer what Jacques Pelkmans has described as a "customs-union-plus" or, at best, a "pseudo common market".[2] It comprises "an area without internal frontiers in which the free movement of goods, persons, services and capital is ensured . . .".[3] As a result, an economic area extends from Edinburgh to Syracuse and Lisbon to Berlin, in which multinationals, conglomerates, small firms, traders, large distributors, banks, insurance companies, and airlines are able not only to compete but also to compete using commercial strategies that, by the very nature of things, have to be different from those that have been implemented in national markets. Naturally, this marketplace is also open to overseas companies from the USA, Canada, Japan, and elsewhere, which are attracted, to an even greater extent than they were in the past, by the numerous advantages of a commercially uniform European market.

The Community has to guarantee that these entrepreneurs have a modern and efficient system of legal protection. This is indispensable if the development of the Community's economy is to take place in an orderly manner, that is, in accordance with the rules and programmes governing, respectively, the free play of competition and competition policy. It was mainly this desire, more than complaints by the Court of Justice about being overloaded, that prompted the Member States to set up a Court "with jurisdiction to hear and determine at first instance . . . certain classes of action or proceeding brought by natural or legal persons".[4]

---

[1] Single European Act, OJ 1987 L 169, p. 1.
[2] J. Pelkmans, "The Institutional Economics of European Integration" in M. Cappelletti, M. Seccombe and J.H.H. Weiler (eds.), *Integration Through Law* (1986), Volume I, p. 318, at pp. 339–387.
[3] Single European Act, Article 13.
[4] *Ibid.*, Article 11.

Notwithstanding the necessarily generic nature of the formula "natural or legal persons", it was not difficult to predict that the main beneficiary of the new configuration of the European court system would indeed be the business sector. This is not because the creation of a court has the immediate effect of making those persons who have access to it more litigious. Rather, the creation of the single market gave rise to a real and objective need for legal certainty in the face of factual and legal situations for which no precedents existed. In other words, the changes in the European commercial and economic context could not help but affect the way in which the Community's antitrust legislation is implemented and interpreted.

For instance, the EC Treaty justifies the prohibitions laid down in Articles 85 and 86 on the grounds that the prohibited activities are "incompatible with the common market".[5] Hence, it was the intention of the draftsmen of the original EC Treaty, that those provisions would be mainly to protect intra-Community trade against attempts by businesses to compartmentalize the common market by means of agreements or abuses of dominant positions. But with the achievement of a market without public economic frontiers, such businesses will probably lose interest in rebuilding barriers that are no longer useful for their purposes, since they will have to confront each other in a single field and, at the same time, fight off competition from outside Europe. In that event, the antitrust rules have to be construed, above all, as provisions designed to protect the individual's right to participate in business activities on terms of free and fair competition. Businesses themselves will then take action against competitors' anti-competitive behaviour in order to secure equality of opportunity and freedom to compete for operators in the supranational single market.

Apart from businessmen, others too will start to knock, or will knock more frequently, on the doors of Community law, in particular consumers or, rather, consumer associations. They will assert their right to purchase goods and services at market conditions that are optimal and uniform throughout the Community. Consequently, the Commission will be called upon to tackle radically new administrative problems, and it is obvious that the solutions adopted to these problems will not invariably meet with everyone's approval.[6] The Community courts will have the task of finding legal solutions, with the awareness that in so doing they will be contributing to the building of an arsenal of case law, which will serve as a genuine code of conduct to all those working in the market and supervisory institutions. Hence, there is the need to establish clearly the preconditions that natural or legal persons must satisfy before they can turn to the Community Court in order to obtain judicial review both of measures taken by the Commission or of the reasons for the Commission's failure to act. This Chapter deals with a number of aspects connected with this theme and refers in particular to several disputes brought before the Court in

---

[5] Article 85(1) EC.

[6] An example of this state of uncertainty is afforded by the continuing debate on the applicability of Article 85 EC to concentration agreements between undertakings.

Luxembourg in the 1980s, as preparations for the internal market gathered pace.

For authorities responsible for supervising and enforcing antitrust legislation "private suits are . . . more of an important supplementary enforcement device. They may be the most effective way of policing the multitude of comparatively local and insignificant violations that will tend to escape the glance of federal enforcement authorities or that, even if noticed, do not merit the expenditure of limited enforcement resources".[7]

This is the philosophy behind section 4(a) of the Clayton Act, which provides as follows: "[A]ny person who shall be injured in his business or property by reason of anything forbidden in the antitrust laws may sue therefor . . . and shall recover threefold the damages by him sustained, and the cost of suit, including a reasonable attorney's fee".[8]

In Community antitrust law there are no so-called "treble-damage actions". Instead, Article 3 of Regulation 17[9] authorizes the Member States and "persons who claim a legitimate interest"[10] to apply to the Commission with a view to its finding that the antitrust provisions of the EC Treaty have been infringed. If an infringement is found, the Commission "may by decision require the undertakings or associations of undertakings concerned to bring such infringement to an end".[11] Consequently, under EC law, a person who initiates antitrust proceedings certainly does not do so because he is attracted by the prospect of a substantial pecuniary recompense. Consequently, at first glance it might appear *easy* to lay a complaint before the Commission because little must be proved; but, at the same time, such a complaint seems pointless because nothing is to be gained. This, however, is not the case. The relationship between the complaint and the Commission has a fairly substantial content in Community law and yields results that are substantially profitable for both parties.

The first point to be clarified is the concept of "legitimate interest". Under Article 3 of Regulation 17, the individual's right to make a complaint is conditional.[12] What must the complainant prove in order for his complaint to be acted upon? The Court has not yet ruled on this question.[13] The view taken by

---

[7] C. Kaysen and D. Turner, *Antitrust Policy* (Harvard University Press, 1959), at p. 257.

[8] 15 U.S.C. § 15 (1982).

[9] EEC Council Regulation No 17: First Regulation implementing Articles 85 and 86 of the EC Treaty, OJ 1962 L 13, p. 204.

[10] *Ibid.*

[11] *Ibid.*

[12] *Ibid.*

[13] See subsequently Case T-64/89 *Automec Srl v Commission* [1990] ECR II-367; Case T-24/90 *Automec Srl v Commission* [1992] ECR II-2223 and Case C-39/93 P *Syndicat français de l'Express International and others v Commission* [1994] ECR I-2681.

one learned writer was that "any reasonably direct and practical interest in the outcome of the complaint would be sufficient".[14] As a rule, nobody will take the trouble to make a complaint unless there is the prospect of obtaining at least something of practical utility. On the other hand, a complaint cannot be regarded as the mere identification of a particular economic fact, with the Commission being free to decide whether or not it should act thereon. If that were the case, the Community legislature would certainly not have required the Commission to inform the complainant (Member State or natural or legal person, as the case may be) of the reasons why it does not intend to act on the complaint.

What then is the legal feature that enables an individual to have the same power of complaint as a Member State? In the first place, when the Commission acts under the provision in question "on its own initiative", it does so essentially with a view to restoring the free play of competition in the common market. This being so, the subject of the application made by the private individual must be directly connected with the proper operation of Community trade so that by adhering to the Commission's intervention, operators in the market—and hence not only the complainant—can carry out their economic activities in complete freedom with respect to the behaviour of the undertaking that was the subject of the complaint.

Accordingly, a "legitimate interest" may be said to exist outside of the confines of the personal sphere of the complainant, transcending it so as to coincide with the general interest of the legal order. In the final analysis, a party who makes an application to the Commission does not assert a right autonomously, as is the case in American law where a person acts in order to obtain damages. A complainant is not even a straightforward informant of the Commission. On the contrary, as a person with a legitimate interest in the complaint, the complainant is entitled to call upon the supervisory authority to act in order to enforce the Community antitrust laws while undertaking to collaborate with that authority.

According to the judgment in *GEMA v Commission*,[15] an applicant under Article 3 of Regulation 17 is not entitled to obtain from the Commission a decision on the existence of the alleged infringement of the Community rules.[16] According to the wording of that provision, "even when the Commission has found that there has been an infringement of Article 85 or Article 86, it *may* [and not "must"] . . . require the undertakings concerned to bring such infringement to an end"[17]. Certainly, the Commission may, for instance, address to the undertakings recommendations for the termination of the infringement.[18]

---

[14] J. Temple Lang, "The Position of Third Parties in EEC Competition Cases", (1978) 3 *ELRev* 177, at 179.

[15] Case 125/78 *GEMA (Gesellschaft für musikalische Aufführungs- und mechanische Vervielfältigungsrechte) v Commission* [1979] ECR 3173.

[16] *Ibid.*, at 3189–3190.

[17] *Ibid.* at 3197 (Opinion of Advocate General Capotorti) (emphasis in original).

[18] See Regulation 17, *supra* n. 9, Article 3(3).

However, it is clear that if the undertaking in question persists in its infringing conduct, the supervisory authority may not stand idly by but will be obliged, *inter alia*, by virtue of Article 155 of the EC Treaty, to order the undertaking to terminate the infringement.[19]

If, however, the Commission takes no action, it must, in any event, communicate to the complainant its reasons for taking no action;[20] and, as we shall see later, the complainant may bring an action before the Community Court to have that communication declared void.[21] Lastly, if the Commission, in order to avoid determining whether the action (or inaction) is lawful or not, refuses to provide the complainant with explanations as to the outcome of his complaint, the latter will be entitled to bring an action for failure to act with respect to that omission under Article 175 of the EC Treaty. It may, therefore, be stated that Regulations 17 and 99/63 confer a series of rights—and, also, obligations—on the complainant, that are justified only on the grounds that the complainant has a specific legal interest.[22] The other side of the coin is that under these Regulations the Commission has precise duties *vis-à-vis* complainants; in return, the Commission may require complainants to take positive action, which, in practice, takes the form of a requirement to collaborate with the Commission.[23]

In this regard, therefore, the individual and the Commission are pursuing the same aim. Having said this, it must be pointed out that the fact that the claimant may and must cooperate with the Community authority does not transform the Commission's inquiry into a direct confrontation between private individuals making accusations and private individuals defending themselves. On the contrary, Article 89 of the EC Treaty is designed to ensure that only the

[19] See R. Joliet, "Lord Bethell devant la Cour de Justice: En avion ou en bateau. . .?" (1982) 18 *Cahiers de droit européen* 552, at 559.

[20] See Regulation No 99/63/EEC of the Commission of 25 July 1963 on the hearings provided for in Article 19(1) and (2) of Council Regulation No 17, OJ 1963 L 127, p. 2268.

[21] See *infra* nn. 30 *et seq*. and accompanying text.

[22] See Case 191/82 *Fédération de l'industrie de l'huilerie de la CEE (FEDIOL) v Commission* [1983] ECR 2913, where relating to anti-dumping proceedings, the Court stated "[C]omplainants must be acknowledged to have a right to bring an action where it is alleged that the Community authorities have disregarded rights which have been recognized specifically in the regulation, namely the right to lodge a complaint, the right, which is inherent in the aforementioned right, to have that complaint considered by the Commission with proper care and according to the procedure provided for, the right to receive information within the limits set by the regulation and finally, if the Commission decides not to proceed with the complaint, the right to receive information comprising at the least the explanations guaranteed by . . . the regulation. Furthermore it must be acknowledged that, in the spirit of the principles which lie behind Articles 164 and 173 of the Treaty, complainants have the right to avail themselves, with regard both to the assessment of the facts and to the adoption of the protective measures provided for by the regulation, of a review by the Court appropriate to the nature of the powers reserved to the Community institutions on the subject".

[23] See Case 298/83 *Comité des industries cinématographiques des Communautés européennes (CICCE) v Commission* [1985] ECR 1105, where the Court, in dismissing the application brought by the Community's Cinematographic Committee, held that "the Commission was justified in requiring the abuse alleged by the CICCE to be proved or at least corroborated [by the CICCE] by examples". In view of the inaction of the complainant, the decision to discontinue the investigation was, therefore, to be regarded as lawful.

Commission will investigate suspected infringements of competition rules. The Commission is, and remains, in control of the procedure. Admittedly, the law confers on the complainant a right to be given all the information that is necessary for the proper conduct of the investigation[24] and—in the case of discontinuance—to be informed of the reasons why his complaints were rejected. This right is accorded to the complainants, because they have an interest coinciding with the general interest of the legal order, which distinguishes them from other third parties. This right also marks the absolute limit of their participation in the investigation. On the other hand, the Commission is under a duty, according to the law and the principles laid down in the Court's case law, to observe and enforce the right of the undertakings under investigation to a fair hearing.[25]

3. THE COMMISSION'S STATEMENT OF OBJECTIONS

When the Commission, after receiving a complaint and carrying out an investigation, has sufficient evidence to determine that an antitrust provision has been infringed, it sends a communication to the undertaking concerned.[26] According to the Court, that communication:

> "must set forth clearly all the essential facts upon which the Commission is relying at that stage of the procedure. That may be done summarily and the decision is not necessarily required to be a replica of the Commission's statement of objections. The Commission must take into account the factors emerging from the administrative procedure in order either to abandon such objections as have been shown to be unfounded or to amend and supplement its arguments, both in fact and in law, in support of the objections which it maintains, provided however that it relies only on facts on which the parties concerned have had an opportunity to make known their views and provided that, in the course of the administrative procedure, it has made available to the undertakings concerned the information necessary for their defence".[27]

In *BAT and Reynolds* v *Commission*[28] the Court ruled for the first time on complainants' expectations and claims with regard to the Commission's state-

---

[24] See Case 53/85 *AKZO Chemie BV et AKZO Chemie UK Ltd.* v *Commission* [1986] ECR 1965.

[25] In this connection, the Court, in Joined Cases 100–103/80 *SA Musique Diffusion française and others* v *Commission* [1983] ECR 1825, stated that the provisions of Regulations 17 and 99/63 "are an application of the fundamental principle of Community law which requires the right to a fair hearing to be observed in all proceedings, even those of an administrative nature, and lays down in particular that the undertaking concerned must have been afforded the opportunity, during the administrative procedure, to make known its views on the truth and relevance of the facts and circumstances alleged and on documents used by the Commission to support its claim that there has been an infringement of the Treaty". See F.-C. Jeantet, "La défense dans les procédures répressives en droit de la concurrence" (1986) 22 *Revue trimestrielle de droit européen* 53, at 53–67.

[26] Regulation 99/63, *supra* n. 20, Article 2(1).

[27] Joined Cases 100–103/80 *Musique Diffusion, supra* n. 25.

[28] Joined Cases 142 and 156/84 *British-American Tobacco Company Ltd and R. J. Reynolds Industries Inc.* v *Commission* [1987] ECR 4487. The facts of the case may be summarized as follows: in April and May 1981, Rembrandt Group Limited ("Rembrandt"), a South African multinational, transferred to Philip Morris, for US$ 350 million, half the equity in Rothmans Tobacco Limited

ment of objections. In that case, BAT and Reynolds brought an action against a decision rejecting their complaints on the grounds, *inter alia*, that the Commission had not explained why it changed its view with respect to the charges brought in the statement of objections notified to Philip Morris and Rembrandt. The applicants thought they could discern the existence of dark plots hatched between the Commission and the companies against which the charges had been brought, and they instituted proceedings before the Court with a view to ascertaining the content of certain documents that they believed would throw light on that sudden *volte face*.

The Court rightly dismissed these claims. It was stated, however, that when:

> "the Commission ultimately decides to reject the complaints it must give as its reasons for that decision its final assessments based on the situation existing at the time when the procedure is closed, but it is not under a duty to explain to the complainants any differences with respect to its provisional assessments set forth in the statement of objections".[29]

Indeed, there is no doubt that any conflicting statements made by the investigating authority, however deserving of criticism, do not entitle third parties to search the files of the investigating authority or the undertakings under investigation in order to substantiate their suspicions. On the other hand, in the context of an antitrust action, the Court's guidance is not to be construed as meaning that the Commission is free to change its opinion without having to give an account to the various interested parties. On the contrary, if the Commission, after having formed a view on the factual and legal aspects of an undertaking's conduct, proposes to close the file, its obligation to provide the complainants with the reasons why it is taking that course of action assumes special importance; in fact, almost invariably it will be a question of casting light on a situation in which lawful and unlawful aspects have been inextricably mingled.

Furthermore, the party, who by making a complaint enabled the supervisory authority to find that the EC Treaty rules had been infringed, must be able to

which in turn had a majority holding in the English company Rothmans International, the leading cigarette manufacturer in the Community. British American Tobacco Co. (BAT) and R.J. Reynolds Industries Inc. ("Reynolds"), disappointed at seeing a transaction thay they thought was within their grasp slip through their fingers, at the last moment submitted a complaint to the Commission concerning the agreement between Rembrandt and Philip Morris, which alleged that the agreement infringed Articles 85 and 86 of the EC Treaty. After carrying out a rapid investigation, the Commission decided that the charges were founded and asked the undertakings in question to alter their agreement—failure to do so would result in annulment of the agreement. Complex negotiations followed and culminated, in 1983, in the conclusion of a new agreement. Under the agreement, Philip Morris obtained from Rembrandt only 24.9% of the voting rights in Rothmans International. The earlier requirements that related to commercial cooperation which caused the agreement to be prohibited, were removed, while the clauses relating to each of the two partners' pre-emption rights were reinforced. However, the price of the transaction remained unvaried. The new approach was deemed to be compatible with Community law and so the Commission decided to close the investigation. This resulted in the applications brought by BAT and Reynolds before the Court of Justice.

[29] Joined Cases 142 and 156/84 *BAT and Reynolds* [1986] ECR 1899 (Order of the Court of 18 June 1986).

know the reasons or the factual basis by which the undertaking's behaviour is now deemed to accord with Community requirements. This is especially true when that party is a direct competitor of the undertaking complained of. In the final analysis, while communication of the objections is an essential safeguard for the defence of undertakings,[30] the decision to close a file constitutes—for the complainants as well as the companies who were the subject of the inquiry—an essential guarantee of legal certainty. Although formally addressed to the complainants, in substance the *BAT/Reynolds* decision constitutes the Commission's view on what, following the statement of objections, the undertaking that was subject of the inquiry has done to regularize its situation in the light of the Community rules.

4. CLOSING A FILE IN AN ANTITRUST INVESTIGATION

Where the Commission finds "that on the basis of the information in its possession there are insufficient grounds for granting the application, it shall inform the applicants of its reasons and fix a time-limit for them to submit any further comments in writing".[31] The Court, interpreting this provision in *GEMA*, held that this commuunication is intended only for information purposes and "implies the discontinuance of the proceedings".[32] However, this does not prevent the Commission from reopening the file, particularly where, within the period allowed by the Commission for that purpose, the applicant puts forward fresh elements of law or fact.

In academic circles, this ruling was the subject of considerable perplexity and there was no shortage of attempts to identify avenues that would give the complainant a means of action in order to protect his initiative.[33] On the other hand, the Commission, on the strenght of that pronouncement of the Court, stated that the communication referred to in Article 3(2) of Regulation 17[34] is "not a *Decision* within the meaning of Article 189 of the EEC Treaty and cannot be challenged before the Court of Justice".[35]

What emerges from these words is a profoundly disconcerting situation. The closing of files in antitrust investigations and the possibility of communication by the Court of the justification for closing the file are left entirely to the discretion of the Commission. To put it bluntly, whether such a measure may or may not be challenged depends on whether the Commission decides to call the com-

---

[30] Jeantet, *supra* n. 25, at 59.

[31] Regulation 99/63, *supra* n. 20, Article 6 (the application in this case is made pursuant to Article 3(2) of Regulation 17).

[32] Case 125/78 *GEMA*, *supra* n. 15.

[33] See, for exampte, R. Joliet, *Le droit institutionnel des Communautés européennes* (Liège, 1981), p. 65; Temple Lang, *supra* n. 14, at 181; M. Waelbroeck, "Judicial Review of Commission Action in Competition Matters" (1983) *Fordham Corporate Law Institute* 179, at 202.

[34] Regulation 17, *supra* n. 9, Article 3 (2).

[35] Commission Eleventh Report on Competition Policy (1982) 118 (emphasis added).

munication a "decision". In brief, we have come a very long way from the idea of cooperation between the investigating authority and the complainant, be it a Member State or a private individual or undertaking. This cooperation underlies the present rules on antitrust, and the Commission must continue to use these rules to guarantee free competition within the single European market.

In the Opinion in the *BAT/Reynolds* case, the author, then an Advocate General, endeavoured to identify the rules upon which the system should be based for the collaborative relationship between the investigating authority and the complainant to be fruitful. In the first place, the communication under Article 6 of Regulation 99/63[36] cannot be intended merely to inform the complainant of the reasons for the discontinuance of the proceedings where that has already been decided. On the contrary, it should enable the complainants to comment on the reasons why the Commission plans to reject the application. Moreover, if this were not true, imposing a time limit for the reply would be meaningless; time limits are imposed when it is necessary to reach a result rapidly. Experience shows that the reopening of an investigation that has just been closed rarely is a matter of urgency. Additionally, an obligation to give notice of these reasons satisfies two interests: it enables the subject of the communication to check whether these matters have been correctly assessed, and it enables the Commission to establish whether, on the basis of the comments submitted, it has sufficient justification for discontinuing the proceedings.

On the other hand, as regards the possibility of challenging the discontinuance of the proceedings, the following principles hold good: first, the right to bring an action, having its origin in the aims of the competition rules, cannot be made conditional upon the form of the measure rejecting the complaint; secondly, although it is not obliged to adopt a definitive decision as to the existence of an infringement, the Commission cannot suspend *ad libitum* an investigation commenced by it. On the contrary, from the provisions of Regulations 17 (in particular, Article 9(3)) and 99/63 (in particular, Article 6), it is apparent that, when the Commission intends to close the file in an investigation, it is obliged to (a) notify the complainant of its reasons for forming that intention; (b) allow him a reasonable period in which to submit his comments; and (c) adopt a definitive measure with respect to the application, not the infringement.

There is a third principle. The closing of the file is binding on the Commission in the same way as a negative clearance, only insofar as the state of affairs giving rise to that particular decision does not change. Since it is addressed to the complainant, on the other hand, that measure has no binding effects on third parties, other than that of restoring to the Member States the power to apply Articles 85 and 86 of the EC Treaty.[37] The conclusion to which these remarks lead is obvious. Since a definitive decision on the application guarantees the certainty of the legal relations between the parties, the complainant will be entitled to exercise his right to institute proceedings with knowledge of the

---

[36] See *supra* n. 30 and accompanying text.
[37] See Regulation 17, *supra* n. 9, Article 9(3).

Commission's response to his observations, and the Court will be in a position to review comprehensively and effectively the legality of the measure adopted with respect to him.[38]

5. CONCLUSION

Article 173 of the EC Treaty, which confers on the Court the power to review the legality of acts of Community institutions capable of having legal effects, distinguishes two classes of persons entitled to institute proceedings for annulment: persons to whom the measure is addressed and persons who, insofar as they do not fall into the first category, must prove that the measure is of such a kind as to be of "direct and individual" concern to them. In the latter case:

> "[p]ersons other than those to whom a decision is addressed may only claim to be individually concerned if that decision affects them by reason of certain attributes which are peculiar to them or by reason of circumstances in which they are differentiated from all other persons and by virtue of these factors distinguishes them individually just as in the case of the person addressed".[39]

It is easy to see that if such criteria were applied literally, actions brought to obtain the annulment of decisions granting exemptions or negative clearances of which the applicants are not addressed would be, in most cases, dismissed as inadmissible. In order to avoid that deficiency, the Court, in *Metro* v *Commission*,[40] ruled for the first time on the admissibility of an action brought by a third party against the grant of an exemption and stated:

> "It is in the interests of a satisfactory administration of justice and of the proper application of Articles 85 and 86 that natural or legal persons who are entitled, pursuant to Article 3(2)(b) of Regulation No 17, to request the Commission to find an infringement of Articles 85 and 86 should be able, if their request is not complied with either wholly or in part, to institute proceedings in order to protect their legitimate interests".[41]

Following that judgment, academic writers, albeit expressing their approval for the solution in principle, pointed out that the Court had failed to clarify the grounds upon which the applicant, Metro, was to be regarded as having been "individually" affected by the decision granting exemption.[42] In the *BAT/Reynolds* case the Rembrandt company, intervening on the side of the Commission, argued that the action, brought against the decision to close the file on the investigation, had to be regarded as inadmissible, because the applicants had to show that the measure in question affected them "directly and

---

[38] See Case 298/83 *CICCE* v *Commission*, *supra* n. 23, at 1122.
[39] Case 25/62 *Plaumann & Co.* v *Commission* [1963] ECR 95, 107.
[40] Case 26/76 [1977] ECR 1875.
[41] *Ibid.*, at 1901.
[42] See Joliet, *Le droit institutionnel*, *supra* n. 33, at p. 93 and Waelbroeck, *supra* n. 33, at 200.

individually", in the sense that it was prejudicial to their specific interests. However, the criticism expressed by those academics is directed against the very obstacle that the Court sought to eliminate; in other words, with regard to the criteria of admissibility that are laid down in Article 173 of the EC Treaty, and were strictly interpreted in *Plaumann* v *Commission*, the formula employed in *Metro* introduces an exception of a special nature, which is justified by the overriding interest of verifying in court proceedings whether the competition rules have been properly applied.

Consequently, for the purposes of the admissibility of the application, it is not necessary in antitrust proceedings to consider whether the contested measure was of individual concern to the applicant. Nor can a decisive role be played in that regard by the fact that he complained or intervened in the course of the administrative inquiry. Indeed, in view of the imperative requirement to secure the proper implementation of Articles 85 and 86 of the EC Treaty, a person may also be held to have standing, although he was not involved in the action taken by the Commission, if he maintains that the Commission's action would prejudice a legal position of his that is directly protected by Community antitrust rules. In the final analysis, to be able to challenge before the Community Court a measure of the antitrust authority that is aimed at third parties, an applicant must show in every case that he has an interest in action. To that end, he will, therefore, have to show the possible repercussions—not the specific repercussions—to his legal position.

14

The European Court of Justice and the External Competences of the Community

I. INTRODUCTION

IN THE AUTUMN of 1994, when the European Court of Justice was called upon to give its Opinion on the Agreement establishing the World Trade Organization,[1] the procedure taking place in Luxembourg attracted much attention from the international public. The long-awaited outcome of the Uruguay Round negotiations was finally at hand and the Opinion of the Court was one of the last hurdles before the entry into force of the Agreement.

Now, some years on, the perspective is quite different: the Opinion of the Court enabled the Member States to ratify the WTO Agreement along with the European Community itself,[2] according to the formula of so-called mixed agreements. Against all odds the Agreement came into force on schedule, on 1 January 1995, and the World Trade Organization is now operating.

The main value of scrutinizing the Opinion at this later stage lies in gaining an understanding of the latest developments of the case law concerning the treaty-making power of the European Community and in analysing its consequences for the conduct of the external economic relations of the European Union. While respecting the duty of discretion incumbent upon a judge, the Opinion is first summarized and then commented upon. An attempt is then

---

[1] Opinion 1/94 [1994] ECR I-5267. Among the comments published to date now see: J. Auvret-Finck, (1995) 31 *Revue trimestrielle de droit européen* 322; R.M. Bierwagen, "Introductory Note" (1955) 34 *ILM* 683; J.H.J. Bourgeois, "The EC in the WTO and Advisory Opinion 1/94—an Echternach procession" (1995) 32 *CMLRev* 763; J.H.J. Bourgeois, "L'avis de la Cour de justice des Communautés européennes à propos de l'Uruguay Round: un avis mitigé" (1994) 4 *Revue du marché unique européen* 11; V. Constantinesco (1995) 122 *Journal du droit international* 412; J. Dutheil de la Rochère, "L'ère des compétences partagées. A propos de l'étendue des compétences extérieures de la Communauté européenne" (1995) 38 *Revue du marché commun* 461; K.S. Eisermann, "Die Luftfahrtaußenkompetenz der Gemeinschaft" (1995) 6 *Europäische Zeitschrift für Wirtschaftsrecht* 331; M. Hilf, "EGAußenkompetenzen in Grenzen—Das Gutachten des EuGH zur Welthandelsorganisation" (1995) 6 *Europäische Zeitschrift für Wirtschaftsrecht* 7–8; M. Hilf, "The ECJ's Opinion 1/94 on the WTO—No Surprise, but Wise?" (1995) 6 *European Journal of International Law* 245; D. Simon, "La compétence des Communautés pour conclure l'accord OMC: l'avis 1/94 de la Cour de justice" (1994) 4 *Europe* (December) 1–3.

[2] The WTO Agreement was concluded by Council Decision 94/800/EC of 22 December 1994, OJ 1994 L 336, p. 1.

made to illustrate its implications—indeed, the complications—it has brought about for the representation of the Community within the WTO and other international fora. Finally, this Chapter examines the advisability of amending the EC Treaty and putting into effect interim arrangements in order to overcome those difficulties and to ensure consistency in the conduct of the Community's external economic policy.

2. BACKGROUND TO THE *WTO* OPINION: THE JUDICIAL POSITION ON EC EXTERNAL COMPETENCE

First of all, let us recall why the Court was asked to rule on the WTO Agreement. The Opinion procedure is just one more peculiarity of the Community decision-making process. According to Article 228 of the EC Treaty, the Council, the Commission, or a Member State may apply to the Court for a prior Opinion on whether the envisaged conclusion of an international agreement by the Community is compatible with the provisions of the Treaty. If the Court considers that the proposed agreement is incompatible with the EC Treaty, it may come into force only pursuant to an amendment of the Treaty. Moreover, the Court has consistently held that its Opinion may be sought on questions concerning the division between Member States and the Community of competence to conclude an international agreement.[3]

This was indeed what happened in the WTO case: the Court was not asked to decide whether this instrument was compatible with the EC Treaty—which was not in dispute—but rather to establish whether the Community's competence to conclude the Agreement was exclusive or merely concurrent with the powers of the Member States. If the former were found to be the case, the Community would conclude the WTO Agreement alone; otherwise, this instrument would have to be ratified by both the Community and its Member States according to the formula of so-called mixed agreements. In this connection, it may be recalled that, throughout the negotiating process, a Community procedure had been applied whereby the Commission acted as the sole negotiator *vis-à-vis* third countries, with the assistance of a committee of representatives of Member States and on the basis of negotiation directives issued by the Council. Nevertheless, it had been agreed that both the Community and its Member States would become original members of the WTO. The Member States' participation in the new body was therefore not really at stake, but the Opinion of the Court would determine whether their membership would correspond to real powers or be no more than a formality.

As regards the legal situation before the WTO Opinion, according to well-established case law, the Community enjoys exclusive competence to enter into international agreements, in the first place, by virtue of the express provisions of

---

[3] See also Article 107(2) of the Rules of Procedure of the Court of Justice.

Article 113 of the EC Treaty, which empowers the Council to act in the field of the common commercial policy.[4] Secondly, the Court has consistently held that the Community has implied powers to act in the international sphere whenever the Treaty has endowed it with power to act in the internal sphere (*in foro interno, in foro externo*). However, as a rule, such a competence becomes exclusive only where the Community has first acted in the internal sphere, thus occupying the field (the so-called doctrine of pre-emption).

As regards the first aspect, the Court's approach in progressively defining the scope of the common commercial policy had been based on the assumption that this concept has an open nature and must cover the same content as in a national context.[5] Therefore, Article 113 had been construed in an evolutive manner, to encompass, beyond the traditional instruments of any regulation concerning trade in goods (tariffs and quantitative restrictions), any measures which become necessary by reason of changes in international trade and trade negotiations. Over the years the Court considered, for instance, that Article 113 could provide the basis for concluding international commodity agreements designed to stabilize trade by operating a buffer stock[6] or for adopting such measures as the system of generalized preferences,[7] which are at the borderline between trade and development aid.

The second aspect, namely the Community's implied powers to conclude international agreements, had been based on the so-called ERTA doctrine. In the eponymous judgment of 1971,[8] dealing with a draft agreement on a classic labour-law topic (the working time of lorry and bus drivers), the Court had said that:

> "each time the Community . . . adopts provisions laying down common rules, whatever form these may take, the Member States no longer have the right, acting individually or even collectively, to undertake obligations with third countries which affect those rules. As and when such common rules come into being, the Community alone is in a position to assume and carry out contractual obligations towards third countries affecting the whole sphere of application of the Community legal system".

Six years later, in its Opinion 1/76[9] the Court held that, in some cases, an internal competence could provide the basis for an exclusive external competence even though it had not yet been exercised in the internal sphere.

---

[4] The exclusive nature of the competence deriving from Article 113 EC has been consistently reaffirmed since the Court's judgment in Case 41/76 *Suzanne Criel, née Donckerwolcke and Henri Schou* v *Procureur de la République au tribunal de grande instance de Lille et Directeur général des douanes et droits indirects* [1976] ECR 1921.

[5] The landmark decisions in this respect are Case 8/73 *Hauptzollamt Bremerhaven* v *Massey-Ferguson GmbH* [1973] ECR 897; Opinion 1/75 (*Local Cost Standard* Case) [1975] ECR 1355; Opinion 1/78 (*Natural Rubber* Case) [1979] ECR 2781.

[6] Opinion 1/78, *ibid.*

[7] Case 45/86 *Commission* v *Council* [1987] ECR 1493.

[8] Case 22/70 *Commission* v *Council* ("ERTA") [1971] ECR 263.

[9] Opinion 1/76 ("*Laying-up Fund of the Rhine* Case") [1977] ECR 741.

Although these principles were laid down in cases concerning a common policy, namely transport policy, it would appear from later decisions[10] that they apply in any area of Community activity.

In particular, the Court has expressly recognized in Opinion 2/91 that the powers conferred upon the Community in the social policy area may provide a basis for its external competence. This competence, however, is not exclusive when the relevant internal rules are directives laying down the "minimum requirements" mentioned in Article 118a(2) of the EC Treaty. In this case, the Member States remain empowered to enact measures designed to ensure a better protection of working conditions or to apply for this purpose the provisions of an international convention.[11] Conversely, if the international agreement deals with an area already covered to a large extent by Community rules based on other Treaty provisions such as Article 100 or 100A, which do not enable the Member States to maintain or introduce more stringent norms, the competence of the Community acquires an exclusive character.[12]

It should be noted that, according to the Court, the typical provisions of international labour conventions concerning the consultation of management and the trade unions may fall within the competence of either the Member States or the Community, depending on the objective pursued by such consultation.[13] Furthermore, in the specific case of the conventions drawn up under the auspices of the ILO—which the Community, not being a member of this organization, cannot itself conclude—the external competence of the Community may, if necessary, be exercised through the medium of the Member States acting jointly in its interest.[14] However, as early as 1986 the Council and the Commission devised a procedure applicable to the negotiation of ILO conventions in the areas falling within the exclusive competence of the Community, in full compliance with the tripartite consultation mechanisms provided for in Convention No 144 concerning Tripartite Consultations to Promote the Implementation of International Labour Standards and with the autonomy of "both sides of industry".[15]

In spite of these significant factors, when the Court was asked to rule on the WTO Agreement, the extent to which the Community needs to have acted in order to acquire exclusive competence was not entirely clear; nor was it clear in what way the envisaged international agreement would have to affect common rules adopted by the Community in order for the Member States to be deprived of competence in the international sphere. There was also room for discussion about the exact scope of Opinion 1/76.

---

[10] See Joined Cases 3, 4, and 6/76 *Cornelis Kramer and others* [1976] ECR 1279; and Opinion 2/91 ("*Re ILO Convention No 170 on Safety in the Use of Chemicals at Work*") [1993] ECR I-1061.

[11] *Ibid.*, para. 18.

[12] *Ibid.*, paras 22–26.

[13] *Ibid.*, para. 32.

[14] *Ibid.*, para. 5 and paras 37–38.

[15] Council Decision of 22 December 1986, unpublished but mentioned in the introductory section of Opinion 2/91, at 1067. The Convention was adopted on 21 June 1976 (1976) 59 *ILO Official Bull.* 83.

The Court had traditionally displayed remarkable ingenuity in both areas, by expanding the notion of common commercial policy and by defining the Community's implied powers on the basis of a substantially federal approach. However, in a changed institutional and political context, after the Maastricht conference had refused to amend Article 113 of the EC Treaty in order to establish a common policy on external economic relations, the Luxembourg Judges could no longer afford to strain the Community's external competences against the will of the constituent power.

3. THE *WTO* OPINION

The WTO Opinion is a complex and intricate judicial document. It builds on previous case law, construing it narrowly yet stopping short of contradicting or overruling it. Nevertheless, it fails to draw all the potential consequences from that case law for the WTO Agreement, especially in the new areas of international trade negotiations, i.e. trade in services falling under the GATS Agreement and the Agreement on so-called TRIPS, the Trade-related Aspects of Intellectual Property Rights.

One should certainly welcome the clear message coming from Luxembourg concerning trade in goods. Putting an end to a long-lasting debate, the Court ruled that the Community enjoys exclusive competence in this area under Article 113 of the EC Treaty, even though the agreement concerns *inter alia* ECSC, Euratom or agricultural products.[16] Moreover, the Community's powers cover the Agreement on Sanitary and Phytosanitary Measures as well as the Agreement on Technical Barriers to Trade.[17] Thus, the Court unambiguously rejected the contention that Article 113 could not confer on the Community powers to conclude an international agreement which requires internal measures to be adopted under a different legal base: this is an important point of principle, although the reasoning of the Court in the rest of the Opinion may appear somewhat contradictory in this respect.

The recognition that trade in services may, at least in principle, come within the common commercial policy is another positive aspect of the Opinion.[18] The Court realized that the tertiary sector has become a vital element of an advanced economy and that nowadays any major international trade negotiation inevitably deals with services. The interpretation of Article 113 must keep step with such a fundamental evolution, if the Community is to maintain substantial powers in the area of international trade.

The trouble with services, however, is that they come in many shapes and forms. The GATS Agreement identifies four modes of supply:

[16] Opinion 1/94, paras 22–29.
[17] *Ibid.*, paras 30–33.
[18] *Ibid.*, para. 41.

(1)   cross-frontier supply not involving any movement of persons (as when a stockbroker advises a client in another country by electronic mail);

(2)   consumption abroad (as when a tourist travels to another country, sleeps in a hotel there, eats in restaurants, and so forth);

(3)   commercial presence (meaning that a branch or subsidiary is established in another country); and

(4)   the presence of natural persons, whether employees or self-employed workers, in a country other than their homeland (as when a plumber is sent across the frontier in order to unblock someone's U-bend or a lawyer goes in order to earn even larger fees than he would at home).

These distinctions were to prove extremely appealing to a cautious Court, anxious to hammer out carefully balanced, if not (as some commentators have pointed out) entirely convincing, compromises.

The Luxembourg Judges noted that cross-frontier supplies not involving the movement of persons are very much akin to trade in goods. Therefore, there was no particular reason why they should not fall within the concept of the common commercial policy.[19] The Court declined to reach the same conclusion for the other modes of supply, the reason being that they involve movements of nationals of third countries, which are covered, it said, by separate provisions of the EC Treaty.[20]

Now, the accuracy of this statement may be questioned. First of all, the Annex on Movement of Natural Persons supplying Services under the Agreement expressly states that the GATS Agreement "shall not prevent a Member from applying measures to regulate the entry of natural persons into, or their temporary stay in, its territory, including those measures necessary to protect the integrity of, and to ensure the orderly movement of natural persons across, its borders". Secondly, the only provision of the EC Treaty dealing with such topics is Article 100c, the scope of which is limited to certain aspects of the visa policy. Moreover, we have seen that an argument of the same kind had just been rejected in the section of the same Opinion concerning trade in goods: the Community competence under Article 113 of the EC Treaty to conclude an international agreement is independent, the Court had said, of the legal base to be chosen for its implementation in the internal sphere. Lastly, the Court disregarded the fact that the establishment of a company incorporated in a third country may take place without the movement of nationals of the third country.

The other remark made by the Court in this context—that the existence in the EC Treaty of specific chapters on the free movement of natural and legal persons shows that those matters do not fall within the common commercial policy—has been found even harder to swallow in certain quarters, since those chapters concern only the situation of Community nationals in another Member State and have nothing to do with trade relations with third countries.

---

[19] Opinion 1/94, para. 44.

[20] *Ibid.*, paras 45–47.

As far as transport services are concerned, the Opinion made clear that they do not fall under Article 113 since they are covered by a specific title on the common transport policy.[21] Again, this reasoning may not seem entirely consistent with the Court's findings concerning trade in goods and it certainly relies on a narrow reading of the *ERTA* judgment. The Court also examined a number of embargoes based on Article 113 and involving the suspension of transport services, which had been invoked by the Commission, but considered that they were not relevant precedents since the suspension of transport services was a mere adjunct to a principal embargo on products. Strangely enough, the Court forgot to mention a 1992 embargo against Libya regarding air transport only.[22]

The Court went on to hold that the Community could not claim exclusive competence under Article 113 concerning TRIPS.[23] Notwithstanding a clear connection between intellectual property rights and trade in goods, the former do not relate specifically to international trade and affect just as much internal trade. Once again, it has been objected that the same could be said of technical barriers, which the Court itself recognizes as belonging to the field of the common commercial policy.[24] However, according to the Court, only the prohibition on importing counterfeit goods falls within the scope of the common commercial policy.

The Opinion then examined whether a Community exclusive competence concerning services and TRIPS flowed from its internal powers, according to the principles established in the ERTA judgment or in Opinion 1/76. Without going into detail, let us say simply that Opinion 1/76 is construed narrowly: the possibility for the Community to claim an exclusive external competence even when a corresponding internal power has not yet been exercised is restricted to those exceptional cases where internal measures will not be effective.[25] On the other hand, as far as the *ERTA* judgment is concerned, the view put forward by certain commentators that the WTO Opinion represents a step back does not seem correct.[26] Admittedly, the Court requires that the Community must have achieved harmonization internally in order to enjoy exclusive external competence to conclude an international agreement which might affect these internal rules;[27] but the extent of such harmonization and the degree to which the common rules need to be affected have not changed, as the Court made clear some months later, in its Opinion concerning the OECD decision on national treatment.[28] Moreover, it is accepted that internal legislative acts containing

---

[21] *Ibid.*, para. 48.

[22] Council Regulation (EEC) No 945/92, of 14 April 1992, OJ 1992 L 101, p. 53.

[23] Opinion 1/94, paras 55–71.

[24] See Auvret-Finck, *supra* n. 1, at 329.

[25] Opinion 1/94, paras 84–86.

[26] See Auvret-Finck, *supra* n. 1, at 333; Bourgeois, (1994), *supra* n. 1, at 781; Constantinesco, *supra* n. 1, at 417; Dutheil de la Rochère, *supra* n. 1, at 466–469; Simon, *supra* n. 1, at 2–3.

[27] Opinion 1/94, paras 95–96.

[28] Opinion 1/92 ("*Re OECD Decision on National Treatment*") [1995] ECR 1–521, para. 33.

provisions on the treatment of third country nationals or expressly conferring on the institutions powers to negotiate with third countries may also provide the basis for exclusive external competence.

In practice, the conclusion is that the Community's exclusive competence based on implied powers covers only certain areas of the GATS and TRIPS Agreements, which means that the WTO Agreement must be concluded as a mixed agreement by both the Community and the Member States. But the extensive Community legislation concerning services, and particularly such sectors as transport services, implies that large parts of GATS fall within Community competence. In relation to TRIPS, the obvious inference is that, since no harmonization measures have been adopted in areas such as patents, industrial models, and undisclosed technical information, they therefore remain outside the Community's exclusive external competence. Nevertheless, the Court vigorously rejected the contention that certain aspects of the enforcement of intellectual property rights are within a domain reserved to the Member States.[29]

Lastly, the Court decided to broach a subject on which its views had not been expressly sought, namely the duty of cooperation between Member States and the Community institutions to ensure unity of action *vis-à-vis* the rest of the world in the implementation of the WTO Agreement.[30] This circumstance alone shows that the Judges were deeply concerned about the practical consequences of their ruling, both for the Community and for the functioning of the WTO Agreement: indeed, a paralysed European Community would have been and would still be a fatal blow to the WTO itself. Moreover, coordination between the Community and the Member States in their respective fields of competence is of vital importance, all the more so by reason of the mechanism of cross-retaliation provided for in the Agreement. It must be conceded, however, that the Opinion does not go beyond a statement of principle, which may not prove very useful for the administration of the Agreement in Geneva.

4. THE AFTERMATH OF THE *WTO* OPINION

This final section of the Opinion shows that the Court perceived the major difficulties inherent in the "mixed agreement" formula: not only the WTO Agreement, but any major trade arrangement—inevitably including trade in services—will require, from now on, sixteen ratifications (fifteen Member States and the Community) and endless discussions to determine who has jurisdiction on any particular point. Why, then, did the Court not accept that the Community's competence must be interpreted broadly from the start? The current political context doubtless played some part in the Court's restraint: judicial power cannot always make up for lack of vision on the part of the political

---

[29] Opinion 1/94, para. 104.
[30] *Ibid.*, paras 106–109.

actors, especially when such action would meet with strong opposition in some quarters. Experience shows that the Member States have always been more open and clear-sighted in designing general constitutional solutions at the highest political level than in the day-to-day administration of specific areas, which is generally left to the egoism of national bureaucracies, whose major concern is to maintain their own prerogatives. Now, the proposal to amend Article 113 of the EC Treaty to establish a common policy on external economic relations was not rejected by some obscure civil servant but by the Heads of State and government meeting at Maastricht.[31]

The 1996–1997 Intergovernmental Conference (IGC) provided a fresh opportunity for reflection and action. With the motto "less action, but better action" President Jacques Santer was certainly expressing a widely held view regarding the role of the Community: its institutions should focus on those matters where their intervention is most useful, or even indispensable. Rather than expand token Community competences in such marginal areas as culture or civil protection, where the institutions may produce little more than meetings of experts in Brussels and badly translated brochures, the crucial need is to deepen integration by strengthening the core of Community policies and by ensuring that the Community can cope with new challenges through an effective decision-making mechanism. See, however, the new paragraph added to Article 113 by the Amsterdam Treaty.

If this view is correct, there can be little doubt that, by any standard of subsidiarity, economic relations with third countries are better dealt with at Community than at national level. Two centuries ago, James Madison observed that what he called intercourse with foreign nations forms an obvious and essential branch of the federal administration: "If we are to be one nation in any respect, it clearly ought to be in respect to other nations".[32]

Madison's remark is just as relevant today, even to the opponents of a European federal supernation. It is understandable that the introduction of majority voting in the field of the common foreign and security policy may be seen as depriving the Member States of essential sovereign powers. But this kind of objection should not apply to external economic relations, since their traditional aspects have been conducted jointly for nearly three decades. Any reform extending the scope of the common commercial policy would merely reflect the changing nature of our economies.

From this point of view, it is clearly necessary that the European Union should speak with one voice in all international trade negotiations and in those fora where such negotiations are held, WTO, OECD, UNCTAD, FAO. Its action would gain in effectiveness, partly because our trading partners need to

---

[31] On the "minimalist" philosophy which seems to guide the Court since the ratification of the Maastricht Treaty see G.F. Mancini and D.T. Keeling, "Language, Culture and Politics in the Life of the European Court of Justice" (1995) 1 *Columbia Journal of European Law* 397–413 and see Chapter 11.

[32] *The Federalist Papers* (1788) No 42.

know who is competent to negotiate without having to listen to lengthy lectures on European law. Moreover, it is likely that they would prefer to have one interlocutor rather than fifteen or, tomorrow, twenty-five, each of them endowed with a power of veto.

On the other hand, European public opinion is more likely to accept a transfer of competences in particular areas where joint action is clearly desirable for everyone's sake—the establishment of a single market is the most recent example—than sporadic and confused interventions in matters of local interest. People may question why the Community should issue eco-labels for environmentally friendly dish-washers, but it seems unlikely that anybody will demonstrate to defend the power of a national transport ministry to negotiate an open skies agreement.

The 1996–1997 IGC, based on a limited agenda, was not intended to overturn the general principles on the allocation of powers between the Community and its Member States. Nevertheless, the example of Maastricht should have taught us some lessons. It would probably have been wiser and more effective to apply the subsidiarity principle in earnest when defining Community competences, rather than pay lip service to it every time a new act is adopted. The institutions, endowed with clear-cut competences in essential areas, should then be in a position to carry out their tasks effectively.

The internal market is virtually complete, several Member States are already using a common currency, which means that the key elements of internal economic integration are now in place. Who would deny that its indispensable corollary is a true common policy on external economic relations, with simple procedures for taking all the essential decisions concerning international trade in goods and services in the Community context?[33]

In the meantime, pragmatic solutions must be found in order to limit and, if possible, overcome the disadvantages arising from mixed competences not only in the WTO framework, but also in other important fora such as FAO or the agreements with Central and Eastern European countries. I am afraid that Member States will not accept that the Community should exercise its virtual competences in order to fill the gaps in its exclusive competence, which would generally suffice to enable it to act alone: as regards the WTO, it appears from the Court's Opinion that not a single provision of the Agreement falls within a domain reserved to Member States. However, it could be possible to reach satisfactory solutions for conducting negotiations as well as for representing the European Union's interests within the relevant international organizations.

---

[33] In Constantinesco's words, *supra* n. 1: "la vision des compétences respectives des États membres et de la Communauté que nous livre ici la Cour ne doit-elle pas aussi être comprise comme un message destiné précisément à ceux qui vont avoir la charge de réviser prochainement les traités? Sans un renforcement des structures et des compétences communautaires dans ces domaines, comment l'Union, première puissance commerciale du monde, pourrait-elle être à la hauteur de ses responsabilités?"

Much depends, of course, on the goodwill of the Member States. In some instances they have been prepared to step back when this has led to a better defence of their common interests and more effective negotiation, just as in the process leading to the conclusion of the WTO Agreement. But these are mere concessions, revocable at any time and bound to disappear whenever the essential interests of a Member State are at stake.

The Council and the Commission are now working hard to frame an arrangement on the Community's participation in the activities of the WTO and it is to be hoped that they will be successful. Without knowing the details of the envisaged arrangement, three main difficulties can be foreseen. First, unless the Community procedure is generalized, any *modus vivendi* can apply only to mixed or national competences, since Community powers may be subject only to the procedures provided for by the EC Treaty. Therefore, a preliminary classification of competences is necessary despite the fact that it is still extremely difficult to determine the exact scope of the Community's jurisdiction in any particular case, notwithstanding the Court's Opinion. Secondly, if Member States insist on being able to present an individual position when no agreement is reached, Community discipline will be fatally flawed. Our WTO partners would be entitled to react to an individual action of a Member State by retaliating against the Community as a whole. Even the dutifully behaved would then be tempted to follow their own course in matters falling within their jurisdiction. Thirdly, our partners may become tired of our internal bickering and require us to spell out in advance who has jurisdiction and who is entitled to vote on any particular point of the agenda, the so-called FAO procedure. That would lead to lengthy debates before any meeting and would inevitably impair the effective representation of European interests.

5. THE FAO JUDGMENT

In 1994 the Court was called upon again to adjudicate on these issues in a case concerning the so-called FAO procedure.[34] The Commission had challenged the Council's Decision giving Member States the right to vote within the Food and Agriculture Organization for the adoption of the Agreement to Promote Compliance with International Conservation and Management Measures by Fishing Vessels on the High Seas. Although not contesting that competence to conclude such an agreement was shared between the Community and its Member States, the Commission contended that the main thrust of the Agreement did not fall within the competence of the Member States. Therefore, in accordance with the relevant section of an arrangement between the Council and the Commission regarding preparation for FAO meetings, statements and voting, the right to vote should have been exercised by the Community.

---

[34] Case C-25/94 *Commission v Council* [1996] ECR I-1469.

In its judgment the Court first rejected the objections to admissibility raised by the Council and by the United Kingdom, holding that the Council's vote, far from being a matter of procedure or protocol, had legal effects in several respects. On the one hand, it affected the Community's rights which attached to its membership of the FAO and its position *vis-à-vis* third countries. On the other hand, it had an influence on the content of the Agreement as well as on competence to implement it and eventually to conclude subsequent agreements on the same questions.

On the substance of the case, the Court's reasoning was that the main thrust of the provision of the Agreement falls within the exclusive competence of the Community to adopt conservation measures within the framework of the common fishery policy—indeed, it does not appear from the judgment that Member States have any competence at all. The Court concluded, therefore, that by deciding that Member States were entitled to vote the Council had violated the duty of cooperation between the Community and its Member States, the content of which, in this case, had been specified in the relevant section of the arrangement between the Council and the Commission.

6. CONCLUSION

The Court's reasoning in the FAO case flows from the need for unity in the international representation of the Community. It can be assumed that, even apart from any specific institutional arrangement, the EC Treaty itself imposes on the Member States and the Community institutions an obligation to cooperate, both in the process of negotiating an international agreement and in the fulfilment of the commitments which stem from it.

If this is the case, any dispute between the Community and the Member States concerning their respective competences within the WTO and other international fora can be brought before the Court. Of course, it is not practically possible to seek a Court ruling every time such a dispute arises in international negotiations. The very existence of judicial control, however, should lead the political actors to comply with the duty of cooperation set forth by the Court. A mere skeleton in the WTO Opinion, this duty has taken on flesh and blood in the FAO judgment. The Court has shown that when the political actors fail to ensure Community discipline it is ready to call them to order.

15

The Incorporation of Community Law into the Domestic Laws of the Member States

DIFFERENT KINDS OF relationship may be established between Community law and the domestic laws of the Member States. According to a now traditional analysis, such relationships are created by four distinct processes which are classified according to the intensity of the impact that the Community provisions have upon the national systems or, to put it another way, the greater or lesser extent to which Community provisions are absorbed into the national systems.

The first and most clear-cut process is known as *substitution*. This derives from the existence of a sector of Community law, comprising in particular certain provisions of the Treaties and a large number of the regulations, which, because of their formal origin, genuinely constitute uniform law in the strict sense: in so far as the Member States devolve powers to the Community—a continuing process ensured by Articles 235 and 236 of the EC Treaty and the corresponding provisions of the ECSC and EURATOM Treaties—Community law occupies the place and rank in the national systems of the legislation for which it is gradually substituted. The second type is *harmonization*. The provisions with which this process is concerned are, and remain, national but they are the result of amendments imposed by the Community to meet Community requirements, and for that very reason they display a considerable degree of uniformity. Naturally, the extent of the adjustments to be made to the various individual systems will vary according to the extent to which the legislation to be harmonized differs from the common provisions adopted.

Then there is the process of *coordination*. In this case Community law does not require the legislatures of the Member States to make changes but confines itself to ordering the effects of their legislation in such a manner as to reduce any tendency to create discrimination against particular categories of persons.

This mechanism produces a lesser degree of uniformity than is achieved by harmonization, but its value should not be underestimated. Coordination involves introducing new concepts, suggesting comparisons and undertaking the role of intermediary; and by such methods Community law—take for example Regulation 1408/71 on social security schemes for migrant workers[1]—ultimately brings together the various systems to a greater extent than is strictly necessary. The fourth and last situation, known as *coexistence*, arises where Community law and national law govern the same area of activity, but in dissimilar ways and with dissimilar objectives. The rules on competition are a typical example.

2. INCORPORATION INTO DOMESTIC LAW OF THE TREATIES, THE *ACQUIS COMMUNAUTAIRE* AND THE SINGLE EUROPEAN ACT

The methods by which Community law is incorporated into the laws of the Member States differ considerably and it would be impossible in the space provided to consider in detail the reasons for those differences.

In the first place, let us consider the Treaties establishing the Communities. As is well known, they contain no provisions concerning their incorporation into the national systems. This process has therefore been achieved by means of legislative approval and official publication in accordance with the rules in each system which govern the implementation of international agreements. In that connection, a distinction must be drawn between the original six Member States and those which subsequently joined the Community. Obviously, all the original six needed to do was to ratify the Treaties, since the process of their implementation had not yet commenced. For subsequent new members, on the other hand, it was necessary to take account of secondary legislation and supplementary law which had developed and had been adopted in the meantime and this was achieved by including in the various acts of accession provisions whereby the new Member States undertook to incorporate the entire *acquis communautaire* into their national law within a specified period.[2]

Other distinctions may be drawn regarding the type of national measure used to implement the Treaties establishing the Communities and the additions and amendments made thereto by the Single European Act, Maastricht and Amsterdam Treaties and also concerning the procedures chosen for consulting the people before any commitment was entered into by the State. As regards the Treaties, six Member States (Greece, Finland, Italy, the Netherlands, Sweden and the United Kingdom) resorted to ordinary laws, whilst in eight countries (Austria, Denmark, France, Federal Republic of Germany, Ireland, Luxembourg, Portugal and Spain) recourse was had to the procedure of constitutional revision, which requires a specific quorum, qualified majorities and, in

---

[1] Regulation (EEC) No 1408/71 of the Council of 14 June 1971, on the application of social security schemes to employed persons and their families moving within the Community, OJ 1971 L 149, p. 2.

[2] With respect to the scope of the provision to that effect contained in the Act of Accession of Greece, see the judgment in Joined Cases 39, 43, 85 and 88/81 *Halyvourgiki Inc. and Helleniki Halyvourgia SA v Commission* [1982] ECR 593.

certain cases, a referendum. Referenda were held, in particular, in Denmark, Ireland, France, Sweden, Austria and Finland. In Denmark, for example, a referendum had to be held in 1972 after the failure to achieve the majority of five-sixths of the votes of the members of the *Folketing* required by Article 20(1) of the Constitution for the devolution of national powers "to inter-State authorities". The Irish electorate, on the other hand, was called upon to approve the constitutional amendment made necessary by the accession of Ireland to the Communities and all subsequent Treaty amendments.[3]

These referenda had to be held in order to comply with a constitutional obligation. However, there was no obligation underlying the popular consultations undertaken by Denmark in 1986. Although it was not bound to do so by any provision of national law, the Danish government simply decided that it wished to test public opinion between signature and ratification of the Single Act. Nor was there any legal reason for the fact that Copenhagen undertook to be bound by the result even if the vote went against the proposal. The same commitment had been made by Norway at the time of the first enlargement and, as is well known, words became deeds. A majority of 53.49% voted against the Act of Accession and the Norwegian government, which had already signed that instrument, did not go on to ratify it. In the case of Norway, history was later to repeat itself in 1994.

The discussion has so far been confined to considering national systems. But, from the point of view of Community law, the differences between the procedures adopted by the Member States in order to become parties to the Treaties and the problems of an internal or external nature which have arisen or which may yet arise from the procedure adopted are of no importance. The Court of Justice has been quite categorical in that regard. In *Acciaierie San Michele*[4] it stated with the maximum possible clarity that by the instruments of ratification the Member States bound themselves in an identical manner and in particular they adhered to the Treaty definitively and without any reservation. Objections based on the procedure adopted by a Member State to give effect to a Treaty as part of its own legal order are therefore unacceptable.

3. INCORPORATION OF COMMUNITY REGULATIONS INTO DOMESTIC LAW:
LIMITS IMPOSED BY THE COURT OF JUSTICE UPON THE ADOPTION OF
IMPLEMENTING AND SUPPLEMENTARY MEASURES BY THE MEMBER STATES

Let us now consider the incorporation into national law of secondary Community law, that is to say the legislation adopted originally by the Council and the Commission and now, in addition, by the European Parliament, in

---

[3] See Article 29(4) EC and the further amendment which, following an anguished judgment of the Supreme Court, the government was obliged to formulate in order to be able to ratify the Single European Act.

[4] Joined Cases 9 and 58/65 *Faillite des Acciaierie San Michele SpA v High Authority of the ECSC* [1967] ECR 1.

order to achieve the objectives of the Treaties. Before reviewing the problems involved here, it is necessary to say something about the basic machinery employed in the various systems to give effect to Community measures.

With the obvious exception of the United Kingdom, the constitutions of all the Member States—including, therefore, those States whose constitutional law was inspired by dualist theories—contain provisions whereby Community measures are granted access to the internal legal order either expressly or by means of fairly general wording which can be construed in that sense (typical examples of the two methods are provided by Article 8(3) of the Portuguese Constitution and Article 11 of the Italian Constitution). Some of those rules antedated the setting up of the Community and others were adopted with a view to the accession to the Community of the Member State concerned. However, even the provisions adopted by way of subsequent amendment are as a rule framed in general terms: in other words they do not mention the institutions created by the Treaties of Paris and of Rome. The only fundamental law which provides specifically for the incorporation of Community law rather than treating it in the same way as laws emanating from international organizations in general is the Irish Constitution. Article 29.4.3 states that "No provision of this Constitution invalidates laws enacted, acts done or measures adopted by the Communities, or institutions thereof, from having the force of law in the State".

In the case of the United Kingdom a similar result was achieved by means of the European Communities Act 1972, a law which, according to British legal writers, is "ordinary" in form but, at least in part, "constitutional" in content. Adopting a technically rigorous formula and, by contrast with the Irish Constitution, using positive terms, section 2(1) thereof provides that the rights, obligations, remedies and procedures established by Community rules having direct effect "shall be recognized and available in law and be enforced, allowed and followed accordingly". At the same time section 2(2) confers upon the government the power to adopt provisions "for the purpose of implementing any Community obligation of the United Kingdom, or enabling any such obligation to be implemented".

Needless to say, the first kind of measure to be considered is the Community regulation which, according to the second paragraph of Article 189 of the EC Treaty, "shall have general application (and be) directly applicable in all Member States". In principle, therefore, regulations do not require the adoption of national implementing or amending measures[5] but are binding in their entirety on the Member States and the nationals thereof as soon as they enter into force. In other words, according to the rules imposed by Article 191 of the EC Treaty, regulations come into force on the date specified in them, failing which on the twentieth day following their publication in the Official Journal of the European Communities.[6]

---

[5] Case 31/78 *Francesco Bussone* v *Italian Minister for Agriculture* [1978] ECR 2429.

[6] Case 98/78 *A. Racke* v *Hauptzollamt Mainz* [1979] ECR 69 and Case 99/78 *Weingut Gustav Decker KG* v *Hauptzollamt Landau* [1979] ECR 101.

The principle is, however, subject to exceptions. Additional or implementing measures may prove necessary as a result of the inevitably general wording of certain provisions or of particular terms employed in regulations, especially where they do not deal with each individual stage of an administrative procedure or, as occurs quite often, they confer specified powers upon a national authority, which they describe merely as "the competent authority". In such situations, the form and content of the measures adopted in the Member States (laws, regulations, or general or specific administrative measures) will of course depend upon the nature of the matters for which they are designed to provide and the persons who are to be affected by them.

The Court of Justice has acknowledged this inevitable reality—it could not have done otherwise; but it has nevertheless expressed serious concern about the undesirable results and abuses to which supplementary measures may lend themselves. Hence, a number of limitations have been placed upon the initiatives which the Member States may take. For example, the adoption of measures designed to incorporate regulations into domestic law is justified only to the extent necessary and appropriate for the proper implementation thereof.[7] Moreover, whilst it may be true that any such measures must be adopted in compliance with the principles and procedures prevailing in the national legal system concerned,[8] it is also essential that, where they are designed to provide the persons concerned with a guarantee of legal certainty and to give guidance to administrative authorities, such measures should satisfy two conditions: they must be formulated in such a way as to ensure that someone who fails to observe them will not be deprived of the rights conferred upon him by the Community rules[9] and—which is of particular importance—they must not take the form of laws.[10]

The unfavourable view which the latter judgment took of measures of a legislative nature is indeed a constant feature of the decisions of the Court and is accounted for by the need to ensure the efficacy of the process which was described earlier as substitution of uniform Community law for domestic law. As is clearly apparent from the judgment in *Variola*,[11] the Community Court fears that, by having recourse to the adoption of laws, Member States might cause "the Community nature of a legal rule [to be] concealed from those subject to it" and thereby adversely "affect the jurisdiction of the Court to pronounce on any question involving the interpretation of Community law or the validity of an act of the institutions of the Community".[12] In a similar vein the

---

[7] Case 39/70 *Norddeutsches Vieh- und Fleischkontor GmbH* v *Hauptzollamt Hamburg-St. Annen* [1971] ECR 49.

[8] *Ibid.*

[9] Case 94/71 *Schlüter & Maack* v *Hauptzollamt Hamburg-Jonas* [1972] ECR 307.

[10] Case 77/71 *Gervais-Danone AG* v *Hauptzollamt München-Schwanthalerstrasse* [1971] ECR 1127.

[11] Case 34/73 *Fratelli Variola S.p.A* v *Amministrazione delle finanze dello Stato* [1973] ECR 981.

[12] See also Case 50/76 *Amsterdam Bulb BV* v *Produktschap voor Siergewassen* [1977] ECR 137.

Court also stated, in its judgment in *Zerbone*,[13] that the Member States must not "impede the direct effect of regulations"; they must not therefore "adopt or allow national institutions with a legislative power to adopt a measure by which the Community nature of a legal rule and the consequences which arise from it are concealed from the persons concerned", in particular by the adoption of "binding rules of interpretation".

Only in exceptional cases, for example where the Community regulation is inadequate for the purpose of governing associations of agricultural producers, so that a combination of Community, national and regional rules is necessary, has the Court held that the incorporation in laws of some elements of a regulation does not constitute a breach of the Treaty.[14]

4. THE EFFICACY OF REGULATIONS WITHIN THE NATIONAL LEGAL SYSTEMS: PROBLEMS RAISED BY THE HIGHEST COURTS IN SOME MEMBER STATES

It is appropriate at this point to consider a matter which, although not directly concerned with the incorporation of regulations into national law, is relevant to the first and most important consequence of that process: the extent to which regulations are actually effective within national systems of law. In this respect reference should be made to the problems raised by the highest courts in certain Member States regarding conflicts of two kinds: first, those which may arise between Community regulations and national constitutional provisions and, secondly, those arising from the existence of domestic laws which run counter to the regulations concerned.

As was to be expected, the Italian and German Constitutional Courts have shown themselves to be particularly sensitive about conflicts of the first type. As early as 1965 the Rome Court raised the question of whether the duty to safeguard the principles upon which the Constitution was based and, in particular, fundamental rights, represented a limitation upon the extent to which the Italian Republic had in fact ceded powers to the Community.[15] And eight years later the same court answered that question at least partly in the affirmative. It stated that the transfer of powers to the Community does not vest in the Brussels institutions powers which, when acted upon, are liable to infringe human rights, and therefore the Italian Constitutional Court is under a constant duty to ensure that secondary Community law does not contravene the key principles of the Constitution.[16]

A concurring view was taken by the German Constitutional Court. Its judgments of 18 October 1967 and 29 May 1974 state that the safeguard represented

---

[13] Case 94/77 *Fratelli Zerbone Snc* v *Amministrazione delle finanze dello Stato* [1978] ECR 99.

[14] Case 272/83 *Commission* v *Italy* [1985] ECR 1057.

[15] Judgment of 22 December 1965, No 98, *Acciaierie San Michele*, in *Giurisprudenza costituzionale*, 1965, 1322.

[16] Judgment of 27 December 1973, No 183, *Frontini*, in *Giurisprudenza costituzionale*, 1973, 2401.

by the existence of the Court of Justice and the judgments of that Court do not constitute an adequate counterbalance to the democratic insufficiency inherent in the Community legislative process in consequence of the absence of any Bill of Rights drawn up with the participation of a parliament elected by universal suffrage.[17] Until that situation is remedied the German Constitutional Court will therefore be obliged to examine Community regulations to establish whether they are compatible with all the fundamental rights upheld by the *Grundgesetz* and, if necessary, to declare them inoperative within the territory of the Federal Republic of Germany.

The danger which such pronouncements represented for the effectiveness (or, rather, the integrity or even the very survival) of Community law is self evident. A number of factors—the most important of which are the greater degree of representativity secured by the European Parliament in 1979 and the spectacular example of judicial activism constituted by the creation by the Court of Justice of an unwritten Community Bill of Rights—nevertheless persuaded those two Constitutional Courts that their fears were groundless or at least were no longer justified. In 1984 Rome[18] and, two years later, Karlsruhe[19] recognized that the legal order from which Community rules emanate is, beyond any doubt, inspired by respect for fundamental rights and, for that very reason, they relinquished the vigilance which they had taken it upon themselves to exercise so long ago. It is nevertheless significant that the German court made its new approach conditional upon the continuing fulfilment of the conditions which prompted it to depart from its previous practice.[20]

The problem of the relationship between regulations and domestic legislation has been resolved without difficulty by the judiciary in most of the Member States in so far as they have held that Community rules enjoy primacy over national provisions adopted either before or after those rules.[21] There have been only two instances of refusal to accept that principle, and even then they are limited to laws adopted after the date of the regulations concerned: in France, by the Conseil d'Etat and in Italy, once again by the Constitutional Court.[22]

---

[17] Judgment of 18 October 1967, in *BVerfGE*, 22, p. 293, reproduced in (1968) *CMLRev* 483; and judgment of 25 July 1971, in *BVerfGE*, 37, p. 271.

[18] Judgment of 8 June 1984, No 170, *Granital*, in *Giurisprudenza costituzionale*, 1984, I-1098.

[19] Judgment of 22 October 1986, in *BVerfGE*, 73, p. 339, reproduced in [1984] 21 *CMLRev* 756.

[20] See also Chapters 1, 3, and 6. Furthermore, as Chapter 4 revealed, a question remark remains, following the judgment of 12 October 1993, in *BVerfGE*, 89, p. 155, over whether or not the German Constitutional Court will be content in future to leave the task of judicial supervision to the Court of Justice.

[21] Judgment of 27 May 1971 of the Belgian Cour de Cassation, Journal des tribunaux 1971, p. 471, reproduced in (1972) I *Common Market Law Reports* 372; judgment of 9 June 1971, in *BVerfGE*, 31, p. 145; judgment of 4 May 1983 of the Symvoulio tis Epikrateias Elliniki Epitheorisi Europaïkou Dikaiou 1985, p. 135; judgment of 21 November 1984 of the Luxembourg Conseil d'Etat, in *Pasicrisie luxembourgeoise*, Vol. 26, p. 174; judgment of 30 July 1986 of the Tribunal de Relação of Coimbra, *Boletin do Ministério da Justiça*, 1986, no 360, p. 307.

[22] Judgment of 1 March 1968, *Rec. Lebon*, 68, p. 149, reproduced in (1970) I *Common Market Law Reports* 406; judgment of 13 December 1985, *Rec. Lebon*, 85, p. 377; and judgment of 22 October 1975, in *Giurisprudenza costituzionale*, 1975, p. 2211, reproduced in (1982) 19 *CMLRev* 455.

In the *Granital* judgment mentioned earlier, however, the Italian Constitutional Court retreated also with respect to the matter under consideration here, acknowledging the primacy of the Community rules and conceding that the Italian courts are obliged not to apply any national law which is incompatible with Community law. The reversal was completed in a later judgment;[23] in it the Italian Court stated that the national courts' obligation to apply directly effective Community law is also binding upon them where the national rule conflicts with a principle laid down by the Court of Justice in preliminary ruling proceedings under Article 177 of the EC Treaty.

5. RECOGNITION OF THE DIRECT EFFECT OF CERTAIN PROVISIONS OF THE EC
TREATY AND OF DIRECTIVES NOT TRANSPOSED INTO DOMESTIC LAW

As is well known, the effectiveness which Article 189 of the EC Treaty attributes to Community regulations has been extended by the Court of Justice to other Community legislation; first of all to the provisions of the EC Treaty itself which (a) expressly confer rights and impose obligations upon private individuals; and (b) impose upon the Member States and the institutions of the Community an obligation which is so precise and unconditional that it can be fulfilled without the need for further measures. By 1987, nineteen provisions had been held to be directly applicable,[24] whereas six other provisions[25] had been held not to have direct effect.[26]

It is worthwhile recalling, at least in outline, the reasoning which prompted the Court to reach its decision in *Van Gend en Loos*, the first and now celebrated judgment on this matter.[27] That decision sets out three propositions which bespeak a profoundly democratic outlook. In the first place, it is stated, it must be recognized that the "objective of the EEC Treaty . . . is to establish a Common Market, the functioning of which is of direct concern to interested parties in the Community" and therefore the Treaty "is more than an agreement which merely creates mutual obligations between the Contracting States". That fact is confirmed by a number of considerations: "the preamble to the Treaty, which refers not only to governments but also to peoples"; "the establishment of institutions endowed with sovereign rights, the exercise of which affects

---

[23] Order of 23 April 1985, *SpA BECA*, in *Giurisprudenza costituzionale*, 1985, I, p. 694.

[24] The first paragraph of Article 189 EC, Articles 9, 12, 13(2), 16—in conjunction with Article 9—Articles 30 and 31 EC, the first paragraph of Article 32 EC, Articles 34, 37(1) and (2), 48, 52, 53, 59 EC, the third paragraph of Article 60 EC, the first and second paragraphs of Article 95 and Article 119 EC.

[25] The second paragraph of Article 32 EC, Article 33(1) and (2) EC, Articles 97, 102 and 107 EC.

[26] Case 9/70 *Franz Grad v Finanzamt Traunstein* [1970] ECR 825; Case 41/74 *Yvonne Van Duyn v Home Office* [1974] ECR 1337; Case 51/76 *Verbond van Nederlandse Ondernemingen v Inspecteur der Invoerrechten en Accijnzen* [1977] ECR 113; and Case 21/78 *Delkvist v Anklagemynd igneden* [1978] ECR 2327.

[27] Case 26/62 *NV Algemene Transport- en Expeditie Onderneming Van Gend en Loos v Nederlandse Administratie der Belastingen* [1963] ECR 3.

Member States and also their citizens"; the existence of a Parliament and an Economic and Social Committee which institutionalize the participation of citizens in the Community decision-making process; "the task assigned to the Court . . . under Article 177" from which it is to be inferred "that the States have acknowledged that Community law has an authority which can be invoked by their nationals before [the national] courts and tribunals". It is therefore possible for men and women in the Community to derive subjective rights from the EC Treaty for the exercise of which no national measures need be adopted.

That argument provoked mutterings in some quarters but nevertheless established itself within a relatively short time. On the other hand bitter opposition, which remains extremely strong to this day, was one of the reactions to the judgments which upheld the direct effect of a number of provisions of directives which had not yet been transposed into the law of the Member States, thus elevating to the status of uniform, and therefore "substitutable", law measures or parts of measures conceived by the Community legislature for the essential purpose of harmonising or coordinating certain areas of domestic law. In particular, an outright rejection of the authority of those judgments was issued by that intransigent custodian of national sovereignty, the French Conseil d'Etat,[28] by the German Bundesfinanzhof,[29] and by the Italian Corte di Cassazione and Consiglio di Stato[30] which, although less brusque from the formal point of view, proved to be no less negative on the substantive issue.[31]

That resistance does not however seem to have perturbed the Court of Justice overmuch, in so far as it has continued to develop its line of reasoning on this point, providing useful clarifications. Its reasoning is based on the following arguments: (a) by virtue of the binding nature of directives it is not in principle permissible to prevent individuals from relying upon the rights deriving from them; (b) the same prohibition follows from the rule whereby directives, like any other legislative measure, must be construed in such a way that their provisions are, as far as possible, effective; (c) Article 177 of the EC Treaty does not draw any distinction regarding the measures in respect of whose interpretation or validity the national courts may or must submit questions to the Court of Justice; and (d) a Member State which has not transposed a directive into its domestic law within the period prescribed cannot rely, as against individuals, upon its own failure to discharge the obligations imposed upon it by the directive (*nemo auditur suam turpitudinem allegans!*). As is obvious, in order to be directly applicable, provisions must not only be sufficiently precise and unconditional but must also have an impact upon relations between a State and the nationals thereof by conferring rights upon the latter. The last-mentioned, or "turpitude",

---

[28] Judgments of 22 December 1978, *Rec. Lebon* 1978, n. 524 and of 16 June 1986, *Rec. Lebon*, 1986.

[29] Judgment of 25 April 1985, *BFHE*, 143, n. 383.

[30] Judgment of 6 May 1980, *Il Consiglio di Stato* 1980 I p. 639.

[31] Judgments of 21 July 1981, *Giust. Civ.* 1982 I p. 995 and 7 October 1981, (1981) *Massimario del Faro italiano* col. 1082.

argument implies that directives which have not been incorporated into national law cannot confer upon a Member State any rights which can be relied upon immediately and which operate with respect to relations between private individuals.[32]

One should perhaps mention that the same principles have also prompted the Court to recognize the direct effect of certain provisions of the agreements entered into by the Community with African and Malagasy States and, before their accession, with Greece and Portugal.[33]

6. PROBLEMS CONCERNING THE INCORPORATION INTO NATIONAL LAW OF DIRECTLY EFFECTIVE RULES OF THE EC TREATY AND OF THE DIRECTIVES

What are the consequences of the aforementioned decisions regarding incorporation into national law of the provisions with which they are concerned? The answer is straightforward as regards the provisions of the Treaties: where the Court has held that they have direct effect, the national authorities need merely do nothing and, if measures are subsequently adopted, the direct effect is in no way affected.[34]

Directives raise more complex problems. Clearly, the fact that they confer upon individuals rights which can be exercised immediately does not relieve the Member States of the obligation to transpose them into national law. However, the process of transposition must take account of that fact: the authorities of the Member States, says the Court, "may not apply to an individual a national legislative or administrative measure which is not in accordance with a provision of the directive . . . or an unconditional and sufficiently clear obligation imposed" by that directive.[35]

It is only national implementing measures that are general in scope which fall within that prohibition.[36] Individual measures, which are based not on Community law but on national law, cannot on the other hand be challenged before national courts and an individual who regards himself as adversely affected by such a measure can only plead that the wider set of rules upon which such measures purport to be based is unlawful.

---

[32] Case 152/84 *M.H. Marshall* v *Southampton and South-West Hampshire Area Health Authority* [1986] ECR 723.

[33] Case 87/75 *Conceria Daniele Bresciani* v *Amministrazione Italiana delle Finanze* [1976] ECR 129; Case 17/81 *Pabst & Richarz KG* v *Hauptzollamt Oldenburg* [1982] ECR 1331; and Case 104/81 *Hauptzollamt Mainz* v *C.A. Kupferberg & Cie KG a.A.* [1982] ECR 3641.

[34] Case 59/75 *Pubblico Ministero* v *Flavia Manghera and others* [1976] ECR 91; and Case 43/75 *Gabrielle Defrenne* v *Société anonyme belge de navigation aérienne Sabena* [1976] ECR 455.

[35] Case 8/81 *Ursula Becker* v *Finanzamt Münster-Innenstadt* [1982] ECR 53; and, in particular, Case 158/80 *Rewe-Handelsgesellschaft Nord mbH and Rewe-Markt Steffen* v *Hauptzollamt Kiel* [1981] ECR 1805.

[36] See Case 51/76 *Verbond van Nederlandse Ondernemingen* v *Inspecteur der Invoerrechten en Accijnzen*, *supra* n. 26.

7. THE INCORPORATION INTO DOMESTIC LAW OF MEASURES WHICH HAVE NO
DIRECT EFFECT: PROCEDURES APPLIED BY THE MEMBER STATES AND THE CHOICE
OF SUCH PROCEDURES

So far the discussion has concentrated on regulations and other Community measures which have direct effect. The problems arising from the reception of measures which do not have direct effect must also be considered; and it should be noted that, of the questions dealt with in this Chapter, this one is the most important. It is in measures of this kind that the most innovative and forward-looking provisions adopted by the legislative authorities of the Community are contained, ranging from tax matters to equality between the sexes, from protection of the environment to the organization of companies. Accordingly, the precise and effective transposition into national law of their provisions is the foundation upon which rests the hope of seeing Europe grow institutionally, in matters of social relations and in terms of quality of life.

First, two straightforward observations are called for. The implementation of directives (because that is the essential issue here) in domestic law involves amendments to existing rules or the formulation of new rules; at least in principle, neither of those obligations can be discharged otherwise than in accordance with the rules specific to each legal system regarding the division of powers between parliament and government or, in certain cases, between the central State and the regional or sub-regional authorities. On the other hand, it is apparent from a review of the way in which the Member States receive Community law into their legal systems: (a) that the procedures employed do not as a rule differ from those which would have been used if the legislation to be put into effect had been conceived not in Brussels but within the Member State concerned; and (b) that, even where the "external" origin of such legislation is clearly apparent, the detailed arrangements adopted for its transposition are the same as those used for the implementation of any international agreement.

It thus appears that, in adopting that approach, the Member States are not mindful of the fact that the principles governing the relationship between Community law and national legal systems are entirely *sui generis*; in particular, to use the words of the Court of Justice, they ignore the fact that "the transfer by the States . . . to the Community legal system of the rights and obligations arising under the Treaty carries with it a permanent limitation of their sovereign rights, against which a subsequent unilateral act incompatible with the concept of the Community cannot prevail".[37] On the other hand it is certain—and those words prove it—that although Community law cannot require Member States to adjust their basic structure to its own requirements, it can require them to choose, within that structure, the most suitable machinery for ensuring compliance with their obligations or, where necessary, to introduce new machinery.

---

[37] Case 6/64 *Costa* v *ENEL* [1964] ECR 585, at 594.

But let us consider matters of detail. It is apparent from an analysis of the various ways in which the Member States incorporate Community law into their own systems that they have used the entire arsenal of the measures available to them. With the exception of France, where the fact that independent legislative powers are vested in the executive confines the use of laws to marginal cases, parliamentary action is the rule in three situations: (a) where there is a more or less absolute requirement that the matter at issue should be provided for by a law (criminal penalties, imposition of taxes); (b) where the Community rules will have to be incorporated within a complex framework of legislation (the classic example is legislation on companies and partnerships); and (c) where the transposition process entails choices which have far-reaching political consequences (for example, where it is necessary to eliminate tax discrimination against nationals of other Member States, the choice between abolishing the tax outright or extending it to the nationals of the State concerned).

In all other cases, the preferred course of action is that measures should be adopted by the executive. The powers delegated to the executive may be general or specific, those of the first kind being provided for by laws which existed before the creation of the Community (Belgium, Luxembourg, the Netherlands and Denmark) or by laws which authorized ratification of the EC Treaty (Germany, Italy, United Kingdom and Ireland). In certain Member States, powers of both types are delegated by virtue of constitutional rules.[38] Finally, in the United Kingdom and Ireland, delegated legislation requires parliamentary approval and in all cases the legislature is entitled to repeal it.

8. CRITICISM OF PARLIAMENTARY PROCEDURE

The academics and politicians who have appraised the benefits and disadvantages of the two methods—parliamentary laws and delegation of powers to the executive—have for the most part declared themselves in favour of the second method. There are three clear disadvantages inherent in the other procedure. In the first place, it is laborious and takes a long time, even a very long time, particularly in countries which, like Italy, have parliamentary chambers which enjoy identical powers. In the second place, there is a risk, which is very high when the principles to be transposed into national law threaten economic or social interests backed by powerful lobbies, that parliamentary debates will challenge the decisions made by the Brussels legislature and will lead to the adoption of rules which are liable to distort those decisions. Finally, there are no mechanisms which, even after many years, ensure the proper implementation of Community law in the face of open revolt or a surreptitious refusal to comply on the part of a national parliament. The increasing frequency of cases of non-compliance with findings by the Court that a Member State has failed to fulfil

---

[38] For example Article 80(1) of the *Grundgesetz* and Article 76 of the Italian Constitution.

its obligations—there is a growing number of "double condemnations"—provides eloquent proof of that unhappy state of affairs.

On the other hand, it is said, legislation through "governmental channels" is usually rapid and straightforward. Moreover, having taken part in the negotiations leading to the adoption of the directive, the executive is in a good position, or at least a better position than parliament, to assess the impact of the Community rules on the national legal system and on the interests protected by that system. Furthermore, whilst it is true that even governments transgress the obligations which they undertake, it is no less certain that their infringements will be most unlikely to take the form of deliberate insubordination; and it is obvious that, from the political, if not the judicial, point of view, there exist a number of appropriate methods for making them overcome any reluctance or persuading them to avoid the ever-present possibility of delay.

The basic point is that Community law imposes itself by its very essence upon the Member States and it is somewhat difficult to reconcile that fact with the traditionally sovereign powers vested in parliaments; in other words, in the implementation of directives the powers of Member States are circumscribed, but national parliaments are nevertheless accustomed to the enjoyment of unfettered discretion. This paradox—which may not evince itself formally but certainly exists in substance—is, even more than the delays and the pressures exerted by interest groups which were referred to earlier, at the root of breakdowns in the systems such as unsynchronized application of directives, the consequent cases of discrimination extending over long periods which are incompatible with the common market, and the general failure to keep up with the schedule envisaged for the implementation of Community policies.

Some may object that such a view fails to take account of the insufficiently democratic nature of the decision-making machinery of the Community; since that machinery, it is observed, is entirely controlled by governments, parliaments which, except in Germany, the United Kingdom, Denmark and now Italy, are excluded from the process of drafting directives, must be allowed at least to participate at the implementation stage. However, that argument is unconvincing or, rather, it identifies a real problem but propounds an incorrect response to it. Whilst it cannot be denied that the drafting of Community legislation takes place in circumstances which are less than democratic, the remedy is to be sought not at national level, but within the Community system. In pursuit of that objective, the European Parliament can play a leading role. It is the responsibility of the European Parliament above all to strive to achieve greater democratization of the legislative process in the Community, by using to the utmost the means made available to it and by contending for institutional arrangements which enable it to play a leading role in that process.

9. PROBLEMS CONCERNING THE INCORPORATION OF COMMUNITY LAW INTO
THE DOMESTIC LAW OF MEMBER STATES WITH A FEDERAL OR REGIONAL
STRUCTURE

A review of this subject would be incomplete if no attention were devoted to the special problems involved in the incorporation of Community law into the laws of Member States of the federal type (Belgium, Germany and Austria) or regional type (Italy and Spain). In such cases, the Community's concern to ensure the uniform application of its legislation throughout the territory of the Member States comes into conflict with either the interests of the Member States themselves or the demands of the authorities in the territories into which the States are divided. Although the Member States are not necessarily opposed to the Community objectives concerned, and indeed support them when they are designed to implement the provisions adopted in Brussels throughout their own national territory, where authorities below State level are concerned conflicts are frequent and on occasion acrimonious.

But in fact those conflicts are largely fictitious. In the case of the German *Länder*, the Italian regions, and the Belgian and Spanish autonomous communities, the real adversary does not reside in the Justus Lipsus and Breydel/ Berlaymont buildings but in their own capital cities: in short, their adversary is the central government which is accused of arrogating to itself the powers delegated to the regions by the Constitution, on the pretext that it is exclusively or at least primarily the responsibility of central government to make certain that international obligations are duly discharged. The "blame" to be attributed to Community law relates, if at all, to its justification of that idea. It is well known that, according to the decisions of the Court of Justice, governments are not entitled, in an endeavour to preclude a finding that they have not fulfilled their obligations, to rely upon the fact that the sovereignty of the State is exercised by means of autonomous powers divided amongst several authorities. Regardless of the authority responsible for the infringement, the State is exclusively answerable for it in every case.[39]

Is there any foundation for these accusations? Doubtless in some of them there is a certain amount of truth. The Italian regions, for example, do not have very extensive powers, restricted as they are by pressure from the municipal authorities, which claim the right to discharge a substantial proportion of their administrative functions, and by the mistrust of the State, a State—let it be noted—which, with respect to the implementation of directives concerning matters which are the responsibility of the regional authorities by virtue of the Constitution, goes so far as to intervene in advance by adopting its own laws laying down the principles with which the measures adopted by the regional

---

[39] Case 77/69 *Commission* v *Belgium* [1970] ECR 237; Joined Cases 51 to 54/71 *International Fruit Company NV and others* v *Produktschap voor groenten en fruit* [1971] ECR 1107; Case 240/78 *Atalanta Amsterdam BV* v *Produktschap voor Vee en Vlees* [1979] ECR 2137.

authorities must comply. In other cases, however, the complaints of those authorities are wholly unjustified. That applies particularly in Germany and even more so in Belgium, where there is not even any provision for the state to take the initiative to adopt measures where inaction on the part of the regions threatens to delay implementation of the national obligations.

That being so, it is the Community authorities, not the regions, which are entitled to protest; and there is no reason to prevent the Community from exerting pressure upon a defaulting Member State, including pressure in the form of recourse to judicial remedies, to persuade it to reorganize its relations with the regions so that they conform both to the principle of *Bundestreue* and to the requirements of European construction.

Index